THE EMERGENCE OF CIVILIZATION

From hunting and gathering to agriculture, cities, and the state in the Near East

Charles Keith Maisels

LONDON AND NEW YORK

To the remembrance of
Hypatia (*c.* 370–March 415 AD) and the Museion-Library of Alexandria

First published 1990
First published in paperback by Routledge 1993
11 New Fetter Lane, London EC4P 4EE

Simultaneously published in the USA and Canada
by Routledge
29 West 35th Street, New York, NY 10001

Reprinted 1995

Typeset by Florencetype Ltd, Stoodleigh, Devon
Printed and bound in Great Britain by Clays Ltd, St Ives Plc

British Library Cataloguing in Publication Data

Maisels, Charles Keith
    The emergence of civilization: from hunting and gathering to agriculture,
    cities, and the state in the Near East.
    1. Sumerian civilization
    I. Title
    935'.01

Library of Congress Cataloging in Publication Data

Maisels, Charles Keith.
    The emergence of civilization: from hunting and gathering to agriculture,
    cities, and the state in the Near East / Charles Keith Maisels.
        p.   cm.
    "Paperback of 1990 hardback"
    Includes bibliographical references and index
        1. Middle East – Civilization – To 622.   I. Title.
DS57.M37   1993   93–7453
939'.4 – dc20

ISBN 0–415–09659–6 pbk

Contents

Contents

List of figures

List of maps

List of tables

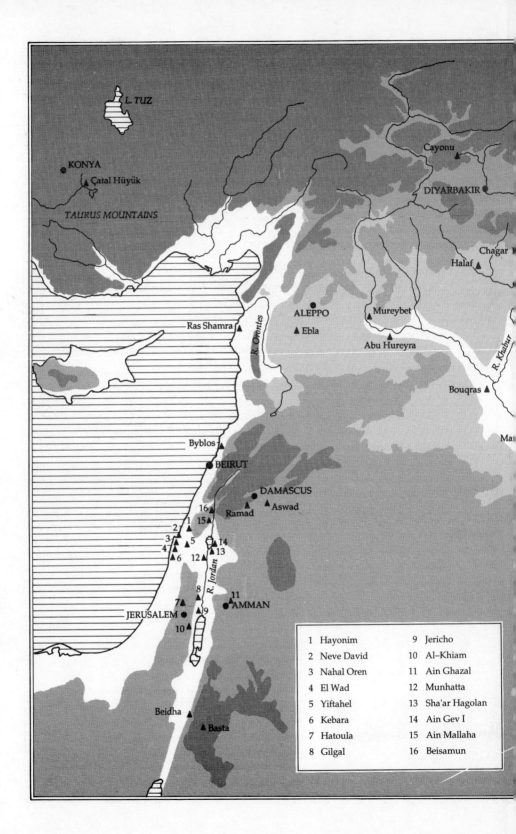

1	Hayonim	9	Jericho
2	Neve David	10	Al–Khiam
3	Nahal Oren	11	Ain Ghazal
4	El Wad	12	Munhatta
5	Yiftahel	13	Sha'ar Hagolan
6	Kebara	14	Ain Gev I
7	Hatoula	15	Ain Mallaha
8	Gilgal	16	Beisamun

L. TUZ

KONYA
Çatal Hüyük

TAURUS MOUNTAINS

Cayonu

DIYARBAKIR

Chagar

Halaf

Ras Shamra

R. Orontes

ALEPPO

Ebla

Mureybet

Abu Hureyra

R. Khabur

Bouqras

Byblos

BEIRUT

DAMASCUS

Aswad

Ramad

JERUSALEM

AMMAN

R. Jordan

Beidha

Basta

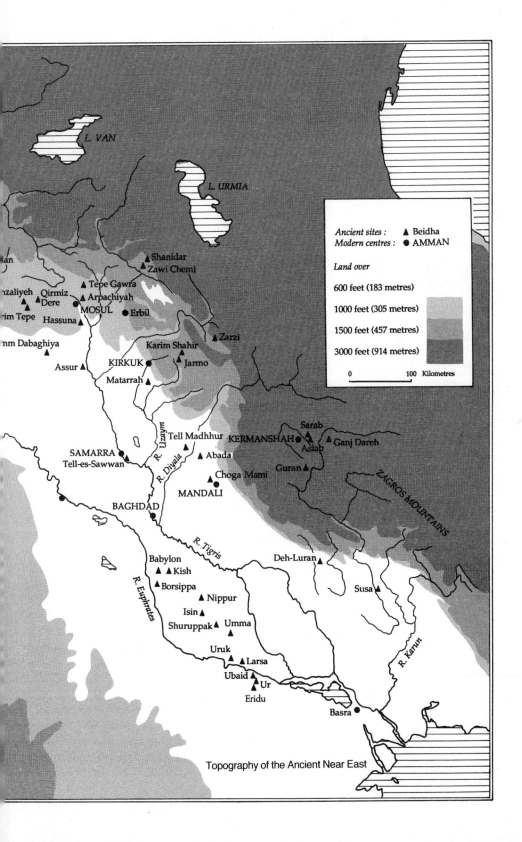

Topography of the Ancient Near East

Glossary of some physical terms

ALLUVIUM: sedimentary deposits of eroded rock fragments laid by the action of rivers. Larger particles, notably gravels, are deposited upstream, while finer materials (usually called *silts*) are deposited downstream, sometimes right into waterbodies, where *alluvial fans* are formed. If offshore conditions are right, *deltas* are formed. As unconsolidated (though usually deep and mineral-rich) material, *alluvisols* are a type of *immature, skeletal* or *azonal* soil, manifesting poorly developed *horizons*, which are bands of different structure and organic activity.

ANASTOMOSING: A condition of rivers in which, due to excessive *deposition* (see above) there is little gradient (slope) in the rivercourse, encouraging the main stream to break up into a network of branches or braids, the number and location of which shift over short periods of time. *Levees* can also result.

CAPRID: goat. *Caprini* is the *tribe* including both sheep and goat. *Capra aegagrus* is the Bezoar, the wild progenitor of the domestic goat, while *Capra ibex* is a type of goat (the ibex) specialising in high altitude and desert conditions.

DISTAL: situated farthest *away from* the point of attachment or connection, the converse of *Proximal*, nearest.

EPIPHYSIS: Peculiar to mammalian vertebra and limb bones, this is the separately ossified end of a growing bone (the *diaphysis*). Separated by cartilage, the two only become unified at maturity.

INCISED: The cutting down of a river into the bedrock, thus taking the river's surface below that of the surrounding terrain.

LOESS: Wind-deposited soil (aeolian).

METACARPAL BONES: Corresponding to the palm-region in man, those are the rod-like bones of the fore-foot in the tetrapod vertebrates, usually one corresponding to each digit (finger or toe). *Metatarsals* are the same bones in the hind foot (sole).

NUCLEATION: A settlement type which has its buildings clustered tightly together leaving little space between (only squares, greens or plazas, not fields and farms).

OBSIDIAN: (Rhyolite) 'Volcanic' glass in extrusive igneous (ie, *magmatic*) rocks. Like glass, it takes a very sharp edge.

OVICAPRIDS: Sheep (*Ovis*) and goat together, used particularly where differentiation from skeletal remains is difficult. However wild sheep (eg: *Ovis orientalis*, or Mouflon) and goat have different environmental preferences and tolerances, goat being tougher and more versatile.

PALYNOLOGY: Pollen analysis. Since many pollens were originally airborne and all are different, identification and counting of different types in sedimentary and peaty deposits can reveal changing vegetation types over time; eg, from woodlands to grasslands where man has cleared for farming and grazing.

SCAPULA: The shoulder blade in man and other mammals.

WADI: An intermittent watercourse without base flow, and thus only running after rains. Not to be confused with a Palaeochannel, which is a course abandoned by a river for geological or energetic reasons.

Acknowledgements

Thanks to: Academic Press for Map 11.1, from W.C. Brice (ed.), *The Environmental History of the Near East and Middle East since the last Ice Age*, 1978.

The Association of Social Anthropologists of the Commonwealth for Figs 8.7, 8.8, 8.9, 8.10 and 8.11 from M. Bloch (ed.), *Marxist Analyses and Social Anthropology*, 1975.

The Athlone Press for Map 8.1, from E.R. Leach, *Political Systems of Highland Burma*, 1970.

British Museum (Natural History) for Map 3.11 from J. Clutton-Brock, *Domesticated Animals From Early Times*, 1981.

Mouton de Gruyter (A Division of Walter de Gruyter & Co.) for Maps 3.8, 3.9, 3.10, from C.A. Reed (ed.), *Origins of Agriculture*. 1977.

Peter J. Ucko for Maps 3.5, 3.6 and 3.7, from P.J. Ucko and G.W. Dimbleby (eds), *The Domestication and Exploitation of Plants and Animals*, Duckworth, 1969.

The University of Chicago Press for Fig. 6.10 from I.J. Gelb, *A Study of Writing*, 1963, and for Figs 5.2, 5.4 and Map 5.1 from R. McCormack Adams, *The Heartland of Cities*, 1981.

The University of Michigan, Museum of Anthropology, for Map 4.2a from F. Hole, *Studies in the Archaeological History of the Deh Luran Plain*, 1977, and for Fig. 4.2 and Map 4.2b from F. Hole, K.V. Flannery and J.A. Neely, *Prehistory and Early Ecology of the Deh Luran Plain*, 1969.

Wadsworth Publishing Company for Fig. 3.4 from Herbert G. Baker, *Plants and Civilisation*, Second Edition, 1970, by permission of the publisher.

Preliminary

What follows is neither a textbook nor a comprehensive survey of the archaeology of the Near East, but a body of ideas with information, some of it archaeological. The work is an exploration in the application of anthropological thinking to the emergence of civilization where it first occurred in durable and unequivocal form: namely on the alluvium of the lower Tigris and Euphrates, a culture area called Sumer.[1] This is where cities and the state first crystallized in any form that could be sustained, but this did not occur in isolation. Sumer is culturally and topographically part of a broader area centred around the rivers Euphrates and Tigris, called Mesopotamia, itself part of the Near Eastern region.[2] It is because Sumer as the 'heartland of cities' is preceded by a long development of towns, villages, and agriculture elsewhere in the region that this work has the shape it has, endeavouring to show a long series of connections forming a trajectory.

The enterprise rests on, and hopefully contributes to, the basic anthropological one: the examination of actual and potential forms of human society, what their logics are and what forces generate, sustain, and destroy them. This is the purpose for which the ethnological[3] examples and ethnographic concepts are introduced, and not as direct analogues for Mesopotamian processes, which, being *sui generis*, must be treated in their own terms, specified below by Larsen. Neither, then, is this work intended as a handbook of Sumerology or Anthropology, though I trust it contributes to and stimulates interest in both.

What is provided is that information necessary to develop the argument, which, as simply as possible, is to explore what succession of interrelated changes in the scale and complexity of societies leads to civilization; where *civilization*, stripped of any normative overtones, is defined as state-ordered, stratified society, which in turn, it is argued, presupposes the levels of productivity derived from plant and animal domesticates in agriculture. *Stratified* means differential access to or control over fundamental resources, those essential to subsistence, conferring differential benefit on the holders (as against, for instance, what mere life-cyclical seniority could command). *State-ordered* means the control of people and territory from a centre, through a hierarchy of offices specialized for this purpose.

In the emergence of stratification and the state I show that hierarchy is generated from the general social characteristics of status and ranking, norms and prerogatives, for central to social morphology is social psychology. Thus attention is also given to ideology and cosmology as essential constituents of any and every society. Ideologies, generated in, and (usually) reinforcing processes of economic integration and stratification, are modelled by employing the concept 'mode of production', seen as encompassing a whole mode of life and not merely production activities; but rendered operational, possibly for the first time, in demonstrating functioning political economies. The mode of production concept applied specifically in regard to Mesopotamia in the proto- and early-historic periods, shows how Clarke's (1968) 'cultural morphology' and 'cultural ecology' cohere in actual, and complex, societies.

Two qualitatively distinct modes of production are identified as seminal in the advent of the state as a pristine, that is autochthonous, institution. One leads to the city-state with relations of production deriving from the process of *synoecism* itself – the divisions of labour and political forms induced by dense nucleation. The other, here designated the '*village-state*' mode of production, but conventionally termed 'Asiatic', is predicated upon the transmission intact of kinship lineality formed into a conical hierarchy, at the apex of which a divine ruler appears with absolute patrimonial prerogatives.

In the former, private property (or narrowly familial property) and monetized relations appear early; in the latter they are long delayed and arrive highly circumscribed and attenuated. The city, where it emerges under the village-state mode, usually as a royal capital, is an instrumental city of functions, overwhelmingly political, based on court, garrison, cult, etc.; while the city-state urbanism is an organic polity, self-centred on its immediate hinterland and largely self-sustaining, therefore usually self-governing through its own specifically 'civic' institutions. Those reflect the fact that while the city-state may be headed by a king it does not owe its existence to kingship and to the spending of royal revenues drawn from the dispersed villages of the territorial state. Rather the *urbs* of the city-state regime owes its existence to its own economic activities, which are largely autonomous from the political, in times of peace at least.

Sanders and Webster (1978:283) have indicated three trajectories from egalitarian society to the state-ordered, the different paths followed being the outcome of differing ecological conditions. Those trajectories are shown in Figure 1. The trajectories which concern Mesopotamia are numbers 1 and 2. Track 2 represents Sumer proper, I contend, and track 1, just possibly early conditions in the north, but with much more certainty later in regard to the Amorites and others on the periphery of Mesopotamia (Maisels 1984b). Track 1 is a clear case of stimulus by a pristine state-form (track 2 representing Sumer) causing chiefdoms to generate the state as a secondary development. *As may be seen, under track 2 there is no chiefdom stage; rather stratification emerges directly from egalitarian society.* In turn stratification (with higher population density and complexity) engenders state organization which consolidates the emergent social stratification. However, Sanders and Webster (op. cit.:282) give no indication as to the stratification mechanisms obtaining in Mesopotamia, to which (along with central Mexico) they

Figure 1 Evolutionary trajectories

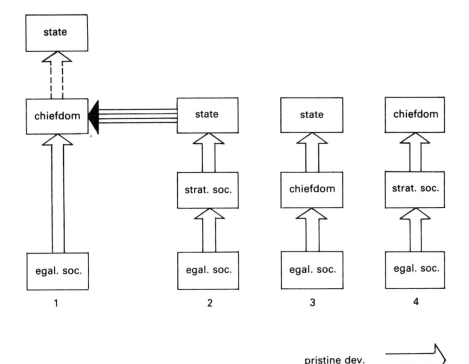

Source : Sanders and Webster 1978:283

think track 2 applies. I believe such a mechanism can now be demonstrated in detail and will attempt to do so below, having first contrasted it with track 3 as the characteristic 'village-state' mode. Track 4, which may apply to pastoral nomads or to Bronze/Iron Age Europe, will not be further considered here.

The environmental variables involved are:

1 potential productivity;
2 inherent risk;
3 topographic diversity;
4 scale.

Those are the variables which will recur throughout this work in seeking to account for the peculiarities of Mesopotamian prehistory and history. For it seems to me that this is essential to the provision of a scientific account in both natural and human sciences: namely, the explanation of how things came to be by showing their generative processes and limit parameters. Such an approach is necessarily both synchronic and diachronic.

Thus even an answer to the apparently 'simple' question, 'why is a tree a tree?', requires the discipline of biology to provide concepts quite additional to such general ones as photosynthesis, biomass, and nutrient cycles, in the case of the tree-form addressing the likes of 'climax vegetation', the nature of canopies, the cellular structure of wood, and nutrient transport. Only when the morphological rationale of trees can be specified in contrast to that of other vegetation can an adequately scientific account be said to have been given.

In the historical sciences an adequate explanation must encompass not only an account of the particularities involved, but go beyond this to seek the forces that have engendered the particularities and even the apparent randomness, for randomness itself occurs only within a frame though rarely is this frame manifest. Neither are simple chains of cause and effect likely to be found, for in social as in natural ecology we have to be alert for systems of positive and negative feedback, and indeed for the factors that cause switching in the system.

As no two histories are ever the same and perceived similarities only polythetically so, without a generative account no encompassing explanation is possible.

Ethnological and archaeological accounts will be employed to see what consequences follow from variation in one or more of those key variables:

1 *Productivity* is the per capita yield of an environment using extant technology and social organization, i.e. it is the input/output ratio of the 'effective environment'.
2 *Risk* can be considered an inherent cost of the above. It indicates

what measure of organization must be undertaken and what costs incurred to smooth the risk-troughs, such as inter-annual variability in rainfall or river-flow.

3 *Diversity* here means qualitatively different resources in association. If too dispersed relative to human mobility, the different kinds of resource – marsh, hill, river, forest, etc. – simply form isolates rather than a complementary mosaic. It will be argued that socio-technical dynamism is an outcome of intra-regional diversity, obtaining at the inter-areal and inter-zonal levels. It is notable however that for all its precociousness there is precious little diversity on the alluvium of Sumer (except with the marsh areas to the south). Instead diversity obtains between the alluvium, the Jazira to the immediate north, the Zagros mountains and foothills to the north and east, the Syrian desert to the west, the Mediterranean coast, and so forth.

4 *Scale* follows from the foregoing, as the geographical dimension permitting or restricting extension: e.g. by colonization; communication, i.e. the formation of partial isolates; and cumulation, in terms of absolute population numbers and disposable surpluses attainable.

As already mentioned, although Sanders and Webster (op. cit.:282) think that trajectory 2 applies to archaic Mesopotamia, they do not suggest what process might be involved. It is one purpose of this work to supply the missing mechanisms, and this is done:

(a) by pointing to the risks involved in the exploitation of the alluvium, where river-flow is critical, and by proposing that this, with associated climatic risks, is whence the Mesopotamian temples assume their catalytic role.

(b) by suggesting that temples formed the nuclei for the crystallization of cities, and that the urban form, which characterized Sumer as what Adams (1981) called the 'heartland of cities' was the consequence both of regional diversity and the relative lack of it at areal level; meaning the absence of metals, wood (other than palm) and stone on the alluvium, with the consequent necessity of deriving those from abroad, and instituting the essentially similar and therefore highly competitive nature of the city-states of Sumer and Akkad.

For further overview, readers are advised to turn to Chapter 11, 'Summary and overview'.[4] They are also urged not to take the first expression of a theme as its full and final one, but to attend to its development in the course of an admittedly rather tortuous argument. In conclusion to the preliminaries, I cannot put the problems and potentials better than has M. T. Larsen in his indispensable study of *The Old Assyrian City-State and its Colonies*:

As pointed out by Oppenheim, assyriologists[5] deal with a dead culture, so in a way their efforts constitute attempts to engage in a dialogue with the dead. There are certain rules set for this conversation however, and it is essential to realise that these rules have been established by the dead. *Only certain questions or categories of questions can in fact be asked*, and unless we observe the rules we cannot hope to accomplish the task of breaking through the opaque wall of strangeness and reach a real understanding of patterns and connections. Our failures are all too often due to our insistence on asking unanswerable questions, or phrasing reasonable questions in such a way that the replies have to be either vague and elusive, or consist of isolated – and therefore useless – statements of fact.

The mere mass of textual evidence – not to speak of the archaeological record which is immensely varied – certainly represents a major challenge, and it is surely not surprising that the purely philological treatment of the texts has come to overshadow the efforts towards interpretation and analysis of basic cultural and historical complexes.

. . . In fact, the distinctive character of Mesopotamian civilisation tends to reinforce the impression of an especially close relationship between assyriology and ethnography and ethnology.

(Larsen 1976:17–18; my emphasis)

Unless we really ponder the implications of this, our dialogue with the dead will turn out to be a dialogue with the deaf, our contemporaries.

Accordingly, the introduction of Mesopotamian material is delayed until Chapter 3, as Chapter 1 seeks to situate archaeology and anthropology relative to one another and prehistory, while Chapter 2 clears a way through some conceptual obstacles.

Chapter one

Introduction

1 The disciplines of archaeology and anthropology

Archaeology and geology are twin sisters of the nineteenth-century enlightenment. It was geology that turned antiquarianism into archaeology. As early as 1836, the antiquarian and customs official Jacques Boucher de Perthes (1788–1868), argued that man had been contemporary with presently extinct animals, and in 1847 he published the first volume of his signally titled *Antiquités celtiques et antédiluviennes* (Daniel 1964:44). Although evidence for the antiquity of Man (long before the Biblical Flood and his supposed creation around 4,000 BC) was accumulating from several locations, Boucher's view did not become the accepted one until endorsed in 1859 by the geologists Evans and Prestwich, who visited his quarry sites at Abbeville in that year (Daniel 1964:45).

However, scholarly antiquarianism, which can be considered proto-archaeology, was pioneered in Denmark and Sweden during the seventeenth and eighteenth centuries, thanks to continuous state support. Thus, since Thomsen's (1836) guidebook to the Danish National Museum, clearly setting out the 'Three Age System' (Stone, Bronze, Iron), systemic classification for the conceptualization of prehistoric societies (and thus encouraging their recovery through excavation), has been by means of this 'Ages System', based upon the materials employed for weapons and tools. Consequently we now think in terms of Old and New Stone Ages (i.e. Palaeolithic and Neolithic, a distinction introduced by Lubbock), then those of Copper (Chalcolithic), Bronze, and Iron.[1] Coupled with William 'strata' Smith's 'principle of superposition', stating that objects found lower in the (undisturbed) earth are older, the nascent discipline of archaeology had found its organizing principles; that is, both its field of study and its means of analysis. As Lubbock proclaimed on the first page of his best-selling *Prehistoric Times* (1865): 'Archaeology forms the link between geology and history.'

With the expansion of archaeology and anthropology both geographically and in depth throughout this century, processes formerly aggregated can now be distinguished thanks to the much finer resolution thus made possible, a process greatly assisted by a range of scientific techniques, foremost among which is radio-carbon (C^{14}) dating for absolute chronologies (when calibrated). It is no longer possible, for instance, to see the Neolithic as a 'revolution' or 'explosion', the immediate consequence of a 'breakthrough' such as the 'invention' of pottery or the sickle.

In 1936 Vere Gordon Childe published *Man Makes Himself*, which Daniel, introducing the fourth edition (1965:x), called 'an epoch-making synthesis of prehistory'. There Childe modified the Three Age System of Neolithic, Bronze, and Iron Ages that he had previously employed, by introducing his own concept of 'Two Revolutions', the Neolithic and the Urban (McNairn 1980: 91–9). For Childe, the term Neolithic represented the advent of pottery, textiles, woodworking, and village life on the basis of regular food production by agriculture and pastoralism, in contrast to (wild) food procurement (Childe (1936) 1965:88). He saw the Urban Revolution not simply as a further growth and nucleation of population, but as a wholly new form of civic existence ('civilization') based upon intensified agriculture, plus further development of crafts stimulated by an emergent stratification into rulers and ruled. With its monumental buildings, didactic art, organized religion, trade, writing, and the appearance of natural science, Childe identified the Urban Revolution with the advent of the state:

> The neolithic revolution was the climax of a long process. It has to be presented as a single event because archaeology can only recognize the result; the several steps leading up thereto are beyond the range of direct observation. A second revolution transformed some tiny villages of self-sufficing farmers into populous cities, nourished by secondary industries and foreign trade, and regularly organised as States.
>
> (Childe 1965:105)

Childe's synthesis (continued in *What Happened in History*, 1942, and *Social Evolution*, 1951), effected a conceptual revolution in archaeology, for 'he supplemented an exclusively chronological by a cultural approach' (Clark 1976:5). The holistic approach which Childe promoted was given further impetus through the work of Grahame Clark. Clark (1952) stressed the 'economic approach' to prehistory, employed to understand the whole mode of life of the people being investigated, ranging from their articulation with the environment to their cosmological reflections upon it.

Shortly after, in concluding a review of technique in archaeology, Wheeler identified the 'problem of numbers' as the 'one problem more than [any] other which demands investigation during the next thirty years' (Wheeler 1956:245). This demographic emphasis, he maintained, was required to illuminate the whole 'social unit' as a dynamic system. Indeed, in that same year (1956) were published a number of ethnologies incorporating numerical data bearing upon demographic issues in contemporary societies (Smith, R. T.; Mitchell, J. C.; Tait, D.). Further harbingers of changing concerns and outlooks had been Taylor's (1948) critique of his colleagues in the United States, *A Study of Archaeology*, and the synthesis by Willey and Phillips in 1958, entitled *Method and Theory in American Archaeology*. This was the work that contained the famous aphorism: 'archaeology is anthropology or it is nothing' (op. cit.:2).

Concerns with economy, environment, and demography were thus very much in the air when, late in the 1960s, the New Archaeology was articulated by Lewis Binford in the United States and by David Clarke in the UK. It was indeed in the very same year, 1968, that Clarke's programmatic *Analytical Archaeology* appeared, while Lewis and Sally Binford edited and contributed to a collection well entitled *New Perspectives in Archaeology*. This latter was perhaps decisive in launching what has come to be called 'processual archaeology', or, with the emphasis on the aforementioned aphorism, *palaeoanthropology*. It also gave rise to a heightened and explicit interest in *ethnoarchaeology*, an approach that seeks to get beyond the use of ethnology and ethnography merely as external sources of analogy for an archaeology going about its traditional business. Instead ethnoarchaeology's function is to integrate social and cultural anthropology as an organic part of the practice of archaeology. This by having ethnography inform the premises employed in the reconstruction of dead societies through excavation.

Inform does not, of course, mean exhaust. There is a great deal in the approach and practice of palaeoanthropology which social and cultural anthropology cannot possibly provide. None the less, what can be done should be done, and hence 'the subdiscipline (of ethnoarchaeology) is defined broadly as encompassing all theoretical and methodological aspects of comparing ethnographic and archaeological data, including the use of ethnographic analogy and archaeological ethnography' (Stiles 1977:87).

Analogy is the use of aspects of the known to construct a model for the unknown. The pitfall is obviously the substitution of a construct for what is yet to be discovered. *Archaeological ethnography* is ethnology undertaken amongst living (or at least recent) societies in order to illuminate aspects of social behaviour either ignored or inadequately treated in conventional ethnology, such as material culture often is. Archaeological ethnography is also known as 'living archaeology'; but Gould (cited Stiles 1977:88), rightly in my view, states that 'Ethnoarchaeology . . . refers to a much broader general framework for comparing ethnographic and archaeological patterning.'

Included in ethnoarchaeology is *historical ethnology*, the attempt to reconstruct ethnology from written sources, here of course Mesopotamian. This, however, is not an analogical procedure, and is more powerful than any such. The next most powerful research tool is analogy derived from archaeological ethnography conducted, as near as can be made out, amongst the 'living descendants' of the society being archaeologically recovered. Examples are Hopi Indian ethnology for palaeoindian research, or rural and upland ethnology in Iraq for ancient Mesopotamian societies, of which much more below. This is also called the 'direct historic' or 'continuous' approach, in contrast to 'external' analogues from other areas, which is termed the 'general comparative' or 'discontinuous' approach. This is by far the weakest procedure, and is best regarded as only suggestive or heuristic.

Explication of those interrelationships is perhaps best done through what can be called the 'Hawkes Ladder', which illustrates levels in social reconstruction and the complementary roles of archaeology and anthropology in producing it. In discussing W. W. Taylor's *A Study of Archaeology*, already mentioned as criticizing his colleagues' practice of archaeology as 'mere chronology', Christopher Hawkes outlined a 'fourfold answer . . . to take you from comparison and analysis of observed phenomena to the human activity that produced them' (1954:161).

In this logical procedure there are four degrees of difficulty, the lowest of which, marked 1 on Figure 1.1 is to know what the artefacts recovered in excavation are and how they were made. Artefacts here means everything wrought by human hands, thus including the likes of ditches, building plans, pits, and so forth, in addition to the more usual sense of pots, tools, and general mobiliary. From animal bones and grains recovered, tools, weapons, and facilities, perhaps as explicit as the finding of sickles in association with storage bins and bread-wheat grains or pollen, or shell-middens and fish weirs, it is quite easy and relatively safe to infer the sorts of subsistence activities underpinning a particular society. This is level 2 in the diagram. What however is neither easy nor safe is to make ready inferences about the sorts of social structure obtaining. Certain things are positively excluded, such as hunter-gatherers grouping themselves into cities while remaining hunter-gatherers, but a great deal else is indeed possible by way of variation. Hawkes (op. cit.:162) gives the example of the uncovering of architectural features whose function ought to be obvious, but is it? If in the excavation of a settlement one hut turns out to be larger than the rest, does one infer: a chief's hut (hence ranking), or a 'men's house' (hence either no ranking on Melanesian analogues, or stratification on that of historical southern Iraqi experience), or is it a temple?

All this difficulty as to social structure in level 3. But assume from the discovery of altars, niches, and statuary in this larger building that we

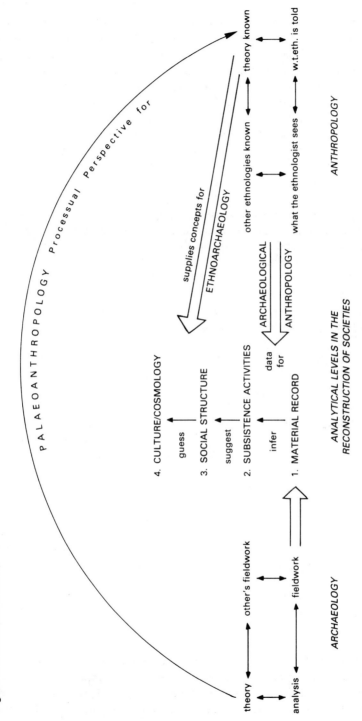

Figure 1.1 The Hawkes Ladder

have decided that it is a temple. What can we know of the religious beliefs held? And beyond this, of that people's cosmology, which is a compound of the religious and the empirical? If the excavated material from Mesopotamia, which is comparatively very rich, was all we had, it would have been impossible even to give the sketchy picture of Mesopotamian cosmology provided in this work. For a fairly sure knowledge of level 4 we need either written texts or ethnology in a continuous tradition; otherwise our inferences are either too general ('hunter-gatherers pray for good hunting, farmers for good crops') or just guesswork, more or less interesting. Archaeology is well able, despite manifold practical difficulties, to uncover the material record (level 1) and to make fairly secure inferences about subsistence activities on that basis (level 2). As we have seen, however, the problems arise in getting beyond this stage, for archaeologists are rightly not content to leave it there (cf. Renfrew 1984:3–19). The problem in getting to the next level (3) and beyond is both evidential and logical.

This is where anthropology comes in,[2] supplying concepts, models, and different data. Archaeological anthropology can sometimes do this in the most direct fashion, in which case data relevant to all four levels can be provided (though this will never be even in quality or quantity). Failing this, not so much ethnology (what the anthropologist sees and is told through participant observation), but the issues raised at the theoretical level (ethnography) can be of assistance to archaeology at its own analytical/theoretical level, that of palaeoanthropology. Palaeoanthropology is in its turn able to provide anthropology with the added dimensions of time–depth and a processual perspective[3] which it currently all too often lacks. Conversely, it is not a matter of *whether* to use ethnology and ethnography in reconstructing the prehistoric past, for our views of other places and different times are already imbued with notions thus derived, as Orme (1981:2) has indicated; but rather *what* ethnological materials and *which* ethnographic concepts should be applied to archaeological interpretation while not substituting for it: 'Archaeological interpretation has depended on ethnography from its infancy in the sixteenth century, through the great growth spurt of the nineteenth century to the present day.' For crucially, 'the idea of a past [qualitatively] different from the present, a keystone of archaeology, was established through the use of ethnography' (Orme 1981:7).

2 Social evolution and anthropology[4]

The 'way was opened' from modern (field) anthropology to participation in the New (processual, social) Archaeology by the 'Man the Hunter' Symposium held at the University of Chicago in April 1966, and published under that title in 1968, edited by Richard Lee and Irven

De Vore. It was a timely impulse because, during most of this century, anthropology 'social' and 'cultural' has tended to eschew developmental classification, such as the evolutionism of its pioneers like Tylor and Frazer. Indeed in the United States cultural anthropology became positively anti-evolutionary after Boas (White 1960:v; Sahlins and Service 1960:1), while in Britain the topic was just generally ignored. Even in France 'anti-evolutionist feeling has been intense for most of this century . . . and to a large extent remains so' (Testart 1988:1).

Those were the conditions under which Murdock (1949:187) could write in his broad synthesis entitled *Social Structure*, which employed a selection of data from the Yale Cross-Cultural Survey (begun 1937), that he had 'weighed a number of such [evolutionary] suggestions against the data from his [*sic*] sample societies, but he has found none which accords with the ethnographic facts'. He complains that Lesser and White in various articles[5] were outrageous enough to suggest that 'hunting and gathering are earlier than herding and agriculture, that a stone age has everywhere preceded the use of metals, and that community organisation antedates the development of any kind of complex political state. It is alleged', Murdock further complains, 'that comparable evolutionary sequences can also be established in the field of social organisation' (ibid.). This indeed has been an indispensable and even commonplace grid since formulated sociologically by John Millar of Glasgow in 1771 (Evans-Pritchard 1981:34; Finley 1983b:10), for it makes the most sense of the widest range of data – prehistoric, historic, and ethnographic – though perhaps less obviously in synchronic than in diachronic perspective.

Yet in rigorous statistical tests employing just such ethnological data, Raoul Naroll (1956:687–715), Freeman and Winch (1957:461–6), Gouldner and Peterson (1962:1–94), and M. J. Harner (1970:67–86), the last-mentioned employing the total universe of the 1,170 societies with codified data in Murdock's own *Ethnographic Atlas*, convincingly demonstrated that there was indeed such a fundamental set of evolutionary relationships.

Carneiro (1967:234–43), employing 205 organizational traits in a total of 100 societies, showed the relationship between population size and the complexity of social organization to be logarithmic, the number of organizational traits being proportional to the root (or power) of the population size.

A decade earlier Freeman and Winch (1957:464) employing scalogram analysis and Murdock's selection procedures on 48 societies from the Cross-Cultural Survey and the Human Relations Area Files, 'clearly demonstrate[d] a scale among six of the eight tested items: punishment, government, education, religion, economy and written language vary[ing] together to form a unidimensional array'.

Previous objections to evolutionism, most a consequence of the a-prioristic schematism of earlier workers that had tended to produce at best a conjectural, and at worst a counter-factual history (Lowie 1946), are thus removed.

The solution has been found to reside in replacing unilineal with multilineal sequences (as best described by Carneiro 1973:100), thus disposing of the presupposition that differing societies represent set stages along a single path. Further, cross-cultural uniformities can be sought, and underlying causation made clear, by measuring the actual type and degree of social complexity obtained along political and economic axes (degree of hierarchy and number of distinct occupations),[6] and by differentiating the social order (system of organizations) from the social structure (network of roles), as discussed in Chapter 8. Thus I employ the term 'succession' to look at a long series of transformations in societies, without prejudging their individual processes, whether their paths are parallel, or how much they may have in common at any particular stage.

In short an acceptable evolutionism (and some such is indispensable), is descriptive rather than prescriptive. By comparison it situates advancing complexity where that is empirically manifest, so that 'despite the many and often justified criticisms of the application of evolutionary doctrine to social facts, only a real flat-earther would now regard the overall history of political systems as static, cyclical, regressive, indeed as anything other than a process of elaboration' (Goody 1980:20).

With fieldwork by participant observation advancing in both breadth and depth during the 1930s and 1940s, social anthropology (and with it cultural anthropology) implicitly delineated 'patterns which are common to all societies of the same general type and patterns which are universal', in the words of Evans-Pritchard (1951:124). And this despite an attitude of indifference to evolutionary thinking going back to Malinowski (Kuper 1973:21). None the less, in their famous introduction to *African Political Systems* Meyer Fortes and Evans-Pritchard could discern three distinct types of political system and social correlates:

> Firstly there are those very small societies . . . in which even the largest political unit embraces a group of people all of whom are united to one another by ties of kinship so that political relations are coterminous with kinship relations and the political structure and kinship organisation are completely fused. Secondly, there are societies in which a lineage structure is the framework of the political system, there being a precise coordination between the two, so that they are consistent with each other, though each remains distinct and autonomous in its own sphere. Thirdly there are societies in which an administrative organisation is the framework of the political structure.
>
> (Fortes and Evans-Pritchard 1940:6)

At the same time Fortes and Evans-Pritchard made two observations which will assume importance as this work proceeds: they regard it as 'noteworthy that the political unit in the societies with a state organisation is numerically larger than in those without a state organisation' (ibid.:7) with the former also more diverse culturally and economically (ibid.:9); while a clear distinction is made 'between the set of relationships linking the individual to other persons and to particular social units through the transient bilateral family, which we call the kinship system, and the segmentary system of permanent, unilateral[7] descent groups, which we call the lineage system' (ibid.:6). It is only the latter which establishes corporate units with political functions.

For Colin Renfrew, like an increasing number, and perhaps now a majority of archaeologists,

> The hierarchy of band, tribe, chiefdom and state has recommended itself to many workers concerned to make generalisations of some kind about culture change, or to fit specific societies under study into some more general perspective. The notion of chiefdom in particular has helped to fill the gap in the workings of earlier anthropologists between the tribe and the state.
>
> (Renfrew 1984:41)

The utility of the 'chiefdom' construct is perfectly clear from Renfrew's own work, such as the widely read *Before Civilisation* (1973a) and in the work of others, for example the contributors to *Patterns of the Past: Studies in Honour of D. L. Clarke* (1981).

Fortes and Evans-Pritchard (op. cit.:6) observe that 'the state is never the kinship system writ large but is organised on totally different principles'. A chiefdom, however, is precisely kinship politics taken as far as it can go (without dissolution), and it is well to point up the fundamental distinction between chiefdom and state. The position (office) of the chief is due to his location in the kinship network and ultimately he is subordinate to it and its values, for he has no major source of power that he can operate outwith kinship relations. Indeed chiefs often have to compete for followers, and they certainly cannot command 'subjects'. But when a chief can so operate, what is occurring (or has already occurred) is the formation of the true state (characterized by a centralized power to command), in which the king (as he has become) is freely able to dispose of major social resources, such as labour and land, untrammelled by kinship relations and guided only by 'reasons of state', that is, by expediency.

The formation of a class of rulers assisted by a class of administrators is simultaneously the process of the transformation of cultivators into peasants, more or less dependent:

> Beyond a certain level of political role differentiation, and assuming its

implications for the role structure of the society as a whole, it is inevitable that authority should progressively be withdrawn from the family, that is, the political aspect of kinship roles is transferred to newly differentiated political roles.

(Southall 1965:124)

In this way the peasant comes to occupy a 'part society' through the specialization of ideological, economic, and military roles which are removed to a distance both geographical and social. Consequently the peasant is always remote from the levers of power, which means that he is the object of politics and not its subject, unless in revolt. Shanin (1971:15) calls this the 'underdog position' bringing with it the dominion of the peasantry as a whole by non-peasants, by outsiders belonging to other strata. This does not mean of course that peasants are a homogeneous mass without internal stratification. Tribesmen, by contrast, who have 'all-purpose' or multifunctional social relations shared by all (*a fortiori*, kinship relations) functioning simultaneously as relations of production, inhabit whole and thus unstratified societies. Bailey's (1961:15) contrast of Tribe and Caste in India is instructive: 'Membership of the clan is, under the system, a condition of holding and exploiting land in the clan territory. A right to land is not achieved by subordination to anyone else, but by equality as a kinsman.'

By 'state' I understand centralized social power deployed through specialized apparatuses, and I follow Haas (1982:157) in comprehending power to be 'the ability of actor, A, to get another actor(s), B, to do something B would not otherwise do, through the application, threat or promise of sanctions'.

Southall (op. cit.:124) goes on to make a distinction between pyramidal and hierarchical states. Pyramidal states are segmentary (though segmental is the more inclusive term), in that they consist of the complementary opposition of similar entities (segments); while in hierarchical states authority devolves from the centre down and in that sense is unitary (ibid.:126–7). Since the term pyramidal applies to 'articulated structures in which the exercise of central authority depends upon consensual delegation to it by the component units in each case' (ibid.), it is clear that the pyramidal states are in fact chiefdoms and only hierarchical states are true states. Indeed, Southall does maintain that 'in a segmentary state the roles at the peak of the pyramid are repeated or at least adumbrated in its subordinate components. The development of unique political roles at the peak of the pyramid turns it into a hierarchy and the segmentary into a unitary state' (ibid.:128); that is, the fully constituted state.

In segmentary states, then (which by my reckoning are not fully fledged states), the subordinate components of political leadership, such as lineage or village heads, owe their position not to appointment by a superior authority, standing, as it were over all; but on the contrary owe their position to its embeddedness (and their own acceptability) within a structural unit like a lineage. And it is further apparent that those constitutive units, to be truly structural, must be corporative in the especial sense of an economically fundamental unit, for without control of its own means of production it could have no political autonomy.

The necessity for such autonomy (*autarkeia*) was central to Aristotle's argument in the *Politics* (Books III and IV), where he defines the irreducible unit of the *polis* (city-state) as consisting in *oikiai*, corporative households composed of the *oikosdespotes* (master), his spouse, dependent children, their spouses, other relatives, slaves and semi-slaves and their mates. 'Aristotle writes of the *oikia* as the minimal building block of the *polis*. Every *polis* is composed of vertical – i.e. segmentary divisions, of which *oikiai* are the smallest discrete units with operational significance. Yet the *polis* is anything but merely an enlarged *oikia*' (Weissleder 1978a:197). The *polis* indeed is an autonomous self-sufficient entity governed by its own citizens who are heads of households. For the *polis* to manifest *autarkeia* in the full sense, there must be as its basis components (households), themselves self-sufficient, self-governing (by the *oikosdespotes*) and complementary in their diversity: they are only structurally not occupationally similar. Internally they manifest a division of labour and between them they cover all the roles necessary to the *autarkeia* of the *polis*.

A state, then, comes into existence only when the population has grown large enough to live well as a political association. . . . Clearly then, the best limit of population is the largest number requisite for self-sufficiency, and which can be taken in at a single view.

More or less the same principle will apply with regard to territory. If asked what kind of land is desirable, all would agree in recommending that which is most completely self-sufficing; and because self-sufficiency consists in having everything without exception, the territory in question must itself produce all that it requires. In size and content it should be such as will afford the population leisure and the means of living at once liberally and temperately.

(Aristotle, *Politics*, Book VII; ed. Warrington, 1959:198–9)

Aristotle consequently did not see the city-state of his time as a 'great household', an *oikos* writ large, but as a distinct political unit emergent from and superior to the diversity of households and undertakings, and in which stratification marked, or rather was the basis of, the division of labour (Finley 1983b:4–5).

With the city-state of Greece we have arrived at a form of political economy similar in many respects to that which obtained longer and earlier in Mesopotamia and which was, indeed, the first form of the state to exist anywhere. As such it is worth providing a brief definition of what Finley (1983b:20) has called the 'basic module' of the Graeco-Roman world until overtaken by the territorial state.

A Greek *polis* (city-state) was a unit of people who (a) occupied a territory containing as its central rallying point a town which held the seat of government and which was itself usually clustered around a walled citadel (*acropolis*) which had originally contained the whole settlement; and (b) had autonomy in that their government was provided by and from their own ranks, not from outside. In some states government might be in the form of hereditary kingship, but not in the early pattern of a theocratic monarch, supreme in his functions, whose decisions could annul the advice of his Council of Elders.

(Jeffery 1976:39)

As '(c)', however, it should be made clear that by city-state is not merely meant the city as an autonomous urban unit, but an (approximately) autarkic entity, requiring the interlocking of the urban centre with its agricultural hinterland, without which none but a few specialized trading cities could have survived. If we substitute a walled temple zone for the *acropolis*[8] the description just given applies in large measure to the Sumerian city-state. And since the city-state is both the earliest and longest-lived form of the state (lasting, minimally, from the fourth to the second millennium) and, with pre-Roman Greece, the most productive (of, for instance, writing in the Sumerian case and demotic script in the Greek), it is indeed surprising that so little attention has been paid to the crystallization of this seminal organization.

Thus the city-state was not just a form of settlement or of government, but a specific form of society. Encompassing as it does the totality of social organization from economy to ideology, the city-state type can be directly contrasted with others, such as the 'village-state' mode usually called 'Asiatic', though by no means confined to Asia. Further, we should be, and are, able to find archaeological manifestations of those qualitative differences in settlement patterns and even construction materials. Thus most of the Shang (*c.* 1,850–1,100 BC) and Chou (1,122–700 BC) 'city' sites of archaic China are large, sprawling, and contain few architectural remains (Chang 1980:129), in complete contrast in all those (and other) respects to the cities of ancient Mesopotamia.

Chinese cities, in common with those characteristic of what I have called (Maisels 1987) the village-state mode of production, were essentially political and cultic, not economic centres. Or rather the wealth consumed in such cities was not produced by them in association with an immediate hinterland, as in Mesopotamia or Greece. Instead they drew revenues – tribute, taxes, corvée, etc. – from a very wide area populated by basically autarkic villages producing largely the same items by largely identical methods. Accordingly, village-states covered territories of orders of magnitude greater than city-states, and cities in them were never clustered, as they were in Mesopotamia and Greece.

The morphology of cities reflects qualitative socio-economic differences, for neither Shang nor Western Chou cities, nor Mayan Tikal, as examples, were nucleated. Their politico-ideological origins and functions are clearly manifest in their layouts. Extending perhaps as much as 10 km around central cultic and elite residential precincts, were dispersed settlements of artisans and other servitors of the elite 'central persons' and 'central practices'. The whole straggling cluster, and particularly the central walled zones separating off the central foci, may archaeologically give the impression of a city (albeit one at a very low population density). But this is illusory, for synoecism is absent; meaning urbanism as a way of life that derives from: (a) nucleation; (b) the ownership of diverse means of production by townsfolk; (c) the civic consciousness and pattern of daily interaction that arises from (a) with (b).

3 Social science and archaeology

This brings us to problems of modelling in particular and problems of theory in general. In archaeology, in contrast to social anthropology, we are dealing with dumb artifacts which must be interrogated, and where only the trivial is obvious. Though basically an empirical and classificatory discipline, archaeology is paradoxically highly theory-dependent because, amongst other considerations, its data are patchy and of uneven quality. There is much arbitrariness and accident as to what remains are discovered and what sites uncovered. Rarely nowadays are sites of any size (and this even includes village-sized ones) wholly excavated even over a period of years. Where wider terrain is tackled it is too often a rush job of rescue archaeology before the sites are irrevocably flooded or otherwise destroyed. Generally, the exigencies of money and politics mean that only selected parts of a site will actually be dug, the rest will be extrapolated from it, and the whole site's wider significance will thus be doubly hypothetical. This pushes problems of theory to the fore, both in regard to what will be asked of the site, thus what (partial) excavation strategy will be adopted, and this in turn will profoundly affect the sorts of overall interpretation given to the site later, both by its excavator(s) and others.

It is important, then, as David Clarke maintained, to have a clear idea of what theory actually is and how it both guides and is informed by practice. Circumstances might now be propitious for such an enterprise as this one, for archaeology seems to have moved on since Clarke (1978:13) could write (originally in 1968) that 'In the theoretical aspect we have the long neglected and festering field of general theory – assiduously avoided by all who wish to preserve their status by concealing their actual method of procedure and dubious mental concepts.' Indeed, emphasis on *explicit* procedures is a hallmark of the 'new archaeology' (Willey and Sabloff 1974:196).

Theory I take to be a corpus of systematically linked concepts sufficient both to define the field of study and to proceed with its analysis. Concepts are delimited and scrutinized 'thought objects' (not any old ideas or images), and as such are usually designated by formal or technical terms. Concepts inform, but cannot be reduced to percepts, that is, to the sense data of empirical reality. Thus the concept 'centre of gravity' is defined by and has meaning within the corpus of theoretical mechanics, a part of the field of physics. Other everyday or transferred uses of the phrase are metaphorical, but to the extent that the meaning then appears obvious or factual, it is potentially misleading.

When a set of concepts can be rendered operational in the elucidation of process by specifying determinate relationships amongst the concepts employed, and between them as a set and the data to be accounted for, then and only then can a theory be said to exist. Thus, like Gandara,

> I hold the view that a theory is a set of systematically related statements, which include at least one law-like principle and which is susceptible of corroboration: that theories are advanced to solve explanatory problems, and that we can evaluate comparatively how well they do this.
>
> (Gandara 1987:210)

Hence the term 'theory' cannot legitimately be applied in that sloppy usage where it is merely a synonym for hypothesis, guess, or worst of all, a belief. Neither can it be the case that a range of theories, if they really merit designation as theory, are equally good in explaining the same data. For the better ones are recognized by more assured premises, and/or are more rigorous in their deductions, and/or are more amenable to empirical (dis-)verification at all stages, the corollary of which is that the best accounts for more data with more ease.

All too often, however, the choice of theory rests on few if any of those criteria, and is simply a matter of predilection. But if prejudice is to be avoided as the (implicit) selection criterion, contending theories can appear to be a matter of choice only for as long as they have not called forth further discriminating data, which the better theories will then account for without special pleading (secondary elaboration). Regrettably, it still has to be said that although a cognitive construct, the power of a theory resides neither in its elegance nor in the satisfaction its proponents derive from it (though this is all the greater when biographical capital has been invested in it). On the contrary, a theory's power is measured by its ability, first to account for extant data with logical consistency, then to predict and be congruent with newly acquired data, and ultimately to allow real objects to be acted upon, or processes intervened in, with the desired effect attained. Where, however, as in macro-social, historical, or prehistoric processes, interventions may not be made directly or at all, the power and purpose of a theory resides in its ability to detail the connections within systemic processes.

It is in this latter sense that the present work should function as a theoretical enterprise.

Chapter two

The premisses of social succession

1 The relationship of demography and technology to social structure

It is a central theme of this work that population growth, technological, and social change are, where present, systematically related and that far from there being a single 'prime mover', one element which drives the whole system, those factors move together in pulses. Further, that a burst of change results in a new social configuration that is stable not only in regard to social organization, but which is also relatively static in its demography and technology. Conversely, where rapid and profound changes are seen to occur in those factors, then we should expect that a new social configuration is coming into being.

A plateau of population density is thus attained which is not destabilized by changes in technology, for the latter is constrained by the overarching mode of social organization and, like the plough, will only 'expand population' when other social pressures dictate its use. Rather, a social configuration is qualitatively transformed either by failure to adapt internal social arrangements to ecological changes, or by the inherent social contradictions when combined with challenges external to the system. For social reproduction is neither automatic nor certain but problematic.

From the hxaro exchanges of !Kung foragers, through the woman exchanges of the Kachin and the matrilateral cycling of foodstuffs in the Trobriands to the grain allocations made by one Bazi, a Sumerian temple administrator (all discussed below), the continued functioning of society's relations of production and their re-creation over time are manifestly conditional upon the political field remaining intact, where politics is defined as the zone of interaction of economic, ideological, and coercive resources. (This use of the term 'politics' to conceptualize a social field is developed at several points later in the work.)

Such relationships are, of course, conditional. The interplay is, for instance, under jeopardy of sectors of the population at some stage declining to play the game, such as the Merina exchange of wealth for blessings (Bloch 1977:321); or being no longer in a position to play the game as hitherto because of changed circumstances (causing, for example, the caricature that the potlach became); or because the ecological basis has been eroded, as exemplified in Highland Burma (Chapter 6, Section 4) with the degeneration of forest to grassland.

What those examples indicate is that, first, there is not an 'ecology' external to society. Second, that there is not, beyond hunter-gatherer society, a relationship to the ecology shared by all the members of a society. Rather, different social categories have different relationships to the environment, more or less buffered, and/or they relate to different facets of the environment, that is, exploit essentially different environments. The Kachin/Shan, hill/valley, swidden/paddy dichotomy is one clear example discussed below, as is the pastoralist/agriculturalist symbiosis of the Near East. These are essentially differentiated groups exploiting complementary niches.[1] Quite a different situation obtains, however, when a land- or herd-owner, experiencing declining yields due to overexploitation of the terrain, simply intensifies the labour inputs of his subordinates to keep output up. Manifestly, such an owner's relationship to the environment is mediated by the labour of others and the political situation by which they are constrained. Thus ecology is not external but is internal to society, to its production and reproduction, and neither society nor ecology are homogeneous entities.

It is, then, to elaborate Polanyi ((1944) 1957), not just 'the economy' which is embedded in the very social structure, but technology and demography also; for of what can 'the economy' consist if not in the application of particular technologies by particular social categories on the basis of population size and density? (Gouldner and Peterson 1962:54–66; cf. also Chapter VII on modes of production for a model of this interaction.)

Population thresholds, like any others, are set by limits. We can represent this (Figure 2.1) as the application of two 'laws' or principles, usually called after Liebig and Zipf.

Zipf's (1949) Law is in fact the well-known thermodynamic Principle of Least Effort. As it applies to human activity it simply postulates that people will preferentially seek to engage in those productive activities which result in the largest margin of return (output) per unit of input of labour. Thus if possible the distance travelled to work in the fields will be minimized, foraging sites will be chosen offering a variety of resources locally, and resources like big-game or shoals of fish will be exploited in preference, say, to small or dispersed animals whose overall density might none the less be the same (Hayden 1981:543–4). Indeed, as will be argued below, a whole mode of life, foraging or swiddening for example, will be preferred to settled agriculture on just such considerations.

Liebig's Law ('of the Minimum') operates to restrain plant or animal growth and reproduction below the level set by the factor of least adequacy (the inhibiting factor) whether that be water, shelter, game, or whatever human populations require (cf. Braidwood and Reed 1957:25); or the minerals, precipitation, insolation required by plants and animals (cf. Odum 1975:109–10). This means that populations that are relatively homeostatic (i.e. do not undergo marked oscillations) are constrained at the level set by the availability of some essential factor at the time of its leanest supply or greatest requirement; obvious examples being water in summer, shelter and calories in winter, protein at any time. It is the removal of whatever the particular bottleneck is that permits population to rise to a new level beneath which it is held either by another limiting factor now in play or by the previous one at its current level.

However, the costs of lifting limits are paid either in increased social complexity, labour, or technological elaboration (Narroll 1956:687–713; Harner 1970:67–86). Thus we can envisage the two tendencies, least cost and least factor, counterposing each other and in the process forming a threshold (Figure 2.1).

The 'effective environment' is of course those aspects of the environment which can be exploited with a given technology, sometimes referred to as the 'techno-environment' (cf. Harris 1971:203ff; Peterson 1979:111ff). Technology is, however, not the single entity usually assumed. What are generally conflated under this head are at least three entities with distinct evolutionary implications:

1 technology in the narrow sense, by which implements and machines are usually meant;
2 facilities, usually fixed, such as storage bins or canals;
3 domesticates, animal and vegetable, i.e. 'processors' under human control.

For the three taken together there is not even an adequate term in English, so here I will use the term 'technics' where I want to draw attention to all three facets. Hassan's (1981:261) term is 'technoculture',[2] but a more common, though contested, compound would be 'productive forces'. They are of course only operational in the matrix of social relations of production, which are invested with the techniques for their use. Full discussion of those points is reserved until Chapter 7. Summarily, relations of production determine what is produced, by what means, by and for whom.

Least Effort can of course be expressed reciprocally as maximal efficiency, which in the foraging and swiddening case maximizes time available for non-subsistence pursuits. Least Effort only applies, however, where people are actually in control of their own conditions of production. Then they will tend to follow the 'satisficer' strategy of prudentially pursuing stability and minimizing risk, with the aim of

Figure 2.1 The demographic threshold

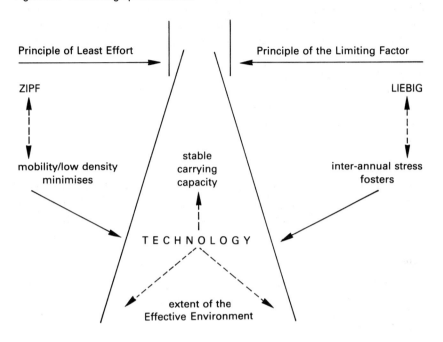

securing subsistence and social integrity even under the worst conceivable conditions. When, in a stratified society, the majority are constrained to work under conditions set by others, then this determining elite will minimize its own efforts by maximizing those of others. Further, it will tend to pursue an 'optimizer' strategy of maximizing output. This is the phase of the 'rise of civilization', whereby local disparities of glut and dearth are smoothed by stocks and efficient transport, regional and inter-regional exchange is promoted, as also is a heightened division of labour by specialization. All of this allows population to rise to new levels, but ultimately continuous heavy surplus extraction exhausts the basis, social and natural (Adams 1978).

The Limiting Factor can also be, and often is, set not just by seasonality (by the amount of a critical resource available in the leanest season of an annual cycle), but in the poorest year of a multi-year cycle, obviously critical in agriculture where sufficient seed must be available every year. It is then this lower inter-annual level which marks the limiting factor and, in social terms, is translated into a strategy of 'least risk' to be attained either passively by containing population or consumption beneath limits set by 'worst-case' conditions (Hassan's (1981:167) optimum carrying capacity); or by embarking on an active strategy of maintaining disposable reserves to meet the worst case (even if those take the form of items to be used in exchange); or by developing production techniques sufficiently diverse or extensive as to provide some sufficiency even under the most adverse conditions (Colson 1979:20–3).

Very low population densities and the mobility that accompanies the foraging way of life set low demands on the environment, keep options open with regard to fluctuations in diverse resources, and offer the greatest security, so making low demands on technological development. It is under severe environmental stress induced by secular resource changes, and in the response to set non-stressful (i.e. optimal) limits to subsistence, that Hayden (1981:520) sees the dynamic of technological change from the Palaeolithic into the Neolithic. The post-Pleistocene tendency to buffer resources by extending the number of those habitually exploited, necessitated, in Hayden's view (op. cit.:520) 'the use of technologically specialised equipment [hence] overall technological complexity increased with staple food diversity'. Innovation, therefore, is 'viewed as a probabilistic event dependent on episodes of disequilibrium'; the point being that when things are going well there is little motive for change (Piggott 1965:26). While this argument will be exemplified below, the 'stress makes change' hypothesis needs to be combined with a postulate regarding *conditions of opportunity*, in the absence of which no amount of stress, say upon the Inuit, can make them develop cereal farming – the permissive conditions are just absent. On the other hand particularly favourable conditions, say for intensive fishing on the northwest (Pacific) coast and Peru, are themselves *inducements* to develop the appropriate technology for the fishery's exploitation.

But this is not the traditional approach to social succession. Founding fathers as disparate as Durkheim ((1933) 1964:336) and Marx and Engels ((1846) 1976:44–5) have attributed the impulse behind the rise of urban society and the state rather straightforwardly to the increased division of labour consequent upon a population growth taken almost as axiomatic, an approach enjoying a current fashion also. Thus for Durkheim, in his well-known discussion of the *Division of Labour in Society* (op. cit.): 'Civilisation is itself the necessary consequence of the changes which are produced in the volume and density of societies.' While for Marx (op. cit.) with the increase of population 'there develops the division of labour, which was originally nothing but the division of labour in the sexual act [*sic*], then the division of labour which develops spontaneously or "naturally" by virtue of natural disposition (e.g., physical strength), needs, accidents, etc.'.

In this vein, but with a heavy technological stress, one of the foremost archaeological theorists of this century, V. Gordon Childe (1958:78), could state: 'the first step towards escape from the rigid limits of neolithic barbarism was the establishment of the metallurgical industry'. This not only 'broke down the self-sufficiency of the neolithic village', but specialization 'overturned the barbarian social order, based on kinship, and evoked a new population of full time specialists. The latter is my excuse for calling it the Urban Revolution.'

Only recently has the view been systematically expressed, for example in Hassan (1973), Cowgill (1975b), or Bender (1978) that the growth of human population (and with it the technology employed) is not a law of nature but an outcome of prevailing social relations. Taking rising population as given when in fact it is not only contingent but called into question by the evidence, only begs the questions that have to be answered in the historical and contemporary worlds.

Indeed Marx ((1867) 1918:692-3) recognizes this problem (though he does not resolve it) when, in opposition to Malthus he holds that each period, or more exactly each type of social organization, has its own 'law of population', which is certainly not to be explained by the alleged natural and ineluctable tendency (in Malthus) for a geometrical rate of population increase to meet a limit in a mere arithmetical increase in food production. And he concludes (ibid.): 'An abstract Law of Population exists for plants and animals only, and only in so far as man has not interfered with them.'

But Malthus did not just rely on the mismatch between two exact ratios (which anyhow only occurs between second and third expressions); his was not really a mathematical or statistical argument but one from nature. Rather his thesis depended upon

> that law of our nature which makes food necessary to the life of man, [means that] the effects of these two unequal powers must be kept equal. *This implies a strong and constantly operating check on population from the difficulty of subsistence.* This difficulty must fall somewhere; and must be severely felt by a large portion of mankind.
>
> (Malthus 1970:71; my emphasis)

Malthus's constantly operating checks are of two types, preventative and positive, evaluated by him as vice and misery: 'The sum of all the positive and preventative checks, taken together, forms undoubtedly the immediate cause which represses population' (ibid.:28); checks necessary if the population is not to exceed what would now be called carrying capacity. Flew (ibid.:27), illustrates this as in Figure 2.2 and calls it the 'neutral system' in contrast to Malthus's 'pejorative system'.

For in Malthus's view:

> there is no reason whatever to suppose that anything besides the difficulty of procuring in adequate plenty the necessaries of life should either indispose this greater number of persons to marry early, or disable them from rearing in health the largest families. But this difficulty would of necessity occur, and its effect would be either to

Figure 2.2 Malthus's neutral control system

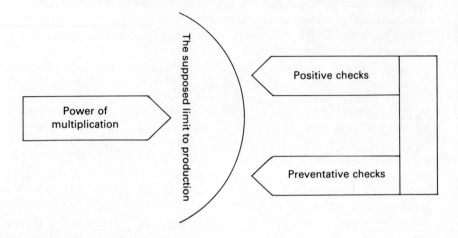

discourage early marriages, which would check the rate of increase by preventing the same proportion of births, or to render the children unhealthy from bad and insufficient nourishment, which would check the rate of increase by occasioning a greater proportion of deaths; or, what is most likely to happen, the rate of increase would be checked, partly by diminution of births, and partly by the increase of mortality.

(Malthus 1970:243)

The former are, of course, the preventative checks, the latter the positive, 'and the absolute necessity of their operation in the case supposed is as certain as and obvious as that man cannot live without food' (ibid.).

Positive checks, then, are causes of premature death in an existing population; while preventative checks are those obviating births, of which Malthus admits only delayed marriage and abstention outside of it. Malthus assumes as constant the 'instincts':

1 to the earliest possible marriage for everyone;
2 breeding within marriage right up to the limit set by procuring subsistence.

Not considered by Malthus as either efficacious or desirable:

(a) birth-control in marriage or out of it;
(b) abortion or infanticide to couples or single persons;

except in so far as either or both measures fall under the dismissive rubric of 'vices'. As for effective birth-control as public or private policy 'from prudential considerations' he could only admit abstinence from marriage, either for a time or permanently, from prudential considerations, with a strictly moral conduct towards the sex in the interval. And this is the only mode of keeping population on a level with the means of subsistence which is perfectly consistent with virtue and happiness.

(Malthus 1970:250)

All other checks, he goes right on to say, whether of the preventative or positive kind, 'resolve themselves into some form of vice or misery', which of course says nothing about their efficacy. Malthus's moralism just could not admit as population regulators other 'checks of the preventive kind', birth-control and abortion, except as vices to be avoided as 'a general corruption of morals with regard to the sex which has a similar effect; unnatural passions and improper arts to prevent the consequences of irregular connections' (ibid.). Regular connections within marriage would presumably not admit of such unnatural inter-ference with the laws of God and nature. Which is particularly interesting, for although Malthus was, in the first instance, writing of his contemporary world, the same laws, he maintained, also held 'In the rudest state of mankind, in which hunting is the principal occupation, and the only mode of acquiring food (ibid.:81). There, amongst

nations of hunters . . . their population is thin from the scarcity of food . . . it would immediately increase if food was in greater plenty, and that, putting vice out of the question among savages, misery is the check that suppresses the superior power of population and keeps its effects equal to the means of subsistence.

(Malthus 1970:82)

Contained in the (First) *Essay* of 1798, the Malthusian argument 'of the superior power of population to the means of subsistence' (ibid.:83) was (and is) still important enough to cause Sahlins (1974:49) to ask 'What are we to make of the popular inclination to invoke demographic pressure on resources in explanation of diverse economic and political developments ranging from the intensification of production to the elaboration of patrilineal structure or the formation of the state?' By 'popular tendency' is here obviously meant not just the journalistic but the academic also. Sahlins observes (ibid.) that very seldom do what he calls 'archaic' economies attain the theoretically possible carrying capacity of their terrain. In regard to the range of resources available and the technology extant for its exploitation, higher population levels can generally be sustained. Is it then not rather the case, he asks, that the social organization of production, in particular the allocation of land, determines demographic levels and constraints, rather than either the natural environment or 'human nature'.

Sahlins (ibid.:41–51) cites many examples of societies 'failing' to populate their terrain to its maximal values. One example of the means employed and not given by Sahlins is contained in Lorna Marshall's account (1967:18) of !Kung Bushman bands: 'The !Kung limit their population by infanticide. They generally space their children at least two and often four or five years apart. Infant mortality takes another toll and keeps !Kung families small.'

And Lee further observes how ideology serves this purpose:

> For example, the fact that women go to the bush to give birth and insist on excluding men from the child-birth site is justified by them in terms of pollution and taboos; but the underlying explanation may be that it simplifies matters if a decision in favour of infanticide is made. Since the woman will commit a considerable amount of her energy to raising each child, she examines the newborn carefully for evidence of defects; if she finds any, the child is not allowed to live and is buried with the afterbirth. By excluding men from the childbed women can report back to the camp that the child was born dead without fear of contradiction.
>
> (Lee 1982:41–2)

Lee (cited Ripley 1980:353) states that the !Kung San practise infanticide at the rate of 6 per 100 births. Similar examples could be dug out of many ethnographies.[3] Consider, for instance, Malinowski (1929:49) on the Trobriands. He reports that girls commence intercourse at or even before puberty, but children are virtually never born out of wedlock, that is, until there is a socially assured place for such offspring (1929:166). Quite clear is the Trobrianders' assertion: ' "Copulation alone cannot produce a child. Night after night, for years, girls copulate. No child comes!" In this we see again the same argument from empirical evidence; the majority of girls, in spite of their assiduous cultivation of intercourse, do not bring forth.' In substance: 'Fecundity in unmarried girls is discreditable; sterility in married women is unfortunate' (Malinowski 1979:108).

Since marriage is socially regulated, it means that population is socially regulated, as Evans-Pritchard (1940:17) found of the Nuer when he stresses that it is cattle, functioning as bridewealth, that beget children. Thus the reproduction rate of humans is tied to the reproduction rate of cattle. As one marries only with cattle, Mary Douglas titles this process 'Where the cattle are, the women are not' (1973:78). Regarding East African pastoralists, amongst whom age-grading also obtains, Bonte (1977:178) observes: 'The two main factors regulating marriage age are the need to assemble a substantial number of animals in order to marry (the livestock being obtained from both agnatic kin and stock associates) and the rule ordering marriages according to seniority.' Indeed Bonte (ibid.:179) goes so far as to say that 'Kinship only exists as part of a wider system of social relations manifested in the circulation of livestock.'

At the other end, Woodburn (1979:260) speaks of 'the neglect and abandonment of the injured, the sick and dying', and states that 'Hadza who suffer injuries [in hunting and gathering] have less chance of survival than if they had been members of a sedentary community with kin who were obliged to provide for them.' But the Hadza recognize few 'load-bearing relationships' and hence social relations, being minimal, like their politics (ibid.), have an implicit tendency to hold population down.

Even this brief review shows that there are many means, institutional and individual, ideological and physical, for the regulation of numbers in a population and that it is not an 'input' external to the social system. Population levels are, rather, a 'condition of state' of all the elements of a system, whose values it has means of regulating, if not exactly, at least within limits that can be set quite narrowly. Consequently we can for the moment conclude with Hitchcock (1982:254) who states: 'These findings suggest that a combination of cultural, nutritional and hormonal factors are related to changes in demographic patterning.' Next the specific logic of population dynamics will be developed. Here it is only necessary to indicate that it did not 'just drift' or push relentlessly upwards with the social structure adapting itself to accommodate ever-rising levels.

2 Is population pressure an historical constant?

In a now quite influential hypothesis M. N. Cohen (1975, 1977) has taken the ineluctability of population-pressure so far as to say that the Neolithic transition is the outcome, not of a concatenation of factors in the Holocene (as described below), but of accelerating population pressures through and from the Palaeolithic period. Cohen admits that such a hypothesis is near impossible to demonstrate directly, so he relies instead on two indirect measures of rising population density: the *necessity* as he sees it (1977:78) of the move to the broad-spectrum and aquatic economy of the Epipalaeolithic; plus expansion of necessity into wholly new environments by the colonization of new regions (1977: 89). This Cohen correlates with the impelled shift from more desirable/easily obtained subsistence resources to those that are, at least initially, less palatable or more demanding of labour (1977:78).

This accounts, according to Cohen, for the observed shift at the end of the Palaeolithic from the pattern of big-game/large-herd hunting toward small-game hunting with fishing (and seemingly increased gathering) characteristic of the Meso- and Neolithic. While some, such as Clark (1973:94), see an undoubted decline in the European Mesolithic, making those 'in all measurable respects inferior to that of their Advanced Palaeolithic forebears', Clark attributes this precisely to the 'altogether exceptional conditions which came to an end with the Ice Age itself' (ibid.; cf. MacNeish 1972, 1977 for Meso-American and Peruvian similarities).

What came to an end were the steppe, tundra, or prairie conditions induced by glaciation that so favoured the large herbivores (Clark 1980:89). As temperatures and precipitation rose so too did both sea-levels and the diversity index of flora and fauna with the advance of boreal forest (ibid.:44–5). But the exploitation of the new resources required an adjustment and learning period (ibid.:45–58; Braidwood and Willey 1962b:342). None the less, as Cohen scans the globe, such regional processes seem to lose their relevance for his argument. Though Cohen reviews (1977: *passim*) a considerable amount of literature to support his thesis, his actual demonstration turns out to be circular:

> I argued in chapter 3 ['The case for the Old World'] that certain changes in human exploitative patterns are likely to be more reliable indicators of population growth than changes in the relative density of sites, since the latter are more subject to sampling error.
>
> (Cohen 1977:129)

However, since most archaeological evidence we have about 'human exploitative patterns' as much else does in fact come from such sites, this is scarcely an analytic distinction that can be made operational.

'On the one hand population pressure, at least as I have defined it, seems to be increasing in post-Pleistocene Europe. On the other hand, there is some evidence that the absolute population of the sub-continent may have declined' (1977:129). This is a possibility, Cohen says, if 'there had been a catastrophic decline in available resources resulting from changing climate' (ibid.). Well, the climatic evidence is to the contrary (Clark 1980: *passim*).

Now, while admitting that hunting-gathering societies socially limit their populations to well below carrying capacity (1977:51, 64), Cohen maintains that (a) the membership flux known to exist between hunting-gathering bands allows of (b) a membership flux over a wide area (1977:64), that, in turn (c) permits a slowly rising and generalized population level in a region since bands do not have fixed numbers and perceive there to be adequate subsistence resources available to them *as individual bands*. This, in Cohen's model, makes a certain 'population-control leakage' possible, tolerable, and even inevitable, because

> despite certain pressures the community can bring to bear, birth control and infanticide decisions are often a private matter for parents alone to decide, rather than a matter of strict group policy. Parents make their choices based on their perceptions of a whole range of relevant variables.
>
> (Cohen 1977:54)

However, rising density leads to declining population flux as outsiders become increasingly resented as bearing more heavily upon available resources (ibid.:82). The maximal exploitation of the available resources, including those hitherto neglected or regarded as of 'low prestige', then demands sedentism with all its liabilities, as Cohen sees it:

> I suggest that sedentism *in most cases* occurs, not because of newly discovered resources which *permit* year round residence in a single location, but rather because of the decline of resources associated with other parts of the traditional annual cycle, or because of territorial impingement by other groups.
>
> (Cohen 1977:83; original emphasis)

Indeed Cohen argues that the groups which did not self-limit population enjoyed a 'competitive advantage' over those that did, and consequently displaced or eliminated them.

In his comprehensive survey of the Neolithic of the Near East, James Mellaart (1975) could discern, from the duration, number, and small size[4] of sites over the period of the Kebaran and Zarzian Epipalaeolithic cultures of the region, that 'they hardly suggest overpopulation, and all one can infer is that there were probably more people in the Epipalaeolithic than in the Upper Palaeolithic' (ibid.:27). And in Palestine, an area more intensively investigated than Mesopotamia, there is just not any evidence for population increase, but on the contrary, 'total numbers of archaeological sites known . . . fall dramatically from the late Kebaran to Natufian PPNA' (Oates 1980:311).

Instead Mellaart suggests that what population advance there was is quite insufficient to suggest any pressure, but is instead a consequence of advancing cultural sophistication that has 'an increasing awareness of the environment' (op. cit.:27). It so happens, too, that Mellaart sees 'the increase of population as the result not the cause, of new technology and economy' (ibid.:22). While the groundwork in terms of tools and techniques was being laid during the Epipalaeolithic of the Levant,

> The sudden changes at the beginning of the Natufian[5] cannot therefore be ascribed to climatic deterioration and resulting demographic pressure. On the contrary they seem to be due to man's awareness of new *opportunities of food conservation and exploitation*, already explored during the preceding Kebaran.[6]
>
> (Mellaart 1975:19; my emphasis)

The challenge of changed conditions in Holocene times was mentioned earlier and, if we are to avoid social voluntarism, we must try to stipulate just what it was that made people 'aware of new opportunities', to invent new (composite) tools and techniques and, most of all, 'facilities' like storage bins. Cohen falls into this trap of social voluntarism when he makes statements maintaining that 'Some [populations] in fact *chose* to limit population at the hunter-gatherer level. Some just as clearly did not' (1975:88; my emphasis). Just one of the things wrong with this explanation is that central to his case is the premiss of parental reproduction choice often violating either group pressures, or group interests, or both. So how does 'social choice' predominate? We may speak of society as an organism, but that is only a metaphor. Both Cohen and Mellaart will have to do without their transcendental subject – Society. Society is not a conscious subject, but a resultant object of systemic processes (Gouldner and Petersen 1962:8–13).

Two considerations are available finally to dispose of Cohen's thesis. If population levels were everywhere rising during the Upper Palaeolithic (at least), why was the Near East the first to Neolithize itself and produce farming and urban clusters? The answer of course resides in the peculiar *concatenations* of processes, natural and human, in that specific place and time, the terminal Pleistocene (H. E. Wright 1977:296–7). While population fluctuated elsewhere, in the Near East it tripped a resonant amplification system of the type that we have recently seen in this Egyptian example:

> The success of the Delta barrage on the Nile was such that, as the cultivated area and the population increased, it became necessary, in 1884, to strengthen the barrage to provide more water to cope with increasing demands and, when this proved inadequate, to build dams and reservoirs.
>
> (Walton 1969:125)

Similar developments occurred upstream at the cataracts where the Aswan dam had to be raised three times this century to cope with its own (previous) success in supplying ever larger populations (ibid.). This is of course an example of positive feedback in one system, that of water-supply; but since positive feedback obtains, other (sub-) systems of the general social system (e.g. food-supply, power, or transport) are necessarily changed. Such systemic changes over time is what is meant by 'process'.

On the crucial question: 'Why the Near East?' Cohen is forced (1977:281) to concede that he 'cannot yet explain satisfactorily why, given the overall buildup of population pressure, agriculture began slightly [!] earlier in some regions than in others nor why it was developed independently in some regions and diffused to others'. Effectively an admission of defeat. However, the final refutation of Cohen's thesis really resides in the case of the Australian continent, which can indeed be regarded as a historico-geographical controlled test (Peterson 1979:122). Upper Palaeolithic people entered Australia not less than 16,000 years ago (Mulvaney (1966) 1976:76–7) and rapidly filled up the continent to densities varying according to differential rainfall and land fecundity. Distribution of population was both uneven and selective; well-watered coastal and riverine districts carrying the most dense populations. Kenneth Maddock ((1972) 1973:22–3) supplies the following estimates for the pre-colonial period:

Gidjingali (Arnhem Land)	2 persons to the square mile
Wanindiljaugwa (Arnhem Land)	1 person to 3 square miles
Walbiri (Central Australia)	1 person to 35 square miles
Aranda (Central Australia)	1 person to 12.5 square miles
Murray River Aborigines	3–4 persons to the mile of river
Sydney Aborigines	5–10 persons to the square mile.

Between New South Wales and the interior, for instance, we have density differences of several orders of magnitude. Maddock comments that:

These figures are not very indicative of land use in different areas, because Aborigines were selective about their surroundings. Expanses of country that yielded little were passed over in favour of more fruitful stretches. The Aranda seldom visited much of their territory, so parts that were relatively bountiful and hence more likely to be frequented would usually have been more densely occupied than the estimate suggests. This is brought out by T. G. H. Strehlow's account of the southern Aranda (1947).

(Maddock 1972:22–3)

Population flux there was aplenty as bands moved around the clan 'estates' (ibid.:35) and as membership fluctuated between bands (ibid.). But of upward population drift there was none, for the bands not only limited their numbers to well below the carry capacity of the gross environment, but indeed kept numbers within the limits of the *optimal* environment! That is, they were not even 'forced' into what was for them sub-optimal terrain. Upper Palaeolithic Aboriginal society even 'Neo-lithized' itself *in situ* to the extent of developing both microliths and composite (hafted) tools from around 3,000 BC (Mulvaney, op. cit.:80). It developed however no pottery, permanent structures, or other aspects of material culture associated with the 'full' or archetypal Neolithic of Eurasia. Most of all it developed no agriculture, and it remained in hunter-gatherer homeostasis until the advent of Europeans.

But worst of all for Cohen's thesis is a comparison of Australia with !Kung (Bushman) foraging territories. Peterson's (1979:111–29) analysis indicates that while the component bands of each population are indeed in constant flux for personal, political, and environmental reasons, band membership is remarkably stable in overall numbers and at least in core membership. Those latter represent what can be called the 'corporate' existence of the group, not in juridical terms but in terms of continuity of a certain number of people habitually and systematically exploiting a territory with which they have long association. This territory, called in the Australian literature the group's 'range' or 'estate' (for there is an element of patrimonialism) and the Bushman's n!ore, is usually centred on waterholes for the latter and on ancestral sites for the Australians. Both territories contain a range of resources necessary to subsistence and Peterson's crucial point is that far from flux leading to ignorance of what resources are available, the strong statistical association of at least core group members to territory that they 'own', 'provides localised feedback making orderly population control possible by creating finite resource areas for definite populations' (op. cit.:122). Thus the 'individual bands' are as much a fiction as Cohen's private individuals who compose them. All exist only in relation to 'resource nexuses' (ibid.:117) which set known limits on who can be supported. Strongly correlated with place of birth, long-term residents have primary rights, incomers secondary rights, and newcomers only conditional rights on sufferance. Thereafter, 'residence is surprisingly stable since n!ore ownership correlates strongly with birthplace' (ibid.:116). This of course cannot apply when new groups are moving into new territories. It does however apply once the territory has filled up.

Such data refute Cohen's thesis at least for the seminal areas of the Near East, and support the concept of 'pseudo-density' outlined by Bennett Bronson (1977:40–2). By pseudo-density two things are meant. The first is that what counts as population pressure depends on the local environment of local populations, say in a single valley. A continental population in prehistory is an abstraction, useful perhaps for some analytic purposes, but certainly not reflecting conditions 'on the ground' in the actual use of the terrain. At the end of a valley with an alluvial fan, certain resources, say wildfowl, may be abundant, while to the population at the other end of the valley this is a scarce resource for which valuables may have to be given in trade. Conversely, though food may be more than ample in the delta, population may be held down there due to a shortage of non-brackish water. It all depends on the highly localized balance, not only of population to 'total' resources but of proportionality amongst resources.

The other, but related, aspect of 'pseudo-density' is that 'In human as distinguished from animal populations, pressure, scarcity, and stress are to a considerable extent *states of mind*' (Bronson, op. cit.:42; my emphasis), not absolute conditions of the environment. Thus preference for a particular local resource, say fowl, may make it scarce locally by overhunting or simple disturbance. Is this an example of population pressure when there are other perfectly adequate, if less preferred, and still local sources of protein? Obviously we could only speak of pressure where one major resource after another had been seriously depleted.

'Hence, we cannot always glibly say that some sorts of scarcity are due to overall population pressures: they may be due to simple overconsumption' (ibid.:40).

We must conclude with Hassan that

Strong emphasis on the role of population growth as an independent causal force in long-term cultural changes thus may present a serious distortion of the intricate reciprocity between population and production, on the one hand, and between population and other cultural factors on the other.

(Hassan 1975:46)

3 Is agriculture the outcome of technological discoveries?

If, then, human populations possess methods of maintaining stability with their environment (homeostasis), what is it that causes demographic increase? Since all human populations are socially constrained, unlike animal populations, logically we must look to changing social organization (Bender 1978:218). But the conventional view tends to see a direct relation between technology and land-use with population pressure ineluctably driving those changes forward. P. E. L. Smith provides the following illustration (Figure 2.3) on the basis of the Boserup model discussed below.

While acknowledging the relevance of social organization and increased work input per unit of land as the move is made from forest fallow to multi-cropping, Smith none the less 'take[s] the position that population pressure on cultivable land is the critical variable, "the engine which sets in motion adaptive changes in a set of related technological and social variables among subsistence cultivators" ' (op. cit.:423, n. 4). The point is, however, that population pressure cannot just be taken for granted as

Figure 2.3 Technological progression on the Boserup model

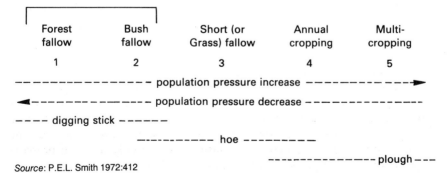

LONG FALLOW

Forest fallow	Bush fallow	Short (or Grass) fallow	Annual cropping	Multi-cropping
1	2	3	4	5

– – – – – – – – – – – – – population pressure increase – – – – – – – – – – →

◄ – – – – – – – – – – – – population pressure decrease – – – – – – – – – – – –

– – – – digging stick – – – – – –

– – – – – – – – – – – hoe – – – – – – – – –

– – – – – – – – – – – – – plough – – –

Source: P.E.L. Smith 1972:412

a 'natural' force that only derivatively affects social organization and technology. Population pressure is not a force outside of society that feeds into it, effecting changes. Here Jack Goody's (1976:20) formulation marks a step forward when he points out that 'the other aspect of advanced agriculture bearing upon the conditions for the emergence of diverging devolution is the expansion of population it allows, another factor making for scarcity of land' and thus affecting inheritance patterns. 'Where such agriculture is dependent on the plough, the increase in production is partly a result of the greater area a man can cultivate: once again, land becomes more valuable, especially the kind that can sustain permanent cultivation by means of the simpler type of plough.'

This puts the problem the right way round – plough agriculture *allows* population to grow further. But why was the employment of the plough necessary in the first place? The usual explanation is, as we have seen, the demiurge of an automatic population growth. Its conventional alternative, or rather complement, is technological 'invention', 'breakthrough', or 'revolution' which, it is suggested, rather pushes population levels upward. For Leslie White (1949:365) the most forthright technological determinist, 'the technology is the independent variable, the social system the depe.1dent variable. Social systems are therefore determined by systems of technology; as the latter change so do the former.' Such a monocausal view results in mere juxtaposition instead of the elucidation of process and produces a sort of evolutionary 'just-so' story. Again, according to White:

As the agricultural arts developed and matured, as plants were improved through selective breeding, as new techniques of cultivation, irrigation, drainage, rotation of crops, fertilisation, etc., were introduced and improved, the amount of food produced increased. Small tribes grew into large tribes and these into nations and empires; villages grew into towns and towns into cities.

(White 1949:378)

While still taking population growth as given, Ester Boserup (1965) does show that this technological determinism explains nothing; explanation must be in terms of what social needs existing and improved technologies serve. Her model has been influential because it is unifying in that it can show sequential changes with a common logic. Attempts have been made to apply Boserup's scheme directly to the origins and development of farming in Mesopotamia (along with a population-pressure prime mover criticized in the foregoing section), most notably in the collection edited by Spooner (1972). It is therefore not sufficient simply to mention her sequence in passing, as is usually done, but to detail it. This done it will later become clear that this scheme, developed originally in regard to conditions in southeast Asia under tropical and monsoon conditions in originally closed canopy forests, does not apply in the sub-Mediterranean climate of the Near East (defined in Chapter 3). None the less there remains the value of the scheme as a conceptual grid for what otherwise tends to be merely 'instances' or 'examples' of disparate land-use without even a common terminology employed to make comparison fruitful.

Boserup (1965) starts by defining different types of cultivation practice based on *length of fallow*, supplying a unifying land-use framework usually absent in discussion.

1 *Forest fallow* represents the best return to labour of any agricultural practice requiring only around an hour's work per day. Known as swidden or 'slash-and-burn' cultivation, and being in extent more truly horticulture than agriculture, it requires twenty times more land in fallow than in use. But this amount of primary forest supplies a complementary range for hunting and gathering.

2 *Bush fallow* obtains when the 'twenty-year rule' is broken with the fallow period lasting only six to ten years, a period insufficient for full forest regeneration. Plots may indeed be in use not for a couple of years as with (1), but may be exploited for from six to eight years. Under those conditions only scrub can regenerate.

3 *Short fallow* prevails when the fallow period lasts a few years only. Then nothing but grasses have time to colonize the fallow and it is of use only to grazing animals. Indeed some have suggested (Stewart 1956:115–29) that as grasslands are seldom true climax anywhere, the 'natural grazing lands' of Africa and Asia are the result of burning off and cutting miombo-type (dry) woodlands, such as are still to be found in parts of Tanzania and Mozambique.

4 *Annual cropping* results in a fallow only during the 'dead months' between crops or seasons in a rotational cycle that includes fallow as ley, as in the Three Field System of medieval Europe.

5 *Multi-cropping* is the most intensive system of land-use, since one plot is made to bear two or more successive crops every year. It is in effect a peculiarity of tropical irrigated agriculture as evidenced in Geertz's (1963) 'Agricultural Involution' with respect to Java.

Now although not the Near Eastern evolutionary process, a succession from (clearing) horticulture to (field) agriculture has much heuristic value since, for instance, true field agriculture demands some type of plough. It is also the case, and an important consideration, that the application of the plough necessitates a form of social organization, and indeed amount of capital investment, quite different from that where, say, the dibble-stick or hoe obtains. The point is that the usual Mesolithic–Neolithic–Bronze Age–Iron Age succession from axe to the metal-tipped plough cannot be seen as *produced* by 'great leaps forward' in productive technique driving society ever onward and upward.

Conversely, Boserup thinks that it is 'natural' population pressure that drives the process of changing land- and tool-use along, demanding ever higher labour and capital inputs. Wherever possible, for sound material-social reasons, swiddening/foraging will be pursued, since:

1 The time used for superficial clearing under the system of forest fallow is but a fraction – perhaps 10 or 20 per cent – of the time required for complete clearing. Pierre Gourou (1971:35) indicates a range of from 25 to about 60 days' work per hectare per year for the cultivation of tubers.

2 Forest horticulturalists are well aware that they obtain the best result for given effort by clearing and cultivating secondary forest, where dry matter can easily be around 160 tons per acre with rainfall a mere 65 inches per year (ibid.:94). Here fire and hoe are the main tools and the plough unnecessary.

3 Operating a primitive plough is hard work, both for the man and the animal, and consequently consumes a lot of energy. In addition to the ploughing itself, the ploughman must take care of animals and keep the plough functioning. Further, unless he keeps a large herd of domestic animals and uses much labour (though not necessarily his own) to collect their manure, prepare composts, and spread it carefully on the fields, he is likely to obtain a much lower yield per hectare under short fallow systems or annual cropping than by cultivating the same land under the system of forest fallow.

> The poverty of tropical grassland results first of all in the slow growth of the animals. A Malgash ox takes six or seven years to reach its full development. And the beasts need a vast amount of space. It is estimated that an acre of tropical pasture can feed only 48 lb of live weight, whilst the same area in Europe can feed 480 lb. . . .[7] In fact, in Madagascar a zebu uses on average some 15 acres of pasture.
>
> (Gourou 1971:64)

4 If the animals are fed exclusively on non-cultivated fodder, the area cultivated in a given year under the systems of short fallow can rarely be more than one-third of the local territory and usually the maximum is much lower. Hence 'To put it briefly, the agricultural systems of the tropics function as if animals did not exist' (ibid.).

Until the advent of mechanized agriculture swiddening is the only form of cultivation that minimizes labour input by maximizing capital input. In burning-off, a huge amount of 'natural capital' in the form of biomass is transformed into nitrogen ash (with other elements) plus soil preparation. Anything from 250 to 450 tonnes of biomass per acre goes up in smoke and 600–900 lbs of nitrogen per acre too, merely to produce 100–200 lbs of nitrogenous ash (ibid.:32–3). Under such conditions fertility lasts only a couple of seasons before the clearing is exhausted. Perseverance after that not only produces meagre crops but makes forest regeneration difficult. Gourou pulls the strands together by suggesting that:

> The ladang [i.e. swidden] system is not an inevitable consequence of the tropical climate and soil; it merely represents a certain stage in agricultural technology. Other methods are possible, as we shall see. It must be recognised, however, that for a population that is small enough to permit a sufficiently lengthy fallow, ladang assures a return per man-hour higher than can be obtained from continuous cultivation by hand, unaided by animals or machines. True, the yield per acre from the latter method is higher, but only at the cost of a greater amount of labour. Fire is a great economizer of energy.
>
> (Gourou, op.cit.:52)

So here we are back to the crucial condition of 'a population small enough', and find a big puzzle why any population should take to cultivation when

> The Bushman figures imply that one man's labour in hunting and gathering will support four or five people. Taken at face value, Bushman food collecting is more efficient than French farming in the period up to World War II, when more than 20% of the population were engaged in feeding the rest.
>
> (Sahlins 1974:21)

In general, then, the more intensive the agricultural system, the more work is required for a unit of food (Harlan 1975:49). Indeed modern intensification demands the application of amounts of work input such that the energy balance is actually negative. More energy (usually fossil) has to be put in (oil, fertilizer, pesticide, etc.) than ever comes out either as food or raw materials (ibid.). The question then is, 'Why farm at all?' Or as the !Kung informed Richard Lee (1968:33) 'Why should we plant, when there are so many mongongo nuts in the world?' Along with eighty-four other species of edible food plants, including twenty-nine species of fruits, berries, and melons, plus thirty species of roots and bulbs (ibid.). And all of this well within a day's walk of the home base.

Where greater production is wanted, leaving aside for the moment the matter of for what reasons, the 'natural' response is to do more of the same, that is to cultivate more extensively but employing the same methods. Depending on the type of social organization either villages 'bud-off' to do this (Forge 1972:374–5), or they 'take-in' to cultivation what had hitherto been waste, commons, or forest (Postan (1972) 1975:57).

35

Only under real *social* pressure would extensification (adding land) give way to intensification (adding labour), and even then this might well *not* result in a 'technical revolution' for 'subsistence is determined more by social than purely technical factors. . . . With the same basic tool array there can be vast differences in the efficiency and productivity of horticultural techniques, nor does the apparent excellence of tools correlate with the excellence of productive technology' (Forge, op. cit.).

When the Yir Yoront of the Cape York Peninsula underwent a leap from Palaeolithic to Iron Age technology with the introduction of the steel axe supplanting the traditional polished stone axes, the heightened productivity was used to provide more sleeping time, 'an art they had [previously] mastered thoroughly' (Sharp 1964:90). When steel axes were introduced to the Siane of the Eastern Highlands of New Guinea, again the indigenous social structure accommodated the improved means of production, and 'As an immediate result of the technological change, the Siane had become more leisured, they had larger and more elaborate ceremonials, and the number and size of ceremonial payments had increased about threefold' (Salisbury 1968:488). It is not that this represents a no-change situation. On the contrary what is being demonstrated is that existing social institutions adapt to accommodate. Indeed Sharp (op. cit.:93) graphically shows that where, amongst the Yir Yoront and in marked contrast to both Siane and Tolai, ideological barriers against adaptation are intrinsic, then only disintegration follows.

A single major technological change can then produce great social shocks, but conversely it is also the case that the application of major new technology requires a prior shock to the body politic if major innovations are to be applied. Hocart provides a down-to-earth example:

> Even if a man had discovered the fertilising effect of manure just by noticing things, he would still have to get his fellows to adopt it. Let anyone who thinks this a simple matter try introducing manure among a people who have never used it; he will meet with incredulity or even disgust. When I tried manuring yams in Fiji, the Fijians thought it disgusting. If people are to adopt such a discovery they must be prepared for it by the general trend at the time.
>
> (Hocart 1954:130)

It is significant that the Fijians were already successful cultivators and saw no need of Hocart's 'improved technique'.

Likewise iron was known as a workable material during the two millennia of the Bronze Age in the Near East.[8] Potentially stronger and cheaper, the technical difficulties to be overcome in working a metal whose melting-point could not be reached by early (bronze and pottery) furnaces were only addressed (by forging) when widespread dislocation in the 'Sea Peoples' period late in the second millennium BC interrupted supplies of tin and copper across the Mediterranean (Maddin, Muhly, and Wheeler (1977) 1979:293). In the few centuries after *c.* 1,200 BC, specifically 'steeled' or carburized iron gave rise to implements such as picks, adzes, and chisels with cutting edges tempered to a hardness equivalent to that of modern hardened steel (ibid.:298). Yet only around 500 iron artefacts, mostly ornamental, are found in the Near East dating from the two millennia of the Bronze Age. Only massive disruption that resulted in the collapse of Hittite Anatolia and Mycenaean Greece with a Dark Age following, made the previously impossible possible because necessary.

In the Iron Age proper, major innovations in the means of production really only occurred at the beginning and end of the Graeco-Roman world, for it was then that the relations of production were qualitatively changing: 'there were not many genuine innovations after the fourth or third century B.C. and there were effective blocks' (Finley 1973:147). Those were social blocks, obstacles in what can be called the 'political economy'. From Aristotle in the fourth century BC to Vitruvius the architect and engineer in the first century AD, there was general agreement between writers on all subjects that since the machines essential to civilization already existed – the ladder, pulley, windlass, wagon, bellows, and catapult – systematic enquiry directed to progress in productive technology was regarded as neither possible nor desirable (Finley, op. cit.:146). The only 'research institute' of antiquity was the Museum of Alexandria, founded and supported by the Ptolemies. Despite its library, building to nearly a million volumes, royal patronage, and eminent scholars, the Museum in its centuries-long existence added virtually nothing to productive technique. Theirs was a tradition of 'pure' not applied research in a society where knowledge was essentially contemplative (Finley 1983b:185; Yonah and Shatzman 1976:303). Though the Romans invented the watermill, the 'mother of machines', it was never deployed on a wide scale as it was in medieval Europe (White 1970:7); and despite the aridity of the eastern Mediterranean in particular, the windmill was never developed from the watermill (ibid.).[9] Accordingly, as Finley points out in his analysis of the ancient economy:

> We must remind ourselves time and again that the European experience since the late Middle Ages in technology, in the economy, and in the value systems that accompanied them, was unique in human history until the recent export trend commenced. Technical progress, economic growth, productivity, even efficiency have not been significant goals since the beginning of time. So long as an acceptable life-style could be maintained, however that was defined, other values held the stage.
>
> (Finley 1973:147)

Similar values prevailed in medieval Britain too, where, as Postan remarks, 'the real problem of medieval technology was not why new technological knowledge was not forthcoming, but why the methods, or even the implements, known to medieval men were not employed, or not employed earlier or more widely than they in fact were' (op. cit.:47). Postan goes on to speak of the 'unmistakable' inertia of medieval agricultural technology and, significantly, states that progress was ' "bunched", into certain periods at the beginning and ends of the era' (ibid.:49).

Even within the 'modern European experience' which is one of sustained change, we have seen that most of the major technologies fostered by the World Wars existed in experimental or theoretical form before the need for the likes of the aviation gas-turbine, penicillin, computers (plus operations analysis and systems thinking), or nuclear fission, became pressing in the social upheavals that armed conflicts represent. It was the First World War that made aviation into a practical proposition and an industry, so that only a decade after the Channel had been flown for the first time (and only just!) the Atlantic was flown by a wartime bomber.

Traditionally the Neolithic has been associated with the advent of ceramics, such wares being both possible and useful to settled agriculturalists. Yet from the famous site of Dolni Vestonice in Czechoslovakia, where Upper Palaeolithic huts have been dated to 23,000 BC and whose associated flint industry is Eastern Gravettian, comes the fired-clay Venus figurine, the oldest identified (Wymer 1982:262). Not an isolated find, the figurine was recovered along with 2,200 pellets of baked clay, some of which were fragments of broken or unfinished animal statuettes (ibid.: 239). Wymer himself concludes, not only that pottery figurines are unknown from any other Upper Palaeolithic site, but that 'this invention of ceramic techniques was a flash which failed to ignite any need or response in the community and probably died with its inventor' (op. cit.:262).

Significantly, there is no further evidence for pottery until the post-glacial period; until, that is, more sedentary conditions made pots desirable, necessary, and practicable. The point, as Renfrew (1984:391) observes, turns on the distinction between invention and innovation, where the latter is the process of adoption and dissemination of an invention. Though the two processes are usually conflated and thus misunderstood, the mechanisms are actually Darwinian. Within limits set by existing social capacities, varieties of 'random' inventions are made, the survival (adoption) of any one dependent upon finding a niche in the social environment.

That technology and productivity are conditioned (often stifled) by social relations can be seen in a particularly germane example, coming as it does from ethnology in agricultural villages of Iraqi Kurdistan. Commenting on 'the lack of efficiency in agricultural techniques and the low level of investment in capital equipment', Barth states that:

> Threshing is generally done with six oxen, without any mechanical appliance or equipment. There does however exist a quite efficient thresher [mentioned by Leach 1940] which could greatly reduce the necessary expenditure of man-hours. The value of this thresher was given as £12, its life approximately 20 years. It is generally considered that 2 mules working 3 days with the thresher do an equivalent of 6 oxen working 10 days without it. If we, to simplify comparison, equate the work value of a mule with that of an ox, that gives a reduction of $\frac{1}{3}$ in man-hours and $\frac{1}{12}$ in expended energy. Though the gain thus seems quite spectacular, the thresher is in fact rarely seen. The labourer himself has no capital to invest in equipment. The tenant farmer pays the labourer the customary share for doing the threshing, whether it is one way or another, and is certainly not interested in assuming any further expenses. Continuing up the hierarchy, there is no greater incentive to such 'investment' for the intermediary or the landowner.
>
> (Barth 1953:23)

4 Mutation and succession

In our culture it is all too easy to take change for granted and assume sustained technical and social change to be a law of nature. But few indeed are the societies where increases in net capital formation proceed as a matter of routine (and competitive pressure), that is, as an intrinsic part of the normal cycle of social reproduction. Surpluses in pre-modern societies, ancient and contemporary, tend to be consumed unproductively by the elite in luxury, ostentation, and aggrandizement. Due to the rigidities of the social order, surpluses left in the possession of non-elites also tend to be unproductively consumed. Accordingly in ancient and pre-industrial societies new capital formation tends to occur in bursts upon qualitative changes in the relations of production. Thereafter development tends to extension of the existing forms, while qualitative changes have to await another period of social re-formation.

 If it is the case that major innovations only occur when social relations are themselves being recast, what are the forces that cause the recasting? Are we simply to look for impacts upon the system from the exterior, and leave it at that, mentioning military defeat or barbarian invasion or some other external source of disaster? Surely not. This might serve where historic state-ordered societies are impacted and destroyed, but even in the case of the collapse of the Roman Empire, which is the archetype of such explanations, can we not more convincingly argue that its internal condition was the primary determinant? When vigorous, Rome could not only repel invaders but expand mightily; when internally weakened it crumbled under attack, encouraging further onslaught.

At any event, this is a description of collapse, but what of advance, in the absence of which there is nothing to collapse? To approach an explanation we must leave the complexities of Roman history for simpler societies and a more schematic model.

Take for instance the model for the emergence of the first agricultural societies from foraging ones. It is proposed in the next chapter that the process commenced with the increasing reliance by foragers upon the wild cereals available in the Near East during the early Holocene. The success of heavy cereal exploitation led to increasing sedentism, which necessitated a new pattern for the exploitation of other resources, particularly animals, and the advent of semi-permanent and then fully permanent villages which the new exploitation patterns made both possible and necessary. New patterns of subsistence allowed population expansion, hence more villages, then larger villages and, with further social change, towns.

At first sight this seems to be a prima-facie case of simple linear evolution, though certainly an internally generated one. Towards the end of the sequence we have monumental architecture, irrigation, administration, writing; somewhat earlier the advent of the plough and wheeled transport, earlier still bone and flint sickles and hoes. Population too has grown by several orders of magnitude to fill cities, so what of the self-constraining interrelations of social systems mentioned previously? The point is, and it is usually overlooked in such discussions, that when we are analysing social succession we are not dealing with one and the same society with greater or lesser dimensions, i.e. one that just grew. There should be a term to distinguish internal evolution of a society at a particular period of time[10] from the succession of social forms to which the term 'evolution' is also, and thus confusingly, applied. We must be clear at what level our analysis applies, such as the three generations alive at any point in time, or other 'real life' periods like that of dynasties. Or are we dealing with artificial retrospective constructs like centuries or even millennia?

In the case of the forager-to-farmer example, therefore, we are speaking of an evolutionary process extending over millennia, and in which what did not occur was that foraging society just got blown up like a balloon to have another scale and complexity. On the contrary, we are dealing with different societies. Foraging society gave way to semi-sedentary society which was succeeded by fully sedentary cultivating society, and so on. Even if they occupied exactly the same areas and were composed of direct descendants, these are not the same societies in terms of internal structure, dimensions, complexity, cosmology, technology, or politics. At each stage the type of social order involved is different. Thus the postulate that a social order incorporates a particular population dimension, with a particular type of technics employed, both intrinsic to the social structure, is not undermined but reinforced by social succession.

This however leaves the problem of internal evolution, or development, to be tackled, unless what is being proposed (which it is not) is that there are only qualitative leaps, and between those fixity in the social order obtains. But manifestly there is *mutation* between *qualitative transformations*, the latter resulting in *social succession*.

Paradoxically perhaps, to look at change through time, that is, diachronically, we must look at relationships at particular points in time, that is, synchronically. To get at dynamics we must be able to see those relationships that persist over time, meaning systemics.

But what exactly do we mean when we speak of a social *system*; is this just a synonym for social structure or social order, concepts developed below? Not at all.

Social system, as here employed, refers to social arrangements seen from a strictly operational viewpoint, as sets of input/output relations between operational entities (sub-systems) chosen for the purposes of modelling.

Thus the economic or subsistence sub-system of foragers divides into male hunting with some gathering (and perhaps fishing), and female gathering with some hunting of small animals, with perhaps some fishing assistance. Subsistence is here our term for a set of different activities, while the cosmology sub-system would consist of a complex of myths, symbols, beliefs, classifications, and rituals that we have grouped together as a (sub-) system for the purposes of study. When we try to show how, for example, cosmology affects subsistence and vice versa, and interacts with other social activities or attributes also regarded as (sub-) systems, we may be said to delineate a *social system*, or more exactly what is indicated is systematicity. This because it is a construct of purely analytical convenience, trying to trace causative relationships between entities of quite different levels in 'real' society, such as marriage (an institution), technology (material culture), and warfare (concentrated political acts).

Human culture would be impossible in the absence of stability, *for culture is about the inter-generational cumulation and transmission of beliefs, institutions, and techniques*. So it has to be stressed that qualitative changes, where they occur, take place over the generations, partially, gradually, and usually imperceptibly, taking perhaps millennia, such as the emergence, from the cultivation of limited hydromorphic soils, of fully-fledged canal irrigation in Sumer. A 'quick' process reaches some kind of fruition perhaps in a matter of centuries, and a hypothetical example will

41

be outlined below. The greater the number of sub-systems present (i.e. the higher the level of social complexity), the quicker will qualitative crises or transformations be reached.

Those truisms stated as prerequisites, we can now introduce intentionality or human purpose, for we must connect systemic modelling with real social phenomena. The intent of human actors is simply to reinforce or improve their existing conditions of life, the only one known to them. An example previously mentioned is the exploitation of a newly abundant resource in the early Holocene, the wild cereal grasses. While initially bolstering a foraging way of life, the next step is to reduce mobility so that this resource can be fully exploited. At every stage people proceed from where they are then – past and future are unknown and unknowable (except mythically). When animals get scarce round the village, then lambs and kids surviving from the hunt must be reared. When natural hydromorphic soils on the edges of springs, marshes, and rivers get scarce, then channels must be dug to lead water. Immediate exigencies are being responded to, not the fulfilment of a plan; and even if it were, the long-range consequences cannot be known, for they are the cumulative result of many and contradictory inputs.

Over time successive increases in complexity, productivity, and sheer scale result in quite different types of society, because each type is able to accommodate (accumulate) so much subsidiary change before the system, formed with earlier parametric values or attribute states, must transform itself into another system. It is obvious that the converse of this is the assertion that social configurations are not infinitely variable and social structure is not plastic.

What causes social mutation to become social transformation I shall call *sub-systemic out-turn*. To illustrate what is meant a hypothetical, but historically realistic example will be given.

Assume a new technique in the working of leather, developed initially let us say for plough-teams, when applied to armour, stirrups, or bridle-bits, puts mounted warriors at a greater advantage relative to peasants. Then the emergence of professional raiders, warrior kings, or warrior castes can alter the system of social stratification, settlement, and land-use, with the most profound consequences for further change.

Say as a result that this society developed into a very rigidly feudal one, but one where a segmental warrior elite are always contesting hegemony one with another. Again, the introduction of a new technology, perhaps iron, or steel, or firearms, while initially only establishing the hegemony of one 'house' or clan, more wealthy or unscrupulous than others, may then allow it to go for supreme power. To secure its by now pre-eminent position it can (for it is now fully ascendant) venture permanently to undermine its rivals by abolishing peasant debts or reducing their taxes, suppressing all sectional warfare, and reserving recourse to arms to itself.

This in turn might well have the consequence of promoting trade, towns, and the new social strata that go with them; all of which quite alters the mode of stratification obtaining, and threatens those interests that brought the new order into being.

Only the simplistic would say that technology *itself caused* all of this. For one thing, we have indicated that invention is never by itself adequate explanation; *what must be accounted for is whether or not it engages with social relations sufficiently to become innovation.* For another, though the example given was in origin technological, others could have been cited that were ideological, like the early history of Islam and the advent of Islamic societies. But any monocausal view ignores the concatenation of forces simultaneously in play. The point is that because of the interconnectedness of all aspects of society, and the concomitant but conflicting desire of its members to improve their own position within it, if one sub-system is substantially altered to further this desire, it has incalculable effects for the protagonists and the system as a whole. Thus one day, slavery or the old gods may be abolished and new men are in charge. The declaration sets the seal, perchance, on a 'revolutionary change' by overt recognition of an outcome. That outcome derives from the fact that the steady-state condition mentioned is not so steady. While a steady-state system is characterized by continuous inputs required to sustain its parameters, these are, in social systems, never maintained exactly or anything like it. Different reproduction cycles, having differential rates, uncertainties, and thus variable mutual influences and outcomes, result in lineaments which are not fixed but intrinsically fluctuating. The consequence is a dynamic not a stable equilibrium. It is this oscillating condition, a composite of processes of varying frequencies, amplitudes, and interferences, that the out-turn of a sub-system can push across the threshold of its limiting values and so transform the system, after inevitable disruption and recomposition, into one with different parametric values belonging to a new configuration of sub-systems. This is the advent of a new society.

I have here used the awkward term 'out-turn' and not (sub-systemic) 'ouput' to stress the potential for change within any sub-system, resulting from particular human actions or intentions; *the key point being that the consequences for the system as a whole are neither foreseen nor intended.*

In Chapter 5 I criticize Flannery's (1972a) attempt to make a general systems approach do service for an evolutionary account.[11] Functional or systems approaches are logically different from evolutionary explanations: the latter both employ a different theoretical framework and must rely on archaeological/historical facts, while the general systems approach is exactly that: one applicable to all systems once their specifics have been reduced. Both functional/systems accounts and evolutionary ones are required for any adequate explanation of social complexity and social change, but the two must be kept separate though connected.

The best and simplest evolutionary accounts have a strict Darwinian process. What this requires is that there be a source of undirected variation and a source of selection. In the biological context the inexact replication of genes is the source of variation and the environment is the source of selection. Differential reproductive success accrues to those individuals whose gene pattern has best 'fitted' them to environmental conditions. That is, the number of those bearing the more advantageous genes will increase preferentially.

This mechanism can be applied to human *societies* if the level at which it is applied is *culture*. Here success is just the same: the dissemination of traits in a given, but now cultural environment, which is the source of selection according to prevailing conditions of social structure and social order (Chapter 8). The source of variation is new or modified ideas or practices by individuals or groups. Variants (innovations) will then be taken up by other groups or individuals according to their location in the social order, and it will succeed, that is be generally disseminated, according to the vigour of competing interests.

Thus the advent of Christianity was an unpredictable variation upon traditional Jewish messianism, taken up and elaborated because it answered a cultural need in the Roman Empire during its first centuries. It thereafter became dominant in the culture of the Mediterranean and Europe because it was ultimately adopted as the Roman state religion. Hence 'fitness' here means (best) fitted to the prevailing cultural and political conditions, and has nothing to do with the adaptation of a society to its physical environment.

As suggested by Rindos (1987:73) in the context of 'go forth and multiply' religions, the process of cultural mutation, while possibly furthering 'fitness' in the sense of proliferating the number of believers, might well be counter-adaptive with respect to economic conditions and the overall quality of life (e.g. freedom from religious wars, tithes, and inquisitions). However, his major theme (1984) is that agriculture became, with the advent of developed agricultural systems, positively maladaptive even for the security and quality of food supplies. Thus 'fitness' and 'adaptiveness' are disconnected when humans are involved, since they are not a population of individuals acting directly on their environment like other animal species; but instead only engage with the natural environment through the social. Accordingly social evolution operates at the phenotypic or behavioural level,[12] from variation in cultural traits selected against the prevailing social structure (of roles) and social order (of organizations).

Chapter three

The ecology of the Zagrosian Arc

This chapter will examine the geographical conditions in the Anatolia–Zagros region of the Near East at the end of the last Ice Age. It will be seen that as the last Ice Age in Eurasia ended, there came into existence in the one region a particular association of plants and animals which were (a) abundant, (b) very useful, and (c) genetically and behaviourally predisposed to domestication. For the first time too in an interglacial, there was present a species of *Homo* who was pre-adapted by behavioural plasticity for manipulating his subsistence resources on an ever-amplifying scale.

Thus in the Near East ten millennia ago, a particular combination of climatic, geographic, biological, and cultural conditions existed, which gave rise directly to permanent settlement and agriculture, indirectly to urbanism and the city-state.

1 Physical geography

The Zagros–Kurdi–Taurus mountain arc forms a crescent of Alpine folds, trending southeast/northwest between the plateaux of Iran and Anatolia, each with a distinct climatic and vegetation pattern (Braidwood and Howe 1962:134). In the north, the Taurus range, running due east, effectively forms the rim of the Mediterranean in Asia Minor; then, as the high (*c.* 1,800-metre) Kurdish Alpines, turns south around 500 km inland to run southeast as the northern littoral of the Persian Gulf, itself a rift running southeast/northwest. The whole arc is displayed in Map 3.1.

This crescent-shaped series of Cenozoic sandstones, conglomerates, gypsiferous marls and limestones, all 'pleated like an accordion' (Hole *et al.* 1971:254–5), totals some 2,500 km in length. It is this great crescent stretching from the Mediterranean to the Gulf which is here called the Zagrosian Arc. Its characteristic altitude is around 1,000 m (Braidwood and Howe 1962:132) and while the western-facing flanks in the central reaches may receive in excess of 1,000 mm (40 inches) of rain annually,

Map 3.1 Some prehistoric and early historic sites in the Near East

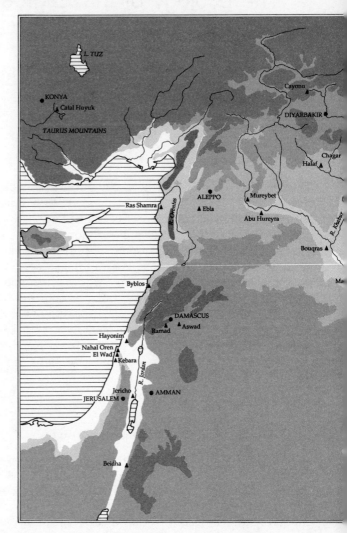

the east-facing slopes are in rain-shadow. So too is the central plain of Syria, which though extending to the west of the Zagros range, is none the less in the rain-shadow of the Lebanon (Jebel Liban) and Anti-Lebanon (Jebel esh Sharqi) ranges that form a line roughly parallel with the eastern Mediterranean coast, at right-angles to the main arc. It is from the lower slopes of the Jebel esh Sharqi that the three main rivers of the Levant: the Orontes (Asi), flowing north and west, the Litani, south and west, and the Jordan, flowing south in its rift valley, have their origins.

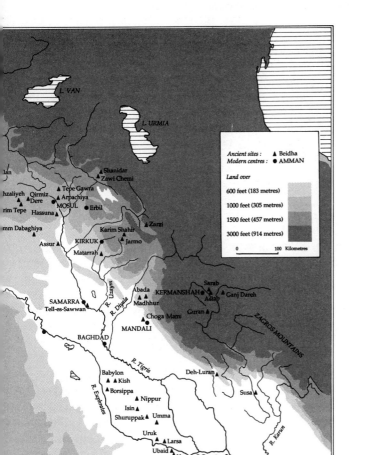

Both the Tigris (**idiglat** in Sumerian) and the Euphrates (**buranum**)[1] originate in Armenia, the former to the south of Lake Van, the latter near Mount Ararat. The westernmost river is the Euphrates which, at around 2,720 km (1,750 miles), follows a more circuitous route south than the Tigris (2,032 km/1,263 miles). Inland from modern Aleppo and ancient Ebla, the modern Euphrates even approaches to within a hundred or so miles of the Mediterranean. The Euphrates drains 163,120 km^2 as against 68,975 km^2 for the Tigris, while the Karun, the other major river responsible for the alluvial areas of Iraq and Khuzistan, drains only

47

Table 3.1 Temperature and precipitation

| | Averages of maximum daily temperature | | Average monthly precipitation | |
	Annual	Warmest month (August)	Wettest month	Driest month
Erzurum	53°F	80°F	3.1	0.9 inches
Mosul	82°F	110°F	3.1	0.1 inches
Baghdad	87°F	110°F	1.1	0.1 inches
Basra	87°F	105°F	1.4	0.1 inches

Source: Air Ministry Meteorological Office, *Tables of Temperature, Relative Humidity and Precipitation for the World. Part V, Asia*, London: 1958, pp. 49–51 and p. 90. Quoted in Larsen, 1975:48.

41,744 km^2 and has a total length of 820 km (Larsen 1975:47).

The other important river in this area is the Diyala, like the Karun to its south a tributary of the Tigris, which the Diyala joins at Baghdad. Still proceeding south to north the Great and Little Zabs, the latter near Mosul, also join the Tigris. Those four southerly tributaries, fed from the Zagros, help make the Tigris a much more torrential and variable river than the Euphrates which has no active tributaries in Iraq, governed instead by rainfall over central Turkey and fed by three perennial tributaries, west to east, the rivers Sejour, Balikh, and Khabur. While the Lower (Little) Zab, between historic Assur and Nuzi, has historically registered a north/south demarcation between the upper Syrian settlement sites and Sumer with Akkad to the south, the Diyala from prehistoric times was a main highway to and from the mountains and over them to the Caspian Gates in the Elburz Range (Mallowan 1965a:18–20). Further, just north and east of where the Lesser Zab joins the Tigris, is where both rivers are intersected by the 200 mm reliable rainfall isohyet trending northwest to southeast. To the immediate south, but still on the east bank of the Tigris, is found the seminal site of Samarra, unable to rely on rainfed farming.

Whereas only a part of central Anatolia (Turkey; see Map 3.3) is *not* potentially cultivable by rainfall alone, rarely falling below 400 mm (Van Zeist 1969: fig. 3), in central Iran the converse holds and cultivation is largely confined to oases (Oates and Oates 1976b:14–15). The overall climatic regime of our region (excluding interior Iran) is an intensification of the Mediterranean 'summer-dry', which means that all crops (excluding, of course, tree crops, rice, cotton, and sesame) are necessarily autumn sown, from October to December (Oates 1980:304). Indeed intensification is such over much of its range that the regime has been characterized for southern Anatolia as 'an extreme continental Mediterranean climate' (Erinc 1980:73). A conspicuous gradient of both temperature and precipitation occurs along a section running from Erzurum, in Turkey, to Basra in southern Iraq. They vary inversely, as can be seen in Table 3.1.

Map 3.2 The reliable 200 mm isohyet in Mesopotamia

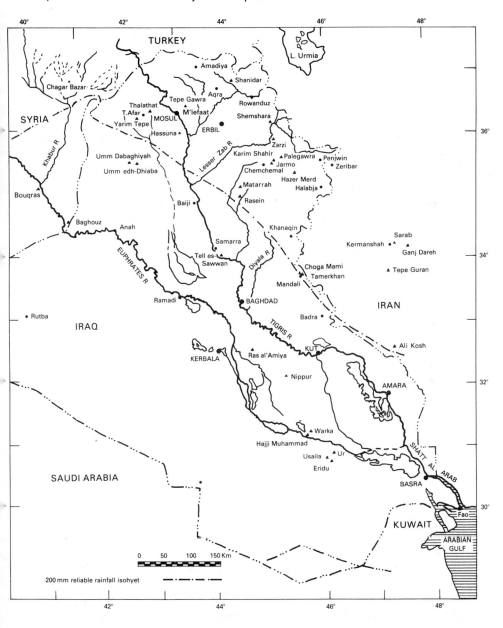

Source: Oates and Oates 1976a:112
Note: Prehistoric sites are indicated by a triangle

Whereas the Mediterranean is summer-dry, on the plains of Mesopotamia there is in fact summer drought, rendering the climate more continental than Mediterranean. On the lower plains what has to be contended with is high mean annual air temperature, large diurnal and annual ranges of temperature, low atmospheric humidity, and scanty, extremely variable rainfall that is concentrated in the winter and spring, most from November to March (R. McC. Adams 1981:11). Actual air temperatures in south central Iraq vary from a January maximum of 26.6°C, with a low of −8.3°C, to no less than 50°C in July, which has a low of 18.3°C (Adams, op. cit.: table 1). Mean variation in precipitation in lowland Iraq can amount to 50 per cent although some rain will occur in any year (Larsen, op. cit.:48). In winter rain-bearing winds from the Mediterranean cross the Syrian Saddle – a gap north of Tripoli between the Lebanon and Amanus outliers of the main Taurus range – supplying precipitation to the westward Zagros slopes (Braidwood and Howe, op. cit.:132).

As previously noted the central Syrian plain through which the upper Euphrates flows, there joined by its tributaries Belikh and Khabur, is in rain-shadow, and south of the Hit–Samarra line which marks the beginning of the alluvium proper, rainfall is less than 200 mm during the main growing season from October to April (Adams, op. cit.:12). As 200 mm is a minimum requirement of dry (i.e. non-irrigated) farming, for 200 mm to be assured every year, it is the 300 mm isohyet that is significant (Oates and Oates 1976a:111). This is clearly indicated on Map 3.2. On it are marked significant sites down to 5,000 BC and from it we observe that all the sites south of the 200 mm reliable isohyet lie, of necessity, on present or former watercourses. Oates and Oates (ibid.), who divide Mesopotamia into three climatic zones – the western and southern deserts, the northern steppes and plains, and the mountains – state that 'only in the northern plain and in the mountains is rain-fed agriculture possible'. Further, 'It may be stated as a generalisation that no significant rain falls in any agricultural area of Iraq from June to September. This includes cultivable mountain valleys at quite high elevations' (ibid.).

Euphrates and Tigris are only about 40 km apart as the latter passes through Baghdad, and they actually join in the extensive marshes north of Basra, whence the rivers, now merged as the Shatt al-Arab, continue for another 100 km to the Gulf. In that final stretch to the sea the river

Figure 3.1 A typical river levee in cross-section

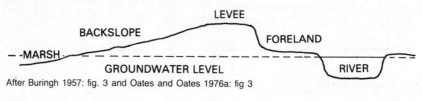

After Buringh 1957: fig. 3 and Oates and Oates 1976a: fig 3

gradient is only 2 m (Oates and Oates 1976b:13).

Although Mesopotamia in Greek means the land between the two rivers (Tigris and Euphrates), a more topographically accurate description would be the plains and piedmonts between the Zagrosian folds and the Arabian massif, with the rivers running down the depositional plains filling the sunkland between (Margueron 1967:201). The Euphrates, the principal river of settlement and irrigation, is deeply incised in its Syrian upper reaches, but on the alluvium proper, which commences around the Hit–Samarra line, forms natural levees (wide raised banks). Levee formation is illustated in Figure 3.1 in cross-section.

With a gradient of only 35 m from Baghdad to the Gulf, a distance of some 500 km, the Euphrates meanders in braided and shifting channels all over the plain, often with disastrous consequences. This is a classic anastomosing regime on an aggradational surface deposited by the river itself, tending thereby to raise its own level in and on the sunkland caused by the compressional forces from crust-spreading along the Red Sea rift system (Larsen, op. cit.:45). In marked contrast the Tigris, a much more torrential river, downcuts through most of its length, making it useless for irrigation without either lifting gear or large-scale works (Adams, op. cit.: 7). Only late, around Sasanian times, was the Tigris extensively employed. Consequently 'there was no band of dense cultivation and urban settlement along the Tigris comparable to what existed along several Euphrates branches' (Adams, op. cit.:158).

Figure 3.2 Distribution of six major biomes in terms of mean annual temperature and mean annual rainfall

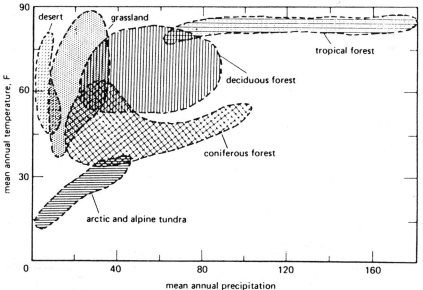

Source: Odum 1975:185

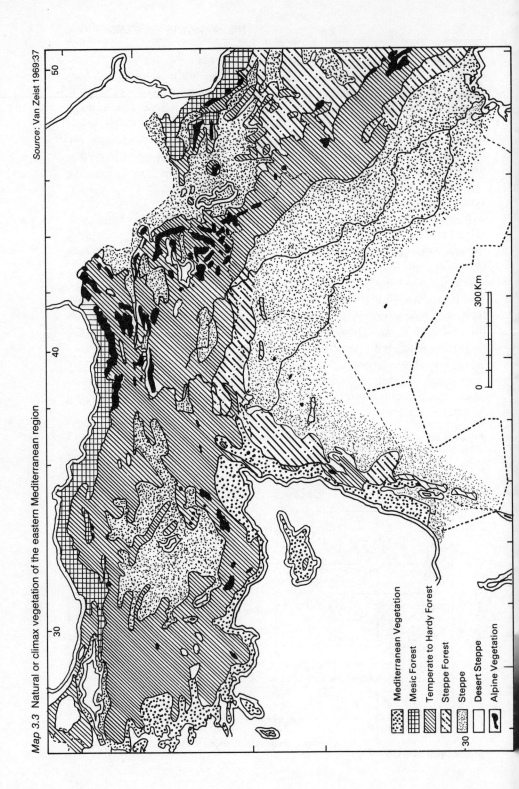

Map 3.3 Natural or climax vegetation of the eastern Mediterranean region

Source: Van Zeist 1969:37

Mediterranean Vegetation
Mesic Forest
Temperate to Hardy Forest
Steppe Forest
Steppe
Desert Steppe
Alpine Vegetation

300 Km

On the twin rivers true navigation is possible on the alluvium and, of course, the Gulf and the Shatt, which rises with the tides. Upstream navigation beyond Hit, where the rivers 'cut their way across a plateau of hard limestone and shale and are bordered by cliffs' (Roux 1964:21), is effectively blocked. Boats and rafts could thus come downstream, but transit up beyond Hit (where there were and are natural sources of bitumen for boat-building) had to be alongside rather than on the rivers, unless towed.

It will be noted, then, that what is here called the 'Zagrosian Arc' is synonymous neither with the mountain ranges themselves, nor merely with the alluvial plains of what was called, following Breasted (1916:100–1), 'The Fertile Crescent'. The term 'Zagrosian Arc' refers to the mountain ranges with their intramontane valleys, their extramontane piedmonts (foothills) and the 'steppe' transition to the alluvium itself. The diversity and contrasts characteristic of the Arc can be seen in Map 3.3.

If there is a common denominator in the flora of such a diverse region, it is the lowest, grass. Legumes need around 500 mm of rainfall to flourish, but the grasses, even cereal grasses, can do well on half that

Figure 3.3 The Pleistocene succession, indicating names of glaciations and earliest (Villafranchian) fossil animals

GENERAL TERMS		NORTHERN EUROPEAN TERMS	ALPINE TERMS	APPROX. TIME BP
		POST-GLACIAL OR HOLOCENE		— 10,000
P	UPPER	WEICHSEL	WÜRM	
L		Last Interglacial		— 75,000 (Homo sapiens appears)
E				— 125,000
I	MIDDLE	WARTHE ? SAALE	RISS ? (MINDEL?)	— 200,000
S				— 265,000
T		Great Interglacial		
O	LOWER	ELSTER ?	(MINDEL?) (GÜNZ?)	— 430,000
C				— 800,000
E		'Cromerian' Interglacial		
N				— 1,000,000
E	BASAL	EARLIER	(GÜNZ?)	
		Villafranchian		— 3,000,000

Adapted from Braidwood 1975:12

amount (Grigg 1970:170). In regions of summer drought, such as
characterizes the Mediterranean and sub-Mediterranean, annuals can
amount to no less than 50 per cent of the total species present (Raven
1971:122). This is a natural condition (of the Holocene), but where
disturbance by man has been considerable, grasslands and low shrub
associations develop in the place of woodlands (ibid.). In Figure 3.2 we
can see how this comes about when the six major biomes are graphed in
terms of mean annual temperature (°F) and mean annual rainfall
(inches). The temperature range of grasslands extends from just above
freezing-point to almost 90°F. At one extreme of precipitation grasses
overlap with desert; at the other, above 20 inches per annum of rainfall,
intruding into the range of both deciduous and coniferous forest, both of
which are highly vulnerable not only to cutting, but also to burning and
grazing.

2 Neothermal conditions

The current Quaternary geological period has been marked by the
Pleistocene Ice Ages in northern Eurasia. There have been four distinct
periods of glaciation during this Great Ice Age, with, of course, three
interglacials. The main glaciations and interglacials are outlined for the
last 3 million years in Figure 3.3 and the neothermal conditions that
mark the current period are indicated as commencing 10,000 years *Before
Present* time. Note the very recent advent of *Homo sapiens sapiens*, only
after 75,000 BP, and that the evidence from pollen samples cored from
lake sediments around the Zagrosian area indicate no major climatic or
environmental changes from around 40,000 to about 12,000 years ago,
when conditions started to improve (Wright 1968:336).

Although those ice-sheets directly affected only northern latitudes in
a line roughly from the Scheldt to the Dnieper (so far as southwest Asia is
concerned), with southerly ice-sheets also over the Alps and Caucasus, its
effect on contiguous latitudes was pronounced, due to alterations in wind
circulation patterns, sea-levels, temperature and, of course, precipitation
as free water was reduced.

Only during the fourth millennium BC, for instance, well after the
onset of Holocene conditions, approximating to present-day ones, does
sea-level in the Persian Gulf stabilize around modern values (Larsen, op.
cit.:57).

Recent palynological evidence (by pollen analysis) in the Near East
shows that the Late Pleistocene climate was both cooler and drier than
subsequently (Wright 1977:290–1). We should therefore not make the
common-sense assumption that during glacials, or interglacials for that
matter, pluvial (heavy rainfall) conditions were necessarily experienced
by more southerly latitudes. That is, unless we have specific evidence for
a certain area, such as is now becoming available for the Arabian

Peninsula which seems to have experienced better conditions (Stevens 1978:263). Circulation/precipitation patterns, after all, are the outcome of a whole range of complex variables, some of which are independent.

3 The advent of *Homo sapiens sapiens*

When the Holocene conditions set in over ten millenniums ago, there was in existence for the first time a creature of large cranial capacity,[2] both cause and effect of a developed culture (Holloway 1975:78), employing language as the central means of communication and possessing a material culture that long included fire, plus a whole range of stone tools and organic implements. Indeed without fire and the use of tools to make both skin clothing and shelters, neither *Homo sapiens* nor *Homo neanderthalis* before him could have spread in the way they did throughout Eurasia (Wymer 1982:246).

At the beginning of the middle Pleistocene there was *Homo erectus*; during the early part of the Last Glaciation there was, for the first time, *Homo sapiens*. Much has been made by Cohen (*supra*) and others of the fact that there had previously been interglacials in the Pleistocene, so why didn't agriculture get started then? This they hold to be support for their views on advancing population pressure. However, a small fact they conveniently, but amazingly, forget is that *Homo sapiens* did not exist prior to the *last* interglacial. Over this period Man with traits most conveniently described as Erectus (and with a brain volume ranging from around 900 cc to 1,225 cc) had evolved to Man with traits most resembling those of modern man, or sapiens (Wymer op. cit.:133); in other words the smallest *Homo sapiens* brain volume equalled the largest in *Homo erectus*.

Homo sapiens sapiens, fully modern man, is at least 40,000 years old (Bordes 1968:224; Le Gros Clark 1971:353). The transition from Middle to Upper Palaeolithic being 'more or less concomitant with the transition from Neanderthal to modern man' (Bordes, op. cit.). It is, then, not fortuitous that the Dolni Vestonice finds of experimental pottery occur when they do (*c.* 23,000 BC), nor that cave art appeared for the first time in this period (Jochim 1983:212).

4 Post-glacial conditions in the Near East

The Zagrosian Arc, together with the northern Mediterranean as far as Spain, was denuded of woodland during the last glaciation (Würm). Instead, its ecology was characterized by Artemesia steppe, comprising grasses and chenopods, as analysed from the palynological record by H. E. Wright (1977:284). The relatively abrupt change to the Holocene raised both temperature and precipitation over the whole Mediterranean

Map 3.4 Zones of natural state or climax vegetation in Iraq

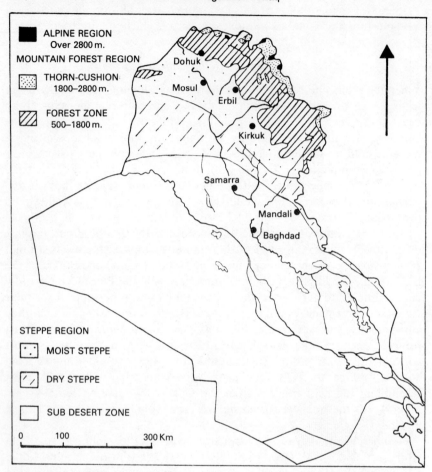

ALPINE REGION
Over 2800 m.

MOUNTAIN FOREST REGION

THORN-CUSHION
1800–2800 m.

FOREST ZONE
500–1800 m.

Dohuk

Mosul

Erbil

Kirkuk

Samarra

Mandali

Baghdad

STEPPE REGION

MOIST STEPPE

DRY STEPPE

SUB DESERT ZONE

0   100   300 Km

Source: Oates 1980:305

basin, bringing with it the present Mediterranean climate of winter rain, summer dry conditions. With orographic rainfall on hills and mountains, tree climax vegetation – oaks, cedar, pistachio – spread right along the Zagros–Taurus ranges, even in some particularly favoured areas forming a closed canopy, that is, a true forest (Van Zeist 1969:40–1). However, most tree cover was Quercetum, open oak woodland or savannah, which occurred not below 500 m in our region. Upland climax vegetation in Iraq is indicated on Map 3.4. Observe that riverine galeria forest, as other lowland features, is not distinguished here. It does not mean that those features were absent. Studies of charcoal by Van Zeist (1970:176) indicate that on the banks and islands of the Euphrates, forests of poplar, with tamarisk, ash, and other species, would have been found.

In most parts, then, only steppe-forest or parkland was formed, placing

56

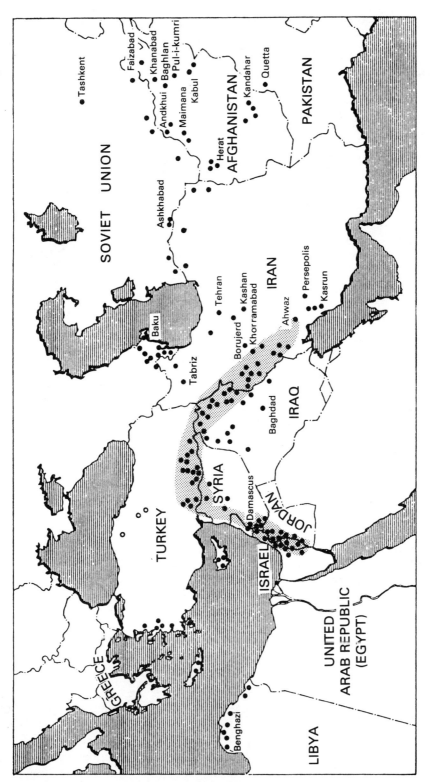

Map 3.5 Natural distribution of wild barley

Map 3.6 Natural distribution of wild einkorn   *Source*: Zohary 1969:50

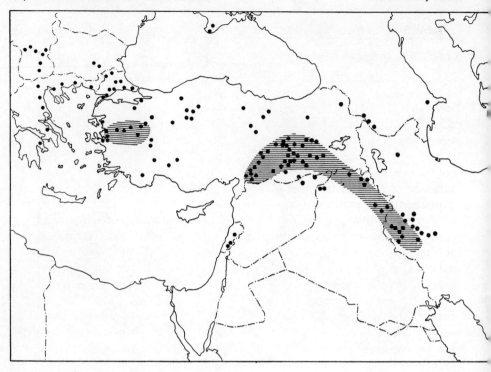

Map 3.7 Natural distribution of wild emmer   *Source*: Zohary 1969:51

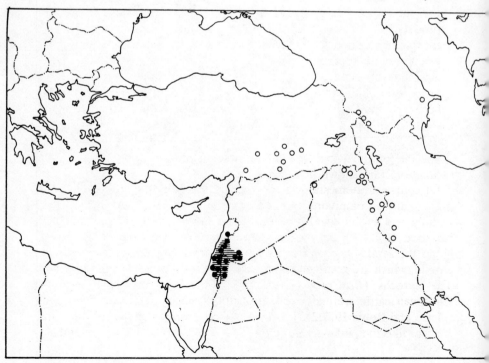

Table 3.2 Comparative productivity of some North American ecosystems

Cedar Creek, Minnesota, primary productivity (kg/ha²/yr)

	Maximum	Minimum
Prairie grasslands	9,700	6,100
Savannah	63,200	54,400
Oak forest	257,100	224,200

Source: Simmons 1974:119.

no restriction on the growth of grasses. Indeed where rainfall was insufficient to support trees, grasses could still thrive. Map 3.5 shows the natural distribution of wild barley (*Hordeum spontaneum*), while that of the wild grasses, einkorn (*Triticum boeoticum*), and emmer (*Triticum dicoccoides*), are shown in Maps 3.6 and 3.7. As can be seen, while wild barley and einkorn are widely distributed across the Near East, emmer – the most useful wheat and thus the one most frequently encountered at prehistoric sites – is confined to a narrow arc from the Levant to the Zagros.

In turn grasses, herbs, and shrubs support grazing animals and, of course, the hunters that prey on them. Their association has been succinctly described by Simmons, who points out that while true forest has by far the highest rate of primary productivity, savannah has the highest secondary productivity – that is, biomass available to animals (since they cannot use the cellulose and lignin in wood):

> the shelter of the scattered trees result[s] in a very high primary productivity at ground level. Here can be seen a fundamental reason for the high densities of wild animals in African savannahs, particularly when specialist grazers of swamps and tree tops are added to the ground-level suite. Because they are adapted to use a greater proportion of the forage than domestic livestock, the biomass of wild herbivores on extensive grazings is nearly always greater than domestic stock.
>
> (Simmons 1974:119)

Specific productivity, albeit from measurements in North America (Minnesota) are shown in Table 3.2.

Of course all domestic livestock began as wild herbivores, though the pig is really an omnivore. Goats feed mainly on leaves and thus can live in hilly and bushy regions, while sheep prefer short grasses and their favoured habitat is that of open pastures (Herre and Rohrs 1977:258–9). None the less, sheep and goats need to drink regularly, in contrast to gazelle, which are relatively indifferent to water supplies (Legge 1977:64). The aurochs (*Bos primigenius*) from which, as its name suggests, European cattle were derived, probably lived in open park-like areas (Herre and Rohrs 1977:263). However, *Bos gauros*, the gaur of India and Burma, like the endangered kouprey (*Bos sauveli*) of Cambodia and the

Map 3.8 Natural distribution of *Bos primigenius*

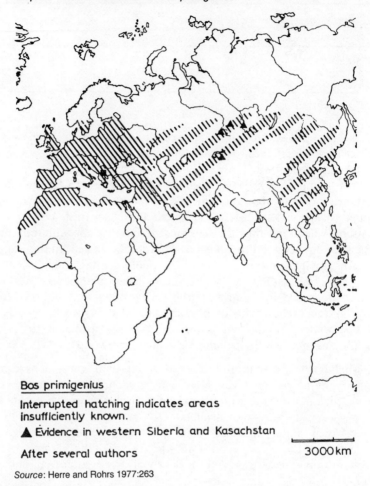

Bos primigenius

Interrupted hatching indicates areas insufficiently known.

▲ Evidence in western Siberia and Kasachstan

After several authors

3000 km

Source: Herre and Rohrs 1977:263

banteng (*Bos |bibos| javanicus*) of Indonesia (also called *Bos banteng*), is at home in the forest (ibid.:264–5). The natural distribution of *Bos primigenius* is shown in Map 3.8.

Bos primigenius was the first bovid to be domesticated, but that was achieved (probably in Anatolia) *c.* 2,000 years later than sheep and goat. The natural distribution of goat (*Capra hircus*), from which the population of *aegagrus* supplied the first domesticated flocks, is shown in Map 3.9, while Map 3.10 indicates the natural distribution of sheep (*Ovis ammon*), from which the *orientalis* group, the Asiatic mouflon, produced the first domestications.

The overlap of the ranges of those plants and animals make it most likely that, as Jack Harlan says of what he calls the 'Near Eastern nuclear arc' (1977:364): 'it appears to be the arena of the domestication of barley,

Map 3.9 Distribution of *Capra hircus*

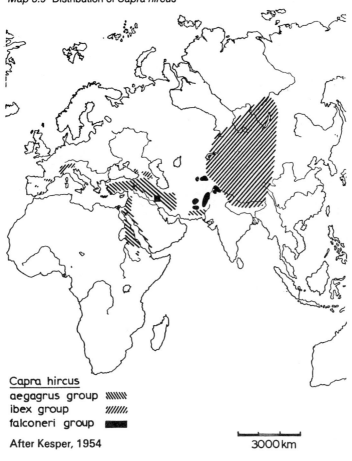

Capra hircus
aegagrus group
ibex group
falconeri group

After Kesper, 1954

3000 km

Source: Herre and Rohrs 1977:257

emmer, einkorn, pea, lentil, flax, chick-pea, broad bean, bitter vetch and other vetches, as well as sheep, goat and pig. Cattle probably were first domesticated within this arc or close to it.' This important point about the Near Eastern nuclear arc is summarized in Map 3.11 which shows the region of overlap at the end of the last Ice Age of the four most important potential domesticates.

This region of overlap (with Trans-Caucasia) turns out also to possess the greatest variety of wheats, as indicated by Kislev (1984:149). He lists 6 species of wheat for Temperate Europe, 10 for the Mediterranean, 16 for Anatolia and Iran, and 18 for Trans-Caucasia. Though what is listed are contemporary distributions, this is further, if indirect, support for the argument that the Near East was the heartland of wild-grains, both sufficient in density and extent to promote early sedentarization, and later to engender their manipulation into key domesticates in the Neolithic

61

Map 3.10 Distribution of *Ovis ammon*

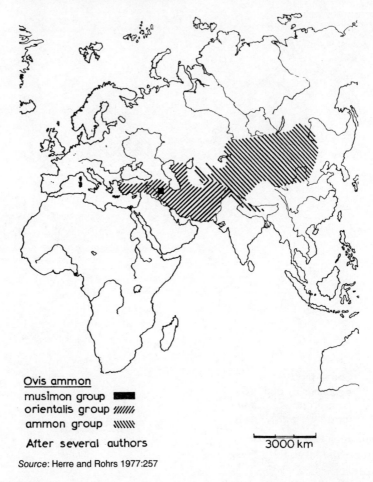

Ovis ammon
musimon group ▪▪
orientalis group ⁄⁄⁄⁄⁄⁄
ammon group ＼＼＼＼

After several authors

3000 km

Source: Herre and Rohrs 1977:257

agro-pastoral system.

For the Levant, Legge (1977:59) has indicated an increasingly selective management of hunted species (gazelle, fallow deer) from the Late Palaeolithic up to and including the Early Ceramic Neolithic, with a relative low dependence upon plant food. He goes on to remark that 'most of the known and densely occupied Natufian sites in Palestine are marked by lack of arable land, though in ecologically varied settings and with good grazing resources'. After the Natufian period such sites as Nahal Oren, Rakafet, Shuqbah, Hayonim, Ain Mallaha, and Kebara manifest 'an abrupt cessation of occupation' (ibid.:61) and it cannot be accidental that arable soils at those sites seldom exceed 20 per cent of the territory. In contrast, some of the major, long-lived tell sites of Palestine, such as Jericho, 'possess roughly equal amounts of arable land and rough grazing within radii of 2 km and 5 km of the site, with the added

Map 3.11 Probable distribution of four main progenitors of domestic livestock

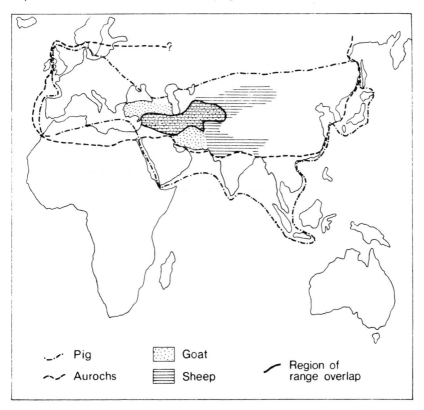

._.⌐ Pig	▓ Goat
∿ Aurochs	≡ Sheep
⌐	Region of range overlap

Source: Clutton-Brock 1981:19

advantage that much of the soil can be subject to irrigation' (ibid.).
Further, the large tell of Megiddo shows a concentration of 62 per cent of
area being arable soils (ibid.).

Broadly, Legge (op. cit.: 62) suggests that from the Middle Palaeolithic
forward we find hunters in the Levant occupying cave dwellings, while
from the Mesolithic onwards we find settlement building up at open sites,
such as Jericho, Hureyra, and Mureybet. This he sees associated with a
shift from gazelle to sheep and goat exploitation resulting in the virtual
abandonment of the *gazella* species, despite its previous importance over
millennia as a food resource (op. cit.:64). Beyond those observed
shifts Legge, following Higgs and Jarman (1972:3–13), is arguing for the
virtual domestication of gazelle, on the basis of 'a pattern of exploitation
difficult to separate from "domestication" were the animals in question
sheep or goats' (1977:62), because 'some degree of manipulation, control,
of deliberate selection is involved', as also for plants, and this right back
to the late Pleistocene. However, such manipulation as there was, and
this is inferred from kill age-ratios (Legge op. cit.:55, 57), seems much

63

more like the 'intelligent predation' cited by Clark (1980:45) in regard to the European Mesolithic, which 'served to maintain the reindeer population at an optimum level having regard to grazing potential'. Human predators in substance displaced other predators, and so, taking this along with the lack of intimacy involved, Clark states that 'it would be going too far to rank it as tantamount to domestication' (ibid.). Indeed, as immature animals are simply easier to catch, this may give the impression of 'culling'. Hence, close contact with, and knowledge of, the fauna and flora upon which they depended is characteristic of most Upper Palaeolithic and Mesolithic populations, and indeed modern hunter-gatherers (Flannery (1968) 1971:81; Harlan 1975:24–8). There can be little doubt that such awareness served as the *prerequisite* to the true domestication of plants and animals. Domestication causes morphological changes in plants and animals under human manipulation, the result of behavioural changes from those obtaining in the wild state. Thus a fully domesticated plant or animal is completely dependent on man for survival (Harlan 1975:64). These are changes in ecological adaptation brought on by cultivation or management but are not reducible to them. But this point about awareness as the prerequisite to domestication, quite in accord with Braidwood's ideas (e.g. 1960, 1972) about the historico-technical bases for farming, is in fact lent support by Legge himself when he suggests that sheep and goats supplanted gazelle (and that fairly suddenly!) because the ovicaprines 'are more readily integrated into a sedentary, crop producing economy, with the "failure" of the gazelle related to its unsuitability for husbandry on a sedentary basis' (1977:64).

Thus there does indeed seem to be a change of kind, and not just of degree, in subsistence strategies involved in 'settling down with true domestication'; whereas what Zeuner (1974:125) terms 'the social parasitism of man on the reindeer' is only possible because 'neither was compelled to adopt any profound change of habits'. In contrast the very substance of domestication is not just 'an efficient pattern of exploitation' but *regulated reproduction under human control*, with all the morphological and behavioural changes that ensue, and which were noted as being absent amongst the gazelle. Most significant, of course, are the social-structural changes involved in 'keeping' animals and raising crops. This is emphasized by the zoologists Herre and Rohrs in their statement that 'the attempt to procure a dependable meat supply must have been the factor of major importance' (op. cit.:254); and whereas Legge (op. cit.) resorts to some rather shaky speculation about increasing desiccation to explain changing man–animal relationships, Herre and Rohrs look to the human end of the equation under which some kind of 'population changes, destroying the balance between man and animal are a more probable cause of domestication than are climatic changes' (op. cit.:254). In any case we have noted climatic change in the Near East to have been in the opposite direction to increased aridity on any but the most localized level.

In the next chapter I shall be looking in detail at the process of permanent settlement, population increase, local density problems and, thus, a 'changed balance between man and animal' which substituted production for procurement. So the next step is to examine the domestication of grasses.

5 The cereal revolution

Thus far we have seen that, due to the soil, temperature, and precipitation conditions of the Zagros and its piedmont, the prevailing Holocene plant association has been one of 'thick herbaceous cover occupying the openings between the well spaced trees (*Quercus ithaburensis* in the west and *Quercus brantii* in the east)' (Zohary 1969:56). This belt receives between 400 mm and 1,000 mm of winter rain (ibid.:55).

The cereals seminal to farming, the wheats emmer (*Triticum dicoccoides*) and einkorn (*Triticum boeoticum*) plus barley (*Hordeum spontaneum*), favour hard limestone and basaltic bedrocks with their associated heavy soils that occur over a considerable part of the sub-Mediterranean quercetum belt (Zohary, op. cit.:55). There the wheats and barley, along with oats (*Avena*) and goatface grass (*Aegilops*) form the dominant annuals. So much so that 'in the *Quercus ithaburensis* and *Q. brantii* formations and related park-forests or "moist-steppes", that stretch from Palestine to South Turkey and Iraqi and Iranian Kurdistan, one finds extensive "natural fields" of wild cereals' (ibid.:56). On uncultivated slopes these natural fields extend continuously for many kilometres, while both in their growth and total mass, wild fields of wheat, barley, and oats are not inferior to their cultivated counterparts (ibid.). In terms of actual grain productivity the robust wild forms also compare favourably with the cultivars. In years of good rain, wild stands of *T. dicoccoides* mixed with *H. spontaneum* in eastern Galilee yield some 50–80 kg of grain per dunam (= 1,000 m² = 0.1 ha. or 0.247 acres) compared with yields of 50–150 kg per dunam of cultivated barley and durum (wheat) employing scratch-plough agriculture (ibid.), with the loss of land to grazing that requires.[3]

Similarly extensive 'fields' of wild cereals extend along the Zagrosian Arc from Palestine, through Syria and southern Turkey into northern Iraq and western Iran, but the species composition varies. While wild barley (*H. spontaneum*) is everywhere present, the Palestinian tetraploid wild emmer wheat (*T. dicoccoides*) is replaced in Turkey, Iraq, and Iran by diploid wild einkorn wheat (*T. boeoticum*), admixed occasionally with tetraploid *Triticum araraticum* (ibid.). Barley is inhibited by cold and seldom occurs naturally above 1,500 m, while wild einkorn, by contrast, is very tolerant of cold and exposure. In Turkey it grows above 1,500 m, and as high as 2,000 m in the Zagros Mountains (Flannery 1973:277). Its primary range appears to be the Zagrosian Arc and the immediately adjacent steppe, while in the Levant it grows as a weed in disturbed habitats (Flannery, op. cit.:277). Palestine is, however, the primary range of robust, large-seeded emmer, where it occurs in very extensive and productive stands. *Triticum dicoccoides* is almost certainly the ancestor of cultivated emmer wheat (*Triticum dicoccum*), hence the name. Extensive natural 'fields' of varying composition thus extend in a wide arc from Palestine and southern Turkey, through Syria to northern Iraq and western Iran (Zohary, op. cit.:56).

Van Zeist (1969:33–45) examining prehistoric environments in the Near East, came to the conclusion that, with warmer/wetter conditions, 'the trees like the cereals would have spread from their refuge areas (only) after 14,000 B.P.'. This would have produced a distribution of wild wheats and barley little different from that obtaining today. Both palaeobotanical and archaeological evidence lead to the conclusion that, while the gross amount of rainfall in autumn, winter, and spring were the same as now, the summers between 10,000 and 6,000 BP were drier than subsequently (ibid.:45). This emphasizes the marked seasonality of the region, to which the deciduous oaks, pistachio, and almond are so well adapted; and also, of course, the annual grasses. The utilization of seasonal resources demands scheduling – the phased consumption of resources – while harvests of nuts and grains provide the material for a storage economy (Testart 1982:523–30). The region is also a mosaic of rich and poor, optimal to highly marginal, habitats, often in close juxtaposition due to vertical layering from piedmont to high slopes, rain-shadowing, the presence of springs, rivers, lakes, marsh, and so forth (Flannery 1969: 73).

The peculiar pre-adaptation of the grains derives from a large seed in an instantly shattering spikelet (wheat) or triplet (barley) that serves to drive the seed into the summer-hard ground within a few weeks of ripeness and before the worst of the dry season (Zohary, op. cit.:57). Indeed the diagnostic feature of wild wheats and barley is their fragile spikes, such that upon maturity their ears disarticulate immediately (Zohary, op. cit.:57). This is the 'brittle rachis' phenomenon. The spikelets/triplets act like arrowheads driving their seeds into the soil.

Wild cereals produce seeds of similar size to domesticated plants, so that a seed with a good reserve of nutrient is buried 'ready to go' with the first effective autumn rain for successful competition in 'the lush, herbaceous communities of the oak park-forest belt' (ibid.: 58). Significantly, the major alteration under cultivation was not to size of seed, but to the brittle rachis' instant seed-dispersal mechanism. Also modified was the 'wild-type' regulation of germination, which in *T. dicoccoides* and *T. boeoticum* causes one of the two kernels on each spikelet to be inhibited until the following year as a precaution against drought. In barley, which has only one seed per dispersal unit, differential inhibition occurs between triplets of the same ear. True domestication, that is induced morphological change, causes barley to become six-rowed instead of two-rowed, with the sterile lateral spikelets fertile (Harlan 1975:129–30).

Natural selection thus produces the brittle rachis to scatter seed readily. Under patterns of human collection this still applies, as the less brittle kernels will tend to be gathered and consumed, while the more brittle will shatter on disturbance and reproduce. Only when the less fragile have been gathered and deliberately retained for subsequent planting, will varieties be reproduced that consistently have the preferred non-shattering qualities. 'Genes for non-brittleness are thus strongly selected for by the system of harvesting *and planting*' (Zohary 1969:60; my emphasis); simply harvesting wild populations does not produce non-brittleness. Once planting was a regular occurrence those preferred traits would fairly readily have stabilized, since wheats and barley are predominantly self-pollinated. This, along with density of stand and large fruit size, being factors 'predisposing' cereals to cultivation; indeed virtually 'presenting themselves for domestication' as J. G. Hawkes (1969:24) put it.

Those grasses, however, are mainly, but not exclusively, self-fertilizing. After a millennium or so of domestication, emmer-durum wheat crossed spontaneously with goatface grass (*Aegilops squarrosa*) whose distribution adjoins, but does not overlap with, the natural range of the emmer-durum wheats.[4] What was formed thereby was the bread wheat, *Triticum aestivum*, a hexaploid plant that has no equivalent in nature, consisting as it does of two sets of chromosomes (genomes A and B) present in the emmer-durum wheats, together with a third set (genome D) from *Aegilops squarrosa* (Zohary, op. cit.:60). As Zohary observes, *Triticum aestivum* (i.e. bread wheat) was formed by hybridization and subsequent chromosome doubling, this fusing tetraploid (4n = 28) emmer-durum wheats with the diploid (2n = 14) *Aegilops squarrosa* and resulting in the hexaploidy (6n = 42) of three sets of genomes. The third set (D) of genomes promotes a hardiness which enabled the spread of 'mediterranean' emmer-durum wheats to both continental and more humid climatic zones. This quasi-natural developmental process is illustrated in Figure 3.4 (p. 68). The diagram should be read from the bottom, while on the right can be noted the ascending order of ploidy.

Not only do the stalks of the inflorescence of bread wheat not shatter upon harvesting, unlike emmer and the diploid wheats, but the glumes that enclose them open easily, permitting the grain to fall out during threshing. Thus they are called 'free-threshing' wheats.

Figure 3.4 Diagram of the history of diploid, tetraploid, and hexaploid cultivated wheats

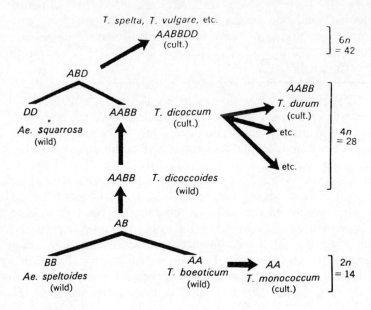

Source: Baker (1965) 1970:66

6 Cereals as the basis of a self-amplifying system

It is no accident that areas of indigenous 'High Civilization' are those – Meso-America, China, the Near East – where the domesticated grasses, maize, millet and rice, wheat and barley, became the staple. Harvesting wild einkorn in southeastern Turkey, first by hand-stripping and then by using a primitive flint sickle, Jack Harlan (1967:197–201) was able to obtain easily 2.05 kg of clean grain per hour by hand, and 2.45 kg per hour using a reconstructed flint sickle. This represents about 50 kilocalories for every kilocalorie expended, a ratio far more efficient than any form of agriculture for which there are figures (Harlan 1975:49).

Compared in constitution with hard red winter wheat of premium quality, the wild wheat turns out to be far higher in protein, as may be seen from Table 3.3.

From the data in the table Harlan concludes (1967:198) that ancient man would have had no difficulty in collecting 'one-half pound of protein per hour during the wild wheat harvesting season': a season which can extend from four to six weeks in the one area (Zohary, op. cit.:57). Harlan's evaluation is very suggestive indeed:

A family group, beginning harvesting near the base of Karacadağ [a basaltic mountain ridge] and working slowly upslope as the season progressed, could easily harvest wild-cereals over a three-week span or

Table 3.3 Nutritional values of wild and domesticated wheats[5]

	% Water	% Ash	% Ether extract	% Crude fibre	% Crude protein	% NFE*
Wild einkorn	7.91	2.77	2.64	2.33	22.83	60.04
Modern wheat	10.60	1.80	1.62	2.78	14.50	68.70

Source: Harlan 1967:198.
Note: *Nitrogen-free extract, which is mostly carbohydrates other than fibre.

more and, without even working very hard, could gather more grain than the family could possibly consume in a year. It seems to be that this would offer a very attractive alternative to living by the chase. To be sure, cereal pottage alone would be dull fare, but the ease of harvesting, the dependability of such a source of food, the assurance that comes with abundant stored food and the high nutritive value all combine to suggest that a way of life more attractive than hunting might be developed, based upon the harvesting of wild cereals. The grain diet would, of course, have been supplemented by hunting, fishing and the gathering of other plant food.

(Harlan 1967:198)

The question then becomes: why adopt agriculture if wild cereals can be so productively harvested? One has, as it were, the productive output of an agricultural cycle without the heavy inputs required. Hence the postulate in the previous chapter that agriculture could not occur as an either/or event – it was a cumulative process. Ultimately, however, there comes a point at which the former balance can no longer be maintained. This is reached when the actively husbanded resources pre-empt the majority of time and effort available, either because ecological relations have been upset by this activity pattern, or because population has grown beyond what the balance will bear. Certainly the accumulation of a tonne of clean grain in a season is a solid staple. Its availability answers the very first question posed about succession – why give up mobile foraging? It is the paths by which a way of life developed from harvesting dense stands of 'free' cereals into being forced to make costly labour inputs continuously that has now to be elucidated. The socio-economic processes involved will be adumbrated in subsequent chapters. Here the evolutionary course followed will be simply itemized as discrete steps in a flow chart (Figure 3.5) with only outline commentary, numbers referring to stages in the flow chart.

1 In the first instance there is a particularly prolific source of calories and protein that is both dense and elastic in exploitation, stable on an annual basis, and eminently storable until the next year's harvest.

Figure 3.5 Flow chart of social evolution from hunter-gathering to city-states in Mesopotamia

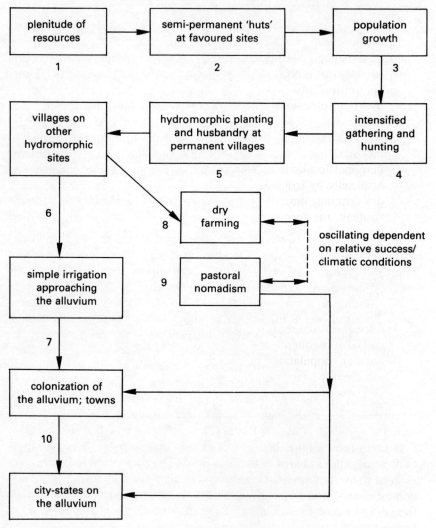

2 Those conditions of exploitation engender the necessity of 'staying put',[6] as harvesting/storing is confined to about one month, and stocks laid down nearby.

3 Sedentism allows population to increase, for reasons already discussed.

4 With an increasing population, resource exploitation must be both intensified and extended to feed more mouths.

5 Planting in hydromorphic locations is now necessary. Further, as animals are rendered scarce by increased human demands and disturbance, husbandry (close herding) of amenable animals (ovicaprids) is required. Settlements are year-round and permanent.

6 As settlements proliferate, cereals are taken from the original hydromorphic locations to others suitable for the activities of a permanent village.

7 As villages spread from optimal through sub-optimal (i.e. hydro-morphic but without many other advantages) to increasingly marginal locations (good soils only), then water must be provided artificially by irrigation, or

8 dry-farming must be undertaken. This latter is the Halafian strategy, the former Samarran.

9 At the same time a niche opens for the exploitation of the extensive low-grade scrub grassland, through mobile herding of sheep and goat flocks. Cattle, where present, are kept at agricultural locations.

10 Successful irrigation agriculture at sites such as Chogha Mami (Oates 1982:25–9), enable colonization of the alluvium proper to take place along the watercourses. Given the tendencies to nucleation inherent in Samarran/Ubaidian social organization (dis-cussed subsequently), towns are quickly formed.

11 Further population growth, combined with the ruin of some settlements due to the vagaries of river-flow, economic and demographic fortune, nucleates population further into cities with an immediate agricultural hinterland, and in the process produces the state in the hands of the leaders of the great households.

In conclusion a note on the bifurcation occurring specifically at steps 6 to 9 of the flow chart, where pastoral nomadism emerges. Sequential evidence to be reviewed in the next chapter shows that plant domestication broadly evolved along with the domestication of animals, though secondary products like wool and milk were probably later. Mixed farming was practised, for reasons of ecological prudence or dietary variety, wherever the terrain allowed. Pastoral nomadism is thus a later specialization not only on temporal grounds but because it is a 'part society' (Barth 1964:71) depending as it does on settled society for its grains, salt, and manufactures. Of specialized pastoralism Barth states, their culture is such as to presuppose the presence of such [sedentary] communities and access to their products. As far as the economic structure of an area is concerned, nomad and villager can therefore be regarded merely as specialised occupational groups within a single economic system.

(Barth 1964:71)

The specific period of emergence of specialized (i.e. full-time) nomadic pastoralism, and not merely seasonal transhumance, Lees and Bates (1974:187–93) have argued to coincide with that of irrigation agriculture on the following grounds: (1) mixed farming allows animals fed either agricultural surpluses or more usually upon waste to function as a nutritional reserve in years of poor cereal crops, and thus herding would not easily be separated out by agriculturalists. (2) The pressure to do this arose only after settlement of the alluvium proper, at which point a number of factors, which tended to be mutually reinforcing, came into play: (a) labour demands of intensive agriculture coupled with the labour required on canals and ditches meant that the labour involved in seasonal movement of stock by members of a family or village could not now be spared, especially when coupled with the extended distance of the alluvium villages from their former areas of transhumance in the hills to the northeast; (b) as population rose with the newly elevated levels of grain output new villages were founded and extra land was taken into cultivation through extended irrigation networks. This, however, would take into cultivation 'next best' land, that is, the more moist land previously offering better forage in its unimproved state. This leaves only the poorest forage grounds nearest the village plus seasonally available field stubble, both too scant to support herds of any size. As good grazing land became scarce on the alluvium, then, in this scheme of Lees and Bates, an important niche was created for non-cultivating pastoral specialists on long-range circuits that did not confine them to the alluvium.

Even if we overlook the fact that the disposition of labour on the alluvium was in the hands of households and temples, not families and villages, extrusion from the alluvium seems too late and localized to account for such an important regional phenomenon. Perhaps some groups of nomads derived from internally displaced elements and others from hill-herding outsiders (cf. Woodburn 1972:205; Mortensen 1972: 293–7); but basically, I suspect, their origins lie in an early (c. 6,000 BC) specialization in Syrian rain-shadow zones, as mentioned below in reference to the ending of the Pre-Pottery Neolithic B period in Syria and Palestine, and exemplified further at Tell Ramad, a site near Damascus, at the end of the sixth millennium.

However there can be no doubt that such specialization, albeit forced by environmental circumstances in the main, allowed fuller use to be made of the region's resources. Contemporary practice, such as that reported from India by Allchin, supports such a construction:

> Throughout India there are communities or castes who specialise in the management of flocks and herds, either on behalf of villages to which they are attached or as independent owners or agents who herd them in remote or uncultivated areas and bring their young stock to fairs and markets at certain times of year to sell to farmers on the plains as draught oxen or milking cows. Today such pastoral people operate in a kind of symbiotic relationship with settled agriculturalists with whose yearly routines their movements are closely integrated.
>
> (Allchin 1972:117)

Allchin stresses the particular importance of this relationship in dry areas.

The emergence of specialized nomadic pastoralism in the Near East was not only of profound economic significance, but equally had major social and political consequences, to be discussed in Chapter 6, section 7.

As to the logic of the very earliest steps outlined in the model, some initial confirmation can be seen in recent work on the *strontium* content of human bones recovered archaeologically from the sites of Kebara and el-Wad in the Levant, where bones from three Epipalaeolithic levels were examined and compared with those from the Neolithic period sites of Ganj Dareh and Hajji Firuz in Iran. Schoeninger's hypothesis was this:

> The level of bone strontium is proportional to the amount of strontium in diet. Since plants contain relatively more strontium than do animal tissues, a diet consisting largely of plant material should contain more strontium than should a diet that includes a large fraction of animal material. If the shift from hunting and gathering to agriculture included an increase in dietary dependence on plant materials, this should be reflected in higher bone strontium levels in the agricultural population.
>
> (Schoeninger 1981:74)

But this in fact was found not to be the case. Instead it appears from comparison of strontium levels of the human specimens with those of the local herbivorous fauna recovered with them, both controlled against modern mink (a pure carnivore), that pre-farming populations already had high proportions of plant materials in their diets. Schoeninger (op. cit.:86–7) illustrates her results in a graph (Figure 3.6) and concludes that

> in any case, both the Levant and Iranian sequences suggest that agriculture in the Middle East did not result in a change in subsistence. Rather, it involved *a change in economy, a change in the management of previously developed subsistence systems.* In the Levant the *previous* subsistence system was heavily dependent on grains. In Iran goats and sheep were far more important.
>
> (Schoeninger 1981:87; my emphases)

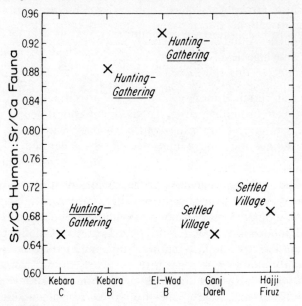

Figure 3.6 Bone strontium levels in Man and other fauna

Source: Schoeninger 1981:86

Note: By comparing the human bone strontium level with the levels in the herbivorous fauna, it appears that there was an increase in use of plant materials among the Kebara B and el-Wad B population relative to the preceding Kebara C population. This can be attributed to the use of cereals that began to spread across large areas of the Levant about the time represented by these site levels. It appears that the populations at Ganj Dareh and Hajji Firuz utilized far less plant material. This supports the archaeological interpretation that in the Zagros area there was a greater emphasis on herding than was true in the Levant

In either event, she argues, as the model does, that 'agriculture provided a means of continuing, with greater control, an already proven, highly productive subsistence system' (ibid.), specified as steps 1 to 5 in the flow chart.

As to steps 5 and 6 – 'villages on hydromorphic sites' – support can be had from the very early agricultural settlement of Tell Aswad in Syria. It is a site some 30 km southeast of Damascus, measuring 275 m north–south and 250 m east–west, extending over about five hectares, part of which is a clayey hillock[7] only 4.5 m high on a lacustrine plain dotted with such buttes (de Contenson 1979:153). Tell Aswad contains no solid architecture, pits being the common feature at all levels, some possibly the basis of dwellings while others, deeper and narrower, are for storage or rubbish. Indications are of mud-plastered reed huts supported by poles, as befits the marshy situation (de Contenson 1979:155). The settlement is preceramic throughout (ibid.:153).

Established early in the eighth millennium, cultivation was practised from the very beginning, the main crop being emmer wheat,[8] plus the pulses, lentil (*Lens culinaris*) and pea (*Pisum sativum*). However, today mean annual rainfall at the site is less than 200 mm and so cultivation relies on irrigation. But the site is located upon Pleistocene marshes between lakes Aateibe and Hijjane, and the assumption that the lake margins and high levels of groundwater made cultivation both possible and desirable in this rain-deficit zone is supported by the proportion of marsh plant seeds and pollens recovered with the Aswad samples (Van Zeist and Bottema 1977:82). Wild barley (*Hordeum spontaneum*) is another attraction of the area, and this would have been gathered along with almonds, fig, and pistachio (Van Zeist and Bakker-Heeres 1979: table 1). From the outset both long sickle-blades and often serrated, notched arrowheads occur. None the less, hunting (including gazelle and boar), fishing, and fowling remained more important than farming in the economy of Aswad, at least until level II, covering the first half of the seventh millennium (Phase II:A = 7,300–7,000 BC; Phase II:B = 7,000–6,600 BC; de Contenson 1979:155). Significantly, no domesticated animals are reported even this late.

In level II, additional to numerous remains of emmer wheat, are found the seeds of einkorn (*Triticum monococcum*) and free-threshing wheat (*T. durum/aestivum*). Barley, both two-row (*Hordeum distichum*) and naked (*H. nudum*) now seem to be the products of domestication, while pulses remain important and wild fruits are still collected (de Contenson 1983:59). But Aswad was neither anomalous nor isolated, for the raw materials used to manufacture small objects such as beads, pendants, tiny cylinders, and balls – namely limestone, alabaster, cornelian, greenstone, soapstone, plus obsidian – indicate widespread exchange relationships.

Thus de Contenson (ibid.) concludes that 'although Aswad II is strongly related to other PPNB sites such as Mureybet, Saaide, Beisamoun, and Beidha, the evidence from clay figurines suggests that it is also linked with northern Mesopotamia'.

Also from the Damascus Basin comes material bearing upon the processes of bifurcation of herding and dry-farming from hydromorphic cultivation continued in different zones as irrigation. Tell Ramad lies on a fertile plateau *c.* 900 m above sea-level, at the foot of Mount Hermon, some 20 km southwest of Damascus. Indeed Ramad is located in the oak–pistachio savannah, where the rainfall amounts permit dry-farming (de Contenson 1971:278), with an average annual precipitation of *c.* 250 mm.

Level I, dating from the second half of the seventh millennium, displays 'a succession of half-buried huts, made of pise (adobe) and furnished with hearths and large basins, probably used as silos, also in pise' (ibid.:279). Wooden bins also seem to be represented. From the very beginnings of the settlement agriculture was practised with the raising of barley (*Hordeum distichum*), emmer (*Triticum dicoccum*), einkorn (*T. monococcum*) and, unusually, club-wheat (*Triticum compactum*). The wild grass, brome, was collected, as was the green vegetable, vetch, but lentils were grown then, as today. Also collected were nuts and fruits, including almond, pistachio, and hawthorn (*Crataegus monogyna*). However, meat was provided by wild game, principally gazelle and deer (ibid.).

Tools, which confirm those activities, form into two groups pointing in opposite geographical directions. One, consisting of tools of fine-grained light-coloured flint flaked into bladelets with an abrupt retouch, produce long sickle-blades, notched arrowheads, burins, and borers. Those point northeast to Mureybet and are also well known in Palestine at Beidha, El Khiam, Jericho PPNB, Wadi Falla, Abu Ghosh, and Munhatta 3–6. The other type points northwest to the Syrian coast at Ras Shamra (V.C.). Those tools, principally rectangular sickle-blades and tanged arrowheads, as well as scrapers and axes with a polished working edge, are made with a flat pressure retouch, on blades of dark brown flint or chert (ibid.:280). And as we should expect from an agricultural regime, other stone artifacts included basalt (the local groundrock) querns, mullers, grinding stones, pestles, and bolas (ibid.).

In addition to clay figurines of humans and animals (bovids, ovids, equids, boars), there is also evidence of a skull cult (possibly of the ancestors), similar to that found at Mureybet earlier, where, however, the skulls were not over-plastered as here and at Jericho. At Ramad the skulls were found supported upon earthen, lime-covered statuettes (ibid.:281). The 'predecessor' cult this indicates, points up the crucial importance of continuity upon the land for agricultural reproduction. Nearly 300 seeds of flax (*Linum usitatissimum*) occurring in both levels, indicate the importance of its cultivation here, although this did not originate at Ramad (Van Zeist and Bakker-Heeres 1975:217). A sample has been radio-carbon dated to 6,250 BC, making the origins of domesticated flax considerably earlier.

By level II at Ramad, in the opening centuries of the sixth millennium, dwellings have assumed the classical rectangular shape, with mud-brick (40 × 30 × 8 cm) walls on stone foundations, and with lime-plastered floors which continue some way up the walls. Those dwellings seem to consist of a single room only, but the skull-cult continues, as does the combination of hunting with agriculture. But an unbaked, coil-made ware called Vaisselle Blanche appears, its surface smoothed and sometimes painted with wide stripes of red ochre (ibid.:283).

Level III, in complete contrast, has not revealed a single building so far (ibid.:284). Yet in this level, true, fired ceramics appear: a crude, handmade, usually dark-coloured ware, consisting of plain bowls and small jars, with the surface entirely or partly burnished. The 10 per cent of the ware which is partly burnished has on the dull parts incised, combed, or scratched decoration applied prior to baking (ibid.). Those are related to pottery from Amuq A, Ras Shamra V.B., Byblos Early Neolithic, and Hagoshrim; which R. Braidwood (Braidwood and Braidwood 1960) originally termed 'Dark Faced Burnished Ware' (DFBW), 'varieties of which can be found as the earliest ceramics from Anatolia to Palestine' (de Contenson 1971:285). In this level, which might date to the end of the sixth millennium, the flint and bone industries, 'are only impoverished shadows of those from Level II' (ibid.). Faunal remains of this phase are almost entirely of domesticated species: goat, sheep, pig, ox, and dog, leading to the striking conclusion that the inhabitants of Ramad had given up agriculture to breed animals, and accordingly had adopted some kind of migratory regime, perhaps only semi-nomadic. De Contenson (ibid.) observes that a similar phenomenon occurred at the same period in Palestine.

This is further remarkable in that the villagers of Ramad were not formerly herders but hunters, and appears therefore to reinforce the suggestion that domestication proceeded from animals, most probably mothers and young, that survived the hunt.[9] But most of all it shows the precariousness of rainfed farming, and that in the face of its uncertainties, even in a favoured area such as Hermon, the mobility and thus flexibility of pastoralism was to be preferred. An early example perhaps, of the sort of oscillation steps 8 and 9 are intended to represent.

Chapter four

The origin and growth of villages

Here archaeological flesh will be put on the bones of the flow chart (Figure 3.5) in the previous chapter. This involves not a comprehensive survey but illustration. The movement will be from west to east, from the Levant to Mesopotamia.

In the Near East the Epipalaeolithic hunting cultures are *Kebaran* in the Levant, *Belbasian* in the Antalya area of southern Turkey, and the *Zarzian* of the Zagros (Mellaart 1975:19). Very roughly they span the period 17,000–10,000 BC. They are succeeded respectively by the *Natufian* in the Levant, *Beldibian* in Anatolia, and by the *Zawi Chemi/Shanidar* phase in the Zagros.

1 The Levant

Nearest the Mediterranean is the Natufian, extending from around 10,300 to 8,500 BC (Bar-Yosef 1983:13). Though centred upon Palestine, it is known from northern Syria to outliers at Helwan south of Cairo. Generally, however, the culture is concentrated south of Beirut and west of the Jordan with no site more than 40 miles from the sea (Garrod 1957:212). Indeed,

> Geometric Kebaran and Natufian sites have quite different distributions. Geometric Kebaran sites are environmentally ubiquitous, occurring along the coast, in high elevations and in the desert lowlands of the region. Natufian occurrences, on the other hand, are confined to those settings which are either at present, or were in the past, within the Mediterranean environmental zone.
>
> (Henry, Leroi-Gourhan, and Davis 1981:52)

Natufians continued the generalized hunting of the Kebarans (but with emphasis upon gazelle and deer, both fallow and roe), to which they added the reaping and storage of wild cereals. To facilitate this, living sites were moved from the coastal plains to the *terra rossa* soils on the limestone uplands, where, in association with oak and pistachio,

The warm humid conditions of [the millennium beginning] *c.* 12,000 BP apparently contributed to the expansion of cereals, specifically emmer wheat (*Triticum dicoccoides*) and barley (*Hordeum spontaneum*), into their contemporary habitat of the Mediterranean hill zone of Palestine (Harlan & Zohary 1966). The pollen diagram of the Hayonim Terrace deposit clearly documents the emergence of a Mediterranean environment at this time in the foothills of the western Galilee.

(Henry et al. 1981:53)

While the Natufians had a hunter-gatherer economy with increasingly heavy reliance on cereal gathering, the Kebaran hunting economy continued in the more desertic areas such as the Negev, or was replaced by other hunting complexes such as the Mushabian in the Sinai, an area never suitable for Natufian settlement (ibid.:52). Accordingly Henry *et al.* conclude that

The appearance of cereals in the Mediterranean zone was apparently the catalyst which initiated the transition of the Geometric Kebaran A into the Natufian. This proposal is based on the observation that: (1) the Geometric Kebaran A – Natufian transition is restricted to the core Mediterranean zone; (2) the Natufian appears at about the same time as the terminal Pleistocene temperature elevation and the emergence of a Mediterranean environment; (3) the distribution of Natufian sites is restricted to the Mediterranean hill zone of Palestine which is the modern natural habitat for cereals and (4) a wide array of artifactual evidence for cereal procurement and processing (i.e. mortars, pestles, querns, grinding slabs, sickle blades and storage pits) appears with the Natufian.

(Henry et al. 1981:54)

Beidha is the site, near Petra on the east bank of the Jordan, of a post-Natufian,[1] Early Neolithic village dating from about 7,000 to 6,500 BC (Kirkbride 1968:263–5). Its elevation at 1,000 m is quite high (to compensate orographically for a southerly and inland position), and it has a remaining area of 0.4 ha, of which around half has been excavated. Beidha is a permanent village lacking pottery, which, along with certain other characteristics, such as the common occurrence of four arrowhead types (Kirkbride 1966:47), associates it with the lowest (earliest) levels at Jericho, called 'Pre-Pottery Neolithic' (PPN with suffix A or B). In this Beidha, a PPNB settlement, is also associated with Tell Ramad, while its use of floor and wall plaster further relate it to similar practices at Çatal Hüyük and Hacilar in Anatolia (cf. Garfinkel 1987:69–76).

Instead of pottery, Beidha people used stone bowls, troughs, and mortars. Baskets coated with lime plaster and bitumen also served as containers (Kirkbride 1968:268). However, wood seems to have been the preferred medium for food preparation, since stone bowls are relatively scarce.

Though parching ovens have not been found (Kirkbride 1966:16), wild barley (*Hordeum spontaneum*) was cultivated (Helbaek's term: 1966:62), as also, in his view (ibid.), was emmer, in a range of forms indicative of transition from the wild race to the domesticated. No less than five gallons of carbonized pistachio nuts were found (Helbaek 1966:62) in the fire-destroyed house that provided most of the floral information at Beidha. Acorns were used, along with other vegetable foods such as field-pea, two kinds of wild lentil, large vetch (*Vicia narbonense*), medick (*Medicago* sp.), cock's comb (*Onobrychis cristagalli*), plus other leguminous plants (ibid.:63). And while still hunting, the people of Beidha herded goats (ibid.).

In later levels (II and III) there was a degree of craft specialization evidenced by the existence of 'corridor buildings' of too peculiar a shape (three pairs of rooms 1.5 × 1 m disposed along a corridor 1 m wide by 6 m), and too full of raw materials – bone, wood, stone, and ochre (malachite and haematite as pigments) – to be other than workshops (Kirkbride 1966:14–15). Distributed throughout the workshops 'chipped and polished flint axes form a very conspicuous class' (ibid.:47).

By the time of level IV, perhaps 200 years after level VI (the earliest), a series of large fine houses, about 5 × 6 m, appear disposed along two sides of an open area like a plaza. Floors and walls were plastered and they had large interior hearths with raised and plastered sills. Stone bowls were set into the plaster near the hearths. The excavator saw the large houses on the body of the tell with the lesser ones 'respectfully removed' to the perimeter, as a 'hint of the presence of a privileged and not so privileged class' (Kirkbride 1967:8). All houses are still, as at all periods, 'semi-subterranean' and entered by a flight of three stone steps.

Between levels IV and III there is a discontinuity, after which the whole village was rebuilt simultaneously, perhaps as a result of earthquake damage to the now more vulnerable stone buildings. Previously fire had been the abiding danger (ibid.:9). For the first time truly rectangular buildings appear (when formerly they were curvilinear or rectangular with rounded ends), integrated into a gridplan layout of the whole village. Summarizing, Kirkbride (1966:22) observes a sequence 'beginning with polygonal houses (Level VI) continuing through round houses (V) and the subrectangular houses with gently curving walls (IV) to the highly complex layout of corridor buildings and large houses of III and II'.

Continuity is manifested, however, in what seems to be the religious function of a large (9 × 7 m) building containing a highly polished table or seat and a circular stone-lined pit at the base of which was a large stone. Both features were outlined in red paint about a metre wide, which ran parallel to the walls of highly burnished white plaster and continuing up them (Kirkbride 1968:270–1). The pit feature, at least, occurs in earlier versions of this house in the same relative position.

But what is clearly a religious complex of considerable size and cost lies at a distance of about 45 m from the village and is perhaps associated with burials or a cult of the dead. It consists of no less than three structures of different periods with associated standing and lying ('horizontal') stones aligned to the cardinal points. 'The materials were obviously hand-picked with loving care, to which may be added the fine workmanship and absolute cleanliness of each one, quite apart from the labour and organisation involved in detaching and transporting the huge blocks of sandstone from the mountains' (Kirkbride 1968:273).

Both Beidha and Petra are located on a shelf of land, about 1,000 m above mean sea-level, and which varies in width from about 4 km at Petra to 6 km at Beidha. This shelf, interrupted by mountain blocks and steep rift-like valleys, extends for most of the distance up the eastern side of the Jordan Valley–Dead Sea–Wadi Araba fault (Kirkbride 1966:54).

In the area of Petra and Beidha the shelf is bounded by the Wadi Araba, largely desertic, and to the east is protected from the high plateau (400 m higher) of the Arabian desert by the ridge of the Jebel Shara, which induces some orographic rainfall. As a result wadis run west from the hills across the shelf into the Wadi Araba, and springs are present due to an impermeable layer about two-thirds of the way up the west side of the sandstone ridge (ibid.).

Beidha stands on the Wadi Gharab, and is close to the spring of Dibadiba. Raikes (1966:70) suggests 'that the first neolithic settlement was situated on a high terrace remnant overlooking a comparatively wide valley floor of loamy sand of which the lower terrace is the surviving remnant'. He further argues (ibid.) that 'during the whole occupation of Beidha the high ridge to the east would have been wooded as it was in recent times', containing pistachio, and inhabited by aurochs and boar (Perkins 1966:67).

Kirkbride suspected the presence of other Neolithic settlements along the length of the shelf, which has indeed more favoured sites than that of Beidha, and by reconnaissance found some (1966:56). As a consequence Beidha no longer stands out as an anomaly in what is now a rather arid southern and interior location. Rather it belongs fully to that group of sites occupying what she calls the 'western arc' of uplands in the Levant, as against an 'eastern arc' in Iraq and Iran, between which 'there is no clear evidence for contact . . . until the much later Hassuna period' (1966:60). In fact, the proto-Hassuna is roughly contemporary.

None the less, this does not mean that there are no early 'intermediate' sites showing both Levantine and Zagros attributes. One newly discovered is Qermez Dere, a small aceramic village site dating to around

8,000 BC and located on the outskirts of Tel Afar, west of Mosul on the Tigris. Qermez Dere, situated on a wadi of that name, manifests lithic parallels with Tell Mureybet on the Euphrates, some 400 km to the west, and also with pre-Jarmo Zagros sites to the east, particularly with Karim Shahir and M'lefaat (Watkins and Baird 1987:3). Those sites are discussed below.

The Hassuna is of course a sixth-millennium Mesopotamian phenomenon. Fully fledged Neolithic village cultures are preceded in the Zagros area by the Early Neolithic sites like Jarmo in Iraqi Kurdistan and Alikosh in Khuzistan (which is discussed below). Jarmo, with Alikosh in this phase, is aceramic, but the contemporary Tepe Guran is ceramic.

The Jarmo–Alikosh–Guran phase, probably of five to six hundred years' duration, is contemporary with the late PPNB of Palestine and Syria and with Çatal Hüyük in Anatolia (Mellaart 1975:80). The PPNA, beginning around 8,300 BC and derived from the Natufian, is the first of the Holocene cultures of the Levant. Always rare in Palestine, the PPNA terminates around 7,350 BC (Mellaart 1975:48). When the PPNB commences at about 7,000 BC, usually at new sites or after hiatuses on old ones (the most famous being Jericho), it manifests a new northern-derived (but probably also Natufian) cultural assemblage (cf. Mureybet below). The PPNB culture, depending on a mix of agriculture and hunting, with domestic goats known from Jericho and Beidha, terminates around 6,000 BC with widespread desertion of sites both in Palestine and the Syrian steppe (Mellaart 1975:67). As no violence seems implicated in what is a very widespread phenomenon, Mellaart (ibid.) follows Perrot in attributing this to advancing desiccation, something he also sees in Mesopotamia, notably at Alikosh in the Mohammed Jaffar phase (discussed below).

Mellaart (1975:68) concludes that:

> The desertion of PPNB sites is widespread in Palestine (Beidha, Jericho, Munhatta, Tell el-Farah, Wadi Shu'aib, Khirbet Sheikh Ali) and in the Syrian desert (El Khowm, Bouqras, Mureybet IV). Only the more favoured Mediterranean littoral and the Huleh-Hermon area would have continued to offer viable conditions; Labwe and Tell Ramad survived.

This led to the exploitation of previously avoided forest zones by those still pursuing agriculture, while others adopted semi-nomadic pastoralism, as at Tell Ramad III.

2 Tell Mureybet

Located on the left bank of the Euphrates near Muskene, about 86 km east of Aleppo (36°N, 05°E), Mureybet is a transitional site in several regards. It is transitional between the Levant and Mesopotamia, and between the Epipalaeolithic and the Neolithic.

Mureybet consists of a truncated conical mound 6 m high and 75 m in diameter, sitting on a platform 4 m high, 125 m wide, and 250 m long from north to south (Van Loon 1968:265). This feature is the reason for the particular location of the settlement, since it constitutes an 'islet' of Palaeocene chalk containing natural beds of lacustrine brown flint (silex). This only occurs here and is superior for fine tools to the grey flint that occurs generally, and which indeed is found in the Lower Quaternary[2] terrace on which the tell rests (J. C. Cauvin 1977:40). Extraction of the brown flint is easy, thanks to the erosion of the 'islet' by the river, exposing at low water the flint embedded in 'chalk cliffs' (ibid.). It is not a site that farmers would choose.

The particular location of the site is important, so Cauvin's map is reproduced here (Map 4.1). The contour lines show the site to approach 300 m above sea-level, while the grid is centred upon the bench-mark at the highest point of the mound, 297.2 m above sea-level (Van Loon, op. cit.:fig. 1). Cauvin's map also shows the two sets of excavations undertaken, first by Maurits Van Loon of the University of Chicago team (1964–5), and later (1971–4) by J. C. Cauvin of the CNRS, Paris. The map, on which both campaigns are separately indicated, also illustrates what was said at the outset about the very limited and constrained nature of modern excavation, even on relatively small sites like this one. Yet this site itself was due to disappear, along with many others, known and to be discovered, under the reservoir for the Tabqa dam in the main valley of the Euphrates. Those campaigns were in effect 'rescue archaeology'.

The earlier campaign distinguished seventeen distinct levels of occupation, beginning around the end of the ninth millennium and continuing until the first centuries of the eighth. Basal levels were suspected of being Natufian, with the discovery of tanged projectile points, but in the limited exposure only 'round-house' and 'rectilinear house' levels could clearly be distinguished (in levels I–VIII and X–XVII, with no houses found by Van Loon in level IX).

Dates now are (Cauvin 1977:48):

Phase IA	8,500–8,300 BC
Phase IB	8,300–8,200 BC
Phase II	8,200–8,000 BC
Phase III	8,000–7,600 BC
Phase IVA	7,600–7,300 BC
Phase IVB	7,300–6,900 BC

In Mureybet we have a site that commences when the Holocene does and extends over two millennia, manifesting continuity of both occupation

Map 4.1 The site and situation of Tell Mureybet on the Euphrates

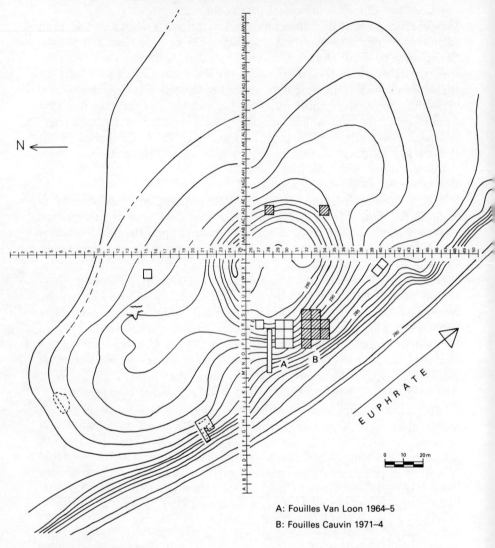

A: Fouilles Van Loon 1964–5
B: Fouilles Cauvin 1971–4

Source: Cauvin 1977:20

and cultural tradition (Skinner 1968:283; Cauvin 1977:41). It is, therefore, ideal for illustrating the hypothesis about the origins and development of sedentarization, and so is treated at some length.

The terrace on which the tell grew up enabled hunter-gatherers to exploit three distinct biomes: the river itself, the floodplain of 3 to 4 km in width, formerly covered with poplar and tamarix, and the steppe beyond, formerly punctuated by oaks (Cauvin, op. cit.:40).

Phase IA

Due to limited exposure and disturbance no structures were found in this earliest Natufian level. However, living floors of reddish compacted clay, similar to the floors of later structures, were located, with hearths of different types. One is a hearth with a raised surface, delimited by a kerbstone in the form of a horseshoe constructed of small pieces of limestone and with an internal diameter of only 50 cm. Another three hearths are pits containing pebbles like the 'fire-pits' uncovered by Van Loon (1968:269) in his middle levels. These earliest examples are however relatively shallow, the largest (structure XXV) measuring 1.5 m in diameter with a depth of 0.6 m (Cauvin 1977:21). Like the others, this was filled with pebbles and charcoal mixed together, in the top 10 cm of which charred fragments of bone were found, suggesting the employment of this largest one, at least, for cooking meats (ibid.).

Tool-making is diverse, abundant, and mostly microlithic, including triangles, flakes, numerous micro-borers, borers, and drill-bits, and fragments of obsidian are also found. Burins, scrapers, picks, and adzes occur, and, significantly, non-denticulated sickle-blades with wear-sheen.

Traditionally this would have been regarded as evidence for the early advent of agriculture, especially when, as here, sickle-blades are associated with pestles (two small ones found, plus a fragment of vase in limestone), and some still try to push agriculture in some form back into the early Epipalaeolithic. However it will become clearer that Mureybet represents hunter-gatherer settlements made permanent by 'broad-spectrum' exploitation from a favourable site. All the resources involved are wild, including the wheat and barley.

Phase IB

This phase is termed by Cauvin 'epi-Natufian'. It has but a short duration, being represented by a bed only 10–20 cm thick. None the less, this is the first phase in which house structures can be positively identified. Structure XXXVII is a round-house of the type traditionally called 'semi-subterranean'. It has an interior diameter of 6 m and is excavated 0.5 m into the soil. The sides of the pit are retained and 'damp-proofed' by a palisade of wooden stakes plastered over to a depth of 10 cm. Since this plaster was flattened and polished at its extant height of 0.5 m, it is assumed that the 'palisade wall' originally rose no higher, but instead was covered over by a roof of light wooden structure supporting perhaps rush or foliage. This in view of the large area to be covered and the absence of central supports (Cauvin, op. cit.:23).

As we should expect with extensive woodworking, excellent adzes are found, one on the very floor of house XXVII. Otherwise the industry remains microlithic, retaining, though in lesser proportion than IA, segments and micro-burins, while other geometrics, such as scalene triangles and trapezes increase somewhat (ibid.). The first notched arrowheads – notched and tanged El-Khiam points – make their appearance, as do small, pedunculated points of diverse type, included in which, though rarely, are 'Harif points' (ibid.). Bone-working, highly characteristic of the Natufian, continues, but the straight bi-pointed objects and pierced phalanxes are now absent. However a flat object in bone, toothed at one end and 'decorated' with seventeen 'acorn cups' in rows, occurs (Stordeur 1974:2).

Phase II

In this level 70 square metres were excavated, exposing no less than seven round-houses in addition to three levels of habitation imposed directly on to house XXVII already mentioned. Accordingly Cauvin (op. cit.:26) asserts direct continuity of Phase II with the preceding Epi-Natufian.

While the floors, as hitherto, are always built up of reddish clay, and no house exceeds 4 m diameter, the houses are no longer uniform. Now more houses are built on the surface than are cut into the ground (ibid.:26). Surface-built houses either have their walls constructed of clay, without stones; or the clay wall has a central spine formed by a line of more or less flat stones set on edge; or, strikingly, given our thesis regarding the exploitation of wild cereals, a clay wall is supported on a foundation of limestone pieces or recycled millstones generally laid flat and extending to one or two courses (ibid.).

No interior hearths were found, but fire-pits containing pebbles and charcoal were found on the outside, adjacent to the wall of the house with which they were contemporary.

Tool-making is overwhelmingly microlithic but with rare geometrics. Micro-borers in places number over 20 per cent of retouched tool-making. Arrowheads, which are small and of abrupt retouch, become abundant. While obsidian is represented by flakes, the rest of the tool-making consists of adzes, borers, and drill-bits, with scrapers and burins, in addition to a small number of sickle-blades. Again small mortars and pestles occur, as do heavy millstones, reinforcing the suggestion that the characteristic fire-pits were used for the roasting of grain prior to grinding. To beads made from bird bone and toothed objects now longer and undecorated, bone-working sees the addition of the first entirely polished awls with rectilinear shaft, with others fabricated on the proximal extremities of metapodes conserving the original epiphysis. The object most characteristic of Phase II however, in that it does not recur, is the needle with eye and sharp-pointed proximal extremity. But another first is the appearance in limestone of a (sexually indeterminate) anthropomorphic figurine and a small head in unbaked clay. As in Phase I no burials were discovered, although there is evidence of cult in the recovery from a built-up clay bank of an entire cattle bucranium, surrounded by three scapulas, two of cattle and one of ass. Also with cultic association are (fragments of) polished batons in hard stone.

Phase III

This phase was exposed over 150 square metres, allowing the juxtaposition of architectural features to be revealed. Round-houses continue to be standard, with their dimensions ranging from 2.5 to 6 m (ibid.:28). Poplar stakes are still employed to retain inner excavated surfaces, with a plastering of clay applied to the stakes; or, manifesting versatility in structural techniques, consolidated by a wall in coarse puddled clay, consisting of a mixture of earth, stones, and bone. Indeed both techniques can occur in the same house. But surface dwellings also continue, such as the large house (Structure XLII), the peripheral wall of which was constructed, at least in its lower courses, of flat stones. This can be seen in Figure 4.1a (p. 88), with the best-preserved house (Structure XLVII) adjoining.

Structure XLVII exhibits the principal novelty of Phase III, namely the internal division of houses by low (0.7 m) murets forming open or closed cells, the latter probably serving for storage (ibid.:30). Particularly interesting is that Structure XLVII was destroyed by fire, preserving the broken and cindered fragments of a flat roof constructed from puddled clay (clay and straw) spread on beams of poplar set edge to edge.[3] This roof in turn was supported on strong uprights of poplar or oak, some positioned around the periphery of the house. Four others, coupled in pairs, formed two pillars on either side of a short vestibule.

Phase III houses show signs of nucleation, with the sharing of common walls, analogous to that of PPNA Nahal Oren (Stekelis and Yizraely 1963). At Mureybet houses rise in tiers up the slope of the tell (Cauvin, op. cit.:30). Houses here are grouped around at least partially paved workspaces, in which fire-pits are found.

In this phase microliths, notably micro-borers, virtually disappear, but long blades formed from 'naviform nuclei', with two striking planes and dorsal hulls, increase. Both the number and dimensions of arrowheads also increase, but those with lateral notches are no longer in the majority, the most numerous now being those that are simply tanged, produced by flat retouching.

Sickle-blades, always fairly numerous, increase toward the end of the phase (ibid.:34). However, scrapers also increase in quantity and quality, which taken with the increase in number and size of arrowheads, suggests an increase in hunting. While 'Mureybet adzes' persist, if in lesser

Figure 4.1a Some Tell Mureybet Phase III round-houses and roasting-pits

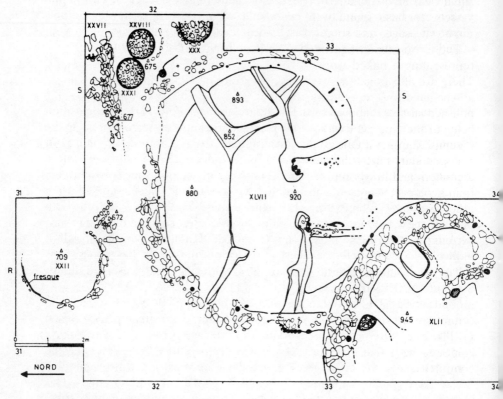

Source: Cauvin 1977:29

numbers, the advent of an axe in green polished stone late in the phase signals the multiplication of this tool in Phase IV (ibid.:34–5).

A novelty is the utilization of ribs for tool-making: spatulas, sometimes pierced, 'polishing tools', and small rectangular platelets. Also new at Mureybet is the manufacture of awls from the distal half of metapodes, though manufacture on proximal halves remains the most usual. Beads in bird bone remain numerous.

But the major novelty in manufactures is the appearance, surprisingly early, of what Cauvin (op. cit.:35) calls 'a genuine ceramic', represented by five small vessels of fired clay all deriving from the beginning of Phase III (near 8,000 BC) and found in houses XLVII and XLII. Their stratigraphic position here leaves little doubt as to their early date (ibid.). Two are cups with flat bottoms and mouths measuring 6 cm and 8.2 cm across the openings, a small cylindrical vase decorated with incisions and containing holes for hanging (and the base of another), and lastly a very small oval bowl (godet). Ceramic experimentation was not confined to vessels, for also found were objects in baked clay of clear form but unknown usage, and some of a type that are very well known.

Those are human figurines, sometimes very schematic and sometimes representing a naked woman with both arms folded under her breasts. There are also female representations in limestone and what seems to be a schematic anthropomorphic statuette also in stone. Batons in green polished stone probably also have cultic significance; the female figurines being of the type later widely dispersed and taken to be fecundity objects ('Venus' figurines). One of the polished batons marks the site of a burial, two secondary burials belonging early in this phase. One, comprising only a cranium and longbones of a female of gracile Mediterranean type, was found compacted under a hearth occupying the angle of a cell; while the other lay some metres to the east, but outside the house, and consisted only of a vertebral column, a pelvis, a thoracic cage, and the bones of the extremities (ibid.:36). It may be that both burials are of the same individual.

Traces of mural paintings were found in two houses, the one in Structure XXII being geometric, consisting of black chevrons on a white ground. Striking, however, in view of what was said in Chapter 2, is that ceramics were not found either in higher, i.e. later, levels of Phase III, or in Phase IV (ibid.:35). This may, on the other hand, just be a consequence of limited excavation, though it must be said (and it is cold comfort) that many other key sites have received much less exposure.

Phase IVA and IVB

Phase IVA was exposed over only 28 square metres in two squares (ibid.:36). No traces of architecture were found, the beds being carbonized black or containing pebbles. However, Byblos points occur, that is, tanged points with foliated retouch. Peculiar to Phase IVA is a particular category with denticulated tang. Denticulation seems to be a special feature of this industry; another, third, being the presence henceforward of polished axes in hard stone. However, the 'Mureybet adzes' in cut flint have disappeared, though a fragment of polished rod recurs (ibid.).

Phase IVB marks the advent of the rectilinear houseform, corresponding to Van Loon's (1968:266) Stratum X (and upwards to XVII), which he calls 'square-house levels'. His Structure 16, from level XIV, reproduced here (Figure 4.1b) can serve to represent this new architecture, since its walls remain standing up to eleven courses.

Figure 4.1b Tell Mureybet
rectilinear houseform

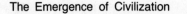

TELL MUREYBIT
1965

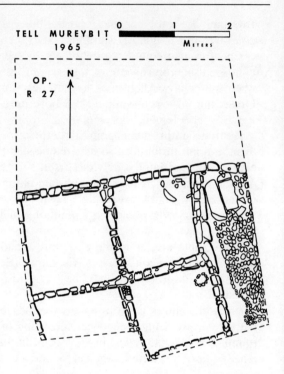

Source: Van Loon 1968:272

Its walls consisted of single rows of limestone pieces fashioned with flint tools into shapes resembling bricks or loaves and surrounded on all sides with thick red clay mortar. . . . Inside this house there were four square rooms measuring only 1.50 × 1.50 m, paved with limestone flags. . . . In Rooms 1 and 4 the pavement was sunk in the northeast corner as if to form a hearth and a bin, respectively.

(Van Loon 1968:271)

Despite those apparently domestic utilities, the small size of the structure overall, only 3.50 × 3.50 m, the division of this very small area into four regular but cramped rooms which appear to have entry only from the roof, plus the appearance of a large carnivore jaw embedded in the wall near the hearth in Room 1, all suggest a ritual function for this building, a possibility heightened by the occurrence of other objects, such as a pierced stone shaped like a millstone, 16 cm in diameter, lying near the centre of Room 1 in association with 'a number of extremely elongated pebbles, possibly used as pokers' (ibid.:273). Pierced also were two interior walls and one exterior, with one stone removed from a course to serve as a peephole.

Cauvin's sounding in Square AD 28 came across the rectilinear walls of a house, the rectangular chambers of which were formed by partition walls in pisé (puddled clay with straw) and with a clay-plastered floor. Under the floor he found two primary burials:

> But on the actual floor of the house several crania were found, placed on mounds of built-up red clay which served as pedestals for them; one of them was found inverted at the side of its pedestal which seems to underline that we are dealing with a sort of 'cultic artifact', freestanding, and not with a partial inhumation. The built-up red clay also served as a pillow for the cranium of a complete burial.
>
> (Cauvin 1977:38)

A small pendant in polished stone representing a bearded masculine head was also recovered.

Lithic tool-making was exclusively on flakes struck from naviform cores, and includes large arrowheads of the 'Byblos point' type, numerous ovular burins with some scrapers and borers on blades, plus some denticulated sickle-blades. The bone industry includes awls on distal extremities of a whole metapode, and axes in the distinctive green polished stone recur (ibid.:38).

Generally materials are either of chert or flint, the former derived from river pebbles, the latter nodular as noted at the outset, and though mostly tan, also occurs as grey, pinkish, or grey mottled with black (Skinner 1968:283). The chert is most useful for 'massive heavy-duty tools' (ibid.), such as 'adzes', 'picks', and 'sledges', with the adzes fashioned for hafting in all cases (ibid.); while the small implements are made on very thin and straight flint blades, used in an increasingly large proportion from bottom to top, obsidian being very rare. Skinner (op. cit.:287–90) notes that the bone industry is poorly developed, and perhaps this correlates with the plenitude of local chert and flint of good quality.

Site, situation, and subsistence

The lithic advantages of the site have been described, but it is the situation of Mureybet at the water's edge in a steppe zone which enabled a fully sedentary community to live there for two millennia (Cauvin, op. cit.:40). The resources available were, as mentioned, those of the river itself, its banks and their immediate environs, and the broad steppe beyond.

Van Loon (1968:279) was rightly surprised at the absence of fish remains in his excavations. This was clarified by Cauvin's team (1977:38–40) who found a great number of fish vertebrae, the largest number being of the species *barbus* or *silurus*, fishing for which is possible throughout the year. Shellfish remains were also abundant, being the bivalves *Unio Tigridis* and *Melanopsis* (varieties *costata* and *praemorsa*), which contributed substantially to the diet (ibid.). The small shells of the species *Theodoxus* were, on the other hand, used for ornamentation.

In addition to a perennial supply of running water, the advantages of which should never be overlooked, the river also served as a route for migratory birds, such as ducks, geese, and pelicans, which fly up the Euphrates from February to April. Though seasonal, they also contributed to a diversified diet.

Due to the peculiarities of the site, the floodplain is non-existent around the tell itself, continuing to the north and south on that ('left') bank (ibid.:40). Of 3 to 4 km in width, prior to deforestation it supported gallery forest of poplar and tamarix. Apart from their uses in construction that we have seen, such dense growth would in its turn have supported boar and Mesopotamian fallow deer at the least, quite apart from steppe animals drawn through the woodland to drink at the waterside. In addition to *Dama* (presumed to be *mesopotamica*) and *Sus scrofa*, Perkins (cited Van Loon 1968:279) also reported remains of *Equus hemionus hippus* (Syrian onager), *Bos primigenius* (great cattle), and *Gazella* sp., presumably *dorcas*, plus *Canis lupus* and *Lepus* sp. (wolf and rabbit/hare). However, cattle, onager, and gazelle comprised at least 95 per cent of Perkins's total sample, in roughly equal proportions for each of those three species. While Perkins (ibid.) could discern 'no noticeable differences in percentage from the early to the late levels', Ducos (1975: fig. 2, cited Cauvin 1977:43) on the basis of a much larger body of remains, detected increased preponderance of *larger* game between 8,200 and 7,500 BC, reaching a plateau at the end of Phase III.

During Phase III, that is in Van Loon's levels IX to XIII, Cauvin (op. cit.:41), from the smaller quantity of fish vertebrae recovered through sieving, sees in this a diminution of fishing, which he correlates with heightened success in hunting large game thanks to the evolution of social co-operative techniques. However, a rise in humidity is also perceptible from *c.* 8,000 BC, that is, at the beginning of Phase III, with the forest pollens *Ostrya* (hop hornbeam), *Corylus* (hazel), and *Cedrus* (cedar) becoming more common. At the end of Phase III, toward 7,800 BC, and extending over Phase IV, increasing humidity is represented by the presence of pollens of *Ulmus* (elm), *Betula* (birch), and *Fagus* (beech), with *Fraxinus* (ash) and *Alnus* (alder), the last a product of damp river conditions, and the others of wetter conditions in the region as a whole, especially the mountains. Coupled with this is a rise in the Leguminosae and a progressive depletion of the Chenopodiaceae (ibid.). Van Zeist

(1970:175) observes that 'Today *Pistacia atlantica* Desf. (pistachio) grows in the mountains of central Syria, while *P. khinjuk* Stocks and *P. atlantica* Desf. var. *kurdica* Zohary (= *P. eurycarpa* Yalt) are native in south-eastern Turkey.'

The steppe consists of a large plain interrupted by hills and normally dry wadis. Throughout the pollen record the scattered presence of oak is manifested, as also wild cereals. Among the charred seeds recovered, Van Zeist (1970:167–8) recognized wild einkorn in the larger and usually two-seeded variety, *Triticum boeoticum*, var. *thaoudar*. Wild barley, *Hordeum spontaneum*, was also gathered and roasted, and fragments of pistachio were encountered.

Olszewski (1986:148) suggests that despite 'the many similarities between the late Epipalaeolithic cultural assemblages in the Natufian area and northern Syria [which] include a dominance of lunate microliths, straight backed bladelets, a heavy tool component, and the presence of circular hut structures and ground stone', we should nevertheless distinguish between the Natufian proper, comprising Palestine with the Negev and northern Sinai, plus Jordan, and northern Syria, while suspending judgement on southern Syria and the Lebanon. She proposes (1986:150) 'that the north Syrian chipped stone industries be called the north Syrian late Epipalaeolithic', and sees this cultural form as a response to the steppic/riparian situation of sites like Tell Mureybet, Tell Abu Hureyra, and Dibsi Faraj East, in contrast to the more wooded and coastal situation of the classic Natufian. She remarks that the ground stone forms in northern Syria, mainly rubbers and querns, are more suitable for grain processing than the mortars and pestles more common elsewhere (the latter more useful for pounding nuts, such as acorns). She sees the steppe around the Euphrates as 'an ideal natural habitat for massive wild grain stands' (ibid.:150), given sufficient rainfall, this grain being wild einkorn, examples of which were recovered both from Hureyra and Mureybet. To Olszewski (ibid.) 'these basic differences suggest the north Syrian assemblages from the Euphrates River area are distinct from the contemporary Natufian developments to the south in several important respects.'

Mureybet is remarkable not only for its longevity but also for its size. Van Loon's expedition excavated roughly 325 square metres, or about 1 per cent of the total surface of the site (op. cit.:280). An average of two structures per stratum were found, about the same in Cauvin's exposures. If such a recovery rate, on 1 per cent, is at all representative of the site as a whole, then each stratum should contain around 200 houses. If each household had on average two adults and three children, then the gross population at any time would be of the order of 1,000, making Mureybet a very large village indeed, by far the largest early village for which there is good evidence. If only half the possible total of houses were occupied at any one time (or if up to half were non-residential structures), then, still employing the conservative figure of five per household, a population of 500 is indicated, still a very large village for so early a date.

For its emergence and duration Cauvin (op. cit.:43) rejects technical inventions, population, or environmental pressures as explanations, singly or jointly. In the first place climate was improving over the life of the site, and with it the diversity and yield of the terrain. Second, population numbers could and did expand with increasing resources (Ducos 1975a: fig. 2) without putting any further pressure on resources (Cauvin, op. cit.: 43–4). Third, technical advances *accompanied* procurement advances but could not be said to cause them. Thus the 'cut adze' in flint is peculiar to the Euphrates, appearing around 8,000 BC right at the onset of the Holocene and the beginning of the site. As Cauvin (ibid.) puts it: 'The Natufians of Phase IA already had it. . . . The presence of those tools is evidently tied to Mureybet's intense need for wood, above all for architecture.' In turn the need for wood was 'caused' by the need for architecture which was 'caused' by permanent settlement which was 'caused' by plenitude and concentration of resources at favoured sites early in the Holocene. This it will be remembered, is where the flow chart (Figure 3.5, p. 70) commences. Instead, Cauvin attributes the success of the settlement to sociological advances, namely to the emergence of forms of social organization enabling a sizeable community to live together permanently, with, perhaps, daughter villages budding off, taking those new cultural forms with them. In so doing, similar well-watered well-favoured sites in an ameliorating environment are sought. Those are hydromorphic sites to which the wild cereals will be taken if they are not already present. Again, no new technology is required for this, only digging sticks, containers, the 'old' sickles and perhaps axes/adzes.

3 The Zagros

Further illustration can be had from the site of Zawi Chemi-Shanidar in Northern Iraq, representing in the Zagros a phase that is the nearest equivalent to the earliest Natufian (Mellaart 1975:70; Solecki 1981:66); though it should be remarked that 'The Zagros Epipalaeolithic to early proto-Neolithic developments are separate from developments occurring in the Levant' (Olszewski 1986:57). For example, a heavy tool component is not seen in the Zarzian (ibid.). Zawi Chemi is a pre-pottery, proto-Neolithic site of 250×275 m (of which 112 m^2 has been excavated to 3 m depth), located in a modern wheatfield on a terrace over the Greater (Upper) Zab. The valley floor is at 425 m above sea-level and surrounded by high mountains (Solecki, op. cit.:67). Zawi Chemi is the open-air site, Shanidar is a cave with a long Palaeolithic occupation.

Dated to the mid-ninth millennium BC, Zawu Chemi is relevant not because of continuous occupation through qualitatively distinct phases but because, in the middle of the region of particular interest (the Zagros), it seems typical of a range of sites of its period, such as Karim Shahir, M'lefaat, and Gird Chai (down-river from Zawi Chemi), with which it has 'close cultural parallels' (Solecki, op. cit.:63).

This was a period in the Zagros already getting warmer and wetter, with trees, cereals, and other plants spreading out from refuge areas, one of which, that of the Rowundaz River (a branch of the Greater Zab), is only some 35 km southeast of Shanidar (ibid.:59). None the less, in the ninth millennium the general environment of Zawi Chemi was characteristically steppe-savannah (Leroi-Gourhan 1981:77) on palynological evidence. As elsewhere in Mediterranean and sub-Mediterranean areas, modern levels of humidity were not fully attained before c. 6,000 BP (Van Zeist, Woldring, and Stepert 1975:139–40). Today the undisturbed vegetation of the area is oak forest (Solecki, op. cit.:56). The Zawi Chemi zone was rich in wild game; species hunted included both large (bear) and smaller animals, with red deer, wild sheep, and goats being preferred prey (Perkins 1964). By the end of occupation at Zawi Chemi (around 8,000 BC),[4] sheep had been domesticated and formed the major source of meat (Solecki, op. cit.:68). Mullers, querns, mortars, pounders, and shaped slabs indicate plant processing. Stone celts, the earliest so far in the Zagros, were probably used as axes, adzes, gouges, and chisels for wood and bone-working, the prominence of the latter again mirroring the Natufian (ibid.:62). The importance of bone-working, in what Solecki (ibid.:68) stresses was a period of experiment, is underlined by the find of a bone reaping knife with a flint blade fixed by asphalt, plus a more 'conventional' sickle handle of bone.

However, in contrast to a post Natufian site like Beidha, occupation at Zawi Chemi appears to have been seasonal despite its considerable area (Solecki, op. cit.:68). Local Kurdi peoples still live in open villages during the warmer months and in the winter move to the shelter of nearby Shanidar cave or others in the vicinity (ibid.:69). A Zawi Chemi occupation level in Shanidar cave has been dated at 10,600 ± 300 BP. Significantly, Shanidar valley lies within the natural range of wild wheat and barley, and palynological evidence suggests, by the definite increase in Cerealia-type graminae pollen around the site in excess of likely environmental augmentation, that cereals were being increasingly manipulated, perhaps planted in cleared fields (Leroi-Gourhan, op. cit.:77). Layers of this date in Shanidar cave contained storage pits, querns, mortars, grinding slabs, and chipped stone tools, together with basket impressions, but the grains involved must have been morphologically wild. Unfortunately no cereal grains have yet been recovered, but the number and diversity of tool types recovered in addition to their applications (e.g. stone-polishing techniques for the production of more efficient and durable cutting edges), means that 'Zawi Chemi may be viewed as culturally transitional between the Epi-Palaeolithic Zarzian and the later, fully settled villages of the region' such as Ganj Dareh or Jarmo (ibid.:67). As such Zawi Chemi, like early Natufian, represents the process of 'intensified food collection'; but Zawi Chemi is at Stage II of mobility/settlement, while Beidha is Stage III of the model detailed below.

4 Khuzistan

Materials for the longest continuous settlement/subsistence trajectory have been supplied by Frank Hole and his co-workers (1969, 1977) in the Deh Luran plain area of Greater Mesopotamia. These show in one and the same location the transition from seasonal villages not only to permanent ones, but to villages in a matrix where towns are nodal. Unlike other sites throughout the region, those excavated in Deh Luran have the great advantage of being undertaken by the same team over a short period, with the 'all-important economic details' (Mellaart, op. cit.:74) prominently in mind, and for whom early and full reports were also a priority. Deh Luran has the additional advantage of reflecting on a small scale the sort of ranges of environment that made for dynamic change in the region as a whole (Kirkby 1977:251; Hole *et al.* 1969:2). Map 4.2a shows inset the location of Khuzistan northeast from the head of the Gulf, with the Deh Luran plain – described by Kirkby (1977:253) as a 'microcosm of Upper Khuzistan' – boxed in the top left-hand corner of the main map.

In Deh Luran (Map 4.2b), proceeding from the Kuh-i-Siah[5] mountains towards the centre of the valley, there are four key environmental zones: 'dry steppe', then the more heavily used alluvial plain, and in the centre the seasonal marsh and floodplain areas (ibid.:285). Surface slope declines from 5° at the edge to under 0.5° at the centre with boulder scatter confined accordingly. Current vegetation changes in the same direction from scattered jujube (*Zizyphus*) trees, via *Prosopis* and *Alhagi* bushes, to salt-tolerant and phreatophyte species in the centre flats and along the river floodplains (ibid.). Though natural salinity is present and some parts have been salinized historically, sodium alkalinity is not the problem in Deh Luran that it is in the Tigris–Euphrates valley where, especially in the south, high water-tables and high salinity are the dominant conditions (ibid.:286).

In order to gain a long sequence covering millenniums, excavation was initially undertaken at two sites in the Deh Luran plain: Ali Kosh (the earlier) and Tepe Sabz. Ali Kosh is a roughly circular mound *c.* 135 m in

Map 4.2a Khuzistan, showing topographic detail

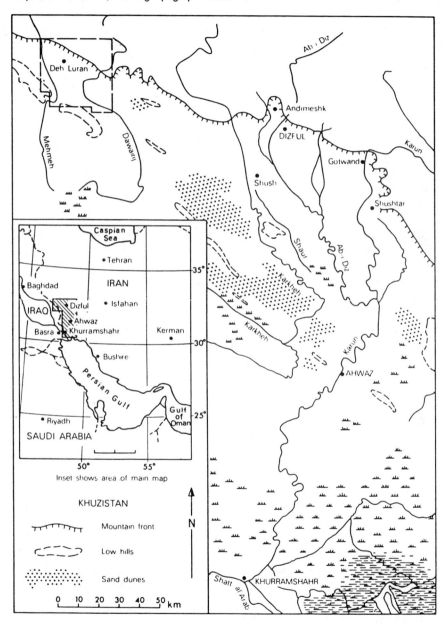

Source: Kirkby 1977:252

Map 4.2b The Plain of Deh Luran in Khuzistan

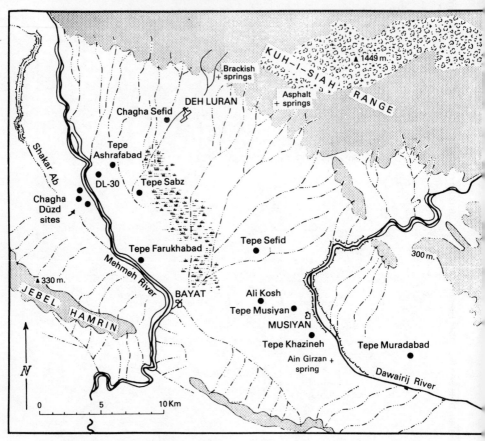

Source: Hole, Flannery, and Neely 1969:14

diameter, 7 m in depth, and with a fairly flat summit rising 4 m above the plain. Tepe Sabz ('green mound' in Farsi) lies 16 km west-southwest of Ali Kosh and of the modern village of Deh Luran ('village of the Lurs'). It is a large low mound, originally 120 × 140 m, 10.5 m in depth, but only 7 m above the level of the plain.

The schematic location of the Bus Mordeh villagers on the Deh Luran cross-section should be noted (see Figure 4.2). The village was established in the southeastern part of the plain, in a sandy, relatively well-drained area only 2 km from the Jebel Hamrin (Hole *et al.*, op. cit.:342).

Small houses or huts, often only 2 × 2.5 m with walls 25–40 cm thick, were constructed by cutting red-clay slabs (15 × 25 × 10 cm) for use as unfired bricks (ibid.). It seems this was the only village on the plain at the time, which, on the basis of artefactual cross-referencing as well as a

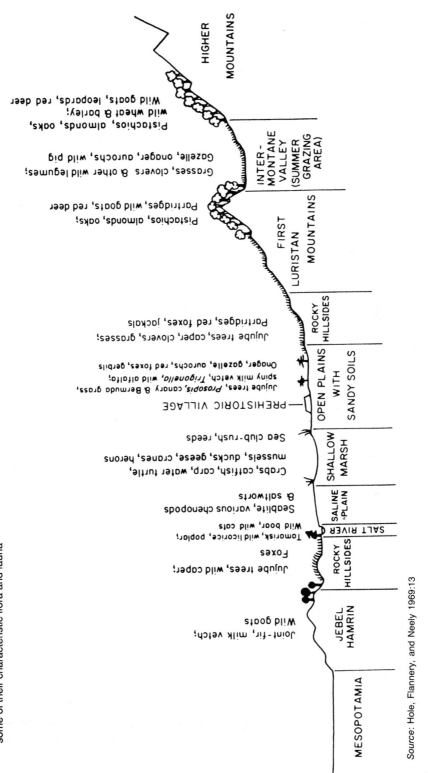

Figure 4.2 Idealized cross-section of northern Khuzistan, between the Jebel Hamrin and the First Luristan mountains, showing microenvironments with some of their characteristic flora and fauna

Source: Hole, Flannery, and Neely 1969:13

radio-carbon date of 7,900 BC,[6] makes the Bus Mordeh phase broadly contemporary with sites like Zawi Chemi-Shanidar, Karim Shahir, Asiab, and Tepe Ganj Dareh, plus, of course, Phase III of Mureybet (ibid.:345).

At this point it is as well to be reminded that

> The Zagros-Taurus Mountains consist largely of folded limestones marked by long ridges and valleys, sharp canyons, broad gravel terraces and other diverse geomorphic features that provide a wide variety of habitat for wild game and edible plants.
>
> (H. E. Wright 1977:297)

Bus Mordeh Phase: 8,200–7,200 BC

Bus Mordeh folk were farmers and herders as well as hunters and gatherers. They planted emmer wheat and two-row hulled barley, neither of which are native to Khuzistan, admixed with goatfaced grass, ryegrass, and wild einkorn wheat as weeds, along with club-rush (*Scirpus*) suggesting they were grown on the edge of the marsh or slough (Hole *et al.*, op. cit.:243). However, nine-tenths of the seeds in Bus Mordeh levels derived from annual legumes and local wild grasses. They included the seeds of medick or wild alfalfa, spiny milk vetch, *Trigonella* (a small plant of the pea family), canary grass, oat grass, and goosefoot. Those are mainly small seeded plants in contrast to the imported cereals (ibid.:343). The latter were harvested with flint sickles, roasted to render the glumes brittle, and then, since these are the primitive non-free-threshing grains, 'threshed' by grinding with flat-topped or saddle-shaped grinding slabs of pitted limestone to produce groats, eaten as gruel (ibid.:343; cf. Harlan 1967:197–201 for experimental preparations).

They also herded sheep and goats with the latter predominating by ten to one, the excellence of North Khuzistan for winter grazing suggesting to the excavators that this had a great deal to do with the beginnings of food production there (Hole *et al.*, op. cit.:344). Originally seasonal utilization would conform to the semi-permanent pattern of occupation suggested above for Zawi Chemi (ibid.:89–90). Further seasonal inducements to early use of Deh Luran in winter are provided by the aquatic resources like carp, catfish, mussels, and water turtle, while from November to March waterfowl visit the area (ibid.).

Hunting was also important and the prey diverse, including onager, wild ox, and boar. Small mammals formed a very small part of the diet but Persian gazelle 'was brought down in tremendous numbers' (ibid.). With four major areas of subsistence, hunting and gathering, farming and herding, it is not surprising to find a large and diversified tool-kit including tens of thousands of flint blades, some only a few millimetres wide, archetypally proto-Neolithic.

Ali Kosh Phase: 7,200–6,400 BC

In the next phase, Ali Kosh still seems to be the only occupied site on the plain (Hole *et al.*, op. cit.:349), and an increasingly successful one. Individual houses increase in size to 3 × 3 m and the walls become a metre thick. Floors were of stamped mud, often surfaced with a layer of clean clay and topped with over-two, under-two mats of reed or club-rush. What seem to be courtyards also existed, containing domed brick ovens and brick-lined roasting pits. No ovens were found inside rooms. These are still not bread ovens but parching ovens, sufficient to lightly fire clay figurines of people and animals (ibid.).

Cultivation of winter-grown cereals increases in this phase to form about 40 per cent of all carbonized seeds left behind in hearths and middens, accompanied by a significant tapering off in the collection of small-seeded legumes. But the hunting of gazelle, onager, and wild cattle also increased and there was a slight increase in sheep numbers (ibid.:347). Domestic goats, now showing clear osteological evidence of domestication in their flattened horn cores, were the commonest animals eaten (ibid.). Small mammals were still of little interest, in contrast to catfish, carp, turtle, mussels, ducks, geese, herons, and river crabs (ibid.:348).

Crops were harvested with flint sickles set into hafts by use of asphalt, which is locally occurring. Grains were probably collected in the simple, twined ('wicker') baskets of over-one, under-one weave, and, after grinding ('threshing') with simple discoidal handstones on grinding slabs, further reduced in the stone mortar and pestle of new advent (ibid.). The innovation was also used to grind pigment, notably red-ochre (iron oxide). Stone bowls, made of limestone or marble, greatly increase in number, used most likely for the gruel (Hole *et al.*, op. cit.:349). Again there are tens of thousands of flint blades, but now imports of obsidian have risen from 1 to 2 per cent in this phase and turquoise is also imported to be made into beads, obtained from nowhere nearer than the Iranian plateau.

With the Ali Kosh site now covering about 1 hectare, and given the size and spacing of the houses, a population of about 100 individuals is estimated, giving a population density for the Deh Luran plain, about 300 km^2, of 0.3 persons per square kilometre (ibid.).

Mohammed Jaffar Phase: 6,400–6,100 BC

By the Mohammed Jaffar Phase the village, now with boulder and pebble foundations and plastered walls, still only covered about 1 hectare, though surface finds indicate it had been joined by two other settlements (ibid.:353). Population density was now approximately 1.0 persons per square kilometre, and the landscape in the vicinity of the villages was being altered to a noticeable degree (ibid.:350). Emmer wheat and two-row hulled barley were still virtually the only crops sown (with occasional lentils suggesting mountain contacts), but the processes of fallowing and grazing had replaced much of the local vegetational cover with pasture plants, such as plantain, mallow, vetch, oat, and canary grass (ibid.). In particular shauk (*Prosopis*) throve. It is a weedy perennial legume which increases with cultivation since, unlike other plants, it does not compete with winter-sown crops. More than a hundred sickle-blades were recovered from levels of this period, an innovation being the trimming of the blades to fit a particular slot in the handle, fixed by asphalt. At the beginning of this phase goats still outnumber sheep, though by its end parity was approaching. The panting mechanism of sheep gives them the advantage on lowland plains. Osteologically, however, both sheep and goats can be considered fully domesticated, and both continued to be eaten young, with only about 40 per cent of the herd reaching three years of age (ibid.:351). Fox, hedgehog, and wild cat were now included in the diet along with gazelle, onager, aurochs, and wild pig.

For the first time pottery appears in Deh Luran with the advent of a soft, friable, and straw-tempered ware of three types employing poorly cleaned clay. The technique was essentially the same as that previously employed in the making of figurines and was almost certainly made in the same ovens. This leads Hole *et al.* (352) to 'point out that, like all innovations, it was simply a recombination of previously existing techniques'. Indeed the lightly baked figurines continue in great numbers. Obsidian, however, remains at around 2 per cent of chipped stone with cowrie shells and turquoise still imported.

The excavators see this as 'a time of population increase and settlement into a variety of habitats' in the Zagros and Khuzistan region generally, bringing with it heightened degrees of social contact and accelerated exchange of techniques (ibid.:354).

Sabz Phase: 5,200–4,800 BC

The Sabz Phase is the first in which fragments of pottery recovered exceed fragments of flint (ibid.:357). Thousands of sherds were recovered but, whereas flint blades had been counted in the thousands during the Mohammed Jaffar Phase, their numbers were reduced in the Sabz Phase to under one hundred in excavations of comparable magnitude (ibid.). Further, there is now a tough grit-tempered pottery in addition to the chaff-tempered friable stuff, decorated with red-ochre paint and probably fired at a higher temperature (ibid.) though still hand-made. Clearly fundamental changes are indicated in this brief period, reflected in what had become one of the commonest tools recovered, a polished stone celt, which is a flat, elongated limestone pebble, chipped into shape and ground until smooth, often with traces of asphalt at one end (ibid.:355). As the other end shows the polish associated with use in sandy soil, the best guess is that it was used for the leading of water to crops under irrigation (ibid.:356). A stronger indication of the onset of irrigation is the shift of settlement away from well-drained, low rises near the margins of the seasonally flooded central depression of the Deh Luran plain, relocating instead to the north where they could take advantage of many small stream channels coming down off the mountains (ibid.:355). As the villages now lie within the 300 mm isohyet making rainfed farming quite reliable, artificial water control may have functioned principally as an insurance against drought or as a supplement to rainfall. Certainly the size of the flax seeds recovered are reckoned by Helbaek (1969:408) to be too large not to have been grown with irrigation. Also grown in addition to emmer was the free-threshing hexaploid wheat, a breakthrough in itself. Two-row hulled barley was still grown, plus lentils, vetch, and vetchling (Hole *et al.*, op. cit.:354), but plants were still processed with the same equipment as hitherto. Obsidian is absent and hide-working tools decline, perhaps giving way to the working of flax and wool (ibid.:356). In this phase goats occur, whose small, helically twisted horn cores make them indistinguishable from the modern Iranian domestic goat. Domestic sheep are found but still in smaller numbers than goat, to which has ben added the domestic ox, much smaller than wild aurochs so much hunted (ibid.). But hunting of gazelle, onager, and boar continued, as did fishing, mussel and turtle collecting, and fowling (ibid.). Domestic dog, like the modern wolf-sized sheepdog of the area, now appears as a village scavenger.

There were at least six villages of this phase in Deh Luran, each with a population of perhaps one hundred (ibid.:358), giving a population density estimate of about 2 persons per square kilometre.

Sabz Phase materials are widespread in Khuzistan and lie mainly north of the 300 mm isohyet, indicating that rainfed cultivation was the principal means (ibid.:358). However, in regard to tools, pottery, and its complex of domestic plants and animals, the Sabz (linked through its pottery types to other lowland sites such as Eridu I, Samarra, Matarrah, and Jaffarabad, and not to the Zagros highlands) is in the mainstream of that tradition which leads on to the Ubaid (ibid.:355) underlying urban Mesopotamia.

It is at this point between the Mohammed Jaffar and Sabz Phases that the excavators perceived a gap associated with the onset of irrigation. The lower levels of Tepe Sabz did not go far enough back in time to yield materials of the Mohammed Jaffar Phase (Hole *et al.* 1969:5). To uncover a sequence that might illuminate this departure, excavations were undertaken at Chogha Sefid (published 1977), a site located only 1.5 km from the modern town of Deh Luran, situated at the lower end of the alluvial fan which was always the locus of the largest settlements in historic times (Hole 1977:41). Other than ceramics and architecture, few differences were found between the earlier series and the later, those of 1977. However, the earliest Sabz Phases were amplified at Chogha Sefid as intended, and found to be a variant of the Chogha Mami Transitional, a period previously known from the site of that name excavated by Joan Oates at Mandali, east of the Diyala in Iraq (1969:115–52). Chogha Mami is a site showing early simple fan irrigation at Samarran levels; it is indeed close to that eponymous site (Oates 1982:26). What Chogha Mami is 'transitional' to is Ubaid and Uruk occupation. Specifically, 'the transitional ceramic tradition of central Mesopotamia is contemporary with Ubaid I and probably early Ubaid II in the south' (Oates 1982:28). At Chogha Mami the full range of Near Eastern domesticates was present – sheep, goat, cattle, pig, and dog – and bread wheat was grown along with flax, naked barley, lentil, large-grain oat, ryegrasses, einkorn, and emmer (ibid.:27).

Short summaries of the supplementary work at Chogha Sefid on the Chogha Mami Transitional and Sabz Phases follow; thereafter the Ali Kosh/Tepe Sabz sequence resumes.

Chogha Mami Transitional Phase (Chogha Sefid site): 5,400–5,100 BC

This is indeed the onset of the 'era of irrigation agriculture . . . and cattle domestication' (Hole 1977:35). Irrigation and cattle not only supplants dry-farming and caprine husbandry, but marks the effective end of the 'broad spectrum' economy that included hunting and gathering. Ground stone and blade tools thus decline in quality and quantity (ibid.:36). However there is no mere addition of cattle and grains to caprines and grains, but a concentration upon barley and wheat supplemented by animals as auxiliary to cereculture, such that:

> This change to an apparent emphasis on farming at the expense of herding is reflected in a marked decline in the amount of meat consumed, from both domestic and wild stock. In view of the history of this region, stretching from the late Pleistocene, this shift in diet is remarkable indeed, and presages modern conditions in which most villagers live nearly exclusively on cereals, supplemented with dairy products and minor amounts of meat.
>
> (Hole 1977:34)

It is under just such conditions that we should expect long-distance herding to develop as a specialism. Simultaneously, for the first time in the Deh Luran sequence, substantial brick houses are found, with walls standing a metre or so high and not founded on rows of stones (ibid.).

Chogha Mami is a phase clearly distinguished by its ceramics, which increases from four to six varieties by the addition of a buff ware with a gritty texture and bearing relatively crude geometric designs. This ware has antecedents in the Samarran tradition in northern Mesopotamia, as does the Sialk Black-on-Red also occurring in Deh Luran at this time (Hole, op. cit.:36). Hole remarks (ibid.) in the light of the decline in the variety of ground stone and other tools, that 'this is a truly transitional phase in that we find the last uses of naturalistic figurines, most ornaments and some of the artifacts associated with butchering'.

Sabz Phase (Chogha Sefid site): 5,200–5,000 BC

Hole (1977:37) regards this phase as the local crystallization of an irrigation tradition – no longer is it transitional, but 'the crystallization of new ways'. The Sabz transformation is instanced in the reduction of earlier tool types to near extinction, along with traditional figurines and personal ornaments (ibid.). Instead chipped and polished celts (perhaps functioning as hoes) are commonly found, as are spindle whorls and perforated stones that could be either loom weights or digging-stick weights (ibid.). Susiana Black-on-Buff predominates, with lesser quantities of Susiana Plain Buff and Sialk Black-on-Red.

Hole (ibid.) surmises that the Chogha Mami Transitional leading to this phase, as a late development of the Samarran tradition which previously is not found in Deh Luran (ibid.:12), is consequently the outcome of an intrusion of a 'separate and distinct' tradition into Deh Luran. For the Deh Luran tradition was related to the mountain regions of western Iran (Zagros) and eastern Iraq (Kurdistan) rather than to those of the steppelands of northern Iraq (Assyria). Here, with the use of hybrid cereal races, domestic dogs and cattle, perhaps already used for ploughing, or at least for trampling and threshing (Hole, op. cit.:34), we have the last major subsistence items that make the rise of cities possible.

Khazineh Phase 5,000–4,800 BC

Khazineh Phase villagers now lived in settlements of around 2 hectares, although larger villages are likely under bigger unexcavated mounds in the area, such as Tepe Musiyan. There were in the Deh Luran plain at this time from six to eight villages, but the geographic range of the Khazineh Phase includes all of Khuzistan (Hole et al., op. cit.:360). The subsistence pattern set by this time continues to be recognizable in small Khuzistan villages to this day: 'hoeing, harvesting, grinding grain, roasting and cooking cereal and legumes, spinning fibre, tending and butchering sheep and goats, and working their hides' (ibid.; cf. Watson 1979:73–118).

In this phase the first examples of coiled basketry from southwest Iran appear, a contrasting technique to the laminated construction previously employed in twilled and twined basketry (Hole *et al.*, op. cit.:359). But no microlithic tools or obsidian occur in this phase, though polished celts continue in importance as do pounders made of flint nodules or cores. However, the variety of ground stone implements goes generally into decline. Free-threshing wheat and two-row and six-row barley, both hulled and naked, were grown, along with the usual complement of vetch, vetchling, lentils, and flax. By now sheep and goats appear in roughly equal numbers, although cattle are few and hunting is slight (ibid.). However, the horn cores and bones recovered from the domestic animals are quite indistinguishable from those of modern domestic breeds in Iran (ibid.). Population density in the Deh Luran plain during the Khazineh Phase is estimated at 4 persons per square kilometre (ibid.:360).

Mehmeh Phase: 4,860–4,400 BC

By now it is clear that the Deh Luran plain is a backwater in Greater Mesopotamia. The major developments are occurring on the Diz-Kharkeh plain, near Susa, and of course around Eridu and Ur on the lower Euphrates (ibid.:363). None the less the Deh Luran architecture is particularly clear for the period, due to chance exposures. Rectangular houses, now easily 5 × 10 m in size, were constructed with outer walls, a metre thick, of untempered sun-dried clay brick in two parallel rows of cobble separated by a band of closely set river pebbles (Hole *et al.*, op. cit.: 361). Floors were covered with twilled (over-two, under-two) reed or club-rush mats and doors swung in stone sockets. The houses, with internal partition walls, could easily accommodate from three to five persons (ibid.). Nine villages of this phase are known from the Deh Luran plain, but now the smallest range between 1 and 2 hectares in extent, while a very large village of this phase may lie buried under Tepe Musiyan (ibid.:362). This produces a population density estimate for Deh Luran at this period of 5 persons per square kilometre (ibid.).

Subsistence activities continue as before but a new type of pottery appears with strong Iranian affinities, Mehmeh Red-on-Red, the temper including both chaff and grit. It is regarded as a real 'index fossil' for the Mehmeh Phase (ibid.). The extremely fine quality of some of the deep bowls of this phase suggests to the excavators not only professional craftsmanship, but also the use of at least the 'slow wheel' for potting (ibid.). The pottery also has representations of bowmen, gazelle, and wild goat tracks, probably reflecting such hunting by ambush along *Tamarix*-lined wadis (ibid.:361). Onager, wild pig, turtles, small mammals, and birds continue to be hunted, though now a small percentage of the diet (ibid.).

Bayat Phase: 4,400–3,900 BC

The Bayat Phase is the last at Tepe Sabz before the settlement was moved, perhaps *c.* 5 km away, to a site like Tepe Farukabad, a shift due almost certainly to salinization of the immediate area. In some parts of present day Deh Luran salination is such that only sesame will grow (ibid.:363). None the less the established plant-animal complex continues until the site is abandoned and it seems that sheep were becoming the dominant herd animal (ibid.). Hunting continues of gazelle, onager, and small game, as also does seasonal transhumance of caprines, a possible explanation for the absence of the domestic pig. Cattle herding remains a relatively minor activity. Houses were large in this period, with rooms in some cases measuring 3 × 3 m. External walls were now bonded at the corners by the interlocking of alternate bricks.

Bayat Phase pottery lies squarely within the Ubaid tradition, corresponding roughly to phases of the Susiana sequence as defined by Le Breton. Ties were overwhelmingly within southern alluvial Mesopotamia and the Susiana sites of the Diz-Kharkeh River area: 'the naturalistic motifs of the Mehmeh phase had vanished, along with most of the other "Iranian Plateau" ceramic characteristics' (ibid.:364). Indeed the excavators doubt whether by this time any of the pottery used at Tepe Sabz during the Bayat Phase was locally made, since even the most utilitarian wares not only appeared mass-produced and standardized, but were indistinguishable from those at Chogha Mish over 100 km away (ibid.:365). But perhaps the clearest indication of evolution on a broad front is the advent of seals as property marks. In a remarkable harbinger of Mesopotamian practice in the historical period, Bayat Phase Tepe Sabz folk sealed jars with clay on to which, while wet, an incised cylindrical bead rolled a unique pattern, such as stylized trees or herringbone designs (ibid.).

There are at least nine villages or towns (some quite large) present in Deh Luran of the Bayat period, one apparently containing a series of temples (ibid.:365). Population density in this period is estimated at around 6 persons per square mile, but the most significant aspect of Deh Luran settlement at this time is that 'The Ubaid *"oikumene"* of which the Bayat phase is just one regional variant, stretched from Syria and eastern Palestine to the Turkoman Steppe' (ibid.:366).

We can now, broadly following Oates's scheme (1973:148), conceive of three broad phases of development from the Epipalaeolithic to large settled villages along the Zagros Flanks. It is in fact a scheme with which Robert Braidwood (1983b:538) has expressed broad agreement.

Phase I is that of post-Zarzian intensified food-gathering in the broad-spectrum economy. Extending from *c.* 9,000 to 7,000 BC, it is roughly

Table 4.1 Approximate ages of the phases in Deh Luran and their relation to periods designated in other areas[7]

	Years BC (Date ×1.03 – 1950)	Northern Mesopotamia	Southern Mesopotamia	Khuzistan
Bayat	4,400–3,900	Ubaid	Ubaid 4	Susiana d
Mehmeh	4,800–4,400	Ubaid	Ubaid 3	Susiana c
Khazineh	5,000–4,800	Ubaid	Ubaid 2	Susiana b
Sabz	5,200–5,000	Halaf	Ubaid 1	Susiana a
Chogha Mami Transitional	5,400–5,100	Halaf	?	?
Surkh	5,900–5,400	Samarra/Halaf		Chogha Mish 'Archaic'
Sefid	6,300–5,900	Hassuna		
Mohammed Jaffar	6,400–6,100	Jarmoan		
Ali Kosh	7,200–6,400	Jarmo (preceramic)		
Bus Mordeh	8,200–7,200	Karim Shahirian		

Source: Hole 1977:27.

contemporary with the Natufian of the Levant and is represented by such sites as Zawi Chemi and Karim Shahir in the Zagros region.

Phase II, extending from *c.* 7,000 to 6,000 BC and generally termed 'Jarmoan', which Braidwood *et al.* (1983:13) characterize as the 'early village farming community', is represented in the Zagros area by such sites as Jarmo itself in Iraqi Kurdistan, Tepe Guran and Ganj Dareh in the vicinity of Kermanshah in Iran, plus of course Ali Kosh to the south in Khuzistan, just below the mountain front.

The type-site of Jarmo at about 800 m elevation in the intermontane valley of Chemchemal is about one and a half hours' drive east of Kirkuk (Braidwood 1983b:537). Jarmo saw only three seasons' work in the much broader problem-oriented research of the Chicago Oriental Institute's 'Iraq-Jarmo Project' investigating 'How the great change from cave to village, from food-collecting to food production came about . . . in the hill-flank country above the Fertile Crescent' (Braidwood and Howe 1960:1).

Presently covering 1.3 ha (3.2 acres) with around one third lost on the northwest to erosion by the Cham-Gawra wadi, only about 10 per cent of the remaining 13,000 square metres has been excavated; even this, in some parts to only 1 m or even less (ibid.:38). The radio-carbon dates are generally what Braidwood (1983b:537) calls 'whimsical', but he is convinced that Jarmo flourished for around 300 years at about 6,700 BC (Libby).

Jarmo was a permanent village establishment with perhaps twenty or more houses and of rather long duration. Its people possessed at least the domestic goat, two kinds of wheat and a barley, and a variety of artifacts adapted to the cultivation, storage, and processing of vegetable foods. Compared to what preceded it the Jarmo assemblage was elaborate, but it retained elements in its flint-working tradition which were at least as early as the Zarzian in ancestry.

(Braidwood and Howe 1960:183)

The wheats recognized were both wild and domesticated emmer and einkorn, plus what seems, from the tough rachis, to be two-row barley (*Hordeum spontaneum*) in the process of domestication (Watson 1983b:501). Sickles are certainly present, but non-cereal gathering was still important, as seen in remains of pistachio nuts and great quantities of snails, particularly the large land snail, *Helix salomonica* (Braidwood 1983c:542). Further evidence of the transitional nature of Jarmo is the fact that in the lower levels wild, and thus hunted, animals, including red deer (*Cervus elaphus*), cattle (*Bos primigenius*), onager (*Equus hemionus*), and gazelle (*Gazella subgutturosa*), are of equal importance (49 per cent) to domestic sheep and goats, according to osteological data (Stampfli 1983:436). In the domesticated category goats were three to four times as numerous as sheep (ibid.). However, even in the later levels domestic animals, which by this time include pigs (but not cattle) amounted to only 60 per cent of identified mammal bones (Stampfli 1983: table 26).

Braidwood and Howe (1960:43) estimate the human population at not more than 150, in a maximum of 25 houses of rectilinear form, at all levels constructed of *tauf* (mud moulded, not poured, in courses on the wall under construction). In later levels those walls were raised on field-stone (unworked) foundations.

Early levels are aceramic, but employ stone vessels instead, such that:

although the making of stone vessels was a normal concomitant of early village life throughout the Near East, there was at Jarmo a rare cultural emphasis on this industry that found expression not only in volume but also in quality of output. Many of the wide variety of shapes that are present are aesthetically very fine, and the regularity of form, the high polish, and the extreme thinness that were frequently achieved reflect a high degree of craftsmanship.

(Adams 1983b:209)

The materials used include limestone, marble, and, to a lesser degree sandstone, all locally occurring. Pottery tended to selectively supplement stoneware at Jarmo, where it seems to be introduced as a technique from without. Adams (1983b:223) makes a most interesting suggestion connecting the obsidian present, the availability of which increased during the life of the village (L. Braidwood 1983:287), with the introduction of pottery; namely that 'its early practitioners at Jarmo may have been women from some distant village, perhaps brought back as wives by men trading for obsidian'. Thus when pottery appears it does so, like the handling of *tauf*, as an accomplished practice, not as 'the fumbling beginnings of a new craft' (Braidwood and Howe 1960:43). This pottery is 'handmade, vegetable tempered, buff to orange in colour, and frequently exhibits a darkened unoxidised core on a clean break' (ibid.). But most striking are the thousands of lightly fired clay figurines, realistic and impressionistic, representing both animals and humans, or more literally their parts, notably pregnant torsos and phalluses, the latter also occurring in stone (Moholy-Nagy 1983:300). Morales surmises that

> the figurines were probably used for daily or regular sympathetic magic of a more or less individual nature. . . . The more realistic forms appear to be 'personal wishes', with the 'desire' expressed in the *act* of modelling the form. The figure was then dried, fired and kept until the wish was fulfilled, or it was discarded immediately after manufacture.
> (Morales 1983:392–3)

More recently another site of this phase (II), Tell Maghzalia, has been found, not in the Zagros, but in the Sinjar Valley piedmont zone in the extreme northwest of Iraq, west of Mosul. Situated on the Abra river just 1 km north of the junction of the uplands with the plains, 4,500 square metres remain of a settlement originally covering 1 hectare (Merpert, Munchaev, and Bader 1981:29). The deposit, which amounts to 8.2 m, derives from clay-walled rectangular structures on stone foundations. There are indeed no less than fifteen clear structural layers with an average depth of 50–60 cm. Walls were of tauf and the floors paved with stone slabs which were plastered with clay and covered with alabaster (ibid.:30). A cylinder-shaped grain bin and a rectangular oven were found, the latter having stone foundations like the house walls, built in the same tauf technique so well known from Hassuna sites.

Many arrowheads occur (which they do not at Jarmo or Shimshara), both tanged and leaf-shaped but all of flint, as do a great variety of sickle knives (many in obsidian which is very common at all levels). Rubbing stones, pestles, and querns are also common. Amongst the querns, mostly small, flat, and nearly rectangular, some have a few shallow holes drilled in their working surfaces, and so could be employed for grinding stone and bone tools, such as awls, needles, and spatulas (Merpert, Munchaev, and Bader 1981:62). Tell Maghzalia was on the verge of pottery-making (a baked-clay statuette was found in addition to other anthropomorphic figurines in stone and clay), and the Soviet excavators relate it to the aceramic levels of Jarmo and Shimshara which share similar traditions of flint-working, while all three employ large quantities of obsidian. However, Merpert *et al.* (1981:62) observe a more marked similarity between Maghzalia and sites in Syria and Turkey, such as Baida, Mureybet, Abu Hureyra, and Cayonü Tepesi. Certainly the variety and number of scrapers plus arrowheads indicate a large role for hunting in the economy, as the varieties of sickle do for gathering.

Merpert *et al.* (1981:31) conclude that

> the assemblage of Tell Maghzalia suggests a culture with a developed flint industry and a developed house-building technique, but still pre-pottery or almost aceramic. The economy was built on hunting and on well-developed gathering which, in all probability, was turning into farming. A great number of tanged arrowheads on blades and animal bones, apparently of wild bulls, indicate hunting activity. At the same time the permanent character of the habitation, the numerous querns, sickle knives, grain bins and other finds suggest that farming predominated,

or at least was coming to predominate. Certainly hundreds of grains of both wild and domesticated barley and emmer wheat were found, and all of this places Tell Maghzalia early in Phase II (i.e. 'Jarmoan') of the overall scheme.

Phase III, commencing around 6,000 BC, is that of the developed village community, the epitome of the Neolithic 'revolution'. In Mesopotamia it is represented by the Hassuna, Samarra, and Halaf cultures in broad order of appearance. They have well-developed ceramic traditions by which they are recognized, but much else regarding origins, duration, and even subsistence is still uncertain (Mellaart 1975:144). What is not in dispute, however, is that those three constitute the earliest distinct agricultural *cultures* anywhere, with the Samarrans specializing in simple irrigation, and I shall argue later (Chapter 6) that: (a) a particular size and type of houseform is associated with Samarran culture; (b) this is not fortuitous but reflects a unique form of social organization; and (c) this line goes forward from the Samarran into Ubaid to serve as the kernel of social organization of the city-state in its formative (Uruk/Jemdet Nasr) periods.

The earliest stage of Phase III, the first actually on the Mesopotamian plain, are sites of the *Sotto* levels of the Hassuna. Those include, in addition to the eponymous Tell Sotto 3 & 4, Umm Dabaghiya, strata 1 & 2 of Yarim Tepe I, the lowest levels of Kul Tepe, Telul eth-Thalathat XV & XVI, plus Hassuna 1a itself (Bashilov, Bolshakov, and Kouza 1980:51). All are founded on virgin soil, where the earliest occupational levels manifest pit-dwellings and fire-pits (ibid.) that seem to represent the colonization process.

Bashilov *et al.* (1980:61) found that when solid architecture emerged at Yarim Tepe I and related sites, in each case it appeared to form a single integrated domestic complex, and they conjecture that

> every above mentioned settlement was founded by one big family. Such families were probably the smallest social units of the early agricultural population which spread in the beginning of the VI millennium BC through the fertile plain laid to the west from the Tigris.
>
> (Bashilov *et al.* 1980:61)

What we seem to have here, then, is a 'colonizer effect' under which the individual, but extended, household unit constituted the basic molecule of an expanding society. This unitary extended form of household may be the one preferred over groups of variously related individual ('nuclear') families, as a response to the need for concentration of resources under tight managerial control, given the difficult conditions of pioneering. Below I argue that the augmented corporate household,[8] called é in Sumerian and *bîtum* in Akkadian, can be traced architecturally as large T-form structures from the Samarran through the Ubaid and Uruk periods, and that this form is still recognizable in the cities of the Early Dynastic period. Hassuna architecture does not manifest the large T-form household structure identified as é and *bîtum* (and referred to below as *oikiai* for convenience). However, I have previously (1987:349) suggested that the *oikos* phenomenon is confined to the Samarran/ Ubaidian line since, like the later Sumero-Akkadians, they were specialists in irrigation and this required a concentration of natural and human resources. Thus while there may be no direct connection between the Sotto Stage Hassunan and Samarran/Ubaidian household forms, a common logic of resource-concentration seems to underlie both.

Hassuna, Samarra, and Halaf cultures overlap both chronologically and geographically (as shown in Figure 4.3), undergoing contrasting and contiguous development. In the Hassunan phases of Yarim Tepe I, Munchaev and Merpert (1987:19) report the finding not only of einkorn (*Triticum monococcum* L.) and emmer wheat (*T. dicoccum Schrank*), but also bread wheat (*T. aestivum* L.) plus club wheat (*T. compactum Host.*) and spelt (*T. spelta* L.). Naked barley (*Hordeum vulgare* var. *nudum*) was grown, and lentils and peas used. They remark (ibid.) that 'from the beginning of the settlement the major cereals are represented here in a much greater variety than in preceding periods'. Flax (*Linum usitatissimum* L.) was also present.

Likewise with animal resources, included in which are domestic cattle (*Bos taurus*), sheep (*Ovis aries*), goat (*Capra hircus*), and pig (*Sus domestica*), plus dog (*Canis familiaris*). Though the proportion of domesticated animals amounts to 82 per cent of bones collected (ibid.:19), also present are wild sheep and goat (*Ovis orientalis*, *Capra aegagrus*), fallow deer (*Dama mesopotamica*), gazelle (*Gazella subgut-turosa*), onager (*Asinus onager*), plus leopard (*Pantera pardus*) and dog (*Canis aureus*). Amongst all of those the importance of domestic cattle is stressed (ibid.). Merpert and Munchaev (1987:8) also mention the existence, from the earliest stages of Yarim Tepe I, of what they call 'a characteristic Hassuna complex', consisting in the ceramic 'husking tray', a platform for drying grain and a grain grinder or mortar.

Samarra, by contrast, is a specifically southeastern adaptation to riverine environments. Joan Oates (1973:166), while remarking that with very few exceptions Hassuna sites lie within the area where rainfed farming is currently possible, contrasts this with 'the area of the middle Tigris, which we now believe to have been the centre of Samarran development, [where] widespread agrarian settlement would have been inconceivable without some recourse to irrigation, even if rainfall was marginally more reliable' (ibid.:172).

Watkins and Campbell remark that 'The Hassuna culture is strictly confined to N. Iraq, and no Halaf culture site outside NE Mesopotamia has yet been shown to have a Hassuna culture occupation underneath' (1987:433). This must not be (mis)understood to mean that Hassuna cultural strata *nowhere* underlie Halafian ones, as, for instance, Yarim Tepe so clearly shows that they do (Merpert and Munchaev 1987:20). Their work, plus that of Watkins and Campbell (1987: figs 2, 3, and 4), indeed demonstrates that the Halaf culture is later in advent than the Hassuna. Although 'the beginnings of Hassuna are not far removed in time from the earliest Samarran levels at sites like Matarrah and Tell es-Sawwan' (Merpert and Munchaev 1987:19), the Halaf, extending through all but the last couple of centuries of the fifth millennium, lasts thereby much longer than the Samarran settlements, which seem hardly to extend even to 5,000 BC.

Similar subsistence resources to those of Hassunan Yarim Tepe were employed at Tell es-Sawwan, an important site near Samarra belonging to the first half of the sixth millennium, and which even at this time formed a compact township of large T-form houses, illustrated and discussed in Chapter 6.

At Tell es-Sawwan, Helbaek (1965:45) reports emmer and bread wheat, and probably einkorn too, plus six-row hulled and six-row naked barley, with two-row hulled barley as the principal crop. Prosopis (shauk) and caper were extensively used, and linseed (*Linum usitatissimum*) was grown under simple irrigation conditions. The site on the east bank of the Tigris was conducive to fishing, so fish and mussels (which include such presently available species as *Unio tigridis* and *Pseudodonopsis euphraticus*) were heavily exploited (Flannery and Wheeler 1967:181). Again, domestic sheep and goats were present, and probably cattle too, while gazelle (*Gazella subgutturosa*) and fallow deer (*Dama mesopotamica*) were hunted.

Unlike Samarran proto-urban sites like Tell es-Sawwan, Halaf[9] settlements were more conventional agricultural villages. None the less 'The Halaf culture is one of the most developed and striking early agricultural societies of the old world', in the words of Merpert and Munchaev (1987:20).

> Its known borders are marked by Tell Turlu and Yunus (Carchemish) in the west, Banahilk in the east, Tilki Tepe, Girikihajiyan and others in the north, and Tell es-Sawwan, Songor B and Chogha Mami in the south. Halaf influence is recorded as far as Palestine to the west and the Transcaucasus to the east.

Halaf culture is recognizable in its very distinctive, and often fine, painted pottery and is characterized by '*tholos*' round-houses, which are not just a developmental stage as they often co-exist with, and sometimes even replace, rectangular structures. Thus the round-house form came to assume a lasting cultural value for Halafian settlements. The presence of *tanour*-type bread ovens, its wide spread and longevity, indicate that Halaf culture settlements employed similar subsistence resources to those seen at Hassunan and Samarran settlements.

From the end of its middle phase, in what can be seen as a harbinger of the subsequent spread of the Ubaid across the Near East, the Halaf expands southwards into areas dominated by the Samarran tradition. Davidson (1977:346–7) considers this to be due to a genuine expansion of Halaf settlement rather than merely an extension of its stylistic influence on ceramics, for 'although widely dispersed geographically, Halaf settlements were culturally well integrated'.

Halaf and Halaf-influenced settlements are found between 5,000 and 4,700 BC from the Mediterranean (Ras Shamra IV) to the Diyala and beyond in the east ('J' ware). By 4,500 BC, some sites were entering the Transitional phase between Late Halaf and Northern Ubaid (Copeland 1979:270). But it was the Southern Ubaid, whose key inputs derive from the Samarran tradition, that was the immediate basis of the Sumerian city-state which emerged in the subsequent Uruk Period. 'In short, the erstwhile Halaf-influenced regions became the Ubaid-influenced regions by about 4,100 BC' (Copeland and Hours 1987:410).

In Figure 4.3 I have tried to show schematically relationships between Hassuna, Samarra, Halaf, and Ubaid; specifically how the Halaf interdigitates with Samarra and Ubaid; also how the latter derives from the Samarran and ultimately supplants the Halaf culture tradition. When more sites are known and better dated, linkages can be shown through proper dendritic branching.

I have placed the transition from Ubaid to Uruk around 4,000 BC, because I cannot accept dating the commencement of the Uruk period as much as a millennium earlier (cf. J. Oates 1987a:474) than that established

Figure 4.3 Interdigitation and succession of prehistoric Mesopotamian cultures

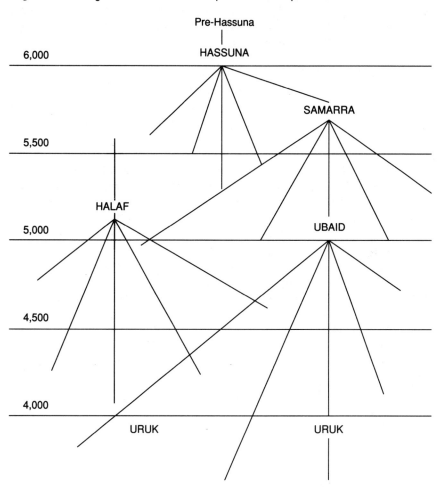

by Sumerologists (i.e. around 3,500 BC).[10] Such drastic archaization seems to be a product of a few dodgy radio-carbon dates, principally from Tell Oueili, where the excavators have themselves urged caution as 'ground and climate are largely responsible for problems of C^{14} dating' at this site near Larsa (Calvet 1987:469). The problems relate both to the small physical size of the samples available for dating by traditional methods (less than 5 g of wood carbon) and in calibrating the results in calendar years (Cal. BC). Accordingly, while Calvet (ibid.:470) would tentatively place the very earliest phase of Ubaid (0) at the end of the sixth millennium, Thommeret (1983:67) prudentially relying only on uncalibrated BP dates, places level 1 at 4,000 BC and level 3 (both of those as in the 1976–8 classification) between 4,240 and 3,700 BC. As level 1 was the latest, and corresponds to the end of Ubaid 4 (Forest 1983:21), this at least provides an acceptable date of 4,000 BC for the end of the Ubaid period, with the beginning towards the close of the sixth millennium, as suggested by Calvet (*supra*).

For the Uruk period, the transition to which from the Ubaid is uninterrupted and gradual (D. Oates 1987:176; J. Oates 1987a:194), I work from the high-precision radio-carbon chronometry of Hassan and Robinson (1987:127), who have compared radio-carbon dates from Egypt, Nubia, Palestine, and Mesopotamia with each other and with the traditional, textually derived, chronologies for those areas.

To locate the Uruk period Hassan and Robinson employ three consistent dates from Grai Resh and Habuba Kabira which average 3,893 ± 88 Cal(ibrated) BC; three measurements from Arslantepe VII that yield an average of 3,586 ± 84 Cal. BC; while four consistent measurements from the widely spread sites of Nippur, Susa, Jebel Aruda, and Godin V, average 3,314 ± 127 Cal. BC.

For the Jemdet Nasr period four consistent measurements from Tall-i-Malyan, Tepe Yahya, Shahr-i-Sokhta, and Godin average 3,400 ± 139 Cal. BC, the period extending to 3,063 ± 132 Cal. BC, according to no less than eight consistent measurements from Arslantepe VI. Thus I understand the Uruk period to extend from about 4,000 until 3,400 BC, when the Jemdet Nasr period begins. This agrees well with Vertesalji's (1987:487) own computations for what he calls 'Chalcolithic IIIB', the Uruk period, which he reckons extends from *c*. 4,100 to 3,400 BC.

The Early Dynastic I period that succeeds Jemdet Nasr has two measurements from Nippur XI, which date it to 2,854 ± 102 Cal. BC, with an almost identical date of 2,855 ± 119 Cal. BC deriving from Gedikli.

A more comprehensive chronology is provided in Chapter 5.

5 The crystallization of the village as a type

If a single feature has to stand for the Neolithic 'revolution', it is the existence of permanent villages of cultivators. The existence of the village has two preconditions: some kind of architecture to provide habitations for all seasons; and the subsistence basis to make it both possible and worthwhile. It is a specific part of the argument, however, that any type of localized abundance tends toward sedentism, and that farming and herding are the outcome of this under certain specified conditions. Agriculture in turn underpins the most permanent form of settlement, which in its turn undergoes evolutionary developments in tandem with agricultural changes.

Flannery's conception (1972b:25) of village formation in the Zagros proceeds from a base camp of hunter-gatherers consisting of around 15–40 persons, from which hunting parties of 3–8 males made periodic trips to 'transitory stations' or vantage points from which they stalked 'the herbivores which provided 99% of their meat supply. This game was sometimes cut into portable sections at temporary "butchering stations" from whence it could be transported back to the base camp' (ibid.). From base camp with temporary 'stations' for specific tasks, Flannery sees the next stage as being the emergence of kraal-type compounds so well known in African ethnography. This 'typical compound [which still shares many of the characteristics of hunting-gathering groups] is a group of 6–8 males with 1–3 women and their children' (ibid.:31). Each adult tends to occupy a separate hut, since the compound is a collectivity which produces and consumes together. 'Generally, the people of a single compound form a basic labour group, and below this level, "full siblings tend to work together" ' while 'the food storage is open and shared by all occupants of a compound' (ibid.).

The compound unit of settlement is subsequently replaced by villages of rectangular houses designed, unlike the huts of a compound, to accommodate families rather than the individuals forming a compound collectivity (ibid.:39). Flannery sees evidence for this in the greater size of the rooms in a rectangular house, with 'no complete house smaller than 15 m^2 and most 25–35 m^2 – large enough in Naroll's terms [of 10 m^2 per occupant] to shelter at least three to four persons' (ibid.:31). In contrast, rarely do circular huts exceed 7 m^2 of floor area and in the rectangular structures both male and female tool-kits are found in the same building. Further, rectangular buildings tend to be grouped in settlements of greater size, typically of 1 to 4 hectares (ibid.:40). Flannery surmises that the rectangular structures represent the emergence of the individual household as the basic unit of production, and indeed consumption, for possessing 'household storage units [they] were not subject to the same kind of obligatory sharing as those of the compound' (ibid.:39), which on size alone would have been a larger kinship grouping. Flannery represents the individual households reciprocating between nuclear and 'extended' (stem?) families, in the accommodation of which they are facilitated in being able to add rooms to rectilinear walls, or block off their openings. However, it is not clear why the addition or subtraction of a circular hut in a compound would be any the more difficult.

Joan Oates (1977:465), however, sees the evolution of settlement structures as representing not so much social changes as the very process of settling down. This is, after all, a first. The first permanent structures are roughly circular in plan because that is the shape of semi-permanent huts. As sites become occupied on a more continuous basis, the huts, in shape and construction, are, so to speak, frozen in place by the addition of stone walling around posts formerly bridged by wattle and daub, as at

Beidha in the Natufian (Kirkbride 1968:266). Later, floors are dug into the ground for about half a metre, extra stones added as walling, and a brush or reed supported clay roof put over the top of what remains a 'round-house'.[11] Oates concludes that

> A tent or hut may be round or rectangular depending on the number of poles employed, but when a permanent structure has to be roofed, the simplest technique is a system of parallel roof beams that are most easily supported on a rectilinear wall plan. A careful examination of the archaeological evidence from Beidha shows precisely this sequence. We need not in fact, postulate changes in social structure or people when the architectural development can be explained more simply.
>
> (Oates 1977:465)

At Beidha a system of uprights dictated the round shape. There the houses were

> arranged in separate clusters like cells in a honeycomb, each individual building roughly circular in plan, erected around an inner skeleton of posts and beams. Stout posts dug in round the perimeter of the floor at regular intervals, usually 30 or 50 cm, were linked by beams to a central post.
>
> (Kirkbride 1968:266)

Indeed she suggests (ibid.:269) that a major reason for the shift from 'post houses', using lots of wood, to free-standing structures of stone, was the frequency of fire in the former, to which we owe the good state of preservation of organic materials at Beidha. Though round forms do indeed evolve throughout the Near East into rectilinear ones, neither the material used nor the juxtaposition of units suggests anything like the 'kraal' settlement type and its concomitant social relationships. It is in principle not safe to see the evolution of the nuclear family simply in the rectilinear shapes of houses.

Figure 4.4 models the settling-down process in terms of reduced mobility.[12]

In the first stage, prior to c. 9,000 BC, hunter-gatherers, with emphasis on the hunting, establish a sequence of campsites as they move around in their annual cycle, exploiting the localized, and especially seasonally restricted, resources at those sites. In the process of exploiting a series of niches movement is altitudinal as well as lateral. But in seasonal latitudes shelter is also required in the worst seasons and so lower ground will be preferred in winter, and particularly, where available, the shelter of caves such as Shanidar, Hayonim, or El Wad, the last mentioned having Middle and Upper Palaeolithic as well as Epipalaeolithic material in it (Garrod and Bate 1937). Shanidar cave has been seasonally occupied from the Palaeolithic to the present (Solecki 1979:318).

Figure 4.4 Patterns of mobility and land use

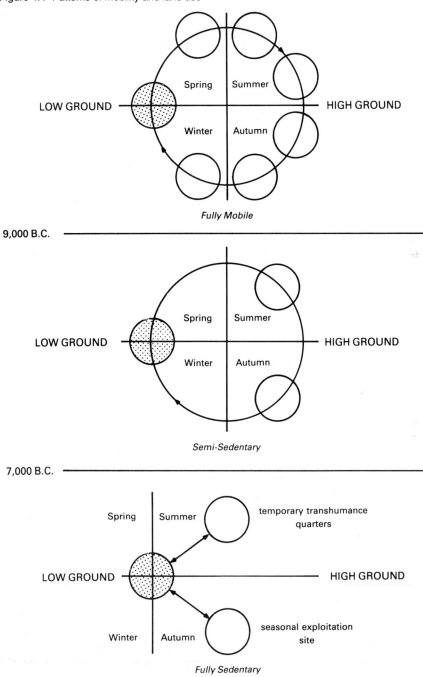

Key: Circles indicate site-catchment areas, centred on camps or settlements

The second stage, extending from about 9,000 until around 7,000 BC, shows a marked decrease in the number of encampments, with a semi-permanent base camp now established on lower ground at which a broad range of resources can be exploited and stored. Bar-Yosef and Goren (1973:67) speak of the most basic cultural feature of Natufian groups as being the ' "base camp" itself, defined archaeologically by the presence of stationary elements, including constructional remains, graves, and grinding implements. Secondary characteristics include sickle blades, lunates, bone artifacts, and occasional art objects.' However, none of the subsistence resources employed was domesticated.

In the Zagros even today the farmers of northwestern Luristan rotate four times seasonally between no less than three types of living structures (Edelberg 1966–7:382). Those are the *zemga*, or 'boulder built village' occupied in December, January, and February; the *siah cador*, or black tent occupied in April and May; the *kula*, 'booths' or 'bowers' constructed at the end of May of posts with leafy branches for roofing and rush mats for walls, and corresponding in ground-plan almost exactly to the tents (ibid.:386–7). Later in the autumn (October and November) the villagers move back into tents, and into the stone-built houses with the onset of winter (December). The distance moved in those changes of habitation and altitude need not be very great (ibid.:392), perhaps only a few kilometres, but it does facilitate the combination of agricultural and pastoral activities over the year, as well as making living conditions more congenial and hygienic.

Edelberg's ethnological work was undertaken to complement that of the Danish Archaeological Expedition to Iran working at that time on the important site of Tepe Guran (Meldgaard, Mortensen, and Thrane 1964). Meldgaard *et al.* describe the present-day conditions around Tepe Guran, situated only 140 m from the river Saimarreh (Kharkeh – which constitutes the border between the districts of Kurdistan and Luristan) as follows:

> Tepe Guran is situated at an altitude of ca.950 metres at the northern fringe of the plain of Hulailan. This very fertile plain stands out between the high surrounding mountains as a wide valley, ca.20 km long and up to 8 km wide, with the river Saimarreh (Kharkeh) winding below the southern slopes. In the early summer the plain appears like one enormous cornfield, dotted with some 30 villages, and traversed by numerous small irrigation channels nourished from the many small brooks in the side valleys. In these valleys, and at the lower mountain slopes, we find the larger part of the population moving around in their black tents with large herds of sheep and goats.
>
> (Meldgaard, Mortensen, and Thrane 1964:104)

Bearing in mind both the relatively short distances moved and the use of the black tents in taking flocks up into the mountains, this settlement/ exploitation pattern could be reckoned more akin to stage III than stage II, were it not that here the whole community moves. However, while the model[12] attempts to represent a prehistoric process of transformation, the ethnological example merely illustrates one possible mobile use of the same terrain.

The third stage, then, obtaining after about 7,000 BC, is that of the permanent village settlement dependent upon agriculture and herding. It is occupied year-round by most of its population, with temporary quarters sited as necessary at task locations; examples being summer transhumance sites at higher altitudes.

6 Demography in the Pristine Neolithic

The particular value of the Deh Luran sequence, apart from its actual existence as an all too rare long sequence, is that the excavators paid particular attention throughout to intensity of land-use and density of population. Extending as it does over about four millennia from the proto-Neolithic to the advent of urbanism, it enables us to check theory against data. In particular it helps us to see how useful different models might be in explaining demographic growth, many of which are reviewed in Hassan (1981). The short and shocking answer must be that none of those models apply; no model of the demographic consequences of the settling-down of hunter-gatherer populations, whether in Africa, Australia, or the Arctic is applicable to the proto-Neolithic Near East.

Instead, ethnography must be used to derive some consistent behavioural principles that integrate with what we know of human reproductive physiology. To me this is the comparative method in full operation. It avoids analogy by identifying independently reproduced behaviour (such as cultural control of fertility) for which it then seeks a rationale underlying the specific cultural contexts in which the relevant behaviour is found.

'Settling down' along the Zagrosian Arc was a long drawn-out process of reduction in mobility by steps, until year-round settlement arrived. This was the outcome of a learning curve which involved the emergence of new subsistence techniques based on domesticates, itself the outcome of earlier stages of sedentism.

A combination of factors raised fertility and lowered infant mortality as consequences of permanent settlement and its subsistence regime. Reductions in necessary mobility, the burdens of child transport, and female workloads are amongst those hypothesized either to produce physiological effects that raise fertility, or those lessened transport demands permit closer child-spacing (cf. Lee 1980:321–46). But reductions in dietary stress, reducing postpartum amenorrhoea consequent upon breast-feeding, reduce birth spacings strongly (Bongaarts 1980a), and birth spacing is the most important variable influencing fertility, while the duration of postpartum amenorrhoea is the most important variable affecting birth spacing (Scott and Johnston 1985:467). Further, malnourished women produce deficient amounts of breast milk and 'breast-feeding not only is superior nutritionally for the developing child but has contraceptive value and extends the period of postpartum amenorrhoea' (ibid.).

In total,

> the fertility of a woman is governed by the length of her reproductive span (menarche to menopause) and the length of her average birth interval: the longer the reproductive span, the larger the number of birth intervals that can be accommodated. The birth interval, measured from one birth to the next, is comprised of the period of postpartum amenorrhoea, the waiting time to a conception *resulting in a live birth*, and the fixed gestation period of approximately nine months.
>
> (John 1985:469; original emphasis)

It is just this lengthening of the reproductive span that Roth (1981:418) encountered in comparing a post-1900 sedentary cohort of Northern Athapaskan women with a cohort of pre-1900 women who were then hunter-gatherers. His Life Table work (e.g. his Table 4) indicates that birth-spacings are only slightly shorter for the post-1900 cohort as compared with the mobile pre-1900 cohort, but that 'rather the difference in fertility resides in the length of the reproductive period utilized' (1981:418). This he attributes to the presence in this century of a stable food base, since the Athapascan settlement congealed around a trading post as a 'contact-traditional all-native community' (ibid.:414).

Of course those are physiological effects, or rather potentials, and do not address cultural factors like coital frequency, taboos (especially postpartum), social constraints, and economic pressures. Hence, seeking to account for the low population density of the horticultural New York Iroquois, Engelbrecht (1987:17) emphasized the heavy labour demands upon women as restricting the number of children they could care for, which indeed exposed children to systematic neglect, leading, on many occasions, to death. Institutionalized raiding meant both reduced coital frequency and also placed a premium on having few children, since escape from raiders was difficult when each woman working in the fields was accompanied by several children. Defensive considerations alone made lengthy birth intervals desirable.

The Iroquois grew maize, beans, and squash, hunted for meat (principally deer), and fished, a diversified subsistence regime; so whereas amongst Athapascan hunter-gatherers the economic restraints were those of food-supply in the northernmost Yukon, in fertile mid-latitude New

York State, the inhibiting factors were largely cultural, centred critically upon women. According to the Jesuit observer Bressani, the woman 'bears the whole burden of the house, cultivates the fields, cuts and carries the firewood, does the cooking, and loads herself, on the journeys, with provisions, etc., for the husband' (quoted Engelbrecht 1987:16).

And Engelbrecht concludes that

> because there were no burden-bearing domestic animals, Iroquois women often hauled crops, firewood, provisions, and game, while caring for nursing children. Many of these activities were probably continued from earlier hunting and gathering lifeways. As among hunters and gatherers, these activities would have been rendered far more difficult with more than one child. Many young children might have impeded a quick escape from enemy raiders. All those considerations would have encouraged a long spacing between the birth of children.
>
> (Engelbrecht 1987:26)

Indeed 'encouraged' might be much too mild a term. One gets the distinct impression that women were in fact 'burden-bearing domestic animals'. Thus while the food-supply problem would be ameliorated by sedentarization at 'broad-spectrum' resource sites in the Near East during the early Holocene, by no means all other constraints on fertility would have been lifted.

Coale sums it up nicely when he remarks that the 'Neolithic Revolution had demographic consequences whose net effect was a slight increase in population growth' (1975:466); a point reinforced by another demographer, Petersen, who states that during the Neolithic 'the growth was so slow as to be imperceptible during anyone's lifetime, and during the whole era fertility and mortality were more or less in balance' (1975:232).

The logic of this becomes apparent when we look mathematically at potential rates of growth in thousand-year intervals. If we accept Flannery's (1972b:25) suggestion that mobile hunter-gatherer bands in the Epipalaeolithic Near East numbered from 15 to 40 persons, we can postulate that the Bus Mordeh Phase settlement in the Deh Luran plain consisted of rather more than this, say 50 persons (Hole *et al.* supply no figure for this earliest phase). However, as we have seen, a figure of 100 persons is given for the next, Ali Kosh Phase.[13] If then we note that there was, as a consequence of sedentism and population growth, but one such settlement in the Deh Luran plains at this time, then it is reasonable to infer that there were not many hunter-gatherer bands in the preceding period of mobility.

Thus the population figure of 100,000 for the whole of the Near East at 8,000 BC given by Carneiro and Hilse (1966:178) as the basis of their

Table 4.2 Calculation of the population of the Near East at 1,000-year intervals for various rates of increase, assuming a base population of 100,000

% increase	8,000 BC	7,000 BC	6,000 BC	5,000 BC	4,000 BC
0.50	100,000	14,700,000	*	*	*
0.40	100,000	5,420,000	*	*	*
0.30	100,000	2,000,000	40,000,000	*	*
0.20	100,000	737,000	5,440,000	40,100,000	*
0.15	100,000	448,000	2,000,000	8,970,000	40,200,000
0.14	100,000	405,000	1,640,000	6,650,000	26,900,000
0.13	100,000	367,000	1,340,000	4,930,000	18,100,000
0.12	100,000	332,000	1,100,000	3,650,000	12,100,000
0.11	100,000	300,000	902,000	2,710,000	8,130,000
0.10	100,000	272,000	738,000	2,010,000	5,450,000
0.09	100,000	246,000	605,000	1,490,000	3,650,000
0.08	100,000	222,000	495,000	1,100,000	2,450,000
0.07	100,000	201,000	405,000	816,000	1,640,000

Source: Carneiro and Hilse 1966:178.
Note: *Above 50,000,000 and therefore considered to be impossibly high.

calculations seems eminently viable, representing as it does 2,000 groups 50 strong; or much more likely, 4,000 groups with a mean membership of 25, the ethnographic 'magic number' for band size (Lee and DeVore 1968a:245–9). Taking 100,000 as a base population and rates of percentage annual increase ranging from 0.07 to 0.50, Table 4.2 emerges.

Significantly, if our generous starting level of 100,000 is cut in half, the picture does not qualitatively change – rates of growth above 0.1 per cent per annum on a sustained basis are impossible, otherwise colossally large populations emerge before the advent of cities (see Table 4.3). Even with the advent of cities over half a millennium later than the terminal date of the tables, we find the following population estimates by Adams (1981:90) of the then most densely populated parts of the Near East: the Nippur and Uruk regions of Mesopotamia (Table 4.4). In round numbers they amount to a mere 60,000 in Early to Middle Uruk times (*c.* 3,500–3,300 BC), and attain 110,000 for the combined areas only in the First Dynastic period, well into the third millennium.

The inference to be drawn is that the very lowest rate in each case, that of 0.07 per cent, is the most realistic, with 0.1 per cent in the nature of a ceiling. Carneiro and Hilse conclude:

> First and foremost, the increase in population that occurred during the Neolithic Period was not 'exceedingly rapid'. It was, in fact, only on the order of one tenth of one percent per year. For a village of 100 this rate of increase is equivalent to a net gain of only one person over a ten year period.[15] Yearly population increments, of course, increased as the Neolithic progressed; yet these increments probably never became very large. Only by virtue of the fact that they were accumulated over

Table 4.3 Calculation of the population of the Near East at 1,000-year intervals for various rates of increase, assuming a base population of 50,000

% increase	8,000 BC	7,000 BC	6,000 BC	5,000 BC	4,000 BC
0.50	50,000	7,330,000	*	*	*
0.40	50,000	2,710,000	*	*	*
0.30	50,000	1,000,000	20,000,000	*	*
0.20	50,000	369,000	2,720,000	20,000,000	*
0.15	50,000	224,000	1,000,000	4,490,000	20,100,000
0.14	50,000	203,000	821,000	3,330,000	13,500,000
0.13	50,000	183,000	672,000	2,460,000	9,030,000
0.12	50,000	166,000	550,000	1,830,000	6,060,000
0.11	50,000	150,000	451,000	1,350,000	4,060,000
0.10	50,000	136,000	369,000	1,000,000	2,730,000
0.09	50,000	123,000	302,000	743,000	1,830,000
0.08	50,000	111,000	248,000	551,000	1,230,000
0.07	50,000	101,000	203,000	408,000	821,000

Source: Carneiro and Hilse 1966:179.
Note: *Above 50,000,000 and therefore considered to be impossibly high.

several thousands of years did they culminate in a population of considerable size.

(Carneiro and Hilse 1966:179)

Assuming an exponential growth model (growth at a *constant rate*, resulting in a population expanding *geometrically* in size through time), the time it takes for a population growing at 0.01 per cent per annum to double is 6,931 years; at 0.03 per cent per annum 2,310 years, and at the likely 'ceiling' level of 0.1 per cent per annum the doubling time is 693 years, only sustainable for short periods and/or in small areas. For comparison the doubling time of an annual growth rate of 3 per cent, currently being experienced by some Third World countries, is only 23

Table 4.4 Changing characteristics of late prehistoric and protohistoric settlement enclaves[15]

Period	Northern enclave	Southern enclave
Early-Middle Uruk	Area: 2,087 km^2 Estimated population: 38,540 Density: 18.47/km^2	Area: 2,010 km^2 Estimated population: 20,110 Density: 10.00/km^2
Late Uruk	Area: 1,619 km^2 Estimated population: 21,300 Density: 13.16/km^2	Area: 2,231 km^2 Estimated population: 41,020 Density: 18.39/km^2
Jemdet Nasr	(Ambiguities in data do not permit comparable estimates)	
Early Dynastic I	Area: 1,184 km^2 Estimated population: 20,240 Density: 17.09/km^2	Area: 2,938 km^2 Estimated population: 86,300 Density: 29.37/km^2

Source: R. McC. Adams 1981:90.

years, and at 1 per cent, which seems like a big reduction in rate, only 69 years.

Carneiro and Hilse's rate of 0.07 per cent that I think is most reasonable, is, of course, one spanning thousand-year intervals. From what we have seen of doubling times relative to annual growth rates, for the early Holocene something like 0.01 per cent per annum growth rate is by far the most plausible, shifting gear to the region of 0.03 per cent with the onset of the Neolithic, even conceivably reaching 0.1 per cent for short bursts in certain localities.

No uniform rate can be right for the whole period under consideration nor indeed can one rate be applicable across the region at any particular point in time, except as a deliberately aggregating device. Certainly in no case is population an independent variable, as Smith (1972–3:5), for one, imagines, but is rather a response to techno-environmental opportunity and socio-economic changes.

The most fundamental of such changes was the process of 'Neolithization', that is, the spread of farming villages across the Near East and into Europe from Anatolia. Thence it spread across Europe from the southeast, at about 25 km per generation (or 1 km per year) in a demic 'wave of advance' (i.e. of population) that reached Britain from Turkey after 2,500 years (Ammerman and Cavalli-Sforza 1984:134). In this process the annual population growth rate may have been of the order of 1 per cent (ibid.:80) but only on the advancing frontier itself, for 'as we move closer to the origin, the tempo of population change slows down and is essentially zero in those places where population has reached saturation level' (ibid.:73).

The demic wave of advance model developed by Ammerman and Cavalli-Sforza sees logistic growth and local migratory activity, on a 'random walk' basis, as producing a diffusionary process that takes the form of a population wave expanding outward at a steady radial rate, and both the archaeological evidence and computer simulations support such a model. However, Ammerman and Cavalli-Sforza (ibid.:116) state that 'another point illustrated in the simulation is that only modest levels of migratory activity are required to sustain a demic event such as the spread of early farming'.

In Chapter 1 it was argued that population density, technology, and social organization are so interactive that each is a function of the others, with population density not itself an independent variable or prime mover. Renfrew's (1975:36–7) specification of population and population density as conditions of state of other variables or sub-systems and not themselves independent variables or prime movers, is particularly relevant to the process of Neolithization envisaged. Different population levels and densities restrain certain processes such as, at low levels, organizational complexity (Textor 1967) and require others, such as the smoothing of inter-annual variability of subsistence production.

The flow chart (Figure 3.5, p. 70) began with a plenitude of resources in the Neothermal Near East. This allowed bands to exploit seasonal abundance, particularly grains, encouraging ever more restricted mobility. Lee (1980:334) describes camp-moves five or six times a year as the 'classic foraging pattern'. Now assume that during the Epipalaeolithic the number is cut to three moves per year with a 'storage' site for harvested grains being the longest occupied, moves being made, perhaps to no real distance and of short duration, to game trails in the spring and to a lakeside site for fowling in the autumn. Such a regime could easily support what is after all only a large foraging band in the range of 25–40 persons. If more grains were harvested and well preserved in storage, that particular seasonal camp would not need to be moved at all, only the adult men going to hunt herd animals with, say, youths fowling from temporary camps in the autumn (cf. Binford and Chasko 1976:139). Indeed, the reverse might well apply where, as in the southern Iraq marshes, aquatic resources of some type (including fowl and other birds) are available on a year-round basis. Such a regime allows the size of the band to be augmented, say from 40 to 50 persons over a number of generations, because of the adequacy of resources available even in the poorest years experienced. People with such a diversified set of procurement strategies are not at the mercy of any one resource. In failure there is always 'slack' that can be taken up from the others. What is to be stressed, however, is that the demographic brakes are *not* now off. Plenitude of resources has permitted a larger population to remain together for more of the year (cf. Lee 1972b:182–4), but the previous means of population control still apply. Though Binford and Chasko (op. cit.:127–31) found the effects of male absenteeism, when the Nunamiut (in Alaska) were still mobile hunters, produced a difference in the mother/child ratio of 6.52 births per thousand mothers as between maximum male absenteeism (amounting in some periods to seventy-six days/household head/year) prior to sedentism and the termination of absenteeism at the end of the sedentarization process, such an effect, they state, would be swamped by random variation in a cohort of 50 women.

Whatever the physiological/environmental factors in play, conscious adjustments of fertility to social requirements can readily be implemented in egalitarian forager society, since as Ripley has remarked:

the ecological pressures indicating need to exert limitations on population growth can be sensed directly, simultaneously, and cognitively by the very figures who, in exerting such controls, would be acting in their own best reproductive interest as well as that of the larger society.[16]

(Ripley 1980:355)

This is obviously the same argument at the level of the individual mother with her direct knowledge of the social and natural environment, as that cited earlier in regard to the band's unmediated knowledge of its core range. Peterson (1976:274) states that in Australia 'Infanticide was not practised through awareness of population problems, but through pressure on individual women in the food quest', while in Africa too the staples are vegetable foods which are gathered mostly by women (Lee 1968:33). This, of course, is particularly the case where gathering is the primary subsistence resource, as it is in societies situated below *c.* 40° latitude, above which hunting and fishing assume heightened importance, as can be seen in Lee's global survey (Table 4.5).

Table 4.5 Primary subsistence source by latitude

Degrees from the Equator	Primary subsistence source			
	Gathering	Hunting	Fishing	Total
More than 60°	—	6	2	8
50°–59°	—	1	9	10
40°–49°	4	3	5	12
30°–39°	9	—	—	9
20°–29°	7	—	1	8
10°–19°	5	—	1	6
0°–9°	4	1	—	5
World	29	11	18	58

Source: Lee 1968:43.

It is worth reminding ourselves that the Zagros/Levant region is broadly encompassed between 40°N (the latitude of Ankara) and 30°N (Cairo); and between 30°E (the longitude of Alexandria) and 50°E (Baku on the Caspian, Bahrain on the Gulf). The Deh Luran plain lies about 32°N and 47°E. Differences in altitude and habitat along the Zagrosian Arc have the effect of sustaining flora and fauna characteristic of higher latitudes and, as we see from faunal remains in the region, hunting plays an important role through to the full and widespread domestication of animals.

With increasing sedentarization the previous *tight* damping of population to retain homeostasis at that level can be henceforward less rigorous because more bands can be supported in an ameliorating environment, sustained at a new level, or rather, sequence of levels. As each band restricts its range to an environmental cross-section now exploited more intensively, a higher overall population density for the Near East can be supported. This looks like 'where we came in' to the Deh Luran in the Bus Mordeh stage around 8,000 BC. By the next phase, that of Ali Kosh, the population has reached about 100, while by the succeeding

Mohammed Jaffar Phase it has grown to around 300, hardly an 'explosion' when a millennium has passed.

None the less, during this time of permanent village fixation, allowing new villages to fill the niches previously exploited seasonally or partially *by one village only* as at Bus Mordeh, the *knowledge and skills* of Natufians, Deh Luranis, etc. are not standing still. The environment is not static, the population is not static but able to inch upward into the new or newly released niches, and their knowledge of plants and animals increases the more they manipulate them. By the time whole new villages require to be set up quite away from the original loci, whether that be Deh Luran or the Judean Hills, not just the plants and animals are taken but necessarily the skills involved in their exploitation. However in new locations new skills and techniques evolve which may well have application back in the original centre and/or in further advance into quite new environments (cf. Kirkbride 1982:11–21). In, say, Khuzistan the supplementing of goat by sheep may allow more animals and thus more people to be raised, who then, with a further extended subsistence repertoire, go forth to exploit areas (e.g. the Negev or the Mesopotamian plains) hitherto only exploited by mobile foraging bands. Thus, contrary to Cohen (op. cit.) and other population pressure theorists (e.g. Earle 1980; Christenson 1980a), it is a very low initial population at the Epipalaeolithic which allows scope for expansion by developing new strategies in a series of new environments; it is not a response to a previously over-exploited environment (cf. Watson 1979:203).

And this remains the case even after millenniums of agriculture on the plains (Oates 1980:308). The fertile moist steppe west of Mosul, with a generously estimated population of 1,200 in the sixth millennium BC, reaching perhaps 6,000 in the Ubaid Period and giving over its 350 km^2 a population density in the order of 8–11 persons per square kilometre

> in an area of fully arable land which even under conditions of hoe agriculture could support a theoretical population of 20,000 . . . with additional grazing land available on the nearby jebel . . . would appear to constitute evidence of population increase but hardly 'population pressure' even assuming the simplest of agricultural techniques.
>
> (Oates 1980:308)

And Halaf sites in northern Iraq near Nineveh 'occupying only prime arable land in the rainfall zone (the deep brown soils of the moist steppe)', leaving unutilized for millennia other excellent soils in the area, some of the richest in Northern Iraq, means that 'there is no conceivable argument for population pressure at this time' (ibid.), which is indeed a time of very widespread expansion of farming. And Flannery (1973:284), in his review of the origins of agriculture in three continents, criticized his own (widely accepted) earlier views as 'coming too close to making population growth and climatic change into prime movers'. Instead he suggests that cultural factors, such as 'changes in socio-political organisation' might provide a more adequate basis of explanation.

To recapitulate: sedentarism at favoured sites enjoying diverse and plentiful resources allowed population to increase, at first accommodated by intensified hunting and gathering. New villages 'budded-off' to new locations, some at least of which were not so well endowed as the old, necessitating the introduction of plants and animals either not naturally present, or insufficiently so. Fully-fledged farming villages employing a well-understood range of domesticates (the Neolithic) allowed population in the region as a whole to rise as it filled up with farming and herding villages in new and sometimes unpromising locations, such as those requiring irrigation.

A revolution in the 'techno-economy', that is, of what was now accessible as the 'effective environment', permitted population to rise further in those areas to which it was applied, able eventually to support nucleated high-density clusters, namely cities.

Can such a series of interactions from the Epipalaeolithic be subsumed under the rubric of 'population pressure'? Only by destroying the very concepts of what a system is and what constitutes adequate explanation.

Chapter five

The heartland of cities

1 Periodization and the beginnings of history

Recorded history commences at the end of the fourth millennium BC, in a seemingly strange location right at the seaward fringe of the southern alluvium. There, in sight of each other, arise Ur, Eridu, and Uruk, 'not far above the Persian Gulf's retreating shoreline, under conditions starkly contrasting with those in the rainfall zone along the Zagros piedmont, where irrigation was much less important or even unnecessary' (R. McC. Adams 1981:58). It is at first sight paradoxical that at the Gulf's edge, of all the parts of the Ubaidian province, the first civilization arose. The landscape (albeit rather poorer than in its pristine state) around the ruins of Eridu at Abu Shahrain, as seen from its ziggurat (see p. 139) by its first modern excavator, R. Campbell Thompson, was described as follows:

From the *ziggurat* as far as the eye can see there is naught but awful solitude; you look down on sombre desert which encircles you for miles. Northwards lie the flat lands, yellow in April and unrelieved except for sparse arabesques of salt spreading like mares'-tails in a breezy sky, while afar, just visible as a little pimple in the mornings but blotted out in the afternoon haze, is the temple-tower of Muqaiyar. Towards the north-east, especially when the sun is setting, the sandstone ridge on the skyline is thrown into vivid relief as a white streak six miles away. Eastwards, not far from the mound, the grass has sprung up, marking the dry site of the winter lagoon which lies between you and the sandstone ridge; southwards towards Dafna and Qusair are the distant low sandstone hills circling round and completing a wide arc to westward. Between you and the sunset is a broad green tract of scrub and coarse grass wherein lie the wells two miles away. Not a tree is in sight, and the only fuel is that provided by the little dry brushes.

(R. C. Thompson 1920:105)

It should be stressed that in this area of the first durable cities there is no long build-up of sites in number and size, represented by sites in the north like Abu Hureyra. On the contrary the first culture known in southern Mesopotamia, in what was to become Sumer proper, is the Eridu (Mellaart 1975:170–1): the first period of Ubaid. But from then on Mesopotamian history can be seen to manifest a fundamental continuity of economy and polity, stretching to the end of the Old Babylonian period in the middle of the second millennium BC. It did so, however, not under centralized rulership in the manner of a territorial state, but in a number of parallel and rival 'lines', one of which could make itself hegemonic for a period without ending the others.

The course of Mesopotamian history was far from smooth, attended as it was by recurrent internecine warfare. But the polity of Greater Mesopotamia was adapted to those conditions, which, if failing to unite the cities of Sumer and Akkad other than transiently, generally provided enough sinew to keep enemies at bay, or even to take the initiative against outsiders as, for instance, in the campaigns to the Mediterranean of Sargonic times. None the less, the millennial continuity of the system of Mesopotamian city-states (a system which also obtained beyond the limits of Sumer and Akkad) was subject to external disruption and despoliation in times of relative decrepitude. Those periods of major disruption, which are three in number, are indicated by the two Zs in the chronology (Figure 5.1), the third attendant upon the ending of the 'Hammurabi Dynasty' in 1,595 BC. However, because power was dispersed among city-states of differing fortunes and was not centralized, though some could be overrun or disputed, others could continue broadly as normal or even flourish, like Lagash under Gudea despite the Gutians. Sumer, Akkad, with Mesopotamia as a broader designation (to include, for example, Assyria), are terms for culture areas and are no more the indicators of a politically unified territory than Greece was in the city-state period (Speiser 1954:14; Hallo 1963b:112–13).

The first severe dislocation occurred late in the third millennium and decisively brought to an end the Sargonic period after that dynasty had overextended the cities' capabilities by continual warfare. The so-called 'Sargonic Empire' was terminated by the irruptions of the Zagros Gutians, the 'snake and scorpion of the mountains' as the plain-dwellers called them. Thereafter it was said 'who was king, who was not king?', such was the turmoil. None the less Sumerian culture continued to flourish at Uruk and Lagash, especially the latter under Gudea (2,141–2,122 BC). Hence we can designate this the Uruk-Lagash period (2,160–2,120 BC).

Continuity resumed with the Ur III or 'Neo-Sumerian' period, after Utuhegal, king of Uruk, had begun to roll back the Gutians by 'setting his foot upon the neck' of their king, Tirigan. The Neo-Sumerian takes its name from the 'Sumerian Renaissance' encouraged by a state that developed central authority and co-ordination to a hitherto unattained

Figure 5.1 Periodization of Mesopotamian history

PERIOD		YEARS BC
Ubaid I	(beginning)	5,500
Ubaid IV	(end)	4,000
Uruk		4,000–3,350
Jemdet Nasr		3,350–2,960
Time of city-states	Early Dynastic I (EDI)	2,960–2,760
	Early Dynastic II	2,760–2,650
	Early Dynastic IIIA	2,650–2,480
	Early Dynastic IIIB	2,480–2,365
	Lugalzagesi	2,335–2,310 (25-yr reign)
Sargonic 'Empire'	Sargon of Akkad	2,310–2,273 (37-yr reign)
	Rimush, younger son of Sargon	2,272–2,263 (9-yr reign)
	Manishtushu, elder son of Sargon	2,262–2,247 (15-yr reign)
	Naram-Sin, son of Manishtushu	2,246–2,190 (56-yr reign)
	Sharkalisharri, son of Naram-Sin	2,189–2,164 (25-yr reign)
Gutians	Uruk-Lagash Period (Gudea, Ur-Ningirsu, Pirigme, Nammahani) terminated by:	c. 2,160–2,120
	Gudea ensi of Lagash	2,141–2,122
Ur III or 'Neo-Sumerian' Period	Utuhegal, king of Uruk	2,122–2,114 (7/8 yr reign)
	Ur-Nammu, king of Ur	2,114–2,096 (18-yr reign)
	Shulgi, son of Ur-Nammu	2,095–2,047 (48-yr reign)
	Amarsuen, son of Shulgi	2,046–2,037 (9-yr reign)
	Shu-Shin, brother of Amarsuen	2,036–2,027 (9-yr reign)
	Ibbi-Sin, son of Shu-Sin	2,026-2,001 (25-yr reign)
Isin & Larsa Period*	Isbi-Irra of Isin	2,017–1,985
	Naplanum of Larsa	2,025–2,005
	Damiq-ilisu of Isin	1,816–1,794
	Rim-Sin of Larsa	1,822–1,763
First Dynasty** of Babylon (old Babylonian) 'Hammurabi Dynasty'	(1) Sumuabum	1,894–1,881
	(2) Hammurabi	1,792–1,750
	(3) Samsuditana	1,625–1,595

Four centuries of Kassite rule in Babylonia were ushered in by the Hittite raid on Babylon in 1595, when Samsuditana was defeated by Murshili I (1620–1595). The Hittites, Indo-European speakers from Anatolia, withdrew after their victory, leaving the way open to the Kassites. In the extreme south, the indigenous Sealand Dynasty lasted from 1793 until 1415, when integrated into Kassite Babylonia which they called Karduniash. Kassite hegemony lasted until 1155, when attacks by Assyria and Elam terminated it.

Key: ⊿ denotes disturbed period of fragmentary and shifting power(s).
   * beginning and ends only.
   ** beginning, middle and end rulers only.

Source: Brinkman 1977:335–7, and Hassan and Robinson 1987:127–8, as discussed in ch.4, sect. 4
Note: See Whitehouse 1983:320–1 for an exposition of 'high' (early) compared with 'middle' chronology

degree. When the Ur III dynasty ended with Ibbi-Sin just at the turn of the second millennium, however, a period of instability and civil war followed. This is termed the Isin and Larsa period after the two cities where continuity was best maintained, against what appears to have been serious problems with nomads and other non-settled elements, 'tribals', prominent among whom were the Amurru or Amorites.

Recovery was achieved under the growing power of the (Amorite) First Dynasty of Babylon (West Semitic intruders), well known to history from the name and works of Hammurabi (1,792–1,750 BC). Though non-Sumerian, this dynasty continued in the mainstream of Sumerian tradition with Amorite innovations. Its termination early in the sixteenth century BC was the beginning of the Kassite period, intruders from the north ushering in a dark age of few texts but seeming stability. This is thus a suitable place to end a historical account.

2 City genesis

At points in more favoured parts of the Near East individual towns had flourished much earlier: Jericho and Çatal Hüyük in Anatolia being the best known. However, those earliest experiments in concentrated living did not continue uninterrupted into historic times and were essentially harbingers (Mellaart 1972:284). Instead, on a semi-arid plain broken only by marsh and dune arose a seminal city-centred civilization on an autochthonous basis, that lasted three millenniums until absorbed into the classical Graeco-Roman world that it had indirectly helped to stimulate.

The location of Ur, Eridu, and the other cities of Sumer proper is in stark contrast to the piedmont northwest of the plain where numerous small springs and alluvial fans offered attractive conditions for early, continuing, and relatively dense settlement (R. McC. Adams 1981:55). By contrast, 'the onset of settlement is first known from relatively small numbers of sites that trace out a gradient of declining density northward from the head of the Gulf. Over most of the region the sedentary communities were widely and fairly evenly dispersed' (Adams, op. cit.:59).

In this first phase, commonly designated the Ubaid I or Eridu period, copious marsh resources were exploited in a sophisticated manner (Wright 1981:323), part of a 'broad-spectrum economy' that employed, for instance, canoes and nets for fishing (Lloyd and Safar 1948:118). Ubaid origins on the southern alluvium were thus almost certainly around the marshes and watercourses: needless to say, their domesticates were not locally derived.

Four sites of this phase are known: Eridu, 'Usaila, Ur, and the type-site of Tell al-'Ubaid itself. Those small communities of only a hectare or so remain occupied into the next, Ubaid II or Hajji Muhammad phase. By this time they had roughly doubled their areas, and at Eridu itself there is already evidence of a 'temple platform' in the 'temple sounding' undertaken by Fuad Safar (1950:28). The same sites continue occupied into the Ubaid III phase, with the continuance also of the broad-spectrum economy. Remains of wild onager, hunted on the nearby alluvial desert, are found, along with domesticated cattle, goats, sheep, or gazelle (Flannery and Wright 1966:61–3). At nearby site EP-104 concentrations of freshwater molluscs show they were also used (Wright, op. cit:323).

By the Late and Terminal Ubaid periods boat models from Eridu show that sailing craft have been developed, and marine fish are being brought to the temple at Eridu as offerings. From Eridu wheat, six-row barley, and dates have been identified and cattle herding is assumed to continue (ibid.). Those are the elements of farming known from later texts and they are all present by the end of the fifth millennium BC (ibid.). By Late Ubaid times not only are we dealing with a variety of large and small settlements served by canals 3–5 km long that it would be 'within the abilities of extended kin groups to build and maintain' (ibid.:324); but Eridu itself has grown to around 12 hectares, while Ur has reached 10 hectares (ibid.:325).

Eridu's earlier settlement mound now forms the nucleus of a broad platform upon which was a temple on a raised terrace (Wright, op. cit.:325). This terrace was shared by some substantial buildings of a residential character. Those, when contrasted with more modest habitations nearby and coupled with differences in burial practices, suggest the advent of some degree of social stratification in this, still Proto-Literate Period. None the less, by this Late Ubaid phase it is unlikely, according to Wright (ibid.) 'that southern Sumer as a whole contained more than 2,500 to 4,000 persons, or about 20 persons per square kilometre of enclave, far fewer than were later supported with a similar technology'. But the succeeding Early Uruk Period, the time of the first city-states, was not the outcome of linear growth in settlement size and density. Rather, with the abandonment of many small settlements and the great expansion of Eridu, we see political rather than demographic forces at work. Consequently Wright (ibid.) estimates the population of the area to be no more than from 6,200 to 10,000 at this time. Thus it seems that population in the south has not so much expanded as been redistributed.

In contrast, by the Early-Middle Uruk phase, the Nippur-Adab environs in the northern area, with some 360 hectares of settlement to the 170 of Uruk environs, had double the population at 36,000 persons (Adams, op. cit.:69). These are calculated on the standard of 125 persons per hectare of actual site area; or about 100 persons per hectare if calculated only from measurement of minimum size of rectangles enclosing sites, instead of the more usual circular or ovoid estimates of area. For an area (Nippur-Adab) virtually devoid of permanent settlement in the Late Ubaid Period, 'this was an extraordinarily rapid, massive process of growth at the very outset of the Uruk Period' (ibid.). Illustrative of relative movement is Table 5.1. Adams's survey uncovered something close to a remarkable tenfold increase in the population of the Nippur-Adab region of the central Euphrates floodplain in just a couple of centuries. He surmises (ibid.:70) that, supplementing vigorous indigenous growth of the settled agriculturalists, there must have been either extensive immigration into the area, or a conversion of the semi-sedentary population into settled agriculturalists, or more probably, a combination of the two. However, later in this same phase, that is during the Late Uruk Period, the weight of population shift is reversed, for the population of the Uruk region doubles while that in the north falls by almost half, leading Adams (ibid.) to conclude that tens of thousands of the inhabitants of small villages abandoned their homes and actually moved southward.

Table 5.1 Gross regional trends in Uruk period settlement

	Uruk environs	Nippur-Adab environs (North of WS-004)
Early-Middle Uruk period:		
Total recorded settlement	173.1 ha	362.0 ha
Percentage of total in sites of 5 ha or less	24.7	35.0
Late Uruk period:		
Total recorded settlement	382.5 ha	200.6 ha
Percentage of total in sites of 5 ha or less	34.8	24.6

Source: R. McC. Adams 1981:70.

Changes in settlement sizes in the two regions between the Early-Middle and the Late Uruk Period are illustrated in Figure 5.2. What the diagrams and the population movements reflect is an increasing hierarchy of settlement type. The city of Uruk, having grown from 70 hectares in the Early Period to 100 hectares in the Late Uruk Period, the largest single centre throughout the period, dominates centres half its size (the next largest in area), with another series of towns half again in size, right down to villages of only half a hectare.

This strongly suggests that by the Uruk Period at least the larger centres were already falling into place at certain steps or intervals that were disjunctively separated by distance, specialised function, and range of religious influence or administrative-political control.

(Adams, op. cit.:72)

From Table 5.2 we can see that already in Uruk times about half the

Figure 5.2 Distribution of Uruk-site-areas by regions and sub-periods

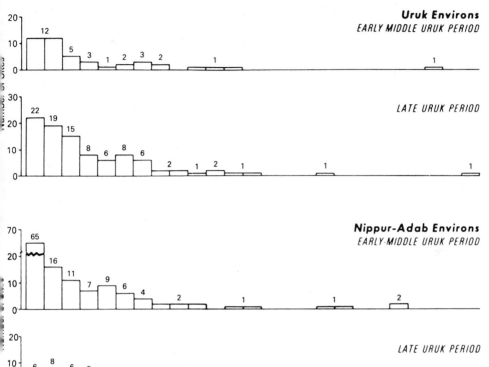

Source: R. McC. Adams 1981:71

total population of Sumer can be classed as 'urban', showing geographically its position as the real 'heartland of cities': hence the title of Adams's (1981) work. Concomitantly, at least in the larger centres, most signally Uruk itself, 'a highly significant segment of the population' must have been enabled to divorce itself from more than token or symbolic involvement in the processes of primary food production (Adams, op. cit.:80). From the quality and quantity of the artefacts recovered at village and town sites of all sizes in the Uruk period, it seems that what we are encountering are flourishing part-time specialisms in communities of a wide range of sizes (ibid.). However, in the largest centres we encounter what seem to be full-time specialists, not least in the advent of scribes, whose 'formalised lists of gods, professions, geographic names, and classes of objects arranged in conceptual categories' exist in addition to the economic and administrative records that lie at the origins of

Table 5.2 Urban and non-urban settlement by region in successive Uruk sub-periods

	10 hectares or less ('villagers/townsmen') %	More than 10 hectares ('urbanites') %
Early-Middle Uruk period:		
Uruk area	53	47
Nippur-Adab area	54	46
Late Uruk period:		
Uruk area	61	39
Nippur-Adab area	30	70

Source: R. McC. Adams 1981:75.

writing (Gelb (1952) 1963:62). Indeed the earliest-known Sumerian characters, still pictographic at this stage, come from the 'Uruk IV' excavation stratum dated around 3,100 BC.

Thus, opposing the formal administrative/information-handling model of state formation propounded by Gregory Johnson and Henry Wright (e.g. 1975), under which the 'objective' necessity of the division of labour calls forth a 'managerial' elite to co-ordinate diverse activities and locations, Adams contends that

> we are dealing instead with a much less simple, less stable mix of relationships between the centres and the peripheries. Among its features were: deities whose cults attracted pilgrimages and voluntary offerings; intervals of emergent, centralised, military based domination of subordinate centres that had been reduced to the status of clients, alternating with other intervals of fragile multi-centre coalition or local self-reliance; coercive extraction of rural resources alternating with more or less freely balanced exchange of subsistence products of the countryside for status symbols and certain limited but important categories of utilitarian goods that could not be produced locally.
>
> (R. McC. Adams 1981:81)

Indeed, writing of his own excavations in the Deh Luran plain that attempted to analyse its import/export relationships, Wright himself (1972:104) stated that the 'area was drawn into a state long before it participated significantly in the transformed exchange network. The latter cannot explain the former.' Quite so, but a cyberneticist approach, dealing only with the input and processing of 'information' which is then transmitted to a lower level as 'policy', seems for him to provide an 'organising principle' for state formation out of a functional hierarchy.

Yet at Eridu in Late Ubaid times, there is evidence of a temple to Enki

(**É-Apsu**), god of the subterranean sweet waters (**Apsu**, whence our word 'abyss'). This is the first firm evidence of a building in Mesopotamia with an explicitly non-secular purpose, and indeed the series of subsequent rebuildings here manifests great cultural continuities. Temples at Eridu developed continuously one upon the other from a small one-roomed shrine (with an external oven) in Ubaid I times, through the sizeable Ubaid 3 temple on its platform, to the yet more imposing Ubaid 4 temple. Lloyd (1978:42), who conveniently illustrates those phases, suggests a date of around 4,900 BC for Ubaid 1, *c.* 4,100 BC for Ubaid 3, and *c.* 3,800 BC for Ubaid 4. Continuity of belief and ritual is seen in the constant relation of altar to offering table, and in repeated use of buttressed structure of highly standardized tripartite layout.

The final protoliterate temple at Eridu is illustrated in Figure 5.3; by this time it had fully assumed the form of a ziggurat, which is a faced, and often painted, stepped pyramid of brick elevating functional buildings. Such was the so-called 'tower' of Babylon.

Sumerians regarded Eridu as the original city and the locus of sorcery, since Enki's source of power was utterance and the word brought order to chaos. Primeval chaos was the undifferentiated waters, which makes a great deal of sense given Eridu's position between sea, marsh, freshwater lagoon, and flat alluvial plain subject to floods.

Figure 5.3 The prehistoric temple at Eridu

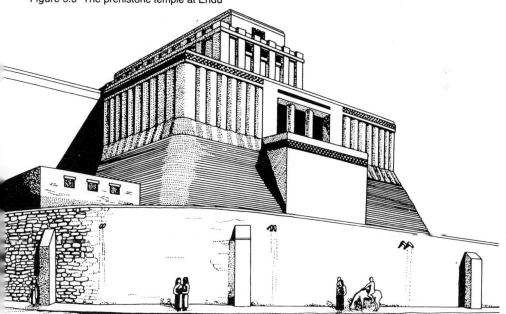

Source: Lloyd 1978:39

As the creation myth *Enuma Elish* relates:

1 When above the heaven had not (yet) been named,
2 (And) below the earth had not (yet) been called by a name;
3 (When) Apsû primeval, their begetter,
4 Mummu, (and) Ti'āmat, she who gave birth to them all,
5 (Still) mingled their waters together,
6 And no pasture had been formed (and) not (even) a reed marsh was to be seen;
7 When none of the (other) gods had been brought into being,
8 (When) they had not (yet) been called by their name(s, and their) destinies had not (yet) been fixed,
9 (At that time) were the gods created within them.

(Heidel 1951:18)

And a related myth goes on to explain that:

1 A holy house, a house of the gods in a holy place, had not been made;
2 A reed had not come forth, a tree had not been created;
3 A brick had not been laid, a brick mould had not been built;
4 A house had not been made, a city had not been built;
5 A city had not been made, a living creature had not been placed (therein);
6 Nippur had not been made, Ekur had not been built;
7 Uruk had not been made, Eanna had not been built;
8 The *Apsu* had not been made, Eridu had not been built;
9 A holy house, a house of the gods, its dwelling had not been made;
10 All the lands were sea;
11 The spring[1] which is in the sea was a water pipe;
12 Then Eridu was made, Esagila (temple) was built –

(Heidel 1951:62)

Contrasting theories of state formation will be criticized in Chapter 7. Here, before proceeding to examination of the Jemdet Nasr and Early Dynastic Periods, it is sufficient to recall Fortes and Evans-Pritchard's observations (1940:19) to the effect that 'myths, dogmas, rituals, beliefs and activities . . . endow the social system with mystical values which evoke acceptance of the social order that goes far beyond the obedience exacted by the secular sanction of force'.

3 Jemdet Nasr to Dynastic periods

While in the north there was no primate city of the rank of Uruk, but rather a number of medium-sized competitors, as we move through the Jemdet Nasr period in the last centuries of the fourth millennium and the first of the third, the peak of relatively dispersed rural settlement in the Uruk environs passes (Adams, op. cit.:81), to be succeeded by further concentration of population within Uruk city itself (ibid.). The settlement pattern of the Jemdet Nasr period is illustrated in Map 5.1.

By Early Dynastic times (EDI) Uruk covered no less than 400 hectares (*c.* 1.56 square miles) and had a population, estimated on the same basis as previously, of not less than 40–50,000. It is, then, scarcely surprising that at its core Uruk contains not one shrine of the cardinal gods in the Sumerian pantheon, but two – Anu and Inanna – respectively, as sky and fecundity, the ultimate repositories of authority and reproduction. Again the disproportions can be seen in the distributions shown in Figure 5.4, where the single bar against the 400-hectare scale at the extreme right-hand edge of the upper chart is, of course, Uruk itself. By this time, it can be observed, there is not even a city half its size in its region. Neither is there a city half its size in the Nippur-Adab region to the north (lower chart). Yet Nippur was historically regarded as the 'navel' of Mesopotamia by the Sumerians, and was for a millennium their cultic centre, as the place where the gods met in council.

Using contemporary ethnological data from Khuzistan, textual records from Early Dynastic Girsu, and modern geographical theory, Adams (ibid.:87) following Jacobsen 1958 (1982), computes the land necessary to support an adult annually, including the alternate-year fallowing system, at 1.5 hectares per person per year. On this basis he estimates the ring of cultivation around Uruk to have a radius of 14 km from the centre of the city.

Figure 5.4 Distribution of Early Dynastic I site areas by region

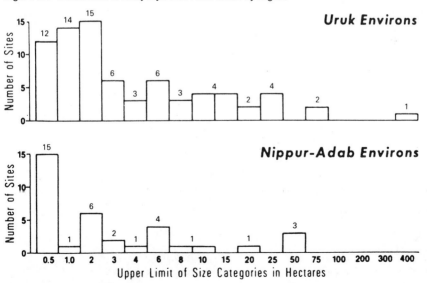

Source: R. McC. Adams 1981:84

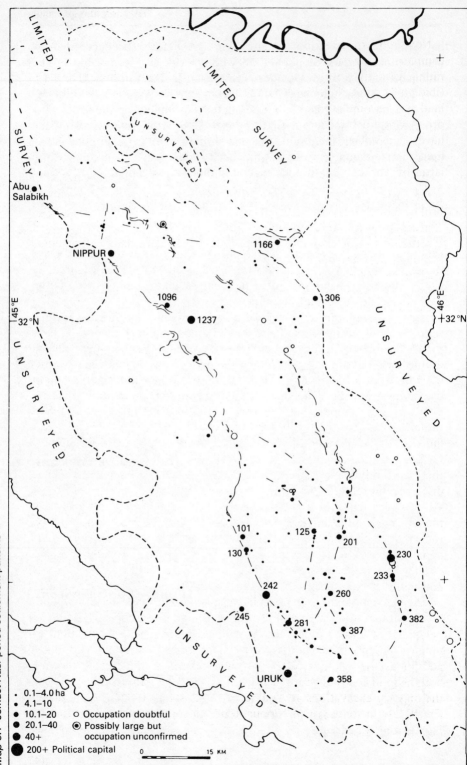

Source: R. McC. Adams 1981:83

Map 5.1 Jemdet Nasr period settlement patterns

LIMITED

SURVEY

LIMITED

LIMITED

SURVEY

UNSURVEYED

UNSURVEYED

UNSURVEYED

UNSURVEYED

Abu
Salabikh

NIPPUR

1166

1096   306

1237

45°E
32°N

46°E
+32°N

101   125   201   230

130   233

242   260   382

245   281   387

358

URUK

0.1–4.0 ha
4.1–10
10.1–20   ○ Occupation doubtful
20.1–40   ⊙ Possibly large but
40+   occupation unconfirmed
200+ Political capital

0   15 KM

Now modern geographical theory (e.g. Chisholm 1968), based on comparison of agricultural societies, suggests that 14 km is far too wide a radius for daily work in the fields from a central point. Indeed Chisholm (ibid.:112) points out that by the time the average distance to cultivated land has become a mere 2.8 km from the settlement, the average net product per hectare has already halved from what productivity would have been when distance to field was only 0.18 km. The former figure, then, corresponds to a distance between settlements of 8 km and the latter of 0.5 km. 'Beyond about one kilometre', Chisholm concludes,

> the costs of movement become sufficiently great to warrant some kind of response; at a distance of 3–4 kilometres the costs of cultivation necessitate a *radical* modification of the system of cultivation or settlement – for example the establishment of subsidiary settlements – though adjustments are apparent before this point is reached. If the distances involved are actually greater than this, then it is necessary to look for some very powerful constraining reason which prevents establishment of farmsteads nearer the land.
>
> (Chisholm 1968:131; original emphasis)

But as we have seen the peak of dispersed rural settlement occurred during the Jemdet Nasr period. Thereafter we observe a collapsing network of Early Dynastic I towns in the Uruk hinterland (Adams, op. cit.:88–9, 160–1). This is especially odd in the light of available evidence (e.g. Maekawa 1974) that agricultural land-use was extensive rather than intensive, with furrows spaced from 50 to 75 cm apart, individual seeds planted (and later drilled) over 3 cm apart within furrows (Adams, op. cit.:87). Indeed the seeding rates were only one-third of those currently prevailing in the region; none the less, there is evidence, discussed presently, that productivity was particularly high at this time. All of which leads Adams to suppose that 'a considerable proportion of the lands around Uruk, or at any rate the entire outermost ring, out to a radius of about 20 km, was worked not by its own citizenry but by dependent labourers from the villages and steppeland beyond' (ibid.).

The nature of this dependency, which need not be taken to be antithetical to citizenship at this stage, is far from obvious.[2] However, if later historical modes are applicable at this time, it may be a consequence of the formation of large temple- and kinship-based estates whose higher personnel at least are city-based; perhaps coupled with a 'taxation' for military defence and capital works made upon non-estate villagers in addition to the voluntary offerings made to shrines and temples known in both historic and prehistoric periods. Certainly the pattern emerging from the ongoing excavations at Abu Salabikh (Postgate 1980a; 1982), ancient Eresh, 20 km southeast of Nippur, tends to support such a construction. Dominating Eresh, a fairly small site, is an enormous temple complex dating from the Jemdet Nasr period and revealing in its copious texts all sorts of administrative activity additional to the cultic and cultural (Postgate 1982:54–9). Temples and, later, palaces tended to dominate the very core of cities, forming as it were, their nuclei. This can clearly be seen at Uruk (Figure 5.5) in the protoliterate period, when perhaps as much as one-third of the city's total area was taken up by temple and other public buildings (Lloyd, op. cit.:48–9). Right at the centre are the precincts of the temple complexes of Anu and Inanna mentioned above, both of which rated ziggurats. From Khafaje in the Diyala, during the Early Dynastic period we have a reconstruction (Figure 5.6) of what a temple precinct looked like and its scale.

In discussing the similarly organized 'palatial' (i.e. palace centred and administered) economy of Minoan Crete from the late third millennium to the early second millennium BC, Branigan (1970:121–2) has suggested that the very process of nucleation of settlement heightens social inequalities. If there are those who 'for varying reasons had been deprived of their inheritance, or rejected by their clan' (and there always are), then their socio-political status is already impaired, and if contributions to the building/rebuilding of socially central institutions are required from all, then all that those people have to contribute is their labour, a role in which they tend to become fixed. This because the localized relative overpopulation, caused by concentration around a particular site, exacerbates relative land scarcity, so freezing out permanently those formerly marginalized.

The consequences, however, are either to put the poorer party into a material, quasi-contractual indebtedness, or into the position of a permanent social junior, and thus in a position of inferiority or clientship. If both the material and social disabilities apply together, then citizenship itself may be lost, since the obligations pertaining to membership of the political community can no longer be met from one's own resources. At a lower level of political organization than protoliterate Sumer, and despite a fiercely democratic ideology amongst the Tolai of New Britain, Salisbury (1966:122–6) speaks of the means employed in the development and maintenance of wealth there:

> The rich men spend about eight times as much tabu (shell-money). Yet, although they spend over four times as much on luxury foods, this item is an insignificant part of their budgets, and is more than covered by their direct earnings. The major part of their financial activity involves the receipt of contributions from rich and poor, and the use of these sums to finance ceremonials, to invest in large capital equipment and in knowledge, and to accumulate for future matamatam [ceremonies in honour of dead ancestors].

And in a further striking analogue of the Mesopotamian complex there is

Figure 5.5 Reconstruction of the temple oval at Khafaje, as rebuilt in the Early Dynastic III period (*c.* 2,650–2,350 BC)

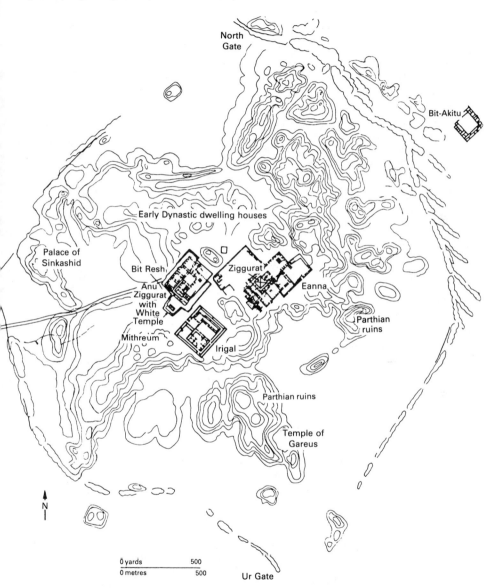

Source: Lloyd 1978:48
Note: Notice the Bit-Akitu, temple of the New Year Festival, outside the city wall in the northeast

Figure 5.6 Site plan of Uruk, showing the Anu and E-Anna precincts

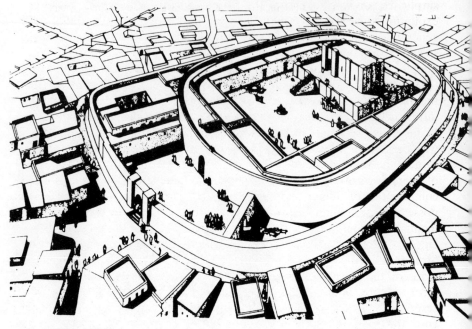

Source: Lloyd 1978:95

a general taxation and the obligation upon everyone to undertake unpaid corvée labour (ibid.:126).

The '**erín** people' of Mesopotamia, who are called in Early Dynastic times **šub-lugal**,[3] worked in groups and multiples of ten in alternate months for rations and wages, but always under institutional control (Maekawa 1976:16). These workers cultivated fields, dug canals, and were liable to military service at least as auxiliaries[4] (Maekawa, op. cit.:18–19). They were not slaves, and being employed only half the year, during the growing season, had the status of institutional clients, a form of subordination seldom analysed, whose importance as an intermediate form of dependency in the early stages of stratification is seen in the *gumsa-gumlao* process (discussed in Chapter 8), and also in early Rome.

4 Subordination and theories of stratification

For Mesopotamia the study of subordination and superordination in the early historic period was pioneered by Soviet scholars, one of the first being V. V. Struve ((1933) 1969a:20, 35) who thought that the tending of sheep and goats was 'performed by a foreign population, probably unfree'. However, Struve's basic characterization of Sumerian (and Egyptian) society was of 'a slave-owners' state' (ibid.:21) whose early basis was rooted in fishing, which alone sufficed to yield 'a sufficient surplus of produce to ensure the maintenance of slaves with a view to exploiting their labour' (ibid.). Those slaves, in Struve's view, were generally collectively owned, and indeed being such were quartered in special 'workhouses', barracks concentrated around the community gods' temples at the focus of Sumerian cities (ibid.:25).

However, Struve's is as much a 'hydraulic' as a *'tempelstadtslehre'*, for the major role of slaves, at least in later periods, he saw as producing the infrastructure of production, that is, the canals, ditches, and earthworks. In his view the needs of large-scale farming based on irrigation, which was organized throughout the area of entire territorial communities, formed the very precondition for collective ownership of slaves. The right of exercising power over slaves belonged to members (i.e. citizens) of the communities of Sumer and Egypt only collectively; and their collective possession of human instruments of production caused the citizens to maintain a communal form of state ownership of land (Struve, op. cit.:22), by which Struve presumably means temple land. According to Struve (ibid.) the '**pa-te-si**', that is **ensí** as it is now rendered, managed the work of the slaves for construction and maintenance of the irrigation infrastructure, and also the work of freemen in the fields. He, too, was responsible for the collection of taxes. This administrative power made **ensís** into despots in both Sumer and Egypt, a power rendered more absolute when 'the whole river valley' came under unified control (ibid.). While land was also individually owned by its citizen proprietors, according to Struve a fundamental condition of its exploitation was the exploitation of slaves in the provision of common irrigation works, the consequence for stratification being that:

> the peasant in an ancient Oriental society with a system of economy based on irrigation, was on the one hand, an immediate producer, in his capacity of a labourer in the field; but he was on the other hand, an exploiter, since he tilled land that could yield crops only with the help of an irrigation system constructed and maintained by the labour of captive slaves. Since the land which he cultivated owed its fertility to the irrigation system, he was in possession of an instrument of production which could not be entrusted to a slave, namely the land itself.
>
> (Struve (1933) 1969a:33)

Now 'unified control of the river valley' certainly marks the beginning of Egyptian history, but never applied in Mesopotamia during the millenniums with which we are concerned. Further, the whole theory of the slave economy has come under withering attack from other Soviet scholars, most notably Professors Tyumenev and Diakonoff. In particular Tyumenev (1954, 1956) could find scant evidence for the separate existence of a class of slave other than some women employed in textiles and the domestic economy. Tyumenev ((1956) 1969b:76) observed that during the Early Dynastic period at least, the collective temple lands were not in fact cultivated by a special temple personnel, and so there was no place for slave labour gangs. Lands as well as draft animals and seeds were turned over to community members for cultivation, and the temple got a share of the crop in return, collected by specially assigned **engars**.

By the time of Urukagina,[5] when temple estates had become ensial or royal domain, they were cultivated by gangs of labourers headed by special officials termed **sag-engar (sag-apin)**; slave labour proper was not employed, Tyumenev argues (ibid.:80–1), and anyway, neither ensial nor temple estates involved the whole population at this period. Tyumenev estimates (ibid.) more than half (perhaps two-thirds) of all the able-bodied inhabitants of Lagaš to have remained outside of those estates and to have remained united in rural communities, being recruited only for temporary labour service on irrigation and construction works. In Tyumenev's view it was through the abuse of corvée labour that had originally been the guarantee of the primacy of the community and the community's (subsequently the state's) ownership rights in the irrigated land (ibid.:70), coupled with 'squeezing' by usurious officials, which meant that by the Ur III period both the estate labourers and free peasants were reduced to virtual slave status under intense exploitation, co-ordinated by the state. Thus 'slaves' by capture or purchase simply merged into a generally unfree population (ibid.:85–6).

With the collapse of Ur III state control and the onset of Hammurabic times, private cultivation and exploitation became predominant and more 'classical' (i.e. Romano-Greek) forms of private wealth and slavery are recognizable.

Reconsidering the extensive economic archives of Umma and Lagash in the third dynasty of Ur period, Struve ((1948) 1969b) none the less reiterated his 'argument in favour of defining the royal estate at Umma as one based on a slave-owning type of economy'. This however begs a number of questions, most notably: (a) on 'ownership'; (b) how representative royal estates were of the whole economy; and (c) the very definition of slavery.

Whereas a fraction of the working population, usually war captives, are indeed initially slaves (**arád** for males, **gemé** for females; Gelb 1973:91–4), Sumerian has only one term, **gemé**, for both female slaves and 'serfs'; in the male case the term is **guruš**. Hence 'in innumerable cases, **gemé**, the largest category of what seem to be explicit references to slavery, is simply the counterpart of **guruš**' (Gelb 1982:92). **Guruš** (*etlum* in Akkadian) is literally a term for 'man' (in the sense of *vir*, not *homo*) and **gemé** an equivalent general term for woman. In Gelb's opinion (ibid.), the term **gemé**, referring specifically to (female) slave status, fits no more than about 2 per cent of all texts. This despite the fact that the word **gemé** occurs much more frequently than the equivalent male terms: **guruš**, **erín**, **arád**, or any other term pertaining to dependent labour. The terms **arád** and **sag** apply mostly to the conditions of (surviving) prisoners of war, which was one of bondage, before permanent allocation within the economy that brought with it improved status (Gelb 1973:91).

The point is that Mesopotamian society was characterized by a structure of subordinations which is neither that of classical slavery, nor feudalism, and in which full chattel slavery tended to be a transient condition of a minority derived from alien elements, as from Subarians in Old Babylonian times (Gelb 1982:90). A hierarchy of subordinations, material and ideological, obtained in which **ensís** and **lugals** appear as the slaves of the gods, their high officials are denoted as the slaves of their employers, and so forth right down to the small percentage of true slaves in Mesopotamian society (ibid.:88). In a re-examination, Struve, while able to distinguish the formally free from the formally subject, none the less goes on to summarize 'the structure of the exploited class for Late (i.e. Ur III) Sumerian society' as follows:

> This class was composed of slaves: men, women and children. They were recruited from war captives, from men and women purchased abroad, from insolvent debtors; and lastly from among younger sons of the holders of small parcels of land. Besides the slaves, royal and temple estates exploited hired workmen who were recruited from the ranks of freemen who possessed nothing but a plot of ground attached to their house, and had to seek additional income in working for hire.
>
> (Struve (1948) 1969b:170)

The fact that the 'immediate producers (hired labourers and the **guruš** and carriers permanently working on the estate) were cruelly exploited by the ruling class' is neither a description of generalized slavery, nor yet does it tell us much about the nature of the ruling class and their sources of power. It is much more instructive as to the structure and evolution of Sumerian society that, in her study of commercial Sippar as late as the nineteenth–sixteenth centuries BC, Rivkah Harris (1975:332) could find that 'the slave population of Mesopotamia was always small and insignificant in relation to the free population', a conclusion earlier arrived at by Oppenheim (1964:76), by Leemans (1968:181), by Gelb (1972; 1982), and by Diakonoff (1972:46). The last mentioned agree in finding that male prisoners of war were often brained on the spot, their corpses 'piled up in heaps' as the likes of Rimuš boasted (2,284–2,275 BC). Only female slaves were used in any number in the state economies due to the difficulty of controlling adult male labourers. Instead individuals, mostly women and children, were incorporated into private households under 'patriarchal ties of the family' (Diakonoff, op. cit.) on the well-known acephalous pattern. Some surviving male prisoners of war were however settled as state colonists in parts of Mesopotamia donated to the service of temples, or employed as groups of **erín** alongside the regular **guruš** agricultural labour force (Gelb 1973:94–6). Gelb (ibid.:83) characterizes both **guruš** and **erín** as 'semi-free', rather like serfs, but stresses the foreign, non-Mesopotamian origins of the latter, most from east of the Tigris, in contrast to native **guruš**.

The absence of widespread slavery may seem paradoxical given the existence of the state in some form from Uruk times onward. However such 'anomalous' data keeps us from forming preconceptions about Mesopotamian society, which is seminal, when compared against later and different societies to which we might like the formative material to conform. Finley (1983a:67), in his rigorous treatment of the classical 'chattel' slavery that has come to colour all subsequent discussion of dependent labour, first points out that slavery as a mode of production is of late Graeco-Roman advent. It is predicated on three preconditions of which it is the 'unavailability of an alternative, internal labour supply' which concerns us here. In Mesopotamia, and for that matter in Egypt, India, and China (in their formative millennia), this certainly did not apply; many types of subordinate labour short of slavery obtained. In the earliest Sumerian records we encounter **šub-lugals**, later **erín** folk (which can best perhaps be recorded as 'the able-bodied') numbering around five thousand in Lagash by Ur III times, 'a considerable proportion of the whole population of Lagash of Ur III' (Maekawa, op. cit.:16). And even in Early Dynastic times the **šub-lugal** formed the core of a stratum called **lu-kur-dab-ba** (ibid.:43). Later there are different terms for different categories of subordinates; **guruš**, **arád**, and **gemé** having already been mentioned.

Finley's other two preconditions are for specifically private ownership of land with sufficient concentration to call for a permanent workforce, coupled with a sufficient development of commodity production, that is, production intended for the market. It will be argued subsequently that in Mesopotamia neither of those two further preconditions obtained. Indeed, in the light of modern research it is what Gelb (1976:204) calls the 'productive slavery' of the Graeco-Roman period that seems anomalous in the ancient world (ibid.).

Diakonoff ((1956) 1969c) also based his analysis upon textual sources from Lagash in the third millennium BC, specifically those of the ED III period, a corpus described by Adams (1981:134) as by far the richest and most informative in regard to economic and social questions yet available. Working from documents giving numbers of the female slave population as a known but varying fraction of total (dependent and free) temple personnel, Diakonoff (op. cit.:176) reckons that it is possible to estimate roughly the total area of temple estates, assuming that the population of the temple of ^dB a-U was probably some 10 per cent of the total temple population of Lagash, which had a score of temples. 'Supposing that the number of personnel was roughly proportional to the estate area, it can be considered that the area of all temple lands amounted to 500–600 sq. km, thus constituting from a quarter to a half of the total area of the Lagaš state' (ibid.). Those figures refer to the 'state cluster' or 'nome' in Diakonoff's terms, not to the city area alone; and to that area constituting Lagash state prior to the loss of over half of its territory at the end of Urukagina's reign.

The rest of the territory was divided between 'community' land, 'in the hereditary possession of patriarchal extended families' (ibid.:177), and aristocratic/royal estates, the latter growing historically with the alienation of the former, while the king (**ensí**, later **lugal**) after the Early Dynastic period progressively gained control of the temple estates. From being a community resource and reserve, they became royal domain.

But temple land itself was not of one type and, even when under royal control, its working was far from uniform. Diakonoff distinguishes three types of land-working of temple domain:

> Temple land in Lagaš at the end of the Early Dynastic Period was divided into three categories: 1) **níg-en-(n)a** land reserved for the maintenance of the temple; 2) **gan-kur** land divided into non-hereditary and interchangeable, strictly individual parcels allotted for their service to men working on **níg-en-(n)a** land and to temple artisans and administrative personnel; 3) **gan-uru-lal** land allotted against a share in the crop to different persons (mostly members of the temple personnel as a supplement to what they got of **gan-kur** land).
>
> There is no evidence that land of any of these categories could ever be bought or sold.
>
> (Diakonoff (1956) 1969c:176)

The land that could change hands lay in what Diakonoff was the first to call the 'private-communal' sector of 'patrial' land, which was sometimes bought up (quite commonly at a nominal price) by important personages, mostly by functionaries in the community administration, kinsmen of the princes, or the ruling princes themselves.

> The land was sold by the head of the family or by several of its members not in the capacity of proprietors of the land but in that of elected representatives (**lu-sa(g)-pa(d)**) of the family commune. As often as not, the sale was effected by a group of family representatives (brothers and other kinsmen).
>
> (Diakonoff, op. cit.:176)

Other family members participated as witnesses, thereby indicating consent, while in the case of large-scale alienations, the whole

Map 5.2 Watercourses and settlement in Early Dynastic Sumer

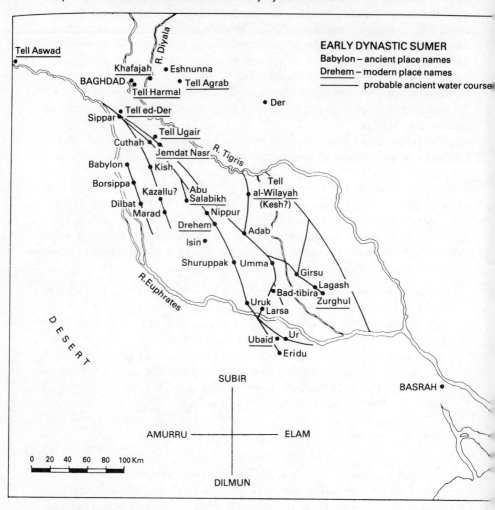

Source: Postgate 1982:49

patrilineage participated (ibid.:177). In the case of really big tracts, the assent of the Popular Assembly of the rural community in question was required, or even of what Diakonoff calls the 'nome'. Such nomes, or cores, for instance the 'nome' of Uruk consisting of Kulab and Eanna, or the 'nome' of Lagash consisting of the separate settlements of Girsu, Lagaš, Sirran, Guaba, and others, were at the outset in Jemdet Nasr times 'closely linked rural communities', with temples at their centre, around which the city-states coalesced (ibid.:187).

A similar view had previously been formed by Henri Frankfort

(1956:64), who had been the excavator of several such temple sites; it was also the view formed by the great Assyriologist, Thorkild Jacobsen (1949:255). Similar considerations apply to Renfrew's (1975:3–59) formulation of 'Early State Modules', which formate at the chiefdom level around 'a central person, resident at a central place' (Renfrew 1977b:100–1).

None the less, Diakonoff cautions us not to expect direct continuity 'of a tribal chieftain's function in the primitive community', but suggests instead (op. cit.:181, n. 10) that during the Early Dynastic wholly new leadership roles arose on the basis of the new urban institutions then emergent. And it is to a detailed consideration of those that we now turn with this sketch of Early Dynastic Sumer in view (Map 5.2).

The institutions of urbanism

Commenting on the 'manifest continuities in monumental temple architecture at ancient Eridu as well as Uruk', Adams (1981:59) posits, from the Ubaid period onward, 'fundamental cultural continuity within the major centres of settlement [as] beyond question'. As the ritual and organizational centre of the original communities, the temples were a special institution in and of the community, not only symbolizing its unity and its relationship to the cosmos, but serving also as the central-place focus. In this sense, as we shall shortly see, the temple supplanted whatever chiefly symbolic or redistributive functions there may have been, and thus served as an institutional barrier to any direct continuity of overall social leadership from a putative tribal condition to an urban one. Anticipating the argument, we can say that the cities of Mesopotamia did not form around a chiefly residence or government centre, as so many did, for instance in Africa. The processes involved are quite different in kind, not in degree alone. The Neolithic of the Near East was on such a broad front technically, socially, and geographically, that, like the Industrial Revolution, it developed both a momentum and a settlement pattern of its own, a distinctiveness heightened by the exigencies of the alluvium.

Stated summarily, agriculture, especially field monoculture, is inherently a risky undertaking (Rindos 1984:xvi), all the more so in an arid zone where there are not many natural resources to which a dense population can turn in crisis (Colson 1979:22). The artificiality and potential fragility of this situation posed unique problems in social reproduction, met by temples as the community reserve and means of co-ordination, as Diakonoff observes:

> Since the produce of temple land was regarded as the grain reserve fund of the community as a whole, it was probably worked by all community members jointly, before, gradually, this task was assigned to specialised groups of the population. During the second quarter of the 3rd millennium BC, people ruined by war, by natural calamities, or

forced to flee from their homes in consequence of strife with their kinsmen, moved to neighbouring communities where they came under the 'patronage' of stronger households, especially of the temple economies, but probably also of the 'houses' of the rulers and nobility. This seems to have been a result of growing property stratification. There is a possibility that the territorial communities themselves detailed special work teams to work for the temples. Also the custom of transferring invalids and sick people to the temples as votive gifts is attested for the different periods of Sumerian history.[1] Thus by the 25th–24th centuries BC a permanent temple labour force had emerged.

(Diakonoff 1982:60)

Had the temple not been both a central and a multiplex institution, it is most unlikely that leadership could have emerged from it. It can also be ventured that the emergence of politico-military leadership in the hands of the **lugal** was in a way a counterweight to the earlier economic and ideological power of temples. At least 'control over the temple estates and their personnel gave the ruler (**ensí** or **lugal**) independent military power' (Diakonoff, op. cit.:66). Such unique configurations made the Sumerian the first, and for a long time the only, truly urban civilization, in contrast to merely royal capitals or administrative centres set amongst, and quite parasitic upon, a sea of peasants and pastoralists. Kings, as we shall see, certainly develop in the city-states of Sumer; but they were the creations of those cities, the urban centres did not crystallize around them.

By *urban*, I mean a population sufficiently numerous and nucleated that the social relations of production mutate to express the principle of synoecism itself (which is interdependence arising from a dense proximity), the emergent expression of which is the crystallization of government. In turn, government manifests itself as the state through administration based on writing, plus monumental building representing the professionalization of ideological, economic, and armed force.

It is not coincidental, then, that the first form of the city, or for that matter the state, takes the form of the city-state.

Temples had the role of catalysts in the formation of cities on the alluvium. To be sure there were cultic centres elsewhere, and the ethnographic record, partly surveyed below, has many accounts of social stores and institutions of economic co-ordination. It is, however, the unique fusion of the three roles in one singular organization that was catalytic. Time and place are, of course, all important, and in temples we see the integration of a great variety of post-Neolithic practices that included the long-distance trade required to import materials, especially metals, wood, and minerals, in which the alluvium was almost entirely deficient, exporting textiles and other manufactures in exchange.

None the less Mesopotamian society, based on the city-state, was not a *tempelstadt* as was thought until quite recently, although as I have suggested, the formative and continuing role of the temple was great. Rather, the society was one of over-ranking households of varying size, importance, and type, grouped into two main sectors: public, that is, temple and crown establishments; and private, namely the 'kinship-centred' groupings we can call, after Diakonoff and Gelb, the private-communal. During the third millennium this sector engendered by alienations of land, such as that of 150 hectares examined below, private-familial and private-individual holdings, often to those eminent in public affairs. Thus social stratification, already inherent in the structure of the household, proceeded on the basis of loss of independent landholding, due to economic, political, and military pressures, and a class of dependents (**guruš/erín**), i.e. able-bodied workers, formed internally. They were not, as were prisoners of war, slaves, who tended to form the royal labour-force, but what Gelb (1979:24) has variously called serfs or helots to indicate their non-slave but only semi-free status. I refer to the **guruš/erín** as dependent or subordinate labour/soldiers.

The Maništušu Obelisk is a **kudurru** dating from the Sargonic period. That is, it is a four-sided record in stone of the sale of fields to king Maništušu, of the dynasty of Agade. It is by no means the oldest **kudurru** extant, but it is, for our purposes, the most important. It records the sale of fields to the king by no less than ninety-eight sellers. But this does not mean that ninety-eight fields changed hands. On the contrary, what were being alienated were coparcenary rights held jointly, if very unevenly, by men patrilineally related through what Gelb has argued to be a clan-type structure (Figure 6.1). By pinning down the meaning of such crucial terms as *dumu* to mean 'son of', *dumu.dumu*, 'descendant', and *šu*, 'of', that is, belonging to or affiliated with (a household), Gelb (1979:44–5) was able to unlock the relationships of the parties to the sale transactions.

Thus on side C of the obelisk we find: PN *DUMU* PN$_2$ *šu* PN$_3$ *ši* PN$_4$ . . . *DUMU.DUMU* PN$_5$ . . . *DUMU.DUMU* PN$_6$; which translates as: 'P(ersonal) N(ame), son of PN$_2$, Of PN$_3$, Of PN$_4$ . . . descendants of PN$_5$, descendants of PN$_6$' (Gelb 1979:27).

There are however complications, as Gelb relates. He observes that:

the discrepancy between the genealogical steps and true generations is further aggravated by the use of such terms as *DUMU.DUMU*, which may mean 'grandchild' as well as 'descendant', and *šu-ši* 'Of', which may denote descent as well as affiliation with a household. In such cases, the terms denoting descent may indicate vertical relationships, those denoting household affiliation may indicate horizontal relationships.

(Gelb 1979:27)

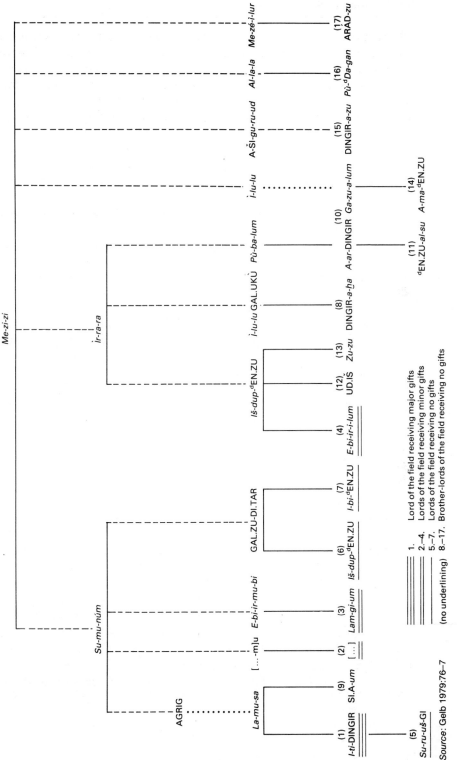

Figure 6.1 Family relationships and their ranking according to Maništušu Obelisk A₁

Source: Gelb 1979:76–7

I think I can show how and why this comes about. Figure 6.1 is the scheme developed by Gelb from side A group 1 of the obelisk, which records 17 sellers in 12 families in 2 groupings (plus 4 attached families), where each grouping is called **DUMU.DUMU** PN, i.e. 'descendants of PN', and all of them are called **DUMU.DUMU Mezizi**, that is, 'descendants of Mezizi', appearing here as the common or originating ancestor. From him descend what are clearly patrilines. Though for convenience we can refer to this as 'clan Mezizi' and they are acting collectively in alienating land, they by no means participate on an equal basis. Some are clearly senior and dominant, some merely present as witnesses, virtually passive onlookers. In the diagram the underlining represents what is stated on the obelisk, namely that, in addition to the price, those marked receive extra gifts in this ratio: of the two major branches of the 'clan', that on the left is clearly senior and I-ti-DINGIR (no. 1) pre-eminent in receiving the major gifts. Indeed of those called 'Lord of the Field' (**lugal gán me**/*bêlú eqlim*), only the senior man in the minor, i.e. central branch, receives other, though minor, gifts. Further the son of I-ti-DINGIR is also called Lord of the Field, in contrast to those not underlined who are called 'Brother-lords of the field' (**dumu gán-me**/*aḫū-bêlū eqlim*). Though of the same generation, their four lineages, of at most three generations' depth, appear to be grafted lineages and are of inferior status.

Descent groups provide access to and legitimation of property and position; they do not necessarily define residential pattern, or even household composition, though here I think that the minimal lineage and its property forms the core of the é, *bîtum* or *oikos*, and further that it takes the form of the extended family at the co-residential level: meaning by 'extended' precisely that it is extended laterally beyond its patrilineal core of three generations. Thus its internal structure could look as in Figure 6.2.

The terms **dagal** (Sumerian) and *rapaštum* (Akkadian), meaning 'wide' or 'broad' and thus 'extended', may be applicable here (cf. Gelb 1979:92). Diakonoff (1969c:179) had previously argued for the existence of 'extended patriarchal families or family communes', and Jacobsen (1957:119) argued that **lú-gal** originally denoted the great householder, great because he commanded the 'great house', **é-gal**, *ekallum*, which, in addition to his own immediate family, was really eminent because it contained 'his personal servants and retainers bound to him by exceptionally strong ties of dominance and obedience'.

We proceed from the father, La-mu-sa, of the senior Lord of the Field, I-ti-DINGIR and his younger or junior brother SI.A-um, who appears without issue, in contrast to I-ti-DINGIR, who is succeeded by Su-ru-uš-GI (no. 5 in Figure 6.1).

Completed family size from this period in Mesopotamia averages 2.2

Figure 6.2 The La-mu-sa *oikos*

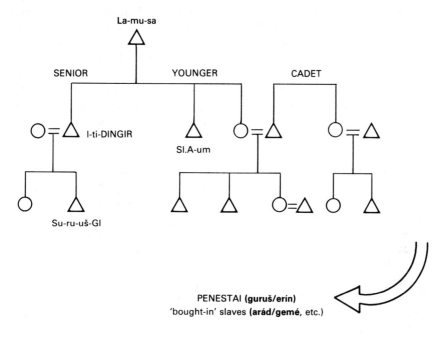

PENESTAI **(guruš/erín)**
'bought-in' slaves **(arád/gemé**, etc.)

(Gelb 1979:75), a very modern figure indicating a static indigenous population level at this time, so we may well assume a sister who marries. As this lineage is well provided her husband assumes matrilocal residence and an inferior position. He brings with him his sister, already or later married, who has offspring. I-ti-DINGIR's sister also has issue which, being the nephews and nieces of the paterfamilias, we will assume to be on the correct side of the kinship blanket, in contrast to those I have shown (Figure 6.2) on the right-hand side of the line as only cadet members of the lineage. None the less, at least up to the end of Sargonic times they are likely to be citizens, as against those below, the *penestai* or **guruš**, able-bodied men with no kinship connection at all, but from nearby ruined households, supplemented perhaps, according to the amount of land to be worked, or grain, leather, wool, etc., to be processed, by 'bought-in' slaves, called (in Sumerian) **arád**, if male, **gemé**, if female.

This is potentially a large grouping and not all its members necessarily inhabit the same building, though if not the whole group at least a substantial core would have been co-resident. One such structure may well be that excavated at Tell Madhhur in the Hamrin area of Diyala in Iraq (Killick and Roaf 1979:534–42). The isometric partial reconstruction by Susan Roaf (in M. Roaf 1982:43) of a late Ubaid two-storey house of about 14 m square on a tripartite plan, with a central cruciform hall, to the north and south of which were rows of rooms, should be compared with the plans of Ubaid temples at Eridu (conveniently in Seton-Lloyd 1978:42). Both share the tripartite layout, which is not surprising since the 'household' basis of Mesopotamian temple architecture has long been recognized. I therefore suggest that such large, multi-family, T-form houses are characteristic of the demands imposed by the concentration of resources and storage where rainfed agriculture is not viable or highly risky. A particularly striking example (Figure 6.3) comes from the Ubaidian site of Tell Abada (also in the Hamrin Basin, which lies at the

Figure 6.3 Plan of Building A, level II, at Tell Abada

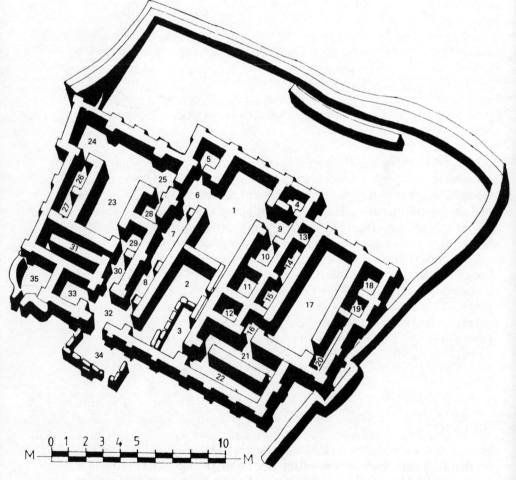

Source: Jasim 1985:II, fig. 15

same latitude as Samarra and Tell es-Sawwan, but between the Diyala River and the Zagros Mountains), especially valuable with over 80 per cent of the site excavated (Jasim 1985:I:16).

However, such conditions are not confined to the alluvium proper. The (earlier) Samarran site of Tell es-Sawwan, near Samarra on the east bank of the Tigris, sits on a bluff overlooking the river, at 220 × 110 m is fairly large, and dates from the middle of the sixth millennium BC. They kept domestic sheep, goats, and probably cattle (Flannery and Wheeler 1967:181), and grew emmer, two-row hulled and six-row naked and hulled barley, einkorn and bread wheat, plus flax (Helbaek 1964:47). Fishing was important and hunting of fallow deer and gazelle occurred, but very important is the presence of small ditches for simple irrigation, running along the edge of the site, supplementing its natural hydro-morphism. Both the type-site of Samarra and Tell es-Sawwan, some 11 km downstream, lie below the reliable 200 mm isohyet needed for rainfed agriculture (Flannery and Wheeler 1967:179); but not too far below it, located between the Assyrian steppe and the alluvium proper. The great importance of Tell es-Sawwan in showing the evolution of the Samarran 'irrigation culture' and in serving as a harbinger of historic patterns, was immediately recognized by its excavators (El-Wailly and Abu es-Soof 1965:24). Stamp seals of clay and stone also occur here.

Mud-brick cast in a mould, long to characterize Mesopotamian architecture, is first encountered at Tell es-Sawwan and from such bricks are constructed large multi-room buildings of the sort shown as early as level I, also in levels II and III, in Figure 6.4. Indeed continuity in architecture is marked throughout all five levels (El-Wailly and Abu es-Soof 1965:24).

1 Ecology and *oikos*

Watson (1978:131–58) has undertaken a comparative review of 'architectural differentiation in seven Near Eastern communities' of the sixth millennium BC. Five are located in northern and eastern Mesopotamia and two (Hacilar and Çatal Hüyük) in Anatolia. She concluded that:

> In spite of rather extreme variation in the categories discussed (overall settlement plan, area of houses, area of rooms), it nevertheless seems clear that the basic residential unit in each settlement was probably the same: a nuclear family. . . . Even the very large Hacilar living rooms contain only one hearth and do not appear to be multi-family dwellings.
>
> (Watson 1978:156)

All, that is, except Sawwan, one of the five Mesopotamian sites reviewed, where, particularly clearly by level III, surrounded by a mud-brick wall,

Figure 6.4 Building plans of three periods at Tell es-Sawwan

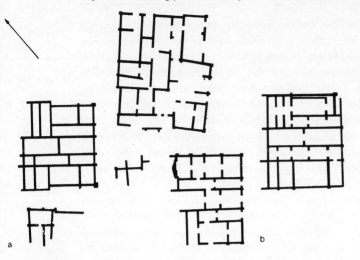
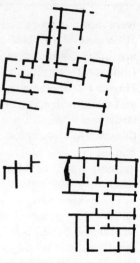

a   b

Tell es-Sawwan: plans of buildings of (a) level I and (b) level II (after Abu al-Soof and al-Wailly)

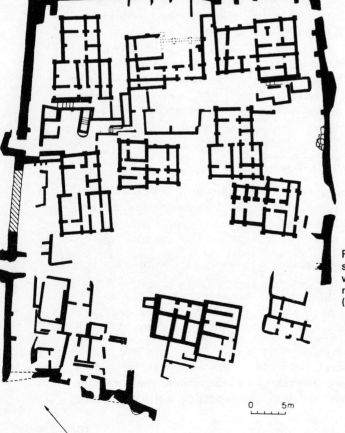

Plan of the Tell es-Sawwan settlement showing circuit wall of level IIIA and multi-roomed houses of level III (after Abu al-Soof)

0   5m

Source: Mellaart 1975:150–1

were 'at least seven, ten to twelve room houses of fairly uniform overall 'T-shaped' plan. These are made of mud brick with gypsum paving. There are also some large structures interpreted as granaries.' Watson (ibid.:145) continues: 'The Sawwan houses differ from the Hasanabad–Hassuna–Matarrah type in that they were not built around courtyards, and were detached from one another, most being freestanding individual structures.' Indeed one can be even more specific, for the excavators (Yasin 1970:10) speak of T-shaped buildings becoming the 'dominating feature' in level IIIa, and of 'rooms in this [upper] phase filled with gypsum granaries' (Yasin 1970:4) which, indeed, were 'scattered everywhere in their settlement' (ibid.:11).

Though the Sawwan structures are much earlier, smaller, and doubtless not socially stratified compared with later Ubaidian sites such as Tell Madhhur, I venture that here are encountered the early physical manifestations of the *oikos*, to be found only in the Samarran/Ubaidian line. But although *oikos* communities are confined to this cultural lineage, which, of course, leads from the Ubaid through Uruk periods into the Early Dynastic of historical Sumer, the number of sites on which *oikiai* occur are not few. Later instances are known as far north as Tepe Gawra (XV) and Erbil, where Uruk Period examples (Figure 6.5) from Tell Qalinj Agha clearly indicate the basic T-form central hall with flanking rooms.

A more complex and earlier example is Kheit Qasim III, a site in the Hamrin Basin, dated by its excavators to the Ubaid 3 period, around the beginning of the fifth millennium (C. Forest 1984:121). A complete building of 10·5 × 14 m was uncovered, constructed of mud bricks measuring 27 × 55 × 6 cm, making the wall 30 cm thick when plastered (ibid.:119). Complete exposure allows the circulation pattern to be specified (Figure 6.6). Entry is from the southeast only, whence access is had directly to the central hall, the stairway to the roof (30 cm-thick walls are barely adequate for a second storey), and to room 9. Chantal Forest (1984:120) points out that the central hall, with its associated rooms – 2, 4, plus 5, 13, and 14 – forms the most independent unit, one which could be closed off by doors. Running at right-angles to the main hall are two secondary halls. From the transverse of the T, access could be had from 17 into 3, 8 into 9, and 11 into 12, but not 13. All of the halls and some of the rooms were paved with mud brick, while 'in every hall were found a fire-place, built on a low rectangular mud-brick platform, and the remains of a storage chest or bin' (J. D. Forest 1984:85).

As for the social relations giving rise to the architecture, J. D. Forest (ibid.) observes that this is clearly a 'private dwelling', indicated both by the facilities (bins, fireplaces), and by the artefacts (pottery, flint, animal bones). Equally clearly, he continues, 'there are three dwelling units, functionally equivalent and self-sufficient, and [so] the house cannot

Figure 6.5 Tell Qalinj Agha

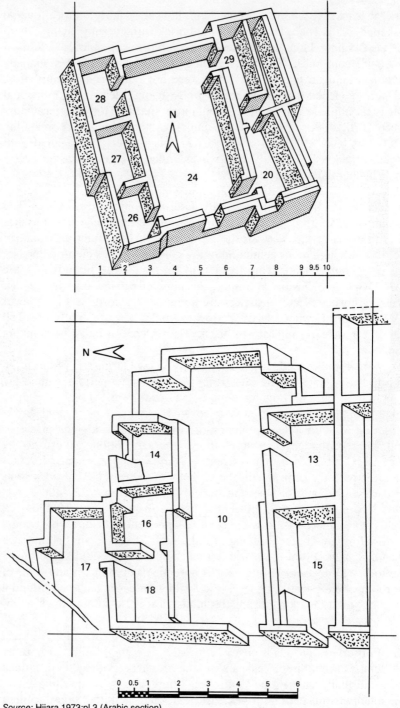

Source: Hijara 1973:pl.3 (Arabic section)

164

Figure 6.6 Kheit Qasim III: an Ubaid settlement in the Hamrin

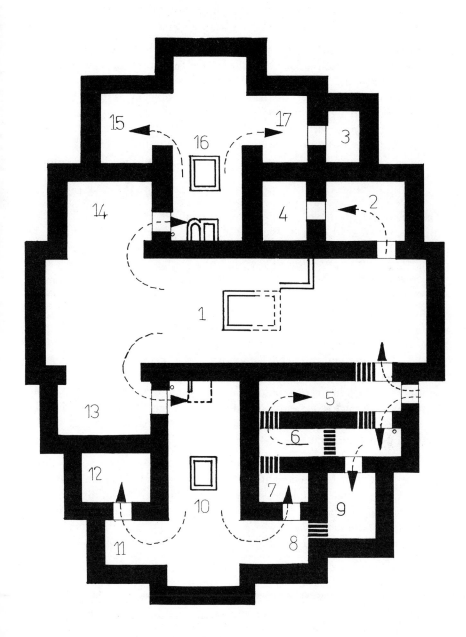

Source: Redrawn from C. Forest 1984:119 and 1980:222

correspond to a nuclear family'. And since the halls are unequal in size and number of attached rooms,

> we can infer that there was some kind of hierarchy within the inhabitants. I think that there are only two ways of extending the household while respecting that notion of hierarchy: it is either by multiplying the number of wives living in the house with their husband, or by multiplying the number of generations. The first hypothesis is to be rejected for several reasons. For example, and I am thinking of Tell Abade, it would be impossible for every male in any village to get two wives. Therefore I retain the second hypothesis until another possibility would be suggested.
>
> (J. D. Forest 1984:85)

That second hypothesis has been detailed above as the *augmented* and *stratified* household, that is, the *oikos*. In the case of Kheit Qasim III the central, dominant hall is likely that of the 'patriarch', with the smaller halls at right-angles to the main one being those of his sons' establishments. Too small overall to contain all the likely dependants, they are seemingly housed alongside in a separate multi-purpose building of markedly different design (Figure 6.7).

Finally, in the peri-historical Early Dynastic I period, *oikiai* are found exactly where we should expect to encounter them, right in the heart of the southern alluvium at Abu Salabikh. There, in what could be ancient Eresh, Postgate and Moon (1984:731), as early as the 1976 season (of a continuing programme), had identified in the West Mound area, 'four contemporary enclosures or compounds occupying the major part of the site during the Early Dynastic I period'. The existence of many such compounds means that they cannot be public buildings, so

> one is forced to the conclusion that each compound housed a single 'private' establishment and if we seek to interpret our plan in human terms, we must visualise a city composed architecturally of large enclosures and socially of corresponding groups of persons, presumably extended families.
>
> (Postgate and Moon 1984:731)

Not actually extended families, but households that include dependants who are non-kin; that is, augmented households structured around a dominant family. Something like this had indeed already been postulated by both Diakonoff and Gelb on documentary evidence, as Postgate and Moon (op. cit.) observe.

However, in a recent discussion of 'extended families' in Old Babylonian Ur, Diakonoff observes that

> the average group of (land)holders consisted of no less than 8 men

Figure 6.7 Kheit Qasim III: the main residence and the multi-purpose building

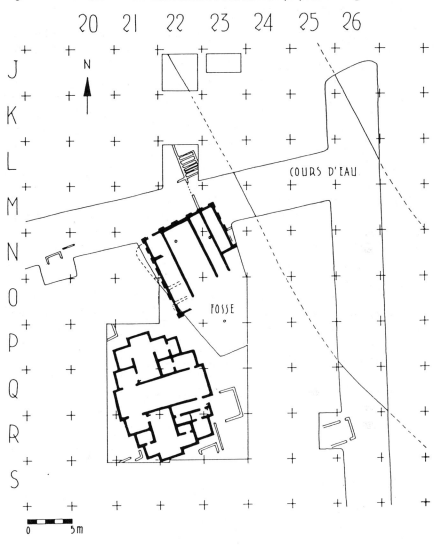

Source: C. Forest 1980:222

enjoying full property rights, which means that including women and children, the group would consist on an average of 30–40 persons, which by the order of magnitude corresponds to the data of Jankowska on the size of the extended families of the much more backward Arraphe in the foothills beyond the Tigris in the 15–14th centuries B.C.

(Diakonoff 1985:48–9)

While the size of the Lamusa Oikos fits this size rather precisely, it only does so if our cadet line agnates are reckoned to have 'full property rights', or if the statement is weakened to 'some property rights'. It may also be that the Lamusa Oikos is at the lower margin of viability, and that is why it is being forced to sell off no less than 150 hectares (Diakonoff 1982:38, n. 91).

That *oikiai* were not merely extended co-residential groups, but were economic entities, is clear from the analysis of archives and record-keeping in Sargonic Mesopotamia. Foster (1982a:17) distinguishes three main types of archive: 'family or private, household and great household', and he observes that the 'great household' archives, though they can deal with very large quantities of property 'are in many respects similar to the household archives, the differences amongst them being often ones of degree and scope'. That scope is illustrated by his profile of an 'ordinary household' archive from Gasur, indicating what the records actually dealt with (Table 6.1).

Table 6.1 Profile of a household archive, Gasur

Subject category	Including	Percentage of subjects counted
Grain		43
Food	Beer, oils and fats, legumes, flour, brewing ingredients	12
Land		10
Personnel management		9
Livestock	Sheep, cattle, goats, pigs, hides, sinews	9
Industrial products/materials	Pottery, textiles, wood, metals	4.5
Legal, commercial		4.5
Learner's exercises		4
Letters, bullae		4

Source: Foster 1982a:9

To this should be contrasted his (1982a:11) example of a 'Great Household' archive, in which grain references have fallen from 43 to a mere 6 per cent, food has risen from 12 to 29 per cent, industrial materials and products tripled from a mere 4.5 to 13 per cent and, accordingly, with personnel management references going from 9 to no less than 22 per cent.

Noteworthy is the very widespread nature of literacy and numeracy, with every such household containing at least one person able to read, write, and calculate.

This is utterly different from the situation elsewhere, for as K. C. Chang observes: 'The invention of writing in China was more associated with social identification than economic transaction, and it was initiated by the common potters rather than society's heroes and geniuses (such as a Ts'ang Chieh)' (1980:247). Most significantly, 'Membership in one's kin group was the first thing writing recorded, because it was the key to the ancient Chinese social order' (ibid.:248).

2 Corporate citizenship

Since all members of the *oikos* depended on the same resources, all would have had to live in close proximity, under the governance of the paterfamilias, such as I-ti-DINGIR. He was obviously one of the 'great', and we know that Mesopotamian cities were run by groups of elders, a king, and an assembly. The clearest picture textually comes not from the south but from the northeast, namely Aššur, where, as documented for the Old Assyrian period, roughly corresponding to the Old Babylonian period further south (*c.* 1,900–1,600 BC), the king was but the chief executive of the council without whom he could not act (Larsen 1976:152–3). We have already seen what has been called 'elders' acting as the Board of Directors of the temples. The term for elders is, in the plural, **ab-ba-ab-ba-me**, which has the same etymology as 'fathers'. City-states were run by a bicameral **unkin** or 'circle of the people', composed of **lú-tur-mah**, or *ṣahir rabi*, the 'small and great'; but literally, the 'young and old' (Jacobsen 1943, 1957).

The Elders' Council, written **AB+AS-uru**, consisted, it seems to me, of men of the standing of I-ti-DINGIR. The Elders' Council was supplemented by the Assembly of able-bodied adult men (**guruš-uru** or **mes**) which we can call the Popular Assembly. Conjointly they ruled with the king, and from their ranks, specifically of the 'senate' or Council of Elders (composed of the **gal**, the great ones or lords), the **lugal** arose, most likely as the leader of the citizen militia. They were always the basic military force, shown in the third millennium representations in tight phalanx formation (cf. Frankfort 1970: fig. 74).

Once the king, **lugal**, and his establishment, the **é-gal** (*ekallum*) had emerged as the palace during the Early Dynastic, sheer aggrandizement for the dynasty is as much a likely cause of the continual conflicts between city-states as were real matters of resources, specifically irrigable land and its water-supply. Sargon is said, by himself, to have conquered fifty cities, and that was not to defend his city of origin, Kish, for he established a new dynastic capital called Agade in the area of modern Baghdad.

Some of those defeated kings were already called **ensi**, and some he established in either a dependent or gubernatorial role, to which the term **ensí** was also applied. For **ensí** is the other term for kings to have emerged in Mesopotamia, and (like **en**-ship) it is older than **lugal**-ship. But rather than emerging directly from the ranks of the *puḫru(m)*, the assemblies or councils, the ensial function seems to have emerged from the temple in collaboration with the assemblies. As late as the reign of the reformer

Nabonidus (mid-first millennium BC), the assemblies retained a decisive role in the selection of temple officials (Dandamayev 1979:590).

By contrast the term **en** ('lord') stresses the priestly function, indeed the supreme priestly function, responsible for securing the fecundity of the land. Enlil, the chief executive of the Sumerian pantheon (whose president was An(u), the sky) was said to be 'the **en** of heaven, the **en** of bounty, and the **en** of the earth' (Jacobsen 1953:181). By contrast gods are never referred to as **ensí**. Under An(u) and Enlil the gods' assembly met in Enlil's holy city of Nippur to confer or withdraw kingship, and generally to shape the affairs of mankind, prominent in which was the ruin of cities.

3 Ensí and lugal as heads of state

Me's are the norms and techniques of civilization instituted by Enki 'the wise, the knowing' (literally 'Lord Earth', operationally 'Lord of the Sweet Waters') to produce world-order at Enlil's behest. With Inanna (Ishtar), 'Queen of Heaven' (and the store-house), Enki was the joint-third most important deity in Sumer and Akkad. Of the hundred or so **me**'s listed in the myth *Inanna and Enki: the Transfer of the Arts of Civilization from Eridu to Uruk*, the **EN**-ship comes first, long before kingship which is merely number nine (Kramer 1963:177). **EN**, the lord high priest, is known as a title as early as the Jemdet Nasr period around the end of the fourth and the beginning of the third millennium. **Lugal**, by contrast, is only known considerably later, the first fairly secure occurrence being from Kish, about 2,700 BC. This concurs with the mytho-historic Kinglist, which states that when kingship was lowered from heaven after the Flood, it was centred in Kish. At Kish too there is archaeological evidence for a royal palace at this time (Moorey 1964:83–98) and a city wall appears at Uruk.

However, while the element **EN** is compounded into both divine and royal names, **ensí** certainly is not so applied, but is reserved for purely human and even mundane functions of stewardship of temples and agricultural activities. Indeed the Akkadian rendering of **Ensí (PA.TE.SI)**, i.e. *iššaku(m)*, survived as late as the Old Babylonian period with the meaning 'agent' or manager of property.

Thus Diakonoff argues that:

> **Ensí** of a city (or the god of the city god) denotes 'priest who lays the foundation (of temples and other buildings)'. The logogram for the term signifies 'overseer laying the foundation (of a building)'. In fact all the most ancient inscriptions of Sumerian rulers are devoted to construction or reconstruction of temples and canals; military exploits

begin to be mentioned much later, at first as a subordinate clause in building inscriptions.

(Diakonoff 1969c:181)

Ensí, then, always had the sense of steward/governor/manager, originally of temple affairs on behalf of the real 'owner' of the household, its chief divinity. Later **ensí** was applied in the sense of a subordinate king or governor to a supreme king, ultimately becoming applied to a steward of private property. Indeed Jacobsen (1957:123) suggests that steward/ overseer was the original role of the **ensí**, as 'manager of the arable lands' and 'leader of the seasonal organisation of the townspeople for work on the fields'.

Lugal, by contrast, never had any connotations other than supremacy. Indeed in the north, as at Assur, the king was referred to as *išši'ak Aššur* (governor or steward of Assur), while the god (also called Aššur) of the city (*ālum*) is referred to as the **lugal** (*šarrum*), the real king of Assur (Larsen 1976:110–11). In stark contrast to 'productive manager' and cultic leadership 'the "king" **lugal**, in contrast to the **en** was from the beginning a purely political figure, a "war leader" ' (Jacobsen 1970d:384) chosen from the scions of the 'great', originally as a temporary commander. 'His residence, the **é-gal**, "great house" had no ties with the temple but is merely his own large private manor which, because of his office, comes to take on the public aspects of a "palace" ' (ibid.). Legislative functions are so far only known in connection with the **lugal**, indicating that his power was more concentrated and multiplex.

Names given to children during the Early Dynastic period are very revealing of the range of roles embraced by the **lugal**. They include: **lugal-ur-sag**, 'the king is a warrior'; **lugal-engar-zi**, 'the king is a good farmer'; **lugal-a-mah**, 'the king possesses great might'; **lugal-si-sa**, 'the king is (or exercises) justice'; **lugal-he-gal**, 'the king (brings about) abundance'; **lugal-za-dah**, 'King (shall we succeed) without you?'; **lugal-u$_4$-sur$_x$** (BU)se, 'may the king (live) unto distant days'; **lugal-u-mah**, 'the king stands triumphant'; and **lugal-pa-e**, 'the king appears in a thunderclap' (Edzard 1974a:142).

Arms and armour in the hands of kings and their soldiery, mostly militia-based, were employed for inter-community hostilities, not for internal policing and control (Watkins 1978:485). Indeed we often encounter kings writing to local authorities instructing them to enforce some law or protect some individuals using their own local resources. For the civil regulatory functions were performed 'democratically', so to speak, by the local councils, through customary law, by ideological pressure, and, when this was inadequate, by application of locally raised armed force.

According to Dandamayev (1982:40), as late as the seventh to the fourth centuries BC, Babylonia remained a complex of conciliar structures. Texts of this period mention *puḫru ša mati*, 'the assembly of the country', *puḫru ummâni*, 'the assembly of the people', and assemblies of cities such as Babylon, Kutha, Nippur, Sippar, Uruk, etc. Hence, while the king had concentrated in his hands the supreme political decisions, especially of war and peace, city and civil matters, including the internal affairs of ethnic groups like Egyptians and Jews, continued to be administered by their own elders and councils.

The early exercises in monarchic enterprise given next for their illustrative value should not blind us to the fundamental political order down the millenniums.

4 Monarchic initiatives

Lagash in southwestern Mesopotamia, probably the largest in area of the third millennium city-states (Maekawa 1973–4:142), due to the accidents of recovery looms large in the textual reconstruction of Mesopotamian society. It included, as well as the city Lagaš (al-Hibba), the city of Girsu (present Tello) and NINA (Zurghul). It also had a port city and area called Gu-ab-ba ('the seashore'), which included the temple of Nin-mar.

If, as argued, all Mesopotamian city-states were distinct entities with particular economic and historical fortunes, then no city-state can be fully representative of others. None the less, as all share key cultural institutions and formal organizations and were in continual interaction, the relations between hierarchies and Lagash society as a whole, well summarized by Maekawa, appear highly illuminating:

> Ur- Nanše established a dynasty, probably in the latter half of the 26th century B.C., and five successive rulers reigned in the city-state of Lagash for about a century. After the short reign of En-an-na-túm II the fifth ruler of the dynasty, En-èn-tar-zi, who had been the highest administrator (sanga) of the temple of Nin-gír-su, and seems not to have had a direct blood relationship with En-an-na-túm II became ensí. Five years later, his son Lugal-an-da succeeded him, and in turn was deprived of his political power by Uru-KA(-gi-na)[2] during the seventh year of his reign.
>
> Changing his political title ensí to lugal (king) after about a year, Uru-KA-gi-na declared his new policies of 'reforms' for the purpose of eliminating the social abuses which, according to his 'reform'-texts, had become grave problems under the preceding ensís.
>
> (Maekawa 1973–4:78–9)

Kings of the Ur-Nanše Dynasty and their successors are shown by Maekawa in Table 6.2 (the last three with the names of their queens).

Eannatum, the third in this series, was a particularly successful ruler in

Table 6.2 The rulers of the Ur-^dNanše Dynasty and its successors at Lagash

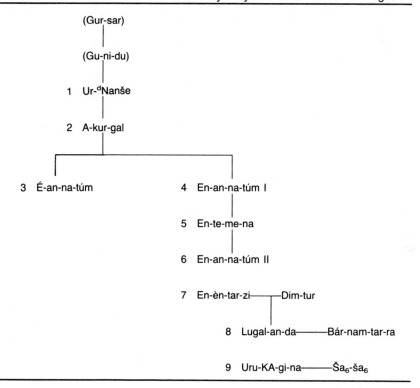

Source: Maekawa 1973–4:79

a line of generally successful rulers, none of whom is actually mentioned in the Sumerian Kinglist. None the less, in the ongoing contest with Lagash's neighbour Umma over productive borderlands called Gu'edena, Eannatum prevailed sufficiently to force Umma's ruler to swear oaths that he would not cross the old canal border (Edzard 1974:971). Eannatum was militarily successful enough to call himself **lugal kiši**, 'King of Kish', implying hegemony over, though not mastery of, the whole of Sumer and Akkad. This because his arms prevailed beyond the bounds of Babylonia itself.

Lugal kiši was always the formula for 'King of Kish'; proper, as the Kinglist states that the very model of kingship (**nam lugal**) derived from Kish 'after the flood'. Umma's rulers habitually referred to themselves as **lugal**, but those of Lagash, such as Eannatum, celebrated the title of **ensí**. And as his is a period (around 2,500 BC) in which lengthy inscriptions become available, it is worth reproducing one at length for the light it sheds not only on elite ideology, but through that to actual events and relationships.

What follows is an inscription translated by S. N. Kramer (1963:309–10), carved on a boulder and dedicated to the god Ningirsu (lord of Girsu), or Ninurta as he is called when worshipped at his temple in Nippur. He is 'lord of the floodstorm' in the Eninnu temple at Girsu, the 'ploughman of Enlil' as Ninurta at Nippur, the main cultic centre of Sumer:

> FOR NINGIRSU – Eannatum, the **ensí** of Lagash, whose name Enlil had pronounced, to whom Ningirsu had given strength, whom Nanshe had chosen in (her) heart, whom Ninhursag had constantly nourished with (her) milk, whom Inanna had called by a good name, to whom Enki had given understanding, the beloved of Dumuzi-Abzu, the trusted one of Hendursag, the beloved friend of Lugaluru, the son of Akurgal, the **ensí** of Lagash – his (i.e. Eannatum's) grandfather was Ur-Nanshe, the **ensí** of Lagash – restored Girsu for Ningirsu; built for him the wall of the 'holy city';[3] (and) built Nina for Nanshe.

This first section, while 'ensial' in that it rejoices in the gods' blessing upon Eannatum as a pious steward nourished by the gods and succeeding with their help (while he succours their houses, namely temples), none the less carries the implicit message that, appointed by the gods, the pious **ensí** was answerable only to them.

Success itself is both the measure and justification of this, for, after all:

> Eannatum conquered Elam, the lofty mountain, (and) heaped up their (that is, the Elamites') burial mounds. He conquered the **ensí** of Urua, who had planted the standard of the city (Urua) at their head (that is, at the head of the people of Urua), (and) heaped up their burial mounds. He conquered Umma (and) heaped up their twenty burial mounds; returned Guedinna, his beloved field, to Ningirsu. He conquered Erech [Uruk]; conquered Ur; conquered Kiutu; laid waste to Uruaz (and) killed its **ensí**; laid waste to Mishime; destroyed Adua.

In the sections immediately above and below Eannatum shows his prowess as a great lord of battle before whom the armies of no other cities could stand. The slaughter of warriors at this time (ED III) is indicative of the absence of application for slave labour.

> With Eannatum, whose name Ningirsu had pronounced, the foreign lands fought. In the year that the king of Akshak rose up (to do battle), Eannatum, whose name Ningirsu had pronounced, smote Zuzu, the king of Akshak, from the Antasurra of Ningirsu up to Akshak and destroyed him. At that time, he (Eannatum) dug a new canal for Ningirsu (and) named it Lummagimdug after his *Tidnu* name, Lumma – Eannatum was his Sumerian name.

If extensive slave labour was not productive in Mesopotamia, developing the infrastructure of canals certainly was, and its glory was such that

Eannatum titled it with his own intimate Semitic name.

> To Eannatum, the **ensí** of Lagash, whom Ningirsu had conceived of (in his mind), Inanna, because she loved him, gave the kingship of Kish in addition to the **ensí**-ship of Lagash.
>
> With Eannatum, (the people of) Elam fought; he (Eannatum) drove (the people of) Elam back to their land. Kish fought with him; he drove the king of Akshak back to his land.
>
> Eannatum, the **ensí** of Lagash, who makes the foreign lands submit to Ningirsu, smote Elam, Shubur, (and) Urua from the Asuhur (canal). He smote Kish, Akshak, and Mari from the Antasurra of Ningirsu.
>
> He reinforced (the walls of the canal) Lummagimdug for Ningirsu and presented it to him as a gift. (Then) Eannatum, to whom Ningirsu had given strength, built the reservoir of (the canal) Lummagimdug containing (?) 3,600 **gur** of 2 **ul** (probably about 57,600 gallons).[4]
>
> Eannatum, whom Ningirsu had conceived of (in his mind), (and) whose (personal) god is Shulutula, built for him (Ningirsu) the palace, Tirash.

Interesting too is the wide geographical spread of those with whom Eannatum fought: from Mari on the upper Euphrates some 280 miles from Nippur, through Akshak, near to Kish in Akkad (Babylonia), to Elam across the Tigris in Iranian Khuzistan, whose centre at Susa was about 160 miles from Nippur. It is worthwhile reminding ourselves at this point that in Sumer with Akkad there were only fourteen major cities in the Early Dynastic period. They were, from north to south: Sippar, Kish, Akshak, Larak, Nippur, Adab, Suruppak, Umma, Lagash, Bad-tibira, Uruk, Larsa, Ur, and Eridu.

5 Monarchy to proto-empire

Eannatum's triumphs foreshadowed the first approximation to the world's earliest empire under Sargon, called 'the Great', after whom the period (2,334–2,154 BC) is named and whose exploits, like those of Gilgameš, entered the corpus not only of Mesopotamian but also of Near Eastern legends. Eannatum's temporary dominance over the other city-states was more after the traditional pattern of 'Kings of Kish', whose military predominance and personal prestige may have been hegemonic, but who did not attempt unified government. That would have been an almost physical impossibility in Frankfort's view (1978:217).

Since states were essentially self-sufficient, competing for the same resources of land and water, government over them came down to arbitrating disputes, such as Mesilim (c. 2,550 BC) King of Kish, did between Umma and Lagash; or extending those same resources by digging further canals. Trade, apart from local circulation, seems to have been more in the nature of negative reciprocity, that is military campaigns and forcible seizure, apart from 'the Dilmun trade' (overseas) and exchanges with pastoralists, discussed below.

There was accordingly no compelling economic basis for a regional ('imperial') government, but certainly there were political advantages in suppressing internal conflict and turning Mesopotamian attention outwards towards a more classical Romano-Greek form of tribute. Sargon faced ferocious autonomatist opposition in trying to add another functional level of rule above the city-state government, such that he not only had to undertake numerous campaigns but even had to found a new 'imperial' city, Agade, whence the name Akkadian derives. Sargon was, it seems, propelled into this role of supplanting city-state conflict by the career of a particularly destructive **ensí** of Umma, one Lugalzagesi who 'burned, looted and destroyed practically all the holy places of Lagaš' (Kramer 1963:58). While there had been traditional (and typical) rivalry between those two cities, this anti-cultural behaviour was the sort of thing Sumerians expected only of the savages of the mountains, such as Gutians or Elamites. It seems, however, that Lugalzagesi was a bona fide berserk for, according to Falkenstein,

> Lugalzagesi of Umma was, like his father, originally an 'ecstatic' (**mah**) in the service of the chief goddess of the city and he joined the community of priests at Uruk in the rank of a 'purification priest' of the god of heaven after he had made Uruk the centre of his kingdom.
>
> (Falkenstein 1979:11)

The suggestion by Peebles and Kus (1977:444), following Gibson (1974), that warfare could be a prime means of upward social mobility in an otherwise rigidly ranked society seems very germane here, especially when coupled to the role of the priesthood as in Lugalzagesi's case, a point stressed by Falkenstein (op. cit.). It should be remembered that the true and presiding 'owner' of the city was its god and both human ruler and priests were his 'slaves'.

Indeed Sargon's own career appears as a parallel case of dramatic upward mobility to dominance. The humble origins of Sargon himself are of course legendary, even archetypal. It was he, an orphan, who was supposedly found floating in a basket upon the Euphrates. Raised as a gardener (in some accounts), he somehow found his way into the court of Ur-Zababa of Kish whom he eventually replaced. However the Kinglist cites four or five others before the termination of the Dynasty of Kish and they must have been contemporaries of Sargon (who reigned for over half a century) for he did not rule all of Mesopotamia the whole time. Indeed, the confusion over who was 'King of Kish' seems to be a legendary confusion (and all legends are confused) between the **lugal**-ship (nominally of all Mesopotamia), and actual rule over the city of Kish.

Hallo and Simpson (1971:55–6) suggest that

> During those fifty years Sargon seems to have been busy establishing himself as an independent ruler at Akkad, the new city he built somewhere on the Euphrates (and still not discovered) and campaigning far beyond the traditional borders of Sumer and Akkad . . . thus he established his authority in a great ring round Sumer and Akkad,

from southeast Anatolia to Elam and Dilmun. Only then, in this reconstruction, do the still independent city-states of Sumer proper, under Lugalzagesi of Uruk, rise against Sargon in his old age. Even then, he seems to have sought an accommodation with Lugalzagesi; but when this failed Sargon moved with great force. Lugalzagesi, 'King of the Land', was taken prisoner along with his 'fifty governors', i.e. **ensís**. But this is best told in terms of an inscription of Sargon's on the pedestal of a statue. What is notable is not only the sheer extent of his campaigns but that he claimed hegemony from the coast of the Mediterranean to the Gulf.

> Sargon, the king of Akkad, the **maškim** of Inanna, the king of Kish, the **guda**-priest of An, the king of the Land, the great **ensí** of Enlil, laid waste the city of Uruk, destroyed its wall; fought with the men of Uruk, conquered them; fought with Lugalzagesi, the king of Uruk, took him prisoner (and) brought him in a neck-stock to the gate of Enlil.[5]
>
> Sargon, the king of Akkad, fought with the men of Ur, conquered them, laid waste their city, (and) destroyed its walls: laid waste E-Ninmar, destroyed its walls, laid waste its territory from Lagash to the sea, washed his weapons in the sea (the Gulf); fought with the men of Umma, conquered them, laid waste their city, (and) destroyed its walls.
>
> To Sargon, king of the Land, Enlil gave no rival; (indeed) Enlil gave him the entire territory from the sea above to the sea below.[6]
>
> Akkadians[7] held the **ensí**-ships (everywhere) from the lower sea and above; the men of Mari (and) the men of Elam served Sargon, the king of the Land (as their master).
>
> Sargon, the king of the Land, restored Kish (and) gave that city to them (the men of Kish) as a dwelling place.
>
> Whoever destroys this inscription – may Utu [the sun god] tear out his foundation (from under him); may he bereave him of his seed.
>
> (Kramer 1963:324)

Much of this is just rhetoric, and as such at odds with likely practice. While city destructions far afield are well attested archaeologically (e.g. Tell Leilan in Subir), total destructions in the heartlands are much less likely. The point was to destroy rivals, not to rule over a desert. Even

Lugalzagesi, after his humiliation, was allowed to return to his base as governor under the (now) supreme overlord. Presumably only **ensís** who had died fighting or who were intractable were replaced by Akkadians as the inscription suggests. Integrated bureaucratic, military, and economic rule did not obtain until Ur III times, and that was a relatively brief episode.

It is interesting that as late as this, and with Sargon commonly and all too loosely regarded as history's first emperor, the standing army at the capital amounted to only 5,400 soldiers. This should tell us something about the numbers of professional warriors at the disposal of rulers of individual city-states, and perhaps why they found it often so difficult to resist incursions by Gutians, Amorites, and other non-city-dwellers. It should also tell us something about the expense of providing bronze arms and armour for warriors, as a result of which its use was probably confined to professionals and the aristocracy; hence its occurrence in the better class of burials (Moorey 1982:32).

In armies almost entirely consisting of phalanxes of spearmen, helmets, shields, and armour would largely have been of leather. In productive uses too, copper and bronze were scarce and precious. Where, as generally, alternatives were available those were employed. 'Until at least the Akkadian period sickles with a flint edge were still the predominant type. . . . Where baked clay, ground stone, chipped flint, bone or wood sufficed for agricultural tools then they continued in use, as in prehistoric craft traditions' (ibid.).

Bronze and even copper ingots (the basic register of exchange values until the Akkadian period) were, then, an elite good, 'subject to rigorous bureaucratic control, constant recycling and use only for essential artifacts' (ibid.). An indicator of the value and scarcity of metal even for the elite is that arrowheads and spearheads

> and where necessary daggers and axeheads, were issued by a central authority in periods of conflict to the main body of troops, and then withdrawn into the city, temple or palace armoury. Significantly, when such arms appear with men of markedly lower status, they are the guards of the 'Royal Tombs' at Ur: presumably the standing royal guard and part of the household.
>
> (Moorey 1982:32–3)

The primary application of metal was thus warfare and warfare is both negative trade and negative production of subsistence. According to Jacobsen ((1957) 1970c:143) 'In the myths (4th millennium) life was on the whole peaceful, with only an occasional serious threat of war.' In the subsequent millennium, however, war became the rule in the epics, cities were ringed with large defensive walls, their rulers thought mainly of war and conquest and thus the danger of sudden attack was an ever present reality. The risks involved in such attacks were indeed real and serious.

G. A. Johnson, discussing 'Local Exchange and Early State Development in Southwest Iran' on the basis of his survey work there, specifically locates state formation on the Susiana plain of Khuzistan in the Early Uruk period of the fourth millennium:

> The first indication of potential external conflict appears in Middle Uruk with a concentration of large settlements on the margins of the settlement system. The first indications of internal conflict do not appear until late Uruk, well after the development of state level organisation.
>
> (G. A. Johnson 1973:157)

Susiana, however, is not, be it noted, in the 'heartlands' of the alluvium, where competition might be expected to be the fiercest. There, work by Hans Nissen on the city wall of Uruk indicates that

> the records of the subsequent Early Dynastic II and III periods are full of local fights between neighbouring cities, such as the one known from contemporary sources between the old centre of Lagash and the new centre of Umma over a stretch of borderland. It is probable therefore that the first city wall of Uruk was a response to feared or actual hostilities from the new emerging centres. This would make the earliest wall of Uruk a product of the changes in the distribution of power at the end of the Early Dynastic I period.
>
> (Nissen 1972:796)

We can see, however, why Sargon's grandson Naram Sin (2,254–2,218 BC) would want to destroy Ebla in Upper Syria, which, an inscription reads, 'since the beginning of mankind no king had ever destroyed'. Ebla was the major power in the north and stood between Akkad and the wood and mineral resources of the Amanus, Anatolia, and Cyprus (Mattiae 1980:174–8). The point was to thrive by monopolizing exchange and extracting tribute, and it seems Sargon only opened the way, as we read from another of his tablets:

> Sargon, the king of Kish, triumphed in thirty-four battles (over the cities) up to the edge of the sea (and) destroyed their walls. He made the ships from Meluhha,[8] the ships from Magan,[9] (and) the ships from Dilmun[10] tie up alongside the quay of Agade.
>
> Sargon, the king, prostrated himself before Dagan[11] (and) made supplication to him: (and) he (Dagan) gave him the upper land, (namely) Mari, Yarmuti, (and) Ebla up to the Cedar Forest (and) up to the Silver Mountain.
>
> Sargon, the king, to whom Enlil permitted no rival – 5,400 warriors ate bread daily before him.

> Whoever destroys this inscription – may An destroy his name; may Enlil exterminate his seed; may Inanna . . .
>
> (Kramer 1963:324)

6 The norms of rulership

Writing of the later (Hammurabic) Dynasty (1,894–1,595 BC), Diakonoff (1969c:199), while observing that by this time a 'centralised despotic monarchy' had formed,[12] yet remarks that 'the validity of the authority of the king over all Babylonia depended on his exercising in every "nome" the function of high priest to its local deity'. And we know too that from the earliest period 'The building and upkeep of temples was of all civic functions the one perhaps most closely linked to chief magistrate or king' (Hallo (1957) 1963b:142).

As 'chief magistrate' the king exercised also the 'chief judgeship', since he ultimately held both divine and physical sanctions; a relationship made clear in the preamble to the law code of Lipit-Ishtar (c. 1,934 BC):

> the wise shepherd, whose name had been pronounced by Nuamnir (i.e. Enlil) – to the princeship of the land in order to establish justice in the land, to banish complaints, to turn back enmity (and) rebellion by the force of arms, (and) to bring well-being to the Sumerians and Akkadians, then I, Lipit-Ishtar, the humble shepherd of Nippur, the stalwart farmer of Ur, who abandons not Eridu, the suitable lord of Erech (Uruk), king of Isin, king of Sumer and Akkad, who am fit for the heart of Inanna, established justice in Sumer and Akkad in accordance with the word of Enlil.
>
> (Kramer 1963:336)

This prologue goes on to assert, in very Confucian 'rectification' terms, how Lipit-Ishtar made all the fundamental social categories (fathers, sons, husbands, wives, etc.) live up to the social responsibilities inherent in those statuses.[13] Indeed the great codices of Mesopotamia are all essentially 'rectifications' of established practices rather than innovations, with, for instance, clarification and updating of compensations for sundry offences. Thus the surviving fragments of Ur-Nammu's (c. 2,112 BC) code at the outset of the Ur III period, consist of the amount due in recompense for loss of foot, bones, or nose, through misuse of weapons or tools. Even the great 'reform' code of Urukagina (i.e. Uruinimgina) (c. 2,300 BC), though having the widest scope known, seeks, like the *mīšarum*, cancellation of debts that accompanied a new reign, to re-establish things as hitherto. This applies particularly to *andurāru(m)* royal acts (in Sumerian **ama.ar.gi₄** or **ama.gi₄**) which from as early as the time of Entemena (c. 2,450 BC) referred especially to the freeing of slaves and the release of cities from oppressive burdens (Lemche 1979:11–22).

Likewise with the most famous because most complete of the Mesopot-amian codes, that of Hammurabi (*c.* 1,790 BC), we see in it 'an Akkadian compilation of laws based largely on Sumerian prototypes' (Kramer 1963:295). It was not the great innovation that previous generations imagined, though it did have enormous influence on the subsequent history of the Near East (ibid.).

But not only transcendental and physical power focus upon kingship, administrative responsibilities did too. Even the great autocrat Hammurabi is inextricably involved in mundane daily routine, as may be seen in a group of texts from Sippar where an agricultural official, Šamaš-hazir, is instructed by the king to collect his records and those of his subordinates and to meet Hammurabi in Sippar to 'go over the books' together (Ellis 1976:14).

Maine, who can have known next to nothing of ancient Mesopotamian kingship since Assyriology was then still in its formative stages, yet wrote most appositely (in *Dissertations on Early Law and Custom*):

> Whenever in the records of very ancient societies, belonging to races with which we have some affinity, we come upon a personage resembling him whom we call the King, he is almost always associated with the administration of justice. The King is often much more than a judge. He is all but invariably a general or military chief. He is constantly a priest and chief priest. But whatever else he may be, he seldom fails to be a judge, though his relation to justice may not be exactly that with with which we are familiar.
>
> (Maine 1883:160)

In those his civil functions, the king was on the one hand constrained by custom and belief, on the other assisted by subordinate but relatively autonomous and equally traditional government organs. Thus, in this Hammurabic period of 'centralised despotic monarchy' as Diakonoff (1969c:199) calls it, even here the state-level royal administration and community organs were linked through the town mayor or village headman (*rabiānum*), presiding over the community Council of Elders (*sibūtum*) and the community court of law, the latter sometimes identical with the former and sometimes a special committee of it. The (*rabiā-num*) and the Council together dealt with problems of landownership and local administrative matters; the *rabiānum* and the community had the duty to arrest robbers on the territory of the community, failing which they had to compensate the victims for their losses.

We noticed above the central role of compensation; and we see here the intrinsic governmental role of 'judging', even by subsidiary organs. There seems indeed to have been no judges by profession (except perhaps for seven 'royal judges' at Nippur), but instead anyone of substance might serve (Kramer, op. cit.:86, where a list of occupations is given). Those criteria also applied to the signatories to court decisions (**ditilla**), both to the actual notary himself (**maškim**) and likewise to the 'witnesses', who functioned either as witnesses in the civil sense (as 'recorders' but not as those giving evidence), or else as a jury. Oaths, however, were not administered in court but in a temple (ibid.:86–7), and none of those 'legal' roles was 'a regular and permanent profession' (ibid.). What we see here is law functioning as the intersection of ideology, administration, and representation.

> Alongside the Council of Elders there existed other organs of community self-government such as the Popular Assembly of a town community (*ālum*) and the assemblage of a city ward (*bābtum*). The functions of the Council, the Popular Assembly and the assemblage of the city ward probably differed in the various communities. The community organs had their own officials (keepers of records, wardens, etc.), a treasury, etc. There existed also undivided tracts of community land, although they were not extensive.
>
> (Diakonoff 1969c:200)

So there was a great deal of continuity, autonomy, and hence a rather circumscribed autocracy, though Diakonoff himself does wrestle with the 'Oriental Despotism' phrase, but, in the light of the existence of 'collective self-government organs' concludes that the sphere of despotism was limited 'so to speak, [to] super-community and extra-community relations' (ibid.:202). That is, to relations between city-states, and between the city-states of Mesopotamia and external forces.

Specifically merchant cities like Sippar, studied for the period from 1,894 to 1,595 BC by R. Harris (1975:69), were if anything even more autonomous, with the town run predominantly by and for merchants and in which the *kārum* (quay) was not only the locus of trade but of administration. And notwithstanding the long strides 'from status to contract' made by this time at least in a predominantly mercantile city like Sippar where, indeed, most of the documents recovered so far have been contracts of some sort, the central role of religious ideology is still manifest, even in specifically commercial affairs: 'In the very early part of the Old Babylonian period, when Sippar is ruled by local rulers, the legal texts specify the curses to be inflicted on the party who breaks the agreement' (Harris, op. cit.:133).

Later, however, action triumphed over imprecations, with contracts threatening plaintiffs that 'their (sic) noses will be pierced, his hands stretched out [in a stock?] and he will (thus) walk about the city square of Sippar' as Harris quotes from one such (op. cit.). Records of those consequences actually ensuing also exist. Further, lawsuits can also be won or lost on the basis of whether or not the oath to be administered in the sanctuary of the temple of Shamash is taken or refused (ibid.:144).

And, as suggested above, in the private economy of buying, selling, and leasing, the king conforms to written contract just like a private, though wealthy, citizen.

Until Hammurabic times, by when the burden may have been confined to *ilku* plot holders (Komoroczy 1976:34), all citizens were obliged to do corvée labour on the infrastructure (roads and canals), or provide substitutes. Indeed 'women are also included and may have been able to substitute for their husbands' (Harris 1975:115). But most significantly, the form of social integration involved in a period usually regarded (e.g. by Diakonoff 1969c:198–9) as one of increased commercial[14] opportunity after a tight Ur III period of state control, is indicated from a document related by R. Harris:

> The bailiff (of Sippar), Abum-waqar, hires a man to carry the divine symbol of Šamaš about the countryside in order to collect the barley tithe from the devotees of the god and bring it to Sippar. Since the first witness to this hire [*sic*] contract is the *rabiānu* (mayor), the bailiff in this case is apparently acting on behalf of the city and not the temple.
>
> (R. Harris 1975:82)

This, it should be noted, in the highly commercialized city of Sippar, and at a time when, Lamberg-Karlovsky (1975:349–59) reminds us, there had long been specialized merchants in long-distance trade and even merchant colonies in Anatolia. Indeed the divine symbols were leased out and carried about the countryside for a number of reasons: to ensure the just collection of taxes and tithes, the fair distribution and storage of the harvest yield, and to further the settlement of disputes (R. Harris, op. cit.: 204). And lest it be thought that such ideological inducements applied only to a traditional and rural peasantry, merchants and their creditors did their final reckoning in the Šamaš temple to liquidate their partnerships and liabilities, there dividing any profits (ibid.:262).

7 Organization of the economy

From Akkadian times, at least (that is, from *c.* 2,300 BC), 'there appears to have been a fairly continuous band of cultivation that varied in width but extended down the centre of the alluvium for virtually its whole length, from Sippar to the head of the Gulf' (R. McC. Adams 1981:147). Large labour gangs, consisting of both men and women (**guruš** and **gemé**) and amounting to about one-fifth of the urban population (excepting Nippur and Ur, privileged by cult and power respectively) were assembled in the south to work progressively northward as the wheat and barley harvest became sequentially due between April and June (ibid.:145–6). None the less, apart from this extensive organization of labour, 'marked regional interdependence was a less constant feature, perhaps confined to the Ur III period' (ibid.:147).

Not only was the return to seed, at 38- to 39-fold in Ur III times, high by European standards up to the present, though in decline from 41-fold in the time of Urukagina to 36-fold for the Neo-Babylonian period according to Jones (1976:60–1),[15] but productivity was likewise high at harvest, the critical time, with texts recording 3.53 hectares harvested per person (although about half of this area should have been fallow) (Adams, op. cit.:146). This is both a creditable and credible figure, for under similar conditions in the same areas the Iraqi Bureau of Statistics (1954) gives the average number of hectares per agricultural worker as 3.24 in harvest.

About half of gross yield was consumed in costs of production, as T. B. Jones's invaluable study of Ur III economic texts (op. cit.:41–61) makes clear. For instance,

> in the territory of Lagash a dozen or more temple establishments were responsible for cultivating most of the arable land. . . . The main crop was barley, and in any given year the yield averaged better than two million bushels. About half of this amount was consumed by the cost of production (wages for workers, feed for draft animals and the like), and a quarter went to the king as royal tax. The remaining 25% accrued to the priests. From this they fed themselves, paid out seed grain, sent large quantities to Nippur, provided the grain for milling, and so on.
>
> (T. B. Jones 1976:57)

The relative amounts expended by an official so charged, one Bazi, are clearly illustrated in the pie chart (Figure 6.8).

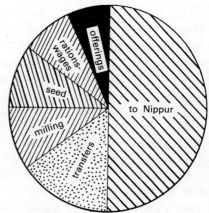

Figure 6.8 Relative amounts of grain (in **kur**) expended by Bazi for various purposes

Source: T.B. Jones 1976:57

Product flows are represented in Figure 6.9, based on the account tablet of Ur-dingirra, **sanga** of the divine Shulgi, the first Sumerian king to be deified in his own lifetime (and indeed at his own instigation) (Klein 1981:8).

Figure 6.9 A production and distribution flow chart

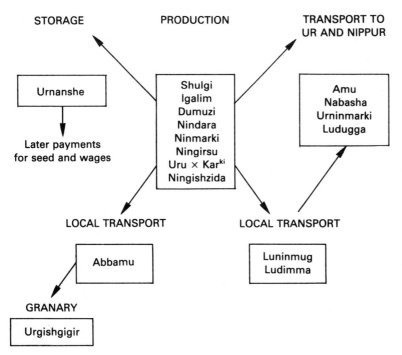

Source: T.B. Jones 1976:59

The core box, marked 'Production', contains the names of temple establishments. Abbamu (lower left) was the ship captain who delivered grain from various establishments to the granary superintendent, Urgishgigir (bottom left). Storage (upper left) was effected by Ur-dam, agent of Ur-Nanše 'for storage and ultimate distribution in the same manner as illustrated by the accounts of Bazi: most of the remainder was stored by Ur-dingirra in local barns' (T. B. Jones, op. cit.:58). Ludimma (lower right) and both Amu and Urninmarki (upper right) are yet more boatmen, while Ludugga and Nabasha are granary superintendents responsible for transport as well as storage. In all, Ur-dingirra, the **sanga**, disposed of 3,700 **kur** where a **kur** or **gur** is 300 litres (ibid.).

In this context it is worth bearing in mind that 'three **silà** of grain per day was the normal subsistence wage for Sumerian workers unable to make special demands upon the economy by virtue of skills or

185

importance' (Jones and Snyder 1961:258). That, at minimum, works out at 2.4 litres of grain per worker per day.[16] While adequate in calories, being in excess of the required 3,000 daily for an adult, such a diet would be intrinsically deficient in both protein and minerals, and vitamins too, were it the sole means of sustenance (Ellison 1983:148–9). Children, on a pro rata diet, would be even more seriously affected. Pastoral nomads, with a much higher protein diet, enjoy better health and hygiene than contemporary and, very likely, historic peasants of the region (Barth 1960:82). However, diet was supplemented by the oil and beer in rations, and by procurement either from the family holding or by purchase. A standard wool allowance (linen being reserved for priests and the wealthy) seems to have been around 10 **manna** (Jacobsen 1970b:221); with one **manna** equivalent to about 500 g; or more exactly 504 g $\pm$ 30–40 g (M. A. Powell 1979:88).

The wool and meat requirements were met by continuous movements from the periphery of Mesopotamia to the temple centres, funnelled largely through Drehem (Calvot 1969:103–13) to supplement the state herds kept on both the alluvial fallow and upon the surrounding non-cultivable (**edin**) steppelands (Adams 1981:148). Steppe, stubble, and riparian verdure were, however, systematically linked in the ecology of pastoral nomadism, tribally organized. To the plains 'steppe nomads came in the spring, mountain nomads in the autumn' (Rowton 1980:294).

To the cyclic and relatively short range movements within or across the borders of states, Rowton (1973a:247–58) has given the designation 'enclosed nomadism'. But those tribal groupings, of whom the best known are from the Mari area around 1,830–1,760 BC, particularly Haneans and Yaminites, exhibit a 'dimorphic structure' (Rowton 1976:17–31), meaning that the tribe has its own settlements also. Since their mobility takes place within the ambit of city-states, the pastoral nomads, while avoiding outright control such as the state exercises over most of the settled population, none the less are symbiotically tied into the economy of the city-state (Matthews 1978:132). As suggested below, pastoral nomadism is a specialized development to exploit terrain otherwise not available to any but hunter-gatherers. In fact this can be seen as a particular form of foraging, mediated by animals, mostly sheep (ibid.). Indeed in its developed, 'historic' form to which the term dimorphic structure applies, with the constant interaction between mobile and sedentary, that is, between the pastoral and the agricultural, we can conceive of this symbiotic relationship also as a kind of extended transhumance by a (differently organized) sector of a regional population.

The necessary but often tense process of the exchange of products and services between agriculturalists and pastoralists is something we see worked out in the myth *Inanna Prefers the Farmer* (Kramer 1961b:101). Here the farmer god Enkimdu and the bellicose shepherd god, Dumuzi, are competing for the hand of 'the maid Inanna' (= Ishtar), goddess of fecundity. In the suitors' dispute Dumuzi is the combative one and he boasts:

> Enkimdu, the man of dike, ditch and plow,
> (More) than I (Dumuzi), the farmer, what has he more (than I)?
> Should he give me his black garment,
> I would give him, the farmer, my white ewe for it,
> Should he pour me his prime date wine,
> I would pour him, the farmer, my yellow milk for it,
> Should he pour me his good date wine,
> I would pour him, the farmer, my **kišim**-milk for it,
> Should he pour me his . . . date wine,
> I would pour him, the farmer, my . . . milk for it,
> Should he pour me his diluted date wine,
> I would pour him, the farmer, my plant-milk for it,
> Should he give me his good portions,
> I would give him, the farmer, my **itirda**-milk for them,
> Should he give me his good bread,
> I would give him, the farmer, my honey-cheese for it,
> Should he give me his small beans,
> I would give him, the farmer, my small cheeses for them.
> (Pritchard 1969:42; see also Kramer 1961b:101)

What is being stressed here by Dumuzi is both the plenitude of his resources and the possibility of balanced reciprocity. Indeed the shepherd goes on, in the very next lines, to promise even more than measure for measure but a bonus of 'extra fat' and 'extra milk'. Despite Inanna's early resistance, opposed to which are the blandishments of the sun-god Utu on behalf of the 'much possessing shepherd', not only does Dumuzi eventually succeed in gaining Inanna, though originally disposed to favour the farmer, but the farmer even invites the shepherd to:

> Let thy sheep eat the grass of the riverbank,
> In my meadowland let thy sheep walk about,
> In the bright fields of Erech [i.e. Uruk] let them eat grain,
> Let thy kids and lambs drink the water of Unun canal.
> (Pritchard 1969:42; Kramer 1961b:101)

Because pastoral nomadism is so specialized, producing only a small range of products – meat, milk products, and wool or hides – and since 'they consume or require a wide variety of agricultural and industrial products' (Barth, op. cit.:69), pastoral access to agricultural resources and their relations to the state were usually buffered through tribal occupation during part of the year, and/or by part of the population, of a town or village within the territory of a city-state. This is the other, more organic, form of 'enclosure'. 'Typically, the dimorphic chiefdom consisted of a town, usually small, from which a local or tribal dynasty exerted a varying blend of rule and influence over the tribes in the countryside' (Rowton 1980:297). Rule, influence, revolt, and conflict, with the nomads acting as raider and levies (sometimes both together), is the political side of economic co-operation and competition (ibid.:296).

What we are dealing with, and what the city-state rulers like Zimri-Lim had to contend with as seen in their correspondence (Matthews 1978: *passim*), is two distinct but interlocking modes of production and hence modes of economic and political organization. Barth clearly brings out the contrasts and the articulation as he encountered them:

> Throughout the South West Asian region . . . the nomads become tied in relations of dependence and reciprocity to sedentary communities in the area – their culture is such as to presuppose the presence of such communities and access to their products. As far as the economic structure of an area is concerned, nomad and villager can therefore be regarded merely as specialised occupational groups within a single economic system; and this fact has great implications for an understanding of the role of the nomads in the life of the nation. Not only are they adapted to an environment containing villages[17] and markets and specialised craftsmen – the other occupational groups are adapted to an economic system which contains pastoral herders as one of its basic elements.
>
> (Barth 1964:70)

None the less this was a turbulent, not a smoothly integrated system (we are, after all, dealing with different modes of production), and it is indeed from disruption, become intense and sustained at particular periods, that Rowton (1980:296–7) sees the nomadic factor playing the dynamic, if episodically destructive, role in the continuity of Mesopotamian civilization. This because the pastoralists' role was neither marginal nor external but intrinsic, as may be seen topographically in the extent of the 'dimorphic zone' shown in Map 6.1. When the state was strong, as was the Mari of Zimri-Lim, the nomads could be closely administered and controlled, even down to their religious observances (Matthews 1978:151). A state weakened, say by warfare, became a tempting prize.

Accordingly during the reign of the divine Shulgi (2,093–2,046 BC), in his forty-eighth glorious year, one text records the processing of almost 350,000 sheep and goats, plus rather less than a tenth of this number of cattle, 'sent to Drehem by royal authority or by priests and officials and representing tribute, offerings and official disbursements' (Jones and Snyder, op. cit.:212). They found that 'the animals were employed for sacrificial purposes and the sustenance of priests, officials, foreign

Map 6.1 Approximate limits of the 'dimorphic zone'

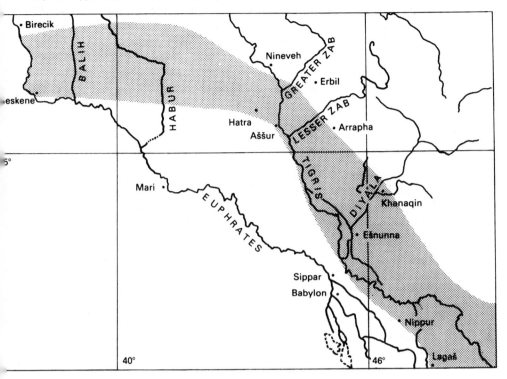

Source: Rowton 1976:31

emissaries and workers. Thousands of animals were brought in and sent out each month' (ibid.).

Such movements led Diakonoff (1972:43) to the assumption that temple sacrifices were the main source of meat for community members. Likewise Dinka and Nuer cattle, so well known to ethnography, have first to be sacrificed before they can be eaten (Evans-Pritchard 1940:26–8).

Also in the Third Dynasty of Ur (under Ibbi-Sin), the Royal Wool Office at Ur was responsible for 6,435 tons of raw wool and employed around 9,000 state-owned male and female slaves in its processing (Jacobsen (1953) 1970b:221). The 'Royal Wool Office' undertook the supply, storage, processing, weaving, and fulling of many fibres, not wool alone (ibid.:223). The actual labour in this period seems to have been done by female slaves under male overseers called **ugala**, themselves grouped under 'headmen' termed **nu-banda**. One establishment, located in a village and specializing in linen, employed an average of 230 women and girls (ibid.).

Textiles and not metals were the major industry of the Mesopotamian world, reflecting not just the exigencies of the extreme climate, but, at least in this period, the need for textiles by the crown as 'the only valuable, lightweight, marketable commodity available in the kingdom's heartland with which to meet the needs of long-distance exchange' (Adams 1981:150). In the ancient world textiles were the only sort of production that could accurately be called 'manufacturing' as against handicraft production or direct extraction. Yet as late as the Roman Empire, which was able to syncretize productive technique from the whole circum-Mediterranean area, the classicist A. H. M. Jones could write of the crudity of the economy in terms that apply equally well to Mesopotamia, right down to the particulars of field rotation:

> It is hard to remember that, despite its great achievements in law and administration, the splendid architecture of its cities and luxurious standard of living of its aristocracy, the Roman Empire was, in its methods of production, in some ways more primitive than the early Middle Ages. Agriculture followed a wasteful two-field system of alternate crop and fallow. Yarn was spun by hand with a spindle, and textiles laboriously woven on clumsy hand looms. Even corn was ground in hand querns or at best in mills turned by oxen: windmills had not been invented and watermills were still rare. In these circumstances the feeding and clothing of an individual demanded a vast expenditure of human labour, and the maintenance of any substantial number of economically unproductive persons laid a heavy burden on the rest.
>
> (A. H. M. Jones 1972:40)

For the Mesopotamian workshop, we may assume that despite some rudimentary division of labour, the actual productive process was but domestic weaving on an enlarged scale. Kramer (1963:104) speaks of three women, using spindles and both vertical and/or horizontal looms, taking as many as eight days to produce a piece of material 3.5 × 4 m. It had then to be fulled, washed, and otherwise got ready for actual use. Wool, by far the most important fibre, was got by plucking and not by shearing, indicating yet again the marginality of metal in production and underscoring the point made at the outset that 'Chalcolithic', 'Bronze Age', etc. are terms of classification and not the primary indices of the mode of production, nor do they indicate the chief materials of production. Still less, as has been argued, do the materials and technologies employed determine the relations of production, for those are essentially historical (turning on previous modes of production) and political, being the current balance of powers.

8 Grain productivity and its stability

The return to seed in Sumero-Babylonian agriculture has been computed by Powell (1985:29–30) to be of the order of 50-fold for barley and wheat.

This is based on conservative assumptions, such as that seeding rates were as high as 12–15 **silà** per **iku**, that is, 12–15 litres per 0.36 hectare (ibid.:7). Harvests of the order of 60 **gur** per **bur** were standard (where 1 **bur** = *c.* 6.48 ha, and 1 **gur** = 300 litres).

Sumero-Babylonian agriculture aimed to maximize returns (to inputs) not yields, and the low seeding rates, at 240 **silà** per **bur**, and the concentration on barley, the most reliable of the grains, were successful methods of achieving this (ibid.:34).

Most importantly, this success was sustained over the millenniums considered here and was not compromised by salinization as was previously thought (e.g. by Jacobsen and Adams 1958; Jacobsen 1982). Instead, Powell is able to show that previous views of salination causing yields to decline in the south from the pre-Sargonic period forwards is a consequence of (a) the unrepresentative nature of much of the textual material formerly relied upon (op. cit.:8) and (b) 'metrological misinter-pretation, by including feed [for the draught animals] with seed [for sowing the crop], and by interpreting records of income as seed' (ibid.:38).

Powell concludes, from textual indications, that far from being a progressive and intractable problem, salinity was understood and routinely mastered by Sumero-Babylonian agriculture (ibid.:37–8). One method, accepted as intrinsic to Sumerian farming, was fallow. Another was the practice of leaching by the application of water when the ground to be leached was in fallow, or at least prior to ploughing. Leaching is of course still the basic anti-salinity treatment the world over.

But in Mesopotamia itself, even in the extreme southerly parts of the alluvium,

> where the land gradient is virtually nil and ground-water always high, a method of 'isolating' salt areas is now employed. Extra irrigation water is applied to cultivated *shitwi* [winter] crops in order to leach salt from the surface soil. As there is a hydraulic gradient, the resulting saline ground-water is 'pushed' to adjacent fields deliberately left 'idle' for the purpose of allowing salts to rise and accumulate on the surface. Effective drainage is, of course, always an answer to salination but it would be difficult to think of a better method of coping with problems of salinity on virtually level land, as in the delta areas of Sumer, than in this clearly very ancient practice.
>
> (Oates and Oates 1976a:124–5)

It would also be difficult to think of a more apposite application of ethnographic analogy in the 'direct' or 'continuous' mode than this example.

Thus from the above, despite the theoretical edifices erected on the contrary assumption, we can confidently assume with Oates and Oates

(1976a:128) that 'Once the basic techniques of water management had been learned, the highly fertile alluvial soils were capable of producing vast and, perhaps more important, reliable surpluses.'

Questions of the rise and fall or waxing and waning of Mesopotamian civilization will have to be addressed on other than simple technological problems. And methodologically, I have already tried to indicate that the technical has no existence apart from its social context, and conversely that 'social structure' and politics cannot be separated from their techno-environmental basis. At the technological level it now seems that Mesopotamian society could cope. The problems must lie elsewhere.

Moorey (1976:101) identifies the proto-Dynastic complex at Jemdet Nasr as a temple: 'the focus for a miscellany of houses and "places of sacrifice" and regularly modified in plan'. Found there were both large and plain-ware jars offering evidence of storage, and the ubiquitous 'bevelled-rim bowls', the likely function of which is described in Appendix D below. Also found were the 'collective sealings' relating a number of cities in the exchange of goods, such deliveries being sent to magazines and storehouses (Moorey, op. cit.:103–4).

Sealing is a special form of 'signing'. Gelb has set out some early, pictographic, signs in Figure 6.10. As between the Sumerian and the Chinese, fundamentally different conceptualizations of the city are apparent, as also is the Chinese anthropomorphization of the sky. While modern Chinese characters are lineal descendants, stylized and rational-ized, of this earliest form of writing, the Sumerian (with the Egyptian) underwent multiple and interactive evolution (Appendix E), which eventuated in the Greek, and hence Latin, alphabet.

Of the many tablets discovered at Jemdet Nasr, none so far read is a literary text, but 'that they are predominantly texts is not in question; primarily administrative checklists of persons, of commodities and of land areas subtly interrelating all three' (ibid.:105). While various deities are named, the term **lugal** does not appear, but there is a group of personal names commencing with the element **EN**, etymologically 'lord' (i.e. chief priest). Moorey concludes (ibid.:106) that we are here (in the thirty-first century BC) encountering an administrative complex within a temple estate, presided over by the **EN** official 'whose cult function was (then) more important than his political role', and whose residence was more sacred than secular in character.

That, no doubt, was the temple's purpose and ideology; its *effect*, however, was to function as buffer in the storage economy. The 'EN' element appears also in the personal names of the culture heroes Emesh and Enten (summer and winter respectively), the former the spirit of husbandry, the latter of 'vital forces' (winter is the rainy season). In their dispute for priority before Enlil, the embodiment of power, Enten declares:

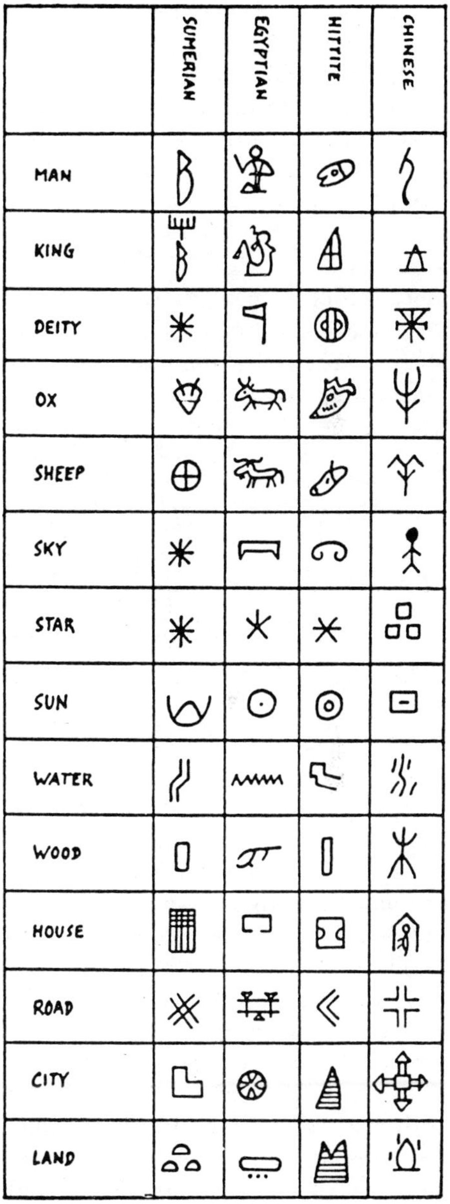

Figure 6.10 Pictorial signs of the Sumerian, Egyptian, Hittite, and Chinese writing systems

	SUMERIAN	EGYPTIAN	HITTITE	CHINESE
MAN				
KING				
DEITY				
OX				
SHEEP				
SKY				
STAR				
SUN				
WATER				
WOOD				
HOUSE				
ROAD				
CITY				
LAND				

Source: Gelb 1963:98

O father Enlil, knowledge thou hast given me, I brought the water of
abundance,
Farm I made touch farm, I heaped high the granaries,
Like Anshan,[18] the kindly maid I cause strength to appear;
Now Emesh, the . . . , the irreverent, who knows not the heart of the
fields,
On my first strength, on my first power, is encroaching;
At the palace of the king . . .

(Kramer 1961a:51)

9 The Old Babylonian period and the end of the ration system

Hired labour, **lú-ḫun-gá**, working for wages, **á**, does not appear until the
Ur III period. Until then most labour was general purpose, dependent
labour, **guruš** and **gemé**, receiving rations from temple and state. As Gelb
sums up the process:

> The semi-free class of the **guruš** workers and the ration system
> dominated the socio-economic life of early Mesopotamia all through
> the periods from Fara (ED IIIa) through the pre-Sargonic and Sargonic
> to Ur III. Beginning with the Old Babylonian (i.e. Hammurabic)
> Period, the term **guruš** for the semi-free class disappeared completely
> and was replaced by others. At the same time the ration system was
> slowly dying out in Babylonia proper, although it continued strongly in
> outlying regions, such as Mari and Chagar Bazar. After a brief revival
> in the Kassite period, the ration system seems to have died out in
> Mesopotamia by the end of the second millennium B.C.

(Gelb 1965:242–3)

Citizens controlled their own means of production, hence Oppenheim's
assertion (1964:90) that staples never appear in the context of trade, for
they were either consumed directly or redistributed socially in the manner
diagrammed above. Temple, royal, and 'private' estates also supplied
their own comestibles to their workers, for the **guruš** in the form of
rations.

The three central staples were barley, sesame oil, and wool, and they
were issued in the quantities shown in Table 6.3 in a form 'very much
standardised all through the Sargonic and Ur III periods, although
deviations of different types are found occasionally' (Gelb 1965:233).

'Besides **še-ba**, **ì-ba**, and **síg-ba**, that is rations of barley, oil and wool,
several other kinds of rations occur in the texts, the most important of
which are **zíz-ba**, **ninda-ba**, **zíd-ba**, and **túg-ba**, that is, rations of emmer,
bread, flour, and cloth respectively' (Gelb 1965:236). In addition,
sheepmeat and beef, butter, milk, cheese and other dairy products,
onions, legumes, cucumbers and other vegetables, plus fruit such as

Table 6.3 Rations

Kind	Time	Men	Women	Children	Measure
Barley	Once a month	60	30	25, 20, 15, 10	Quarts
Oil	Once a year	4	4	2, 1½, 1	Quarts
Wool	Once a year	4	3	2, 1½, 1	Pounds

Source: Gelb 1965:233.

dates, figs, apples, also beer and wine, regularly supplemented the rations during festivals, such as sheep during the **Akitu** (New Year) Festival. During scarcity or glut some items replaced others (Gelb, op. cit.:238) and we may further assume that regional variations, such as the availability of fish in the south, played a role in allocation too.

Indicative of the economy's low productivity overall is the fact that a sheep produced only about one pound of wool annually,[19] barely enough for a child's ration, and that the yearly output of a cow is only around 5 dry quarts of butter and 7½ dry quarts of cottage cheese (Gelb 1967b:68). Interestingly, the value and amount of dairy products from cows are identical with those from goats (ibid.). Further, calves had a low birth-rate, and the growth of a herd of cattle from 6 to 32 in ten years seems quite typical (ibid.), suggesting poor pasture and reinforcing the suggestions above as to the role of long-range nomadic pastoralism. In present-day Zagros village husbandry, sheep and goats average around one pint of milk each in a full day (total of all milkings), while a cow will produce around 1 *mann* (7 pounds, about 0.75 gallons) of milk per day (Watson 1979:98). But even those low figures are for the period of optimal grazing in the spring, and the current state of deforestation in the area means that each villager can maintain only a few animals, so gross yield is also low (ibid.).

Given the latitude and the rudimentary nature of preservation techniques, we should bear in mind that fresh foods, or at least animal foods, must have been locally consumed (Gelb 1967b:68–9).

As well as disbursements in kind, the state received its income in kind also, apart from some taxation of merchants who had the specie to pay in silver. As for a general taxation, there seems to have been none. Instead there was a general corvée, one that Gelb (1967a:7) has called 'the everybody works principle', in 'the form of labour or military service (*rēdû*) and of obligatory sacrifices, at least as far as the third millennium and the first part of the second millennium are concerned' (Diakonoff 1972:44).

The bulk of state income, as indicated, was directly produced from what can be called, following Maria de J. Ellis (1976:12), the State Land Fund. The summary of its disposition during the reign of Hammurabi[20] is given in Table 6.4.

Table 6.4 The allocation of state land

Type of land	**Biltu-**land	**Ilku-**lands	
Tenure	Retained by state	Assigned to beneficiaries on the basis of service (**ṣukussu** & **ṣibtu** fields)	
Method of cultivation	Administered by officials: worked by lower ranks of state personnel (**nāši bilti's**)	(a) Worked by beneficiary	(b) Administered by 'cultivator'(**errēšu**) for owner by rental contracts worked by state personnel
Destination of crops	To state after deduction of production costs	To beneficiary	'Owner's' share (⅓ or ½, called either **biltu** or **miksu**) to beneficiary; cultivator's share to state after deduction of production expenses

Source: Maria de J. Ellis 1976:12

The terms of tabulation by Ellis are elucidated further:

The word **ilku** in general describes the service which an individual performed for the state, and which by extension also came to be applied to land held in return for (or subject to) such service.

Šukussu is used to describe a subsistence allotment, usually held in return for service. The term does not however refer to such service. **Ṣibtu** also is used of land; the word simply means 'holding'.

Finally, **biltu** in agricultural contexts can be used in general of goods which are paid as rent or income, and can also be applied to land which produces such income.

(Ellis 1976:12–13)

In sum, state personnel in the Old Babylonian period either received rations or they received land in lieu of rations (Ellis, op. cit.:18). One imagines that those awarded lands were rather better off, not least in personal autonomy, and indeed Ellis remarks that 'fields were assigned by the central administration to groups of artisans and workers, as well as to individuals because of their membership in certain groups, or their service to the state' (ibid.:15). Gelb (1965:243) remarks that this is indicative of a devolution of the control of land toward small landholders and artisans and away from the largest landholders, temple, state, or private, part of a general fragmentation.

It is worth looking 'in close-up' at an administrative text of the period (from the Musée de Louvre, *Textes Cunéiformes*), translated by Norman Yoffee. The text nicely brings together a number of relationships discussed above:

> item: 24,630 litres barley measured according to the standard 30 litre measure, which is 27 payments of 900 litres plus 11 additional payments of 30 litre measures.
>
> item: 2,610 litres 'late grain' measured according to the standard 30 litre measure, which is 2 900 litre payments plus 11 additional payments of 30 litre measures.
>
> total: 27,240 litres grain measured according to the standard 30 litre measure.
>
> Received according to the 'thick' standard, including 'late grain', from the fields of Kar-Samas under the responsibility of Beliyatum, the *iššakum* of Lamassani, *nadītu* of Šamaš, daughter of Sin-iqiša, the *mu'errum*-official. Brought in to the granary, received by Lamassani, *nadītu* of Šamaš, Sin-rimeni, and Baza.
>
> overseers: Etel-pu, **dumu-e-dub-ba-a**, Sumumlibsi, and Beliyatum, *iššakum*.
>
> date: 28.4. A-s 13.

(Yoffee 1977:120)

A *nadītu(m)*, such as Lamassani was, and for whom the *iššaku(m)* and *mu'erru(m)* officials were acting, was a daughter of an elite family who remained unmarried and instead entered into seclusion in an establishment dedicated to the service of a god, in this instance Šamaš. In a clear example of the 'diverging devolution' of property (Goody 1976:23), the *nadītum* had at her disposal some of the familial property, in this instance amounts that would at least be equivalent to a dowry, to engage in commercial and real estate transactions. The term '*nadītu*' means 'fallow', which meant she did not marry and produce children, but her money was far from fallow. It was actively employed in augmenting her own wealth (Harris 1975:xii), which could be left to adopted 'children'.

The *nadītum* institution was an elite and quasi-state institution, and hence Lamassani's supervisor, Beliyatum, was an *iššaku(m)* official, in the Old Babylonian period 'a manager of crown lands, not a private farmer; he could be paid either a fixed wage or a proportional share of the harvest; workers in his precinct were always paid fixed sums' (Yoffee, op. cit.: 108). The *iššaku(m)* of the Old Babylonian period was an official answerable to a *mu'erru(m)* and he to an *abi ṣābim*, at least after the reign of Ammiditana (ibid.:144).

Now, *iššaku(m)* is a loan word in Akkadian from the Sumerian **ensi(k)** – usually written (in cuneiform) **PA.TE.SI** – and he 'seems to have been originally the leader of the seasonal organisation of the townspeople for work on the fields: irrigation, ploughing and sowing' (Jacobsen 1970a:384n). Manifestly it survived in this (original and technical) sense of something like 'agricultural co-ordinator' into Old Babylonian times, by which time **ensik** was obsolete as a political term.

The lengthy chapter which follows is not essential to understanding the trajectory by which Mesopotamia emerged as the world's first complex civilization. A theoretical expansion, it interrupts the flow of the argument to show how social stratification arises from rudimentary inequalities of power in 'egalitarian' hunter-gatherer society.

Using a range of ethnologies, the chapter also contains a lengthy discussion of kinship as the organizing principle of pre-state society – horticultural, agricultural and pastoral – where kinship functions as the relations of production.

Accordingly, those without special anthropological interests would do best to move on directly to Chapter 9.

Chapter seven

Theories of the state

As suggested at the outset, chiefs rule in chiefdoms and kings reign over states, while meritocratic entrepreneurs such as big-men, famed hunters, or shamans have merely influence in more acephalous societies. States possess a unique power centre manifesting sovereignty, characterized by *ultimate control* of the populations which are their subjects. In chieftaincies only hegemony obtains: autonomous foci of power exist over which the centre is merely preponderant (perhaps only for reasons of tradition or prestige) and any of which might secede to form the nucleus of another chiefdom. Yet most theories of state formation fall at the first hurdle through their authors' failure, or their formulation's inability, to distinguish chiefdom from true state. There is governance in the former, only in the latter is there government: overall social regulation by specialized apparatuses of control emanating from a unique power centre. Unlike the chiefdom, 'the state is never the kinship system writ large, but is organised on totally different principles' (Fortes and Evans-Pritchard 1940:6) which can be summed as the contrast between statuses and offices.[1]

Generalizing, villages are characteristic not just of the Neolithic but of a chieftaincy, whose capital is but the village writ large. By contrast the state necessarily has an urban focus, due not only to elevated population densities and clusters (Lenski 1966:145-6), but to a more ramified division of labour in general, not least in the process of government itself. Further, small-scale societies and chieftaincies are relatively homogeneous in language, belief, and custom, while states tend over time to become inclusive and composed of groups and individuals of disparate ethnic origin. This is possible because the subject's primary relationship is vertically to the state and not horizontally to the rest of society, as it necessarily is in a less stratified social order where identity and cohesion are at a premium.

Social complexity, stratification, and urbanization are usually discussed in the light of the theories or models of state formation obtaining. It is thus necessary, having previously outlined the spread of villages in the

Near East, and also some of the archaeological evidence for the advent of cities, to analyse the theories of state formation currently held.

1 Evolutionary underpinning to theories of the state

It is to Elman Service's work *Primitive Social Organization*, first published in 1962 (with a second revised edition in 1971), that we owe the full and rigorous distinctions[2] between band, tribe, chiefdom, and state forms of what he calls 'levels of sociocultural integration'. So fecund has this approach proved that implicitly or explicitly it informs most contemporary ethnoarchaeology and, typically, the likes of *Studies in Honour of David Clarke* (Hodder, Isaac, and Hammond (eds), 1981) that add much depth to the subject. It is indeed difficult to imagine how ethnoarchaeology could be practised without such a framework, and because this is so, Service's formulations first need to be outlined prior to the elucidation and criticism of the specific models developed by others.

For Service, then, 'a band is only an association, more or less residential, of nuclear families, ordinarily numbering 25 to 100 people, with affinal (i.e. marriage) ties allying it with one or a few other bands' (1971b:100). The loose structure of bands will be developed subsequently, but for Service the salient feature of the band level of sociocultural integration 'is simply that all of the functions of the culture are organised, practised, or partaken of by no more than a few associated bands made up of related nuclear families' (ibid.:98).

From those loose aggregates a tribe is formed (under certain circumstances) through the crystallization of 'sodalities' which become 'pan-tribal'. These stabilize the fluid groupings and give them cohesive structure in both depth and extent. 'Probably the most usual of pan-tribal sodalities are clans, followed by age-grade associations, secret societies, and sodalities for such special purposes as curing, warfare, ceremonies and so on' (Service, op. cit.:102). This structuration is brought on by pressure, not so much from the natural as from the human environment, what Service (ibid.:103) calls the 'superorganic environment'. Hence, though 'a tribe is a fragile social body compared to a chiefdom or a state . . . it seems likely that without foreign-political problems overall tribal integration would not take place; it is always such problems that stimulate the formation of large political bodies' (ibid.). Thus while it is the extension and elaboration of pan-tribal sodalities that 'make a tribe a tribe' (ibid.:105), the process is associated particularly with the Neolithic, for 'The competition of societies in the Neolithic phase of cultural development seems to have been the general factor which led to the development of integrating pan-tribal sodalities' (ibid.:103).

Other than mentioning the transformative influence of competition in general and warfare (or its threat) in particular, Service does not elaborate on the reasons for intensified competition and conflict during the Neolithic, though he maintains that even at the band level it is precisely hostility, actual or latent, that calls forth social organization (ibid.:108). In regard to tribe formation, Service does suggest that this has something to do with increased population around the Neolithic, and this is a crucial consideration we shall have to pursue later.

While 'it is possible that intense competition and frequent warfare among tribes was an important condition for the rise of chiefdoms in the first place, inasmuch as planning and coordination have obvious advantages in war' (Service, op. cit.:141), we see that this is not a sufficient condition, because 'incessant warfare' amongst New Guinea or Amazonian horticulturalists, for example, fails to generate the state or even a chiefdom. This is a point not lost on Carneiro (1970:735), who advocates his own conquest theory but for whom warfare is a necessary but not sufficient cause. However, redistribution seems an efficient cause to Service, since 'most chiefdoms seem to have arisen where important regional exchange and a consequent increase in local specialisation came about because differentiation in habitat was combined with considerable sedentariness' (op.cit.:136). Instead of people moving to exploit different ecological zones, they stay put and their goods move (ibid.:135).

Sedentariness, as I have argued, has a lot to do with it, but as for local specialization and overall re-integration by the chief, Earle (1977a:223) shows quite plainly that territories within the Hawaiian proto-state were specifically organized to ensure local autarky, and that what was 'centralized' and 'redistributed' (only to the elite) were sumptuary items marking their status, a conclusion generalized by the broad survey of Peebles and Kus (1977:444–5). Thus neither warfare nor quasi-marketing agency can explain the evolution of chieftaincy and the state.

However, Service himself has unconsciously produced the best argument against the 'necessity' of chiefly redistribution for the complementary exploitation of diverse habitats. He observes, in regard to specialized nomadic pastoralists, that inasmuch as they are part societies dependent on exchanges with settled agriculturalists 'economic symbiosis must have been well-established *before* pastoralist chiefdoms could become so specialised as herders' (op. cit.:136; his emphasis). But he goes on in the mistaken belief that 'primitive reciprocal exchanges', since they are of interest to the whole group, though they are undertaken by individuals, demand 'organisation – which implies some form of leadership' (ibid.). On the contrary, we have seen above that it is density of settlement and economic specialization which generates nomadic pastoralism (Chapter 3). None the less, for Service, 'a fully developed chiefdom is likely to have both regional specialisation and individual division of labour tied into the redistribution' (ibid.:138).

The redistributor-chief, whom it is suggested commenced his career not, significantly, as a war leader but as a 'big-man'-type distributor of the fruits of his own labours (ibid.:139), 'having control of the magazine', can then subsidize further specialization, particularly of crafts for his own utility. This chief is also able to mobilize large amounts of labour for both military and productive purposes. Instancing the creation of water-control schemes amongst the latter, Service concludes (ibid.:141), 'Once this kind of project was well under way, the societies were transformed to a new level – the classical archaic states – thereby obliterating the antecedent chiefdoms after a brief lifespan.'

Service does not discuss archaic states in *Primitive Social Organization* (1962/1971b) but does so in a later work, *Origins of the State and Civilization* (1975). There he continues to stress the development of a permanent redistributional system as 'closely associated with the origin of chiefdoms' (ibid.:91), for 'it is the basic supply system – and hence it is obviously necessary to the whole society' (ibid.:92). It is further reiterated that 'big-man systems did in fact sometimes turn into hereditary chiefdoms' (ibid.:294), but once established 'all chiefdoms [become] theocracies and an important aspect of the bureaucracy is its function as a priesthood' (ibid.:296). The development of bureaucracy is stressed (ibid.:321), in addition to 'the immense benefits of fitting such different niches and skills into a centralised redistributional system' (ibid.:285). Hence we find the chiefdom/state distinction now rendered as the 'relatively peaceful theocratic mode of rule [of the chiefdoms]; states, on the contrary we have thought of as having more prominent secular sanctions backed by force or the threat of it' (ibid.:294).

Remarkably, however, in his chapter of final conclusions, Service (1975:304), while maintaining that 'Chiefdoms seem to be clearly distinct from segmental societies', postulates that since archaeologically 'there seems to be no way to discriminate the state from the chiefdom stage', he wishes to conflate bands and tribes 'into a single segmental stage' (ibid.), while chiefdoms and states proper are to be merged under the rubric of 'caste societies in the fullest sense of the word' (ibid.:301). This despite the fact that the former classification into bands, tribes, chiefdoms, and states 'may still have its uses in characterising contemporary (or historically known) primitive societies [but] it does not seem so useful for prehistoric archaeology' (ibid.:303); a matter surely for archaeologists to gauge and a modification that Renfrew (1977:99), for one, finds distinctly unhelpful.

Further, in the shift from *Primitive Social Organization* to the *Origins of the State and Civilization*, Service's emphasis has shifted from strife to benefits in causing heightened social organization, while armed conflict now appears (1975:298) as a failure of governance. From conflict to co-operation by way of the centrally administered division of labour, what is now proposed in 'the evolutionary route from big-man society through chiefdom to civilisation' is that 'political evolution can be thought of as consisting, in important part, of successfully "waging peace" in ever-wider contexts' (ibid.:297, 305).

Service, having provided some fundamental elements for a theory of the generation of the state, has attempted an eclectic synthesis and must be judged to have failed to provide a clear conceptualization. His leading factors were redistribution at the stage of chieftaincy and, at the level of the state proper, the benefits of administration. As such his model of state formation comes under the heading of 'managerialism' and accordingly it will be treated below in the appropriate section. The valuable aspect of this has been in drawing our attention to political means of gaining power over the labours of others and in so doing obtaining differentially favourable conditions of life for a ruling minority.

2 Models of state formation

Modern ethnoarchaeological models of state formation fall under two broad categories: (A) the Managerial and (B) the Stress, whose rationale may respectively be rendered as 'benefits' versus 'conflicts'.

Both Managerial and Stress theories divide again in two, so that under Managerial we find explanations in terms of (i) benefits of provisioning, specifically in redistribution, and (ii) benefits accruing from information processing and the co-ordination of a complex division of labour. Stress theories divide broadly into: (i) 'circumscription theory', whereby internal stress is induced by the society meeting external barriers to its expansion, geographical or socio-military. The internal stresses thus set up cause a portion of the population to be circumscribed in their range of options, leaving only that of subordination to an emergent state centre to which they must render taxes or tribute; (ii) 'stratification theories' under which internal stresses induced by emergent class stratification cause the privileged classes to defend their position by building the state.

It is clear that none of those models are mutually exclusive and most contain elements of the others structured around one major principle of causation. Service's theory can thus be seen to contain two main strands, that of warfare and supply benefits (though as his 'warfare' is in fact effective defence, both reduce themselves to varieties of 'benefit'). And in his own classification (1978:22), Service's scheme comes under the head of 'Integrative Theories', albeit a synthetic one.

A: Managerialism
(i) Service

Service's theory has been extensively reviewed so now his more specific model will be evaluated. In *Origins of the State and Civilization*

(1975:76–9) he provides a 'sketch of villages in an area of diversified resources' (Figure 7.1) to show how a chief can be generated from a big-man.

Such villages lie along the course of a river which flows from a hilly region through 'good bottom land' debouching into a productive swamp. These are villages C, A, B respectively (in Figure 7.1). The original settlement is A on the most productive farming land. Thriving, population grows and buds off to form village B at the edge of the swamp where farming is poorer but marsh resources of fish and fowl, plus reeds, are ample. Then a related group comes over the mountains to settle at the upper reaches of the river, which it does unopposed since the land there is relatively poor for farming. But this is compensated by ready access to forest products and to mineral outcrops in the hills, especially flint.

Those villages peacefully exchange the resources in which they are favoured. However village A is in a way 'most favoured' for 'not only is its status highest, because it is the original site, and its production higher, because it is in the best all-round location, but for these reasons it may also be larger' (Service 1975:76). Being in the middle, Service continues, it is easier for B to deal with C through A and vice versa instead of directly. All this still at the level of balanced reciprocity.

> A, then, by simply storing the goods acquired from B and later giving a part of them to C (along with some of its own production), gradually becomes in part at least the 'magazine' of the valley, and A's reciprocities at that time turn into true redistribution.
>
> (Service 1975:76)

Or, according to the next passage, they do when 'an adequate big-man' at A is able to take matters and the magazine in hand, making redistribution 'his own' and turning himself, or at least his successors, into a chief in the process. 'Meanwhile, the local specialisation is so advantageous that it naturally augments, so that C village may give up maize-growing altogether, depending on A for its supply, while B may give up tobacco growing' (ibid.:78).

As production and population further increase, A becomes the chiefly village wielding power by consent that is rooted in economic advantages (both to A and the other two villages) and in emergent kinship seniority (Service, op. cit.:78). This becomes the instituted power of permanent offices as the system extends itself and the chief becomes invested with charismatic authority, while 'a chiefly line is likely to become a priestly line' (ibid.) and so priest-king with an aristocracy come to rule over an extended society become a state. In summary

we are considering essentially the evolution of a bureaucracy of

Figure 7.1 Sketch of villages in area of diversified resources

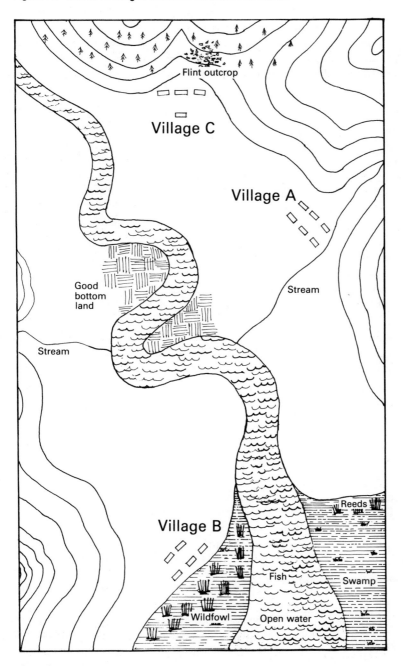

After Service 1975:77

theocratic authority, a bureaucracy that was also the creator and administrator of the important parts of the economic system. Even in the earliest, simplest systems, this political power organised the economy, rather than vice versa; and it was a redistributive, an allocative, system, not an acquisitive system that required personal wealth in order to acquire personal power.

(Service 1975:xiii)

Thus there could be no question of the state emerging to contain an economic class struggle.

The greatest lacunae in Service's argument, both in his 1971 and 1975 works, reside precisely in the transition from chiefdom to state. Indeed the latter is scarcely defined but, rather, described in such terms as 'the power of force in addition to the power of authority [either charismatic or theocratic] is the essential ingredient of "stateness" ' (1975:15). The lack of clear articulation is, of course, a major drawback when attempting to account for the 'Origins of the State and Civilization'; but especially so when this statement contradicts the key process of advancing benefit. But this is not even the major defect. The problem is that all the generative assumptions are contradicted by ethnography.

In the first place it is not the villages that function as corporate entities, rather their component families or lineages are the active entities. Exchanges may affect villages of residence in some fashion but it is individual households or lineages that exchange, for it is they who produce (Vayda 1967:494–500) even at 'trade-feasts' conducted *en masse* between 'sub-tribal villages'. And in particular it is those groups that produce and exchange women, the key exchange 'good' as Service himself originally recognized (1971b:32–40), a realization which is central to modern alliance theory. Since there will be many cross-cutting links (and antipathies!) between and within villages, it is hard to see how a clear politico-economic ranking would arise *between whole villages*, rather than their component groups, unless the 'villages' are merely hamlets or lineage compounds. One could say it might arise as a 'statistical tendency', but it might just as well be random too. Further, affinal links and prestation, which played such a role in the *Primitive Social Organization* scheme, now do not figure in this purely economic, functionalist one of 1975. As for the key magazine/redistribution function at A, are we to assume that A takes on the role of emporium, storing ducks and (dried?) fish against supplies of flint from upland? Again by and for whom? Big-men are no help here, for the functioning of big-men is as instigators of intensified local production for essentially free *distribution*, what is received in exchange being credit, not commercial credit but social prestige. A big-man (or 'centre-man') is a *faction* leader who has built up a *personal* following by being prepared to demonstrate that he possesses the kinds of skills that command respect – magical powers, gardening prowess, mastery of oratorical style, perhaps bravery in war and feud. Typically decisive is the deployment of one's skills and efforts in a certain direction: towards amassing goods, most often pigs (in New Guinea) shell monies and vegetable foods, and distributing them in ways which build a name for cavalier generosity, if not for compassion.

(Sahlins (1963) 1968:164)

The big-man's is not an office that can be transmitted and stabilized but, on the contrary, a personal capacity that ends not even upon his death but with his decreasing vigour in 'fishing men'. Big-man mobilizations are thus inherently unstable, depending as they do on personal prowess and conditional faction: 'in its superstructure it is a flux of rising and falling leaders, in its substructure of enlarging and contracting factions' (Sahlins, op. cit.:166). The 'big-man route' is thus a dead end and cannot serve as the point of departure for what Service calls (1975:308) 'the final benefits of a form of centralised and expanding political organisation that began in the simple attempts of a big-man to perpetuate his social dominance by services to his fellows'. Other institutional structures are required for this which, however, still allow the rising chief to appear as public benefactor.

Figure 7.2 Service's model of the evolution of the state

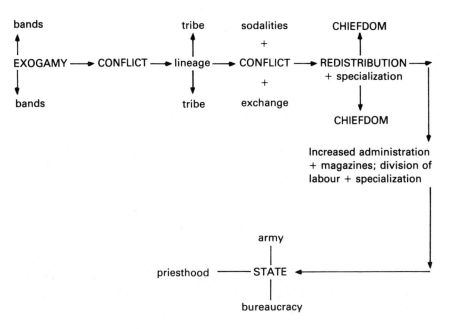

For purposes of comparison and coherency, Service's model for the evolution of the state might be represented as in Figure 7.2 (p. 207).

Page references (which appear on subsequent models) need not be given for each of the elements in Figure 7.2 in view of the previous citations. Instead we will conclude with a final quotation from Service. Prior to empires, he states,

> the earlier origins of institutionalised power and its development en route to the classic forms was clearly associated with increased bureaucratic mobilisation of resources in several ways, but most striking in creating specialisations (of skills and of regions) is an organismic redistributional system that so typically involves complex administration.
>
> (Service 1975:302)

(iia) Flannery

It is precisely the benefits of 'complex administration' that the 'information' school of thought singles out as prime determinant if not prime mover. In fact this other stream of managerialism, perhaps best known from the work of Flannery (1972a) and Wright and Johnson (1975; and each individually), posits the state as primarily and pre-eminently the regulator (and executor) of a flow of information between social sub-systems, many of which are of the state's own creation (Wright 1978:56). In such a scheme, 'regulation involves information flow, even if it is expressed in flow of material items' (ibid.). This is, then, a reversal of Service's causality which explains administration from material provision-ing, in contrast to the 'information' view which seems to value regulation for its own sake. As Wright explains:

> For my purposes a *state* can be *recognised* as a society with specialised decision-making organisations that are receiving messages from many different sources, recoding these messages, supplementing them with previously stored data, making the actual decision, storing both the message and the decision, and conveying decisions back to other organisations. Such organisations are thus internally and externally specialised.
>
> (Wright 1978:55–6; original emphasis)

This is, then, an extreme synchronic and cybernetic view that not only omits but virtually precludes diachrony, such as was central to Service's account. And just in passing, one wonders how orders passed from the state to, say, the village headman, makes him, the focus of a network of cross-cutting local relationships, into a 'specialized organization'. But the outcome of this type of explanation is to see the emergence of the state as the 'promotion' of a hitherto existing 'specialized organization' from a lower and integrated level to a more nearly apical one, at which position it reacts back upon the whole structure, re-ordering it. In the process of its 'promotion' the institution moves from being a 'system-serving' or special-purpose institution toward being a 'general-purpose' or self-serving institution (Flannery, op. cit.:411). Such would be the emergence 'of the Sumerian palace out of the secular residences included in southern Mesopotamian temple complexes at 3,000 BC, with its implications for the evolution of kingship out of some kind of "priest-manager" role in the preceding chiefdom stage' (ibid.:413). For it is the lower-order institutions that are charged with maintaining their own output within certain ranges, while higher-order institutions function not directly in meeting those goal ranges but in supervision of the functioning of the institutions so charged.

Such a hierarchy, by which Flannery means to model 'a simple human ecosystem' (ibid.:409), is illustrated in Figure 7.3. Of it he remarks that

> it consists of a series of subsystems arranged hierarchically, from lowest and most specific to highest and most general. Each subsystem is regulated by a control apparatus whose job is to keep all the variables in the subsystem within appropriate goal ranges – ranges which maintain homeostasis and do not threaten the survival of the system. Management of crop plants, for example, might be regulated by a lower-order control issuing specific commands; the distribution of harvests and surpluses (the 'output' of the latter subsystem) might in turn be regulated by calendric rituals or group leaders somewhere in the middle levels of the hierarchy.
>
> (Flannery 1972a:409)

Should, however, the lower-order entities fail in meeting their targets, 'as in the case of socio-environmental stress', then the next one up can take over its function at least temporarily. This however is dependent upon spare capacity and buffering such that the limits set allow room for manoeuvre and the institutions are not too integrated vertically, a process known as 'linearization' (ibid.:413). Under linearization a failure in one is likely to jeopardize the whole system. A failure in this, the 'hypercoherence' mode, in which signals are not buffered, allows the system no time to generate new organizations to cover changing circumstances, 'which means that more complex, more "highly evolved" systems may be less stable or more demanding, with more direct influence of one subsystem on another, and thus with a need for stronger and more centralised management at the top of the hierarchy' (Flannery, op. cit.:411). From the logic of the system the state emerges 'when segregation (of ramified institutions) and centralisation reach a certain threshold' (ibid.:423).

'Thus, one of the main trends in the evolution of bands into tribes, chiefdoms, and states must be a gradual increase in capacity for information processing, storage and analysis' (ibid.:411). Well so it

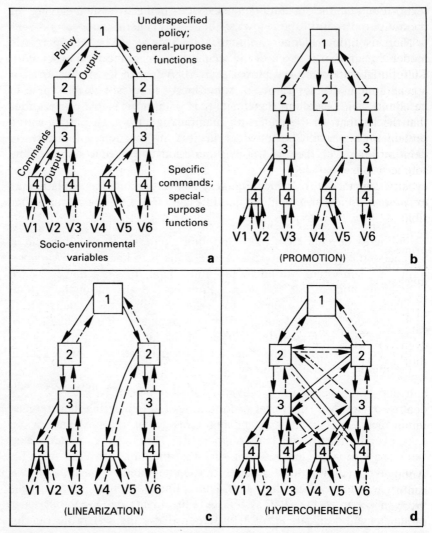

Figure 7.3 Models for the operation of control hierarchies

a — Underspecified policy; general-purpose functions / Policy / Output / Commands / Output / Specific commands; special-purpose functions / Socio-environmental variables / V1 V2 V3 V4 V5 V6

b (PROMOTION) — V1 V2 V3 V4 V5 V6

c (LINEARIZATION) — V1 V2 V3 V4 V5 V6

d (HYPERCOHERENCE) — V1 V2 V3 V4 V5 V6

Models for the operation of control hierarchies: (*a*) the model for a control hierarchy as described in the text, with socioenvironmental variables (*V*1–6) at the bottom regulated by low-level institutions (4), and each successively higher level (3–2–1) regulating the output of the level below it; (*b*) an example of 'promotion', with one function of a third-level institution rising to assume a position of importance in the second level; (*c*) an example of 'linearization', with a second-level control bypassing level 3 and directly regulating the output of a fourth-level institution; (*d*) an extreme case of 'hypercoherence', with too great a degree of direct coupling among institutions on various levels.

Source: Flannery 1972a:410

must – where would we be without palace and temple cuneiform texts – but recording and communicating are means, and not ends in themselves.

There is little that can usefully be said about this general systems model[3] except that it can apply to many systems. Its application to 'The Cultural Evolution of Civilizations', which is Flannery's title, or 'Toward a generative model for the state', which heads his conclusions, brings us, he admits (ibid.:421), not much nearer to solution. This despite the fact that the last part of the paper draws upon the topographic hierarchy of settlement types (cities, towns, villages) in 'hexagonal lattices' as demonstrations of the evolutionary processes involved in Sumer and southern Mexico (Maya) (ibid.:418–22). But the problem is that this cyberneticist model is not really a generative processual model, rather an *ex post facto* construction, compatible, as Flannery himself suggests (ibid.:421), with virtually all the established models, many of which he reviews and classifies as 'prime movers' (ibid.:404, 407). While those prime movers (e.g. population growth or social circumscription) as 'socio-environmental conditions' may represent in his terms 'either evolutionary mechanisms or pathologies' (Flannery, op. cit.:421) of societies, it is hard to see in the Sumerian instance how our understanding of the emergence of (or the distinction between) **ensís** or **lugals** ('kings') is advanced by categorizing the advent of the palace as a case of 'promotion'. There is even very little true 'ecologism' here, where, one suspects, at least the thoroughgoing 'cultural materialism' of Marvin Harris (e.g. 1975, 1978) would be more suggestive in explaining the cluster of states on the alluvium of Mesopotamia. It does not advance our understanding a great deal to be reminded that for systems to be stable they must incorporate redundancy.[4]

(iib) Wittfogel

Another, but traditional, version of managerialism arose early this century and now is associated with the name of Karl Wittfogel. From a 'hydraulic thesis' saying that states arose from the bureaucratic necessity of managing irrigation systems on the great rivers of Asia, he derived the necessity of an 'Oriental Despotism' (1955, 1957), the actual title of his best-known work. Wittfogel suggests that the term 'hydraulic society' applies to 'agrarian societies in which agro-hydraulic works and other large hydraulic and non-hydraulic constructions, that tend to develop with them, are managed by an inordinately strong government' ((1955) 1971:560). This latter attempt to grapple with the Asiatic mode of production will not detain us as it is treated systematically in Chapter 9. A diagrammatic representation of his scheme is reproduced in Figure 7.4. The fact that the final term is 'differentiated leadership' and not the state, is symptomatic, as will be shown below.

Figure 7.4 A managerial theory of state origins (Wittfogel 1957)

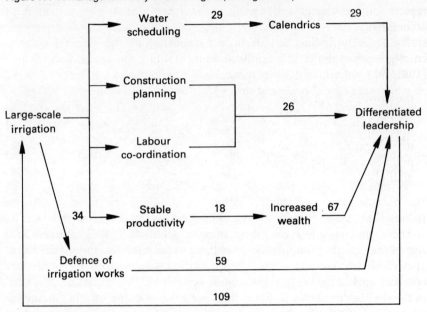

Source: Wright 1978:51
Note: Numbers refer to page references in Wittfogel 1957

Wittfogel's central premisses fall on a number of counts. In the first place, the hydraulic regimes and topology of all the 'rivers of civilization' are quite different, from the regular and limited inundation of the Nile floodplain (so narrow that it never attains more than 12 miles in width from Aswan to the Delta), to the uncontrollable braiding and shifting of the Euphrates on the alluvial sunkland, a river whose regime is quite distinct even from its 'twin', the torrential Tigris (Chapter 3). The annual inundation of the Nile dividing the agricultural year into its three seasons: 'Inundation', 'Going down of the Inundation' (Cultivation) and 'Drought' (Harvest), made irrigation subsidiary, while the distances involved tended to make the ditches (except in the Fayyum) short and narrow (Kees 1961:48).

On the Euphrates an aggradational regime built levees (banks – Figure 3.1, p. 50) which were locally breached and maintained (Jacobsen 1982:62), as also in the quite different regime of Mexico, where 'traditional canal irrigation in the Valley of Oaxaca is a small-scale affair, managed autonomously by each community in its own way' (Flannery 1972a:416). Wittfogel, however, tries to save his scheme against the facts by making this local, unstructured type into a 'loose' variety ((1955) 1971:563) of 'hydraulic society' in contrast to the 'compact', i.e. integrated, network to which managerialism might apply. Such a dilution

Adams (1966:67) regards as further impairing a scheme that he anyhow rejects for the 'compact' or 'core' variety supposed to obtain, and that archetypally, in Mesopotamia. But further, into this 'loose' category, states of early India and China are also said to fall (Wittfogel, op. cit.:563), yet of the birth of civilization on the Indus, Allchin and Allchin (1982:192) remark that

> the principal food grains (wheat and barley), would have been grown as spring (rabi) crops: that is to say, sown at the end of the inundation upon land which had been submerged by spill from the river or one of its natural flood channels, and reaped in March or April. In modern practice such land is neither ploughed or manured, nor does it require additional water.
>
> (Allchin and Allchin 1982:192)

In other words we have a regime similar to that of the Nile.

The archaeological facts are quite simply that irrigation precedes the rise of the state in Mesopotamia (Helbaek 1964:45–8; Oates 1982:25–7) as also 'in Egypt where a good nomarch or monarch would cut canals to conduct water further, but could do nothing about the height of the Nile in flood (Kees, op. cit.:52–3). In his review of 'The indigenous origins of Chinese agriculture', Ping-Ti Ho (1977:428–9) dismisses Wittfogel's hydraulic thesis for China as 'completely without foundation', since the location of the more than 1,000 Neolithic sites known shows them to be located on 'loess terraces or mounds at varying altitudes ranging from fifteen or twenty to hundreds of feet *above* riverbeds', and so demanded 'sophisticated water wheels and water pumps before irrigation could be practised' (ibid.:428). 'Clearly', Ho continues,

> the rise of Chinese agriculture and civilisation bore no direct relationship whatever to the flood plain of the Yellow River, and of all the ancient peoples who gave birth to higher civilisations in the Old and New World, the Chinese were the last to know irrigation.
>
> (Ho 1977:428)

Irrigation began in China during the fifth century BC, by which time the state form had already existed there for at least one millennium and indeed several large states were in competition. This relates directly to the next point: the ethnographies present a case the reverse of that given in Wittfogel's scheme.

Big-men *distribute* the product of their own entrepreneurial activity; chiefs *redistribute* the fruits of others' labour, while kings (states) extract resources from the peasantry, only a fraction of which is ever redistributed, not in recirculation as by feasting and hospitality in chiefdoms, but either as largesse to retainers or to the politically important. It is also used for public display, religion, and for the maintenance of servitors, chief among which is the state bureaucracy (Eisenstadt 1965:218–19). To raise the absolute levels of extraction (and thus their own consumption, personal or political), states *mobilize* labour directly to further the productive infrastructure.[5] Just such a state → mobilization → irrigation/taxation also obtains in Madagascar (Bloch 1977) and Ceylon (Leach 1961c) and it further obtains *after* the advent of the Aztec state (Brumfiel 1983:274–6). Thus once the state has arisen, it tends to involve itself heavily in major irrigation facilities since water is the major constraint on production in low latitudes. But this is exactly the *reverse* process to that envisaged in Wittfogel's form of managerialism, leaving the fundamental origins of the state still to be explained. Indeed, it is only because irrigation in general, and competitive irrigation in particular, is so central to Mesopotamian history that it has been worth dwelling on Wittfogel's model with its popular currency, a view with no ethnographic or archaeological basis and which he admits (1981:xxxix) was really devised to account for a quite different political problem: namely for what he calls Asiatic Despotism and which will be dealt with in Chapter 9 as the Asiatic mode of production.

B: Stress models

(i) Competition and conquest

Carneiro's model (1970, 1978), best known from its concept of 'social circumscription', is fundamentally a conquest theory with ecological aspects. Its prime mover is simply competition for land brought on as a result of the Neolithic, 'when human numbers began to press on the carrying capacity of the land' (1978:210). Villages proliferated to occupy all the good land, leaving little that was of much value.

> As population density in such areas increased and arable land came into short supply, competition over land ensued. This competition took the form of war, and those villagers vanquished in war, being unable to flee as they might have done in areas of uncircumscribed land, had to remain in place and be subjugated by the victors.
>
> (Carneiro 1978:207)

The ecological coda to this straightforward (and very traditional) conquest-state model (Figure 7.5), resides in the notion of circumscription providing the 'container', as it were, for the state. Within such boundaries natural or social, however, no actual process for internal generation of state structure is advanced. Subjugation is accepted, the theory runs, because the original territory of the cultivators is bounded by geographical barriers like deserts or mountains, making escape to 'freedom' and new farmland impossible; while being hemmed in by other societies has the

Figure 7.5 An external conflict theory of state origins (Carneiro 1970)

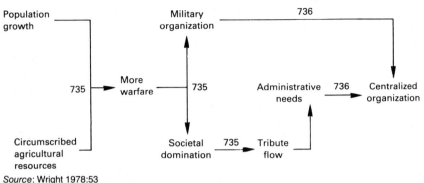

Source: Wright 1978:53
Note: Numbers refer to page references in Carneiro 1970

same effect. Unless, of course, they, the conquerors, are in their turn conquered, and such pyramiding is precisely Carneiro's model: 'through the conquest of village by village, chiefdoms, the first supra-community political units, came to arise . . . from village to chiefdom to state to empire, is the direct consequence of competition between societies' (ibid.:210).

Well, it's simple but does it work? It actually tells us nothing about the rise of the state, still less of ranking or stratification, except that the rulers consist of (or employ) warriors who exact tribute. And the earlier strictures made above on the possibility of 'social augmentation through successful competition', to use Carneiro's (op. cit.:208) own words, are certainly not dispelled by his assertion that 'the political unit warranted being called a state' is one 'so much larger, stronger, and more highly organised than the small chiefdoms out of which it had arisen' (ibid.). This is merely description and fragmentary description at that.

The Neolithic transition to settled village agriculture was, as has already been indicated (Chapter 4), a slow and uneven process, that for millennia depended upon continued foraging as much as cultivation. This provided established settlers and new colonists with all manner of flexibility, not least for new combinations of resource exploitation and, indeed, for new specializations on new terrain.[6] Even after millennia of city-states in Mesopotamia there were always significant numbers 'voting with their feet' as they alternated between and around cities and fluxed from agrarian villages to nomadic niches and back again. Very often indeed, such fluid elements posed problems to the stability of states. Stability neither of watercourses nor of population or politics could be taken for granted. Further, despite Carneiro's 'Principle of Competitive Exclusion' taken from Hardin (1960), whereby 'two species occupying and exploiting the same portion of the habitat cannot coexist indefinitely', the city-states of Sumer and Akkad did just that with basically only

215

boundary variations, despite engaging in frequent warfare. But perhaps several millennia are not indefinite enough.

Most tellingly, however, it has been shown that states arose not in the original Neolithic upland hearths where demographic pressure would have been greatest. On the contrary, they emerged on the alluvium precisely under those environmental constraints in contrast to which favoured focal areas *are supposed to make cultivators stay put and accept domination*. It was the breaching of any 'circumscription' that took settlers down from the fertile piedmont on to the plain, and it is there in a semi-desert punctuated by marshes that we find 'The Heartland of Cities' (Adams 1981: title) whose advent demands explanations less schematic.

(ii) The stratification model

I. M. Diakonoff, the eminent Sumerologist, has consistently pursued a class-stratification model for the rise of the state in the Near East (1969b:15). This is not a model peculiar to him but a fairly orthodox Marxist one, which may be found in one form in Engels's *Origin of the Family, Private Property and the State* (1884) and in contemporary sociological literature in the work of Morton H. Fried (1967, 1978). Diakonoff's model is reproduced in Figure 7.6 from Wright's construction.

This approach is too well known to need extensive discussion at this point. Briefly, it maintains that the state comes into existence to protect, by politico-military means, an order of stratification arising from control of society's means of production by an economically powerful class. In this process class struggle between 'haves' and 'have-nots' develops over control of social resources. In reaction the state emerges to contain class conflict, and it does so in the hands, and in the interests, of those already economically powerful. Or, as Fried (1978:36) summarizes this position: 'Central to the concept of the state . . . is an order of stratification, specifically a system whereby different members of a society enjoy invidiously differentiated rights of access to the basic necessities of life.' This engenders a 'formal organisation of power [which] has as its central task the protection (and often extension) of the order of stratification' (ibid.).

The problem here is twofold. On what basis did economic stratification arise in the first place, and secondly, just how does this translate itself into state power? The latter, it must be stressed, is fundamentally *political* power, which, in general, I take to be the contest over publicly endorsed (and/or enforced) means to private or sectional ends.

The onset of major economic disparities is usually accounted for with some kind of 'trade' postulate (cf. Alden 1982:613–40; Friedman and Rowlands 1977b:204),[7] implicitly retrojecting into prehistory the role of mercantile capital in the rise of modern European capitalism. The bourgeoisie arose, however, by trade and investment within an already

Figure 7.6 An internal conflict theory of state origins (Diakonoff 1969)

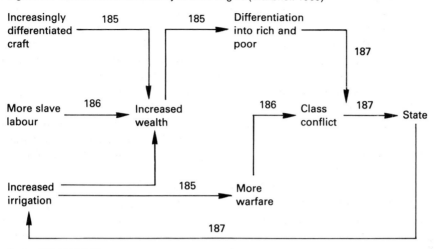

Source: Wright 1978:51
Note: Numbers refer to page references in Diakonoff 1969a

highly stratified and state-ordered society. Such an analogy cannot account for aboriginal stratification. The ethnographic literature abounds in accounts of exchanges affective, ceremonial and utilitarian, both between individuals and between corporate groups of band, tribe, and chiefdom societies without any of the parties thereby becoming enriched, for the whole point is reciprocity (Sahlins 1974:185–91). Indeed 'negative reciprocity' is *the* anti-social statement, being either latent hostility or open warfare (raiding); giving without receiving in the first case, taking without giving in the second (ibid.:196–200). But even if wealth was to be accumulated 'in exchange', yet another mechanism would need to come into play to translate this into control of the means of production. Again, the analogy with capitalism, where everything is open to sale, purchase, and amassment, and where private prerogative has displaced social responsibility, is entirely misleading for prehistoric conditions (Dalton 1981:18–22).

One gets some inkling of an entirely different 'mode', not least of 'exchange', where the greatest good in, and the strongest bonds for, the reproduction and cohesion of society, are brought about by the exchange not of commodities but of people, i.e. women. In return for this 'good', goods and services flow in return from the 'wife-takers'. Are we to reckon this as the 'sale' of women? Only if we apply our totally inappropriate market categories; one is tempted to rejoin, in the words of Paul Lafargue (1891:16), that: 'If political economists so confidently refer capital to the childhood of humanity, it is because they indulge themselves in a convenient ignorance of the customs of primitive peoples.'

217

Both Henry T. Wright (1969, 1972) and Gregory A. Johnson (1973) have conducted field research in southwestern Iran aimed directly at testing monocausal explanations for the rise of the state. This area, centred upon Susa and which was to become the early historic state of Elam, is directly relevant as it lies southeast of the Tigris and forms part of Greater Mesopotamia. In their joint summary (1975:283–6) they maintain that while local exchanges make for regional cohesion and self-sufficiency, 'there is some inter-regional movement of metals, but little else'. And having dismissed 'the hypothesis that population growth in a circumscribed area is in itself a necessary and sufficient condition for primary state formation', since population had actually fallen in the preceding centuries, they conclude that 'there was not primary expansion of exchange just prior to state formation. Inter-regional exchange did not increase markedly until the end of the Uruk Period' (ibid.), which is in fact the period *after* the advent of the world's first states.

Hence neither from ethnography nor archaeology is there any support for the prime role of trade in Sumerian state origins, whatever its role may have been later (Adams 1974:239–56); and if a stratification model is to be pursued it must find other transformative mechanisms.

In fact a stratification model *type*[8] is possible if, and only if, a number of considerations are met:

1 it concentrates upon control of the means of production, that is, it rigorously deals with the *relations of production*;
2 it ceases to be a monocausal model relying upon a single prime mover;
3 accordingly, it stresses simultaneity of processes and does not look to pre-existent economic classes to secrete the state;
4 it sees the state as a 'total political system', not simply a bundle of apparatuses, but as the arena of contest and exchange between ideological, economic, and military forces; and hence one, as Fried (op. cit.:36) justly remarks, that is 'a source of revolutionary transformation of culture in general'.

In a processual sense this must imply that power gained in any major field – ideological, production or distribution, war-leadership, dispute resolution – is able to crystallize other sources of power around itself to the extent that the organizational locus of that initial position of power is itself sufficiently central in the social structure. In Mesopotamia there were two such leading organizations: the temple and the settlement nucleated around it, the urban settlement itself; generating respectively, and in chronological succession, **ensí** and **lugal**. But they personally were not the state; that, as we shall show next, is an outcome of certain relations of production.

3 Relations of production and the advent of the state in Mesopotamia

Having dispensed with the presently encountered types of models as either too general, too partial, or just contradicted by the evidence, it is possible to outline my own working model of state formation, based on the Mesopotamian material adduced in previous and subsequent chapters (see Figure 9.7, p. 272).

Since we are dealing with agriculture, we are dealing at this point with landholding, of which there are two basic forms in pre- and early-historic Mesopotamia. Temple land, the agrarian property of the community as a whole, but run by temple personnel for cultic purposes and as community reserve. Second, but originally of greater extent, land held corporatively by 'patriarchal clans'. Over time this twofold landholding tended to produce a tripartite division of arable land, resulting in temple lands, community land, and a private sector of lands held by eminent individuals from land alienated by the 'kinship' sector. While cultivation was originally by community labour on temple domain, with the labour of kin on the 'patriarchal', both came to rely increasingly (during the Early Dynastic period) and preponderantly thereafter on the varieties of dependent labour specified previously. As weaker clans and lineages went under, they were forced to alienate land, while their members eventually became either seasonal wage labourers or formed types of client subordinate labour, most typically receiving rations, in the other (now three) sectors.

In parallel the supreme temple functionaries had gained control of the 'public' land and its reserves, due in large measure to the fact that they never came to 'own' temple resources as their own property, since the city god 'owned' the temple as his household. Such 'corporate control', however, served to crystallize state apparatuses from temple personnel at the highest levels (**sanga, en, ensí**).

With continual inter-community conflict a warrior elite led by a **lugal** (literally 'big-man') like Gilgamesh emerged from the ranks of the citizenry of good family. When this office, originally transient because reversionary (**bala**), supplanted and dominated the emergent temple hierarchy, it became permanent and the locus of all the levers of power – ideological and economic, as well as military (Diakonoff 1982:66). In this fusion it is particularly important to note 'the Mesopotamian conception according to which *royal* piety is the warrant for national well-being and fertility'[9] (Hallo 1975:212; original emphasis). The stabilization of such concentrated (but far from absolute) power characterizes the Early Dynastic period and reaches its archetype in the Sargonic period.

The following chapter will examine the mainsprings of such processes in the movement from status to state, from intrinsic role differentiation to the formal concentration of powers giving quite a new dimension to relations of super- and sub-ordination. But if a single solvent is sought to commence this process on the alluvium, it can be found in the ruination of households differentially exposed and succumbing to demographic (internal) and environmental (farming) pressures.

Chapter eight

From status to state

1 Status as the prerequisite of all social roles and offices

All peoples have status and rank, not all have had stratification and the state. It is possible, however, to show that the latter is rooted in the former and that no external inputs are required to produce social classes and the state.

By status I do not mean the usual conflation of prestige with rank, nor of charisma with power, but instead employ status in the literal (Latin rooted) sense of 'standing', particularly in the life-cyclical sense, as we currently use the the term 'marital status'. Both roles and statuses are, of course, culturally conferred; however, status is an individual *condition* derived from (ascribed to) belonging to a particular category of persons, while the role or the office held is always active and (interpersonal) relational.

One can have the status (kinship-position) of son or son-in-law, but not the status of priest, which is an *office* embodying roles of ministry and pontificacy. The 'status' of priest is an idiomatic usage for the prestige which many associate with the office.

The important thing from the point of view of the present discussion, is that to hold the office of priest one must have the *status* of male + adult, as prerequisite to all other requirements.

'Status' is then a 'position' held by an individual in the overall system of social relations, which refers to that category of persons' fundamental fitness or capacity.

'Role' refers to the operation of sets of relationships by someone with the right status. Thus 'father' is the role set played by a male – having adult status and having contracted a legitimate marriage – toward spouse, children, affines, etc.; he is not necessarily the begetter of the children.

One *has* a status, one *performs* a role, and one *occupies* (or 'holds') an office, which is a role in an organization. Hence 'Status is an elementary form of office' (Hughes 1958, cited Fortes 1962:61), since what is held by the individual, not *qua* individual (like a particular office), but as a member of an appropriate social category, is a social position, no matter how many other people share that status.

Consequently 'kinship terminologies are built up from the initial specification of statuses fixed by criteria of sex and generation that reduce to filiation and siblingship' (Fortes 1972:293). Indeed the life-cyclical statuses of infant, child, youth, adult, and senior, coupled with the invariants of sex, are the fundamental status sets, and the ones prerequisite to the holding of all others. Consequently, 'It is because a man is invested with (licensed for) husbandhood that his children are able to be born into their "ascribed" status' (Fortes 1962:84).

The very process of making fundamental discriminations that categorize groups of persons as to their fundamental social capacities, lays the basis for ranking. The most fundamental categorization is, of course, male and female. Relations between the sexes are inherently non-symmetrical, due to the brute facts of superior male power (or, more anthropologically, due to hominid sexual dimorphism). Culture might overlay, modify, sanction, or suppress this fact to greater or lesser degree, but it always inheres in social relationships, whatever type of social order obtains.[1]

Citizenship, full membership in the society, is thus the ascription *par excellence*.[2] As Fortes (1962:87) puts it: 'Citizenship, surely, means the sum total of all the legitimate offices, statuses and roles a person can have in his society.' And conversely, Finley (1983a:75), defines the ascription of slavery as the absence of 'offices, statuses and roles', the slave thereby having assumed object 'status'; that is, having no status at all in the sense developed here.

By 'prestige', now separated out from status, I shall mean differential respect or esteem, and that only. But the usual conflation of prestige with status is now easy to understand, since those of 'eminent standing', performing public roles or holding important office, enjoy prestige. It is, however, obstructive to analysis.

'Rank' I shall employ exclusively to mean relations of superiority and inferiority in a way that applies much more generally than social class. Thus Gluckman, analysing such relationships in the traditional state of the Lozi in Zambia, speaks of:

> Rank – the relationship of lord (*mulena*) and underling (*mutanga*); of parent (*mushemi*) and child (*mwana*); of warden or owner (*mung'a*) and a person (*mutu*) or thing (*nto*) – is implicit in every Lozi relationship. Each of these three types of relationship, these three kinds of ranking, is contained in the others. The parent is lord over his child and owns him; the husband is lord over his wife and owns her; the king is parent of his followers and owns them.
>
> (Gluckman 1959:43)

And while 'social stratification is present wherever an objectively differential distribution of life chances and situations obtains among categories or groups of persons ranked as superior and inferior within the social aggregate' (Smith 1977:29), the use of the term social *class*, meaning distinctly identified social strata, will be restricted in my usage to *those with a shared position in the relations of production*. This in preference to the more usual, indeed implicitly standard, 'shared relations to the means of production'.

The relationships between the foregoing can be systematized as follows:

Society I take to be the association of living persons, patterned by place and time, that is, by geography and history, and therefore sharing (at least elements of) a common culture.

Culture is then their mode of interaction with one another and their environment, deriving from the cumulative intergenerational transmission of beliefs, behaviours, and techniques. Hence culture is something that pre-exists each generation, and their induction to it is called *socialization*. Culture is, therefore, something that each generation modifies somewhat, but does not make anew. It is both a product of past social structure and serves to reproduce social structure.

As Fortes observes:

Culture is universally the vehicle of the constraint that is the essence of society; and language shows this paradigmatically because it exemplifies more rigorously than any other constituent part of culture what I describe as the sovereignty of rules in social life.

(Fortes 1983:4–5)

Status is social location setting out capacities and (potential) competencies, attaching, for example, to those of a certain age, sex, or birth. Those ascribe to categories of individuals the ability to perform certain roles.

Role is repeated, because culturally stabilized, interpersonal relationship(s), ultimately dyadic (1:1). They are the specific practices that status allows. Accordingly, roles are patterns of expected behaviour, directed to certain social ends. It is, then, the grid of social positions, which are role-bearing locations, that I consider to be the *social structure*.

Institutions are integrated clusters of roles invested with norms. Institutions, examples being marriage, ancestor veneration, or trial-by-jury, are goal-directed, in the case of marriage toward social reproduction through the domestic unit, with the simultaneous reproduction of statuses also. However, marriage and the domestic unit (which it launches), as institutions, require a particular organization to come into existence for their goals to be realized; in this case that organization is the household.

Organizations emerge to expedite institutions. They are thus *goal serving* while institutions are merely goal oriented or directed. Organizations consist in offices, which are narrowly specialized roles, being task-specific and thus rule-bounded. The structure of organizations I regard as the *social order*.

Though the original rationale of organizations is to serve the institutions – thus, church/religion, courts/retribution, household/domestic unit[3] – the two can often conflict at both the politico-economic (i.e. public) levels, and the private (role-playing) levels. Contradictions between social structure and social order, that is, between institutions and organizations, are of course a major source of social conflict, not least because organizations develop their own justifications, momentum, and innovations, often conflicting with or undermining the institutions they are meant to express. This of course is quite additional to the contradictions within the institutions as a group and the organizations as a group.

Social system, to repeat, designates social arrangements seen from a strictly operational viewpoint, as sets of input/output relations between operative entities (sub-systems) chosen for the purposes of modelling. Thus the economic or subsistence sub-system of foragers divides into male hunting with some gathering, and female gathering with some hunting, in most latitudes. Subsistence is here our term for a set of *different activities*, while the ideological sub-system (which would certainly affect hunting), is separated off as a set of myths, symbols, beliefs, classifications, and rituals that *we* have put into a single 'cosmology' box for the purposes of study. When we try to show how, for example, cosmology affects subsistence and vice versa, and interconnects with other social activities or attributes also regarded as sub-systems (such as technology or warfare), we may be said to be modelling a *social system*. It is a construct of purely analytical convenience in the attempt to trace causative relations between entities of quite different levels, such as marriage (an institution), technology (material culture), and warfare (concentrated political acts).

2 Intrinsic sources of rank

At the outset I made the perhaps surprising statement that all peoples had status and rank embodied in their social structures. In order to be correct, this statement must hold for the least organized and most egalitarian societies known to ethnography.[4]

Hadza hunter-gatherers live in small, fluid, and mobile bands in Tanzania, and are as acephalous as might be, hence Woodburn's description of them as exhibiting 'minimal politics' (1979:245). They have no formal leadership even to the extent of people dodging positions to which any responsibility attaches, and conflict is resolved 'by scattering' (ibid.:250). Yet there is still some ranking, for:

> The initiated men hold jointly the right to eat in secret certain specific portions of the best meat of each large game animal killed. Which portions they are depends on the species of animal but they always consist of the fatty meat which the Hadza value particularly highly and are cut from the carcass with great care. The men must eat the meat together well away from the women and children; they must not be seen eating and they deny to the women and children that they have eaten.
>
> (Woodburn 1979:254)

This is clearly a privilege, a prerogative of rank held by men on the basis of their status, that of being adult male initiates. It is also a privilege expressing their superiority to women and children that is maintained on the basis of their collective power, for, against them 'the men guard their privilege of eating the sacred meat with the greatest rigour' (ibid.), the sanctions ranging from assault and the destruction of property to rape; while serious illness is usually attributed to unknowing consumption of the sacred meat by non-initiates.

What is manifested here, then, in such relations of super- and subordination, is rank, conferring differential access to resources on the basis of fundamental status. This is quite clearly visible amongst Australian hunter-gatherers also, for whom, for example, 'every active relationship among the Yir Yoront involved a definite and accepted status of superordination and subordination' (Sharp 1964:88). So much was this the case that 'a person could have no dealings with another on exactly equal terms. The nearest approach to equality was between brothers, although the older was always superordinate to the younger' (Sharp, op. cit.:88). Harner (1975:128) speaks in similar terms of the Jivaro Indians of the Upper Amazon who practise a mixture of hunting, fishing, gathering, and horticulture and where 'women are both formally and informally subordinate to men'.

The two axes of social differentiation are thus age and sex (La Fontaine 1978b:3). However, the whole point is that 'the classification of human beings differs from the classification of animals or plants in that it constrains the behaviour of those classified. Members of a society identify themselves and others in terms of distinctions and act in relation to these identifications' (ibid.). This is, of course, the whole point of kinship terminology and of status in general as it is defined above. At another level, that of the classification of things, knowing their 'secret names' is thought, as amongst the Baruya of New Guinea, to confer upon the magical practitioner the power of constraining the things thus known (Godelier 1977:197). As people act implicitly according to their classification of each other, they generally imagine that the non-human world is similarly constrained.

Drawing upon her own fieldwork amongst the Gisu of Uganda, La Fontaine describes how

> The boys who are initiated by the ritual both experience and express the underlying principles of age-differentiation: that life is an ordered series of stages, that experience confers authority and demands respect, that traditional knowledge is the basis of the elders' power. Two further points are of relevance to this discussion: first, that immaturity and maturity are ranked stages in the life-cycle. *Their relationship is thus one of intrinsic hierarchy, not complementarity.* Secondly, boys are equated with women and men with the role of husband, that is, initiation confers domestic *authority* on men.
>
> (La Fontaine 1978b:12, my emphasis; cf. Meillassoux (1960) 1978a:134)

While kinship and descent obtain in all societies, in some, such as ours, they function to provide or deny access to other social prerogatives (and thus might be called 'vectoral'), whereas in what is conventionally called 'tribal' society kinship relations *are themselves* polyfunctional relations of production (Godelier 1980:6; Bloch 1973:86–7). Fortes (1969:276) describes, *inter alia*, the 'modern Euro-American family' as inhabiting 'a system in which simple filiation is the sole and exclusive source of full civic, moral and ritual status [and] in which no cognisance is taken of ancestry antecedent to the parents for any social purposes'. If not for 'any' social purpose, at least for most this distinction applies in contrast to 'kinship-ordered' societies. And whereas

> filiation[5] is the relation that exists between a person and his parents only, descent refers to a relation mediated by a parent between himself and an ancestor, defined as any genealogical predecessor of the grand-parental or earlier generation. *A grandparent is therefore a person's closest ancestor.*
>
> (Fortes 1970:108; my emphasis)

Relations of production are analysed extensively in Chapter 9. Here we simply cite Godelier's theoretical summary in order to say what is unique to the 'kinship mode'. For Godelier, then, relations of production are

> all social relations whatsoever, which serve a threefold function: first to determine social access to and control of resources and the means of production; secondly to redistribute the social labour force among the different labour processes, and to organise these processes; and thirdly to determine the social distribution of the product of labour.
>
> (Godelier 1980:6)

Thus, the components of kinship-ordered relations of production are:

1 production for the direct use of the producers (organized by age and sex only), with human labour (and correlatively natural abundance/fertility) the main force of production.
2 production by associated households which are also the consuming units.
3 direct access to both instruments and objects of production by all producers, who are thus technically competent to make or manage their own tools, domesticates, etc. ('instruments'), and have the 'right' to apply them to their productive ends ('objects'), restricted if at all only by sex and seniority.
4 the unit of production coincides with the unit of reproduction, the domestic group; with the notable exception that spouses must be found from households other than those of origin.

The main point here is that social reproduction is a matter of replacing the requisite individuals in their 'rightful places' to 'continue the corporation', with consequently strong jural implications, connected as such places are with specific rights and obligations (Fortes 1969:300).

As a society of 'domestic economy' outlined above is one of direct production of use-values for the sustenance and replacement of its members, it is one necessarily ordered by conceptions of kinship.

> Where the living are thus decreed by custom to be, and see themselves to be, their progenitors . . . incarnate, so to speak, extension of the category of the person from the filial-parental relationship to the most distant relationship of actual or presumed kinship is not logically difficult. That is how it comes about that the notion of the juristic person may be extended, in however attenuated a degree, to include the members of a widely dispersed clan, as among the Ashanti and the Alur.
>
> (Fortes 1969:305)

Fortes's point is that descent groups form corporations as the very 'organizing principle' (into structurally similar units) of a society where reproduction of people is of the greatest moment. Hence the 'corporations' or social molecules are acting as if they were biological entities obeying the fundamental rule of organisms – simply to stay in the game. Hence 'particular forms of property relations are contingent upon, not constitutive of corporate group structure; and this applies to every aspect of property relations, no matter what may be the customary ways in which title arises and is devolved or disposed of' (Fortes 1969:302).

What is being transmitted is always a specific cultural property, even if only a particular identity; but often too, songs, dances, myths, and rites are 'handed down' genealogically (Fortes 1970:111). It is however generally when rights in land or animals are transmitted through descent, manifesting the 'strong' or 'pedigree' principle of genealogy (ibid.:107) that what crystallizes is the classic 'tribal'[6] system constructed of lineages and clans with rights 'descending from' an apical ancestor, in contrast to the essentially 'filial' form of foraging bands in which there is little contrast between family and public relationships (ibid.:122).

Lee and DeVore (1968b:11) made a couple of fundamental assumptions about hunter-gatherers which they characterized as 'nomadic style'. If we elaborate their points (1, 2) that:

1 they live in small groups;
2 they move around a lot; therefore
3 they accumulate few possessions;

we can readily understand why

4 social arrangements are very flexible.

This can be contrasted with what can be called 'cultivator's style':

1 they live in larger groups (typically by factors of 4 to 8);
2 they do not move much;
3 they tend to accumulate possessions (both luxuries and equipment);

from which we can see why

4 social arrangements are highly regulated, not least in rights to land.

Given demographic and environmental fluctuation, the matching of people to resources means that one or the other must be mobile. In foraging it is of course the people who move, as also with slash and burn horticulturalists. When fixed-site agriculture has been adopted it is the produce that must circulate. And when cultivable land is short, it must be matched to demand in the most efficient way so that none goes underexploited and, if possible, none is overtaxed. When restrictions on available land are great, artificial restriction of access by the rigidities of lineal descent are inappropriate and cognatic principles are by far the most efficient (Goodenough 1968:146).

In the classic case of Trobriand island horticulturalists, with villages and their gardens fixed, it is subsistence resources that move to knit up producing and consuming units into a whole, a society. In this matrilineal society, foodstuffs, in particular *taytu* tubers (small yams) which are the staple, move matrilaterally from the adult male producer to his nearest lineal female, usually his sister. This means that 'there is the main garden, *kaymata*, the yield of which is chiefly devoted to the supply of the female relatives' (Malinowski 1979:125), in particular his sister(s)' marital household. This transmission, called *urigubu*, consists of the majority and the best tubers produced. After every harvest they are ceremonially transmitted to another village where the lineal female recipient lives patrilocally. While the clan is the unit of exogamy, 'it must be emphatically stated here that it is not the clan which acts as a unit in this complementary division of functions' (between production, residence, and reproduction of the matrilineage) 'but definitely the group consisting of brother, sister and her offspring' (ibid.:128). Yet on such a basis is the whole of society linked up in systemic exchanges, with yet further redistributions at feasts, ceremonies, and rites (ibid.:39).

But circulation serves not only to link together the autonomous social units; it serves also, and paradoxically, as the basis of an over-ranking authority in the chief, which further reduces autonomy. However, this is not a contradiction, for in the Trobriands the chiefly institution and its revenues exist 'by virtue of his position as a glorified brother-in-law to the whole community' (ibid.:132). At whatever level of eminence, from village headman to paramount chief,

> most of the chief's tribute, though not all, is given as a glorified contribution from wife's brother to sister's husband, only in the case of a woman married to a chief, her whole sub-clan would labour for her and not merely one of her male relatives.
>
> (Malinowski 1979:131)

And since chiefs are traditionally polygynous, Malinowski estimated that a paramount chief with around sixty wives was in receipt of some four hundred times as much income as an average commoner. A commoner was also liable to render his chiefly brother-in-law 'a much wider range of services than is normally due from brother to sister's husband' (ibid.). Those revenues, to which are added some other tithes and dues, are used for political instrumentalities, in particular the financing of large projects such as the construction of the long-distance trade and warfare canoes, large store-houses and dwellings, in addition to public ceremonies (ibid.:51–2).

The creation, disposition, and significance of surplus is dealt with below. Here we simply enter a further consideration on incorporation and the descent principle, also examined ethnographically below. Where 'local contiguity', instead of being complementary to the descent principle as it is, for example, with the Nuer or Tiv, becomes dominant, as it has in the Zambesi floodplain of the Lozi or in the rice valleys of the Malagasy Merina, then the descent system 'closes around' the property as it were, and itself collapses, producing for the Merina a valley-localized endogamy in which there are no affines or neighbours, only cognatic[7] kindred, and no external kinship ties to other valleys, only strangers (Bloch 1977:307). The 'organizing principles' of society have altered from a descent to a territorial principle dependent on joint residence and simple cognatic filiation (Fortes 1969:131), because the mode of production has itself evolved. Here Godelier's definition of 'mode of production' is again relevant. It refers to a specific combination of determinate productive forces and of determinate social relations constituting both material and social conditions, and the internal material and social structures through which society acts upon its natural environment in order to extract from it a series of socially useful goods.

(Godelier 1980:6)

3 Loci of authority in the conditions of reproduction

As far as the pastoral Fulani are concerned, Stenning is particularly clear that social cohesion does not inhere at the level of production but of reproduction, specifically at the level of the conditions of reproduction:

> In the context of seasonal variations and irregular natural hazards, the agnatic descent group and the clan are agencies for the re-establishment of the viability of their constituent families. This function emerges primarily when non-viability is caused by shortages of cattle. Indeed the ability of an agnatic descent group to act in this way is contingent upon the dispersal of its constituent families. Only by endowing household heads with full responsibility for the fertility of their herds and full authority for their deployment is it possible to succour any member of the agnatic lineage group whose family cannot maintain its viability.
>
> (Stenning 1958:114)

In other words the 'full authority' of household heads for the autonomy of the individual households is not opposed to, but the pre-condition of, enduring relations at a societal level, in this case through the medium of the agnatic descent group. This must be so for all societies in which living labour with its accumulated experience and skills is not crystallized in the form of technology with the extensive control of the environment this permits (Meillassoux 1978a:153). Social control in such 'synergistic' societies instead resides in control of people, most notably women, with the central axis of authority running from senior to junior males (ibid.:137). Specialists after the manner of Trobriand canoe builders are not specialized in equipment but in accumulated technique, and even then are not full-time experts (Malinowski 1922:133). The great sea-going canoes differ from the lesser types only 'in the amount of time spent over their construction and the care given to details, rather than in essentials' (ibid.:113).

The clan and the lineage, then, secure for their component units their conditions of production in terms of shared access to land, water, game, etc., that Marx calls 'the great workshop, the arsenal which furnishes both means and material of labour as well as the seat, the *base* of the community. They relate naïvely to it as the *property of the community*, of the community producing and reproducing itself in living labour' (Marx 1973:472; original emphasis).

Rather than being just a position of domestic authority, headship of the basic productive and reproductive unit of society is the prime prerequisite for political influence and office. The *paterfamilias* is simultaneously a function of, and the bridge to, the 'politico-jural order' in Fortes's terminology. 'Indeed in most societies, male adult status, headship of a household and an independent role in public affairs are closely associated' (La Fontaine 1978b:16). Being *in patria potestas* in particular and in general dependent towards the father's generation ('seniors'), crucially for wives, can be tolerated by juniors because it can appear to be but a stage in the life-cycle towards headship and seniority, open to all men, 'in due course', and in which the establishment, upon marriage, of a household under his own authority is the fundamental step (Meillassoux 1978a:139).

In contrast to a kindred organization which is ego-centred, in a lineal organization structured through ancestors ('pedigree focussed' – Fortes 1969:281), it is easy to see the co-residential unit as the 'live' end of the descent group (or, better, 'principle') and thus as the living realization of that principle in a segmentary structure. The classic case of segmentary (opposed and complementary) social structure is, of course, the Nuer. In the diagram (Figure 8.1) we see that 'A whole clan is thus a genealogical structure, and the letters in the diagram represent persons from whom the clan and its segments trace their descent and from whom they take their names' (Evans-Pritchard 1940:192–3).

Apical clan A is segmented into maximal lineages B and C and these bifurcate into major lineages D, E, F, and G. Minor lineages H, I, J, and K are segments of major lineages D and G, and L, M, N, and O are minimal lineages which are segments of H and K.

Figure 8.1 Segmentary kinship structure

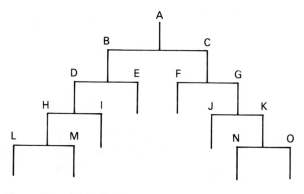

Source: Evans-Pritchard 1940:193

231

It is important to realize that this segmentary lineage structure is, as it were, the framework of an acephalous (stateless) society, a framework for actual relations 'on the ground'. The lineage structure serves only as a skeleton, it does not determine each and every decision and relationship, for those are the outcome of 'a lack of fit between local (i.e. residence) structure and lineage structure . . . due to the needs of cattle and the changing seasons'; also to fluctuations imposed by the state of war or peace prevailing at any time, where if fighting obtains lineages need to regroup for purposes of solidarity (Bloch 1973:84–5).

A minimal lineage is a group with at least three, more usually four or five generations' depth (Evans-Pritchard, op. cit.:196–7) and not to be confused with the domestic group, which is a co-residential group. Lineages as lines of descent are schemata of reckoning and indeed morality (Bloch, op. cit.:85) and so neither co-residential groups nor villages can be reduced to lineages, if only because spouses necessarily derive from other lineages and (in the Nuer case) matrilateral kin are readily attached to the co-residential group.

> A single living hut (*dwil* or *ut*) is occupied by a wife and her children and, at times, by her husband. They constitute a simple residential family group. The homestead, consisting of a byre and huts, may contain a simple family group or a polygynous family and there are often one or two kinsmen living there as well. This group which we may call a household is often referred to as the *gol*, a word which means 'hearth'.
>
> (Evans-Pritchard 1940:114)

In Figure 8.2 the relation between a three-generation (proto) lineage and their residence pattern in a segmentary structure, can readily be seen from this mapping of Tiv genealogy onto the typical compound arrangement. It was this sort of '*kraal*' pattern that was raised in Chapter 4 in regard to the formation of villages in the Near East as seen by Flannery.

In Figure 8.2 we can see from the solid triangles of the deceased males in this patrilineal system, how the lineage structure is a 'mode of relation' for all the people of the compound (*ya*), whose composition may range from two or three to forty huts, but in which *a minority of the people present* actually belong to the lineage in question, the lineage of 'ownership'.

So it is with village clusters too. While the (agnatic) descent structure forms a skeleton for settlement, the flesh of daily life is filled in by all those who live and work together in the village.

> Nuer villages are not corporate, localised, communities, though they are frequently associated with territorial units, and those members of a

Figure 8.2 'Genealogical map' of a Tiv compound

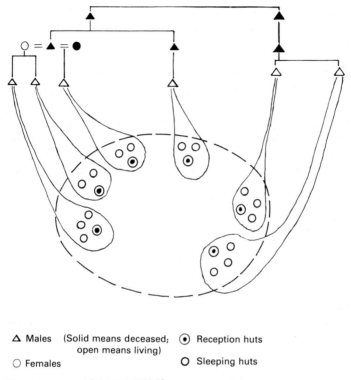

△ Males   (Solid means deceased;   ⊙ Reception huts
           open means living)
○ Females   ○ Sleeping huts

After Bohannan and Bohannan 1968:15

lineage who live in an area associated with it see themselves as a residential group, and the value, or concept, of lineage thus functions through the political system. Every Nuer village is associated with a lineage, and, though the members of it often constitute only a small proportion of the village population, the village community is identified with them (the *dil* lineage) in such a way that we may speak of it as an aggregate of persons clustered round an agnatic nucleus.

(Evans-Pritchard 1940:203)

In this clustering process individual and minor or sub-lineages will be attached to the dominant or 'aristocratic' (*dil*) lineage of a village by turning a relationship through marriage to one of the *dil*'s daughters into a fictive-agnatic descent over time (Gough 1971:83). Thus the residential-territorial reality is squared with the politico-jural.

In this way the rules of exogamy isolate the dominant lineages within each tribe as a whole and permit their segmentary structure to provide a rough framework for the segmentary oppositions between territorial sections, while at the same time each local lineage of the dominant clan is fused with other elements to form a solidary community.

(Gough 1971:83)

Speaking of 'The community and domestic group among Nilo-Hamitic pastoralists', Bonte summarizes the relationship of domestic to residential and kinship group by pointing out that

the domestic group is an independent production unit. It is also a kinship unit based on the polygynous family (2–3 wives on average) itself a part of a larger group, the patrilineal extended family, made up of three generations: fathers, married sons and their offspring. Within the family, most of the work is allocated according to sex and age.

(Bonte 1977:177)

To summarize the argument so far, and to anticipate the discussion to come on kinship and property, ranking and stratification, all of which are political in idiom, we can say that what a lineage represents above all is the descent *principle* – that rights and duties shall be transmitted according to criteria of membership (types of filiation) which do not obtain in society at large. In fact to be a fully functioning member of a lineal society one must first have membership in a corporate lineal group, i.e. be 'affiliated' to it by real or fictive kinship. Ancestor worship, so prevalent in China and Japan, is thus the hypostatization of the continuity and authority of the corporate group. Lineages exist to transmit (allocate) social standing or social (real) property (i.e. not personal possessions), but basically, control of land (Ember, Ember, and Pasternak 1974:74).

Where the property thus allocated *is* social standing it is, structurally, political position. Then revenues, rather than accruing from the ownership of land (privately or in trust) accrue from the 'ownership' of ('right to') office in a political organization. In the case of Roman politics, for instance, to be a member of the political classes, one had first to be a member of the large landowning classes, which were at least in Republican times also the most prestigious because venerable (Finley 1983c:129–32).

However, in China, without private property in land, revenues were derived from position in the state apparatus, which gave access to private wealth accumulation. Clans held land and their representatives held the offices of state:

In these societies, the kind of authority and right here at issue is generated and exercised through social relations created by kinship and descent. Jural authority vests in a person by virtue of kinship status or of office that, in the last resort, depends upon descent. Ancestors symbolize the continuity of the social structure, and the proper

allocation, at any given time, of the authority and right they held and
transmitted. Ancestor worship puts the final source of jural authority
and right, or to use the more inclusive term, jurisdiction, on a pedestal,
so to speak, where it is inviolable and unchallengeable, and thus able to
mobilize the consent of all who must comply with it.

(Fortes and Dieterlen 1965:137)

The 'inverted tree' form of (segmentary) genealogy given above
(Figure 8.1) as characteristic of acephalous lineal society, while
containing seniors and juniors, heads of strong lineages and client
lineages, though it provided a basis for rank, none the less did not
manifest social stratification, which denies free access to the means of
production by the socially inferior who thus become subordinate.

The point, then, is to show how the ranked but essentially egalitarian
structure is transformed into another kinship structure in which a real
hierarchy prevails that can in turn serve as the basis for the cleavage into
rulers and ruled. Such a transformation can be represented as in Figure
8.3.

Referring to Figure 8.3, as lineages 'branch away' (ramify) from the
direct line back to the mythical ancestor and venerated founder, other
branches of the 'noble' line diminish in prestige and power. Then they
just merge into commoner lines which are of short genealogical depth.

For the group to increase and include a greater number of lineages it is
essential, if one is to respect the principle of identifying age with
power, to project into the past the source of authority claimed by the
living senior. This projection into the past then justifies the power of
the senior over a group more or less proportional to the number of

Figure 8.3 Scheme of ranking of chiefly ramage, reflecting in genealogy the rank and
precedence of the villages

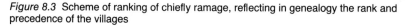

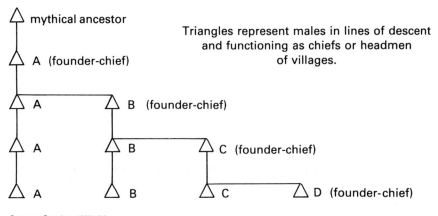

Source: Service 1975:80

235

generations which separate the dead ancestor from the living senior.
(Meillassoux 1978a:147)

4 The 'Asiatic' mode of stratification by conical clans

Just how stratification can arise directly from the ranking of lineages has
been shown in the context of Southeast Asia by Jonathan Friedman,
drawing especially upon Leach's (1954) classic study of Highland Burma.
This deals with the political structures of the 300,000 people of the
Kachin Hills area, thinly but unevenly scattered over an area of some
50,000 square miles between Assam and Yunnan (see Map 8.1). They are
culturally disparate but politically interlinked through common ritual
practices and a kinship system under which 'all Kachins recognise the
existence of an elaborate system of patrilineal clanship elaborately
segmented. The lineages of this clan system ramify throughout the Kachin
Hills Area and override all frontiers of language and local custom' ((1954)
1970:57). Leach himself observes (1970:159) that what makes the Kachin
particularly interesting 'is that they have a society which is simultaneously
segmentary and class stratified'.

The Kachin are swidden horticulturalists of the monsoon upland
rainforest (where it has not been degenerated from climax) and their
principal crop is dry rice, supplemented by humped cattle, chickens, and
pigs, with buffalo meat available at major sacrifices.

It is the growing of rice by swidden methods (called locally
taungya = ladang), not any ethnic criteria that distinguishes the Kachin
from the Shan paddy cultivators of the valley floors, where buffalo are
employed for ploughing and harrowing (Leach 1970:32). Kachin adopting
Shan settlement and cultivation practice 'become' Shan and Buddhist,
and Kachin society in the hills oscillates between a more or less
hierarchical order in its periodic variation between the *gumsa* and *gumlao*
condition. While *gumlao* society is ranked but acephalous, *gumsa*
ideology represents society as a large-scale feudal state (ibid.:50) under a
prince or chief, though between *gumsa* and *gumlao* the mode of
production does not change; which is why, for the Kachin, those political
processes are reversible (where the ecology remains intact). Shan society,
by contrast, is a stable hierarchy with permanent 'princes' (*saopha*) ruling
over tenants (ibid.:288). None the less in the Highlands the terrain
suitable for Shan-type systems is severely limited, being confined to river
valleys and basins. Only the large sustainable surpluses that paddy makes
available allows the emergence of permanently stratified Shan society,
which is accordingly ecologically constrained (ibid.:40). Naturally such
areas are permanently and relatively densely settled, centring upon a
Shan township adjacent to irrigated rice lands (ibid.:35).

A Kachin village, by contrast, may contain any number of households

Map 8.1 The hill peoples of the Burma frontier   *Source*: Leach 1970:19

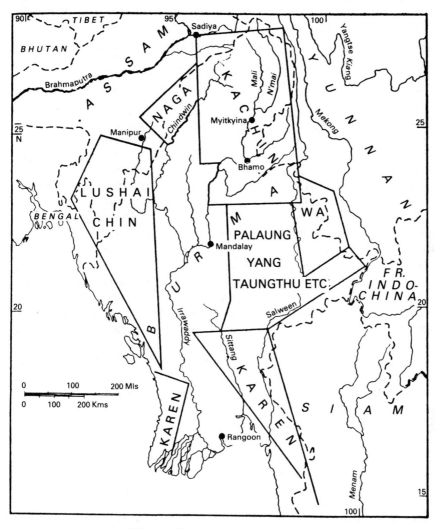

from one upwards (ibid.:114) with a usual range between 10 and 20 households; while the 'villages' in turn agglomerate into (or are sub-divisions of) a 'village cluster' (*mare*). Each village has a hereditary 'headman' from the lineage said to 'own' the land of the village, for 'land title is vested in lineages rather than individuals' (ibid.:68–9), but most villages contain members of half a dozen or more lineages (ibid.). Village sites may move about on their ridges and the land under cultivation shifts each year, but the territory owned by a village in which its reserves are found (of 10 to 20 times the area presently being worked), is permanently held (ibid.:115). Usually the village is named after the lineage owning it, and this lineage is the principal one of the village, its headman *ipso facto* head of the principal lineage (ibid.:116). But though land is corporatively held, it is worked by the component households:

> Usually, in any one year, the members of a village combine to clear a single area of jungle, though sometimes it is only a section of a village group that combines to make a clearing. Once felling, burning and fencing [and sowing, see below] is completed, communal activity ceases. Within the total clearing (*yin wa*) each household cultivates its own independent plot (*yi*) and there is no communal ownership of produce.

> (Leach 1970:116)

However, the head of the senior village in a cluster, the *duwa* or chief, if politically independent, is entitled to have certain work done on his rice plot without incurring any reciprocal obligation and in some cases is entitled even to tribute of one or two baskets of paddy per household per year (ibid.:121). Such chiefs are called 'thigh-eating' since they are able to claim from all persons not of their own lineage, a hind leg of every four-footed animal within their territory killed either in sacrifice or by hunting (ibid.:121). The economic significance of this prerogative of receiving 'thighs' is not great (ibid.:155); what seems to be of greater significance is that both *gumsa* and *gumlao* chiefs are entitled to summon labour to perform free services on their own behalf, most significantly perhaps, having the field hut built and the field sown, as a right, not as part of the usual reciprocity of obligation such as applies between villagers when assistance is rendered in house-building or sowing (ibid.:135). None the less, 'Within any one domain there is no substantial difference in standard of living between the aristocrats and the commoners – members of both classes eat the same food, wear the same clothes, practise the same skills' (ibid.:162). As for the third class in Kachin society, 'Master and slave live in the same house under almost the same conditions' (ibid.), with the exceptions to be examined below.

'Monsoon *taungya* does not normally produce a crop surplus to the immediate requirements of the cultivator' (ibid.:232) and a politically influential *gumsa* chief must be able to dispose of real economic resources (ibid.:233), which under the above circumstances must be derived either from trade, such as the jade mines, from levies on caravans from China, or by tribute from the surplus-producing Shans (ibid.:237). Conversely, in the deforested area where grassland *taungya* obtains and where accordingly productivity is less and the hill-dwellers dependent upon the valley-dwelling Shans for at least part of their rice supply, *all* political organization is of the *gumsa* type (ibid.:235). Not all forest cultivators are *gumlao* by any means, but the potential at least, exploited by some, exists. By contrast, whether Shans politically dominate hill-dwelling

Kachin in the grassland areas or vice versa, 'the isolated hill community which repudiates all links and interdependence with neighbouring valley communities is not really a practical proposition' (ibid.).

But what is pre-eminently exchanged between lineage units is not so much foodstuffs or labour, as women, means of reproduction. The women are exchanged not bilaterally between two lineages in a reciprocal way, but in a pattern called 'generalized exchange', by which lineage A gives to B which gives to C that gives to D, which in turn supplies A with wives. All Kachin (like other societies of the area) are thus connected into exchanging loops, which are themselves interlinked by changes in lineage membership and shifting alliances through time. The loops are consequently only relatively closed.

Kinship in those societies is the dominant relation of production not only because genealogy is the very basis of the lineage, and the minimal lineage (*htinggaw*) of from one to ten household heads is corporative, but also because women are the predominant means of societal interrelation. This means 'alienating' lineage women's productive and reproductive capacities to another lineage. Conferring this 'ultimate good' upon another lineage calls forth prestige as an implicit counter-prestation upon the conferring lineage. This latter is called the *mayu* lineage, while the receiving lineage, which thus becomes inferior through being in the debt of the donor, is called the *dama* lineage. Hence 'the crucial distinguishing principle of modern Kachin social structure is the *mayu-dama* marriage system' (Leach, op. cit.:249), and these are fundamentally relations of inequality. Therefore 'a *gumlao* community which adheres to *mayu-dama* marriage rules rather easily slips back into practices of a *gumsa* type' (ibid.:211).

It may however seem contradictory that in a system of generalized exchange, where

$$A \rightarrow B \rightarrow C \rightarrow N \rightarrow A$$

it should eventuate as:

$$A > B > C > N > A \qquad \text{where} > = \text{is superior to,}$$

or as Leach illustrates it in Figure 8.4.

Technically what is a system of matrilateral cross cousin marriage (a bar on marriage with the father's sister's daughter) and at least a preference for marriage with the actual or classificatory mother's-brother's daughter (MBD), i.e. an exogamous patrilineage, may not give wives to its wife-giving lineages (*mayu*) nor may it take wives from its wife-taking lineages (*dama*) (ibid.:116); 'is thus a correlate of a system of patrilineal lineages rigged into a class hierarchy' (Leach 1970:256).

However, the exchanges are neither synchronous nor certain and the symmetry of exchanges is only a tendency over time, not an institution of

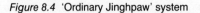

Figure 8.4 'Ordinary Jinghpaw' system

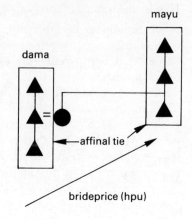

Source: Leach 1961b:121

instantaneous or balanced prestation. Thus lineages which have recently given women are at that point superior in prestige to those upon whom they have recently conferred the women; all things being equal, that is. But is is not only prestige which flows in exchange for women: 'A fixed quantity of wealth or labour circulates from lineage to lineage in exchange for women' according to Friedman (1979:36); especially *hpaga*, prestige goods permitting the possibility 'of a valuation of women, of an alliance, *or of a lineage itself*, all expressed in the variation of the brideprice' (Friedman 1975:170).

Wealth in food, principally buffalo, rice, and rice-beer, is shared in feasting the allied lineages and celebrating the local *nats* (spirits) (ibid.). This in turn confers prestige upon the feast-givers,[8] who, next time they have a marriageable woman, can require a higher brideprice for her higher 'worth'. Conversely a prestigious lineage preferentially attracts available women (ibid.:171) who, of course, add to the productive labour force (and future supply of daughters), so enabling greater feasts to be held adding further to the pre-eminence of that prestigious lineage. While others go into debt trying to keep up, a few lineages emerge that can well afford to play the prestige/production/distribution game, especially since debtor lineages tend to have to work for their superiors to meet their obligations, and so boost the surpluses available to the successful for feasting and boosting brideprice and so forth in a positive feedback system.

The combination of accumulation processes, the production of surpluses, their transformation into control of cattle and the consolidation of rank positions by means of the wife-giver/wife-taker relationship produces an ordered set of lineages.

(Friedman 1979:39)

This is illustrated as follows:

Rank $\qquad$ A > B > C > D ....

Quantity: $\left\{\begin{matrix} \text{Cattle} \\ \text{Brideprice} \end{matrix}\right\}$ A > B > C > D ....$\qquad$ where > = is greater than

Surplus $\qquad$ A > B > C > D ....

There is not, however, one linear ordered set, but a number of 'more or less closed circles of allies capable of paying a similar brideprice, i.e. *a spiral of ranking*' (Friedman 1975:171; my emphasis). Friedman (1974:454) has outlined the flows involved in the emergence of this ranking as shown in Figure 8.5. He calls it the 'Political economy of the minimal segment' and it, 'the motor of the system', is a combination of marriage alliance and feasts:

Community feasts are religious feasts whose dual function is the distribution of surplus/accumulation of prestige and the propitiation of higher spirits in order to increase the wealth and prosperity of the

Figure 8.5 The political economy of the minimal segment

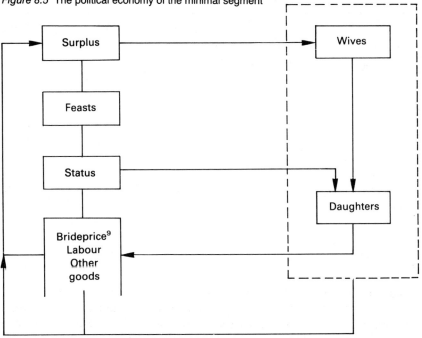

Source: Friedman 1974:454

entire group. We might best characterise this as a religion of productivity in which the real work process is inverted in its immediate appearance. Surplus is represented not as the product of surplus labour, but as the 'work of the gods'.

(Friedman 1975:172)

Feasts are transformed into prestige which as social standing means a higher brideprice for women of elevated position, particularly since male hypogamy (marrying upward) is a requirement for men if they are not to lose rank.

The amount of a girl's brideprice varies according to the rank status of the patrilineage to which she belongs. If her father, her father's father, and her father's father's father have each in turn married women of higher class than themselves, then the girl may be able to claim a brideprice which is higher than that to which her patrilineage would otherwise be entitled.

(Leach 1961b:116)

If what we have just been dealing with is the political economy of the minimal segment, what we now have to explain is what can be called the ideological economy or political ideology of that segment, the minimal patrilineage. As such it projects its (lineage) relations of production and reproduction out into time and space; that is, into the cosmos perceived as earth and sky. Thus we have the segmentary structure extended 'back' and 'up' from the (spiritized) ancestors of the lineage, through the celestial spirits, to the supreme spirit and bisexual progenitor-progenitrix of everything, *Chyanun-Woishun*, in a structure looking like this:

Figure 8.6 The hierarchy of *nats* (spirits)

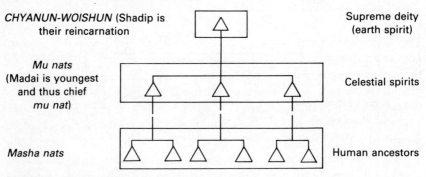

Adapted from Friedman 1979:41

'Conceptually Kachin spirits (*nats*)', Leach (1970:173) observes, 'are "magnificent non-natural men". They simply extend the human class hierarchy to a higher level and are continuous with it.'

Figure 8.7 Gumsa incorporation of village nats

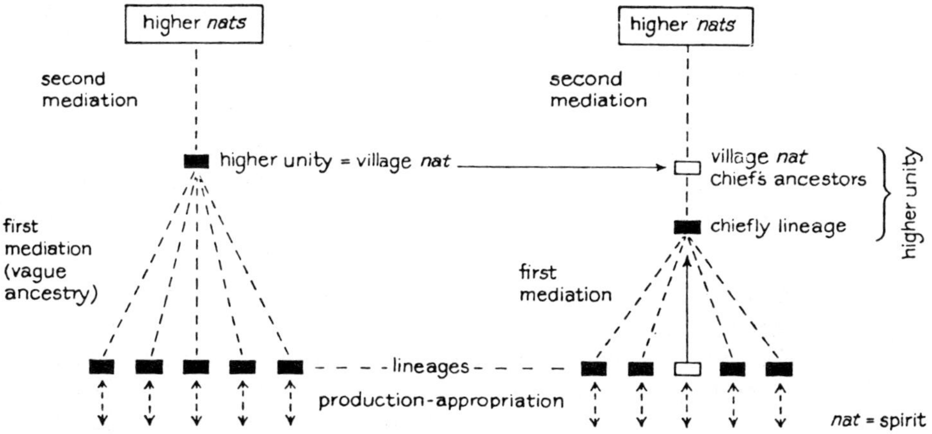

Source: Friedman 1979:44

What is crucial is that for all groups the sources of power, fertility, and security have to be approached through the lower levels of ancestor spirits and celestial spirits. But some groups' ancestors are lower than others, and thus farther from the source of Power, as manifested in their lack of efficacy in providing the wherewithal to feast the village and obtain prestige. Distance from the central power is, as it were, demonstrated by differential ability in tapping it; success breeds success, and success is an index of blessing.

The earth nat [ga nat] who controls production (fertility) is usually approached by the community as a whole through the village priests. The single most important transformation that occurs in the process of hierarchicalisation is the monopolisation of the village spirit by a particular local lineage.

(Friedman 1979:41)

The village spirit (nat), it should be realized, initially 'belongs' to nobody, not even the priests, because it belongs to everybody in its representation of the village community; or, in the emic view, the earth and sky nats 'manifest' the collective existence of the village in its environment. This is the condition indicated on the left in Figure 8.7.

On the right in Figure 8.7, however, the chief's ancestors have become identified with the village spirits,

local spirits who control all lands belonging to the community. The celestial spirits are now ranked by age following earthly rules of succession and the chiefly lineage can now be traced back to the chief celestial deity to whom it is affinally related. Since the chief is genealogically and thus sociologically closer to the forces that control the well-being of the group he is entitled to special privileges.

(Friedman 1979:41)

243

This has been achieved as a result of success in feasting the village and in sacrificing animals to the spirits on the collectivity's behalf, thus assuring the blessing of the spirits on village activities in this 'religion of productivity'.[10]

> The right to sacrifice to Madai and hence to hold a *manau* (feast) is a special prerequisite of the chief. Other rich and influential men do sometimes hold *manau* but in order to do so they must first purchase permission from the chief by means of an appropriate exchange of gifts.
>
> (Leach 1970:119)

As success is thought to ensure success, that lineage best able, that is, engaging in the best distributions, comes permanently to take on the job of representing the village to the *nats*.[11] This results in the village shrine for both the territorial spirit (*mung nat*) and the celestial spirit (*madai nat*) being taken into the eminent lineage's compound, there to be the lineage's 'own' ancestral shrine (Friedman 1975:174). Indeed Leach (1970:113) shows the physical incorporation of the *madai nat* shrine into the chief's household under *gumsa*, and remarks that then 'The chief's house is more than a dwelling house, more than a palace, it is also a kind of temple to the *Madai nat*.'

'Thus the chief', as he has become in his role as head of the 'chief' lineage, 'becomes the mediator between the community and the forces of nature which provide for its prosperity. He is able to do this because his lineage has become the territorial or community lineage', as Friedman (1979:41) expresses it. Now the chief not only represents the community and is thus 'responsible' for it, but in a way, since duties imply rights, he can be said to 'own' it. Since he is now in a superordinate position, he has relations of equality, that is, 'horizontal' relations, only with similarly elevated lineages in adjacent territories. This because relative and mutable affinal ranking has been converted into absolute social age with respect to a fixed common ancestor (Friedman 1975:175). It is this last transformation which Friedman maintains is decisive, 'in that it determines the specific form of the *gumsa* (hierarchic) domain. In the emergence of the chiefdom the *Mayu/dama* relation is RE-presented simultaneously as an elder/younger relation between lineage ancestors' (ibid.). Since we are speaking of social age and ultimogeniture prevails among Kachin, this makes YoS (youngest son) senior and the rulers of a domain (*mung*) modelled on the properly territorial Shan-type domain.

The interdomain structure looks as in Figure 8.8 where the lineages at the apex exchange women and prestige while securing alliances, and the intermediate levels ('aristocrats') confer women on lower lineages thus obligating and subordinating them. However, by receiving women only from their peers in other domains, pre-eminent lineages can engage in

Figure 8.8 Gumsa domain: structure and marriage relations

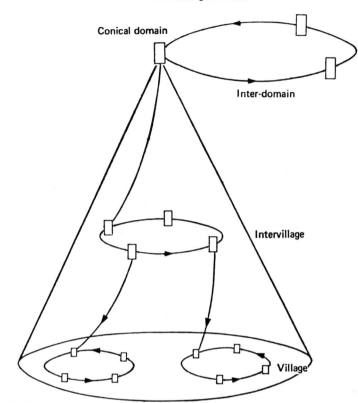

Source: Friedman 1975:177

balanced exchanges which do not obligate them in any way to inferiors, thus securely distancing themselves from inferior lineages.

In his seminal work on the conical clan (originally 1935) entitled 'The principles of clanship in human society', Paul Kirchhoff described this process as follows: Whereas the egalitarian clan (that Kirchhoff calls the 'unilineal-egalitarian') 'divided the tribe into a number of solid blocks with clear cut boundary lines each homogeneous within', the inegalitarian

> results in a type of society which may be likened to a cone, the whole tribe being one such cone, with the legendary ancestor at its top – but within it are a larger or smaller number of similar cones, the top of each coinciding with or being connected with the top of the whole cone. The bases of these cones, representing the circles of living members of the various clans at a given moment, overlap here and there.

> (Kirchhoff (1959) 1968:267)

245

This situation has arisen from a few lineages from those formerly equivalent, through mechanisms similar to those we have seen, moving their lineage closer, as it were, to the common tribal ancestor and thus to the supreme deities. They then appear to represent in a *living lineage* an axial or senior lineage from which all others, their 'inferiors' are 'descended'. *All in fact are minimal lineages*, but some have been converted by ranking into minor, fewer into major, and one perhaps into the 'maximal' lineage from which the whole clan or even tribe appear to descend. As Kirchhoff remarks 'it is precisely the *nearness* of relationship to the common ancestor of the group which matters' (op. cit.:266). And in turn, for the other lineages, nearness to those who are nearest is what matters. Kirchhoff continues, 'The first of the two principles of clanship results in a group the members of which are of absolutely equal standing, as far as this standing is determined by membership in the group (leaving aside the question of age)' (ibid.). In contrast to this elementary type based on simple and parallel (coeval) descent, the conical principle according to Kirchhoff

> results in a group in which every single member, except brothers and sisters, has a different standing: the concept of the *degree of relationship* leads to different *degrees of membership* in the clan. In other words, some are members to a higher degree than others.
>
> (Kirchhoff, op. cit.:266)

In other words for the very lowly their very status as members of society is threatened, and from this we may readily see how members who fall down upon or out of certain social relationships, say through debt (or indeed by capture), become non-members and over time reduced to the level of things. They become as a consequence the objects, not the subjects of society, no longer the bearers of statuses and offices but slaves; further their offspring can become fixed in this position by ascription, that is, by a specification appropriate to their position in the *altered* set of social relations which they inherit.

The debtor relation is particularly important in eroding status amongst the Kachin, and simultaneously heightening exploitation, since *equal* obligation (obtaining from the formerly egalitarian clan) under conditions of unequal access to resources, works to the advantage of those in the process of accumulation. The latter can readily discharge their end of the 'social contract' (e.g. feasts, offerings, funeral and marriage payments) and so attract further resources by being 'creditworthy'. However, for those producing only around subsistence levels, maintaining social status is a burden that could well be crushing, for their surpluses are slight (Kirchhoff, op. cit.:270; cf. Salisbury 1966:124).

This process is accentuated by an established Kachin chief, for instance, being entitled to tribute and corvée labour due to his position as descendant and representative of the community spirit upon whose largesse community well-being depends.

> The *masha nats* of a 'thigh-eating chief' are of a special category. The house of such a chief contains two shrines, one devoted to the chief's own ancestors, the other to the *mu nat* Madai, who is now *mayu* to the chief's ancestors. . . . The chief is chief because he represents the 'youngest son line', he is the *uma*. The chief therefore can trace his lineage back to the founder ancestor of his chiefly line, the *uma nat*, who is *dama* to Madai. Hence, ritually speaking, the status of the 'thigh-eating chief' as owner of a domain rests on the fact that he alone can make offerings to the *uma nat* of his lineage. Through the *uma nat* he can approach Madai. Through Madai he can approach Shadip. Shadip controls the fortunes and fertility of all things. Hence the prosperity of the domain depends upon the proper ritual observances of the chief. Hence the chief is entitled to the ritual tribute of thighs (*magyi*) which he receives from his adherents.

> (Leach 1970:176)

And a chief confirms his rank by redistributing a part of his 'income' in the great *manao* feasts. But this is in large measure a redistribution from his dependants to the community at large, in contrast to the 'big-man' principle where a following of fellow producers must be built up from those one cannot compel but must propel: 'Any ambitious man who can gather a following can launch a societal career' (Sahlins 1968:165). A big-man's position depends on his ceaseless activity in distribution to outsiders while his personal faction must 'eat his glory'. Pushed too far, his following deserts and a new or established rival takes over his role of 'pushing production' and distributing it 'outwards' (ibid.:176). While a Kachin *gumsa* chief's position is more institutionalized, his following can still desert him by leaving his domain for another, something the Shan peasants are unable to do, given the scarcity of irrigable land in upland Burma (Leach 1970:255). Kachins can also have the means to undertake *gumlao* egalitarian revolts against overbearing chiefs or to repudiate excessive social indebtedness.

In the light of what was said of the relation between debt and status, it is logical that among the Kachin, slaves belong to the chief or village headman, although an aristocrat may often possess several (ibid.:160). Treated as permanent children, or permanent debtors (ibid.), to whose brideprice their owners are entitled, their possessors are able to appropriate all the production of slaves living in the household, called 'internal slaves' (*tinung mayam*). Those living externally (*ngong mayam*) in their own houses pay heavy tribute, such as every alternate calf born. 'Internals' are treated as very inferior family members in permanent dependence, while the 'externals' are regarded as commoners of particularly low degree (Friedman 1979:182–3).

What is particularly interesting is that the Kachin slaves are not in the position of chattel slavery, as they were for instance in Greece or Rome, 'the first genuine slave societies in history' (Finley 1973:71); that is, they have not been reduced to a purely object status but are assimilated to the lowest grades of social membership, which is to the lowest grades of kinship ranking. Indeed the contradiction of being subordinate *within* kinship relations, rather than being a totally statusless outsider, has been caught by Kirchhoff, who remarks: 'In the cone-shaped clan on the contrary, everything that strengthens the clan strengthens, above all, its core and correspondingly whatever any member contributes to the wellbeing of the clan as a whole benefits above all, the *aristoi*' (op. cit.:269).

In order to accumulate prestige and surplus, aristocrats must collect debts and people; in the process the houses of chiefs can grow to 100 yards in length (Leach 1970:108), including within them a *Madai Nat* shrine room as we have seen. None the less, as indicated at the outset, the productivity of swidden agriculture depends on any area being worked only one year in twenty if the forest is to remain intact. As a very minimum a ratio of 1:12 years clearing/fallow will permit secondary forest regeneration where rainfall is sufficient (as it is in the Triangle, the area north of Myitkyina (Map 8.1), where it ranges from 75 to 150 inches per annum). None the less the 'dozen year cycle' is a step down to a lower plateau of productivity. Here intensification is degenerative, so extensification is required, though chiefs do try to 'circumscribe' their population in a given territory. But as ranking, surpluses, and people concentrate, the population must expand outwards (historically westwards) to keep the density within that which dry-rice swiddening can support, a process achieved not consciously but by the outbreak of *gumlao* revolts before permanently damaging levels of extraction are reached (Friedman 1979:186). The build-up of contradictions, particularly indebtedness, brought about by increasing pressure for production and concomitant inflation of all 'social values' is outlined by Friedman (1975:184) as the 'Internal expansion of the Gumsa domain and its contradictions' (see Figure 8.9).

Rupture of *gumsa* stratification comes when the chief (*duwa*), acting increasingly as landlord over tenants, increasingly fails to fulfil his obligations to kinsmen. Leach states that:

> The overlord extorts services from his subordinates without obligations of reciprocity. Kinship implies a symmetrical relationship; a *mayu-dama* (affinal) or *hpu-nau* (lineage brother) relationship between a chief and his follower may imply one-sided obligations from the follower towards his chief, but it also implies that the chief has obligations towards his follower. The weakness of the *gumsa* system is

Figure 8.9 Internal expansion of the *gumsa* domain and its contradictions

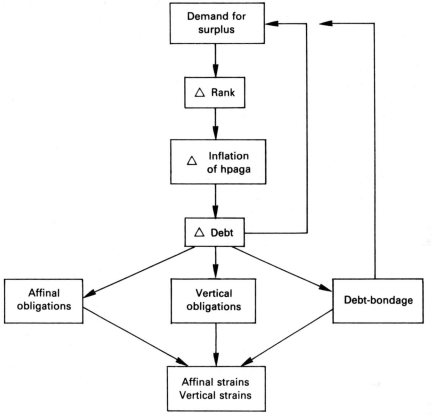

Source: Friedman 1975:184

that the successful chief is tempted to repudiate links of kinship with his followers and to treat them as if they were bond slaves (*mayam*). It is this situation which, from a *gumlao* point of view, is held to justify revolt.

(Leach 1970:203)

With their continued dispersal and political checks the Kachin are alone in the region in having achieved an overall settlement density (*c.* 10 per square mile) that permits the *gumsa/gumlao* cycle to replicate itself, for its environmental conditions are intact (Friedman 1979:186). While neighbouring tribes also experience a kind of 'short cycle' of oscillating political relationships, they do so against a 'long cycle' of deteriorated (deforested) environment, increased population density, and endemic warfare. Friedman (1975:188) shows the short cycles for the different tribes inset tangentially to the envelope of an overall production function, since productive technique is similar for all the tribes (Figure 8.10).

Figure 8.10 The long cycle of declining productivity

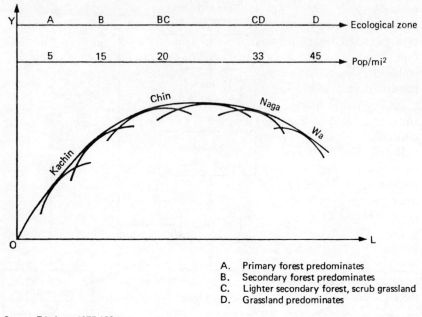

A. Primary forest predominates
B. Secondary forest predominates
C. Lighter secondary forest, scrub grassland
D. Grassland predominates

Source: Friedman 1975:188

As the trajectory curve indicates, production can be intensified in swiddens beyond the level of exploitation characteristic of the Kachin. But in so doing the ecology is permanently damaged, being changed from Primary Forest to mere grassland, and with it social relations alter too, along with both culture and diet. By the time the densities of the Wa ($c.$ 45/mile^2) are reached, settlements contain as many as 700 houses, and are defended by heavy ramparts, for 'war is a daily condition of life and famines are frequent' (Friedman 1975:193). Having reduced the terrain to mere grassland without a trace of forest, the Wa, with their institutionalized headhunting and cult of denial, or rather negation, centred upon the *tevo*, supposed descendant of the sacred founder, have attained a 'political equality founded on the ritual negation of everything (by way of consumption patterns) that led the society to destroy its own conditions of production' (ibid.).

The Chin, on the other hand, whose density is nearest that of the Kachin, have of necessity (outlined initially) 'a rather intricate agricultural adaptation including elaborate cycles of crop rotation [which] has been able to develop on the basis of land-title accumulation' (ibid.:190). A small number of dominant lineages have been able to engross most or all of a village's land because land was divided up into heritable titles. The land became parcellized in fixed titles because, due to political circumscription, the system could no longer expand. And 'as there is no longer any continuity between local spirits and the higher supernatural powers, there can be no position equivalent to a *gumsa* chief, direct descendant of the territorial deity' (ibid.:189). Instead ferocious competition between big-men, accumulating land-titles and throwing potlatch type 'feasts of merit' for prestige, makes for an ever-shifting rather than stable-oscillatory type of polity, for the political superstructure no longer has its former coherence.

As suggested above, topological transformations follow demographic shifts, reflected in a greater lineage depth for the Chin and settlement clustering (Figure 8.11).

By the time (or rather place) that Naga densities have been reached, with the production curve turning downward, the clan has begun to counter the political independence of the minimal exchange unit, making internal differentiation more difficult (Friedman 1975:190). With the great shortage of land its allocation has become a communal responsibility, a direct concern of clan elders, while all land not in use reverts immediately to the clan as a whole. Uneven density between groups of Naga does allow of some oscillation between a village chieftaincy and clan hegemony, that is, can allow for a partial recrudescence of 'local lineage political economy', where and only where some territorial expansion can be had, as indeed with the expulsion of the Ao Naga by the Sema and Lhota Naga (ibid.:192).

> Even so, as density continues to grow, wars become more frequent and their results more deceiving for the internal economies of the groups involved. In most areas hereditary chiefs are entirely replaced by big-men or by clan elders. Individuals can still gain prestige through feasts of merit, but it is impossible to convert this into lineage rank because such feasts are isolated from the alliance network and the ancestral hierarchy. Furthermore labour productivity is too low to permit the acceleration of surplus necessary to interlineage competition. Among the majority of Naga groups big-men have prestige but little power. Among the Ao in particular, political functions are all transferred to the village council of elders. Here competition leads only to a kind of unstable and negative egalitarianism.
>
> (Friedman 1975:192)

The instability and negative egalitarianism are a consequence of a mismatch between demography and techno-environment in this area of hill-swiddening. The established relations of production were predicated upon an expanding system (Friedman and Rowlands 1977b:213); indeed in geo-historical terms, upon an open frontier, necessary for elasticity of settlement, even if not for any absolute dispersal of population. When territory became circumscribed, and, at least in certain directions, closed,

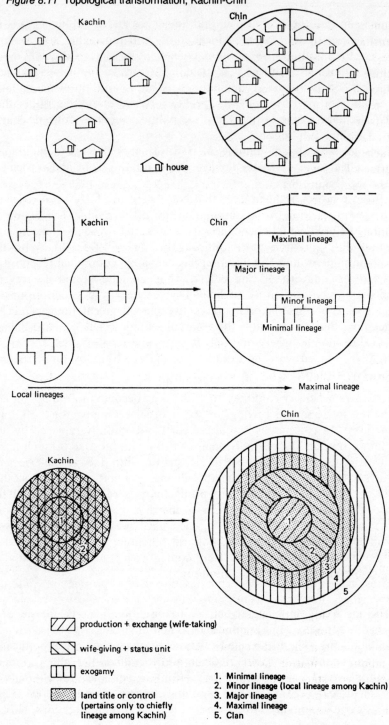

Figure 8.11 Topological transformation, Kachin-Chin

Kachin

Chin

🏠 house

Kachin

Chin

Maximal lineage

Major lineage

Minor lineage

Minimal lineage

Local lineages

Maximal lineage

Kachin

Chin

▨ production + exchange (wife-taking)

◧ wife-giving + status unit

▥ exogamy

▦ land title or control
(pertains only to chiefly
lineage among Kachin)

1. Minimal lineage
2. Minor lineage (local lineage among Kachin)
3. Major lineage
4. Maximal lineage
5. Clan

Source: Friedman 1975:191

an unchanged system of swiddening proceeded to increasing degrees of intensification to support heightening population densities without the necessary revolution in the relations of production that would have instituted a new mode of production with new tools, crops, and techniques. Since they persisted with the old in only minimal adaptation, the result was the degradation of the ecological basis caught in a downward spiral, and for the Naga and Wa in particular, a concomitant degradation in the security and quality of life.

Such a transformation did occur, however, on the valley floors and riverine plains where the irrigated rice regime became standard. There, where annual surpluses could be guaranteed at a given high level, even at the cost of sustained high labour inputs, the Shan states emerged. The (vertical) relation with the supernatural at the expense of (horizontal) relations with other lineages were accentuated by the chiefly lineage to the extent of virtually breaking its 'earthly' connection with the others. Absolute genealogical distance at the apex of the conical clan is decisive in producing the ruler of a territorial state; his pre-eminent position no longer depending on his own generosity in feasting or as a wife-giver. Indeed such is now the king's elevation above society from which he draws tribute, that the donors are privileged if he receives wives from them, for this is his due as the link between heaven and earth (cf. Leach 1970:218).

From his 'due' as ultimate 'owner' of the land, in that the land would be 'useless' without his ministrations on behalf of its village possessors (i.e. producers), the king (as he now is) becomes able to sustain a large and ramified court. Indeed with production likely to rise to political demands, and facilitated by the wider polity, higher absolute state consumption can for a time be masked by growing relative productivity. The burdens of state would of course be felt when state consumption absorbs a higher fraction of stagnant or declining production, at which point revolts are a possibility.

From the royal kinsmen, courtiers, and dependants, develop ministers who have functions in 'administration', that is in operation of the state apparatus itself, some of whom have a putative role in the administration of material production. Even the king himself, through his performance of rites, can be said to have such a function. But as production continues at the village level as it were 'automatically', an administrative role can really only reside in the overseeing of the levying of taxes or tribute from the existing domain (Chang 1980:216), or in its extension by military or colonial means as outlined below. However, by participating in a division of labour no matter how construed, kinsmen/courtiers/ministers can function as a state bureaucracy (clearly in post-Chou times) without any necessary kinship to the royal line and depending only on royal (or factional) appointment.

Above we have seen the approach from ethnography to stratification in the village-state mode. The textual and archaeological materials from China further support this construction, as may be gauged from Keightley's outline of the ideological basis for the dominance of the Shang king at the apex of the royal clan, the *Tzu tsu*:

> Shang religion was inextricably involved in the genesis and legitimation of the Shang state. It was believed that Ti, the high god, conferred fruitful harvest and divine assistance in battle, that the king's ancestors were able to intercede with Ti, and that the king could communicate with his ancestors. Worship of the Shang ancestors, therefore, provided powerful psychological and ideological support for the political dominance of the Shang kings. The king's ability to determine through divination and influence through prayer and sacrifice, the will of the ancestral spirits legitimised the concentration of political power in his person. All power emanated from the theocrat because he was the channel, 'the one man', who could appeal for the ancestral blessings, or dissipate the ancestral curses, which affected the commonality. It was the king who made fruitful harvest and victories possible by the sacrifices he offered, the ritual he performed, and the divinations he made. If, as seems likely, the divinations involved some degree of magic making, of spell casting, the king's ability to actually create a good harvest or a victory by divining about it rendered him still more potent politically.
>
> (Keightley 1978:212–13)

5 Divergent Neolithics

The situation under which 'the authority of the ruler is seen as a manifestation of something which has always existed, which is given in nature by the order of the world' (Bloch 1977:319) is quite different from that which obtained at least in the proto-historic and historic Near East (Lambert 1974; Kramer 1974). The ecological rationale for the qualitative distinction between East and West Asia, between what I have termed the village-state and the city-state mode of production, was outlined as early as 1961 by M. D. Coe in comparing the rise and precipitate collapse of Classic Maya (AD *c.* 300–900) and Angkor Period Khmer (AD 802–1431) civilizations. Both practised extensive cereal monoculture in tropical seasonal-forest zones, respectively of maize and rice. Both supported for a time an elaborate superstructure consisting of temples, palaces, and other monuments (Coe 1961:69).

The superstructure so generated from tribute and corvée may even have put something back into the infrastructure, but the societies concerned failed to generate the city. There were cultic, administrative, and other centres but there was no organic city. No centres of population maintained continuity when the extant superstructure collapsed. Indeed even the capital was but the court temporarily in residence. The Shang capital moved no less than seven times during its hegemony (1,766– 1,122 BC), its longest stay being 262 years, the shortest only 8 years ('Keng' 1,525–1,517 BC). Similarly the Classic Khmer capital was also peripatetic, a new capital being built by the king on his accession (Coe 1961:71). Abandonment and reconstitution were the easier given that even palaces were made of wood and tiled, while lesser structures were the ubiquitous wattle and daub and thatch (illustrated in Wheatley 1971: figs 5 & 6). Indeed,

> The traditional capital removals attributed to the Shang, whose former kings, according to *Shang-shu* ('P'an Keng') 'did not perpetuate their cities' . . . may represent a dim memory of periodic shifts in 'centres of operation' as the kings exhausted their ability to exploit certain areas. State power travelled with the king and his court of diviners and retainers, who prayed and sacrificed to legitimate the orders and expropriations that he levied on the populations and groups that came into his intermittent view.
>
> (Keightley 1983b:552)

This was the general pattern in East Asia, that of a royal, administrative, and cultic centre surrounded by a sea of peasant villages, producing basically the same subsistence crops by similar methods over extensive and largely uniform terrain. Coe (1961:67) called this state of affairs 'unilateral' to stress its segmental, essentially vertical nature, in contrast to 'organic solidarity' and horizontal relations such as are represented in the true city; for 'areas which are environmentally undifferentiated will tend to lack an early growth of urbanism, as opposed to regions which are divided into more or less strongly contrasted sub-areas' (Coe 1961:67). Only situational diversity and an organic inter-dependence with an immediate hinterland engenders urbanism as a way of life.

While China as we now know it is topographically and floristically a highly diverse country, this was not so with regard to the formative Neolithic cultures which underlay the earliest states.

The most succinct summary of this formative situation is Wheatley's:

> Urban forms first developed in China on the great northern plain, a vast embayment of alluvial deposits, enclosed by peripheral uplands on north, west, and south but open to the sea at two points on its eastern rim. Structurally this plain comprises an enormous composite alluvial fan to the west and a composite sub-aerial delta to the east, both built up by the Huang river, its distributaries, and other streams flowing

from the western mountains. The hearth of Shang culture occupied the higher parts of the fan, stretching in an arc from the neighbourhood of present-day Ch'ing-yuan in central Ho-pei to the vicinity of Po-Hsien in northern An-hui, and comprising the territory known to the Chinese in later times as the Chung-yuan, or Middle Plain.

(Wheatley 1971:20)

The very extent of this plain, the fact that only a portion was occupied by the early farming villages, namely 'the southeastern part of the loess highlands which consists of the entire Wei river valley in central Shensi, southern Shansi and western Honan' (Ho 1977:419), and the fact that it was open to the east, meant that villages could simply proliferate without recourse to nucleation. Upon the advent of Shang and Chou states, this process was reinforced by the stimulation effect of contact with peoples on the edges of the stratified domain. Crucial, however, were the formative Neolithic phases centred upon the aforementioned semi-arid loess steppe environment, where only millets grew well in the summer-rainfall regime, and with a topography too interrupted and gullied and with too little grass cover to support grazing animals. It was this seminal pattern, which Ho (1977:469) has called 'lopsided in favour of grain production'[12] that became the dominant one, forming the dynamic core of the Sinitic culture realm.

Phytogeographically and physiographically China is divided into three by the mountain ranges Ch'in Ling and Nan Ling, the former running roughly along the 35th parallel of latitude, the latter along the 25th, a few degrees north of the Tropic of Cancer. This results in three distinct vegetation belts: (1) North China continental/temperate; (2) South China sub-tropical; (3) South Asia belt, an extension of the tropical phytogeography of Burma, Thailand, and the Indochinese peninsula (Li 1983:51). Thus the area between the Ch'in Ling Shan and the Nan Ling Shan forms the South China belt, dominated by the floodplains of the Yangtze. The North China belt, whose southern limit in the eastern coastal plain runs between the Yangtze river and the Huai to its north (Li 1983:22), consists essentially of the Huang Ho basin, the loess highlands, and the plains of North China (ibid.).

Consequently, 'the cold-winter wheat-growing region of North China, with its limited precipitation, can be contrasted with the moist, rice-growing climate of South China' (Li 1983:22). And while 'botanical and phytogeographical evidence of great differences between the environments of North and South China points to the existence of two separate centres of plant domestication' (Li 1966), whereby, as Li (1983:50) puts it, 'each centre produced a well-rounded complex of crops independently capable of nurturing human culture', it was the northern culture that came to dominate and absorb the southern, through the engenderment of powerful state forms.

As summarized by Te-tzu Chang:

> From the dawn of agriculture in the central plain down to the Spring and Autumn period, *chi* and *shu* were two dominant crops. *Chi* was such an important crop in the loess highlands that the people of the Chou dynasty gave the name Hou Chi 后稷 (Lord of millet) to their legendary ancestor. *Su* (millet) and soybeans were predominant crops during the Warring States period. *Su* and *mai* (barley and wheat) were the principal cereals through the Han period.
>
> (Te-tzu Chang 1983:70)

The first of the 'classic Chinese' Neolithic cultures sufficiently known is the Yang-shao, originating in the middle Huang valley, around the confluence of the rivers Fen and Wei.[13] Thereafter diffusion was eastward onto the western part of the plain proper, and north and westward down the valleys leading into central Shansi and eastern Kansu (Wheatley 1971:23). This was already a pottery Neolithic, and its economy combined hunting, fishing, and gathering with cultivation based on two millet domesticates (*Setaria italica* and *Panicum miliaceum*), the raising of hemp and silkworms plus the animal domesticates, pig and dog; indeed 'it is no exaggeration to say that animal husbandry in Neolithic China was very largely pig husbandry' (Ho 1977:466).

Significantly, the architectural features of longhouses and semi-subterranean clustered pit houses which characterize the Yang-shao culture 'suggest planned and segmented village layouts, and on these grounds and others, lineage and clan types of kinship groupings could be postulated' (Chang 1977:108). Further, the placing and layout of village cemeteries leads Chang to conclude also that 'the cult of the ancestors to symbolise lineage solidarity had already been initiated' (ibid.:110).

The successor culture, with the village of Lung-shan as a late, developed end-point, reached all eastern and southeastern China after *c.* 3,200 BC, forming regional traditions that are characterized as 'Lungshanoid' (Chang 1977:144).[14] On the basis of an augmenting economy (in the process of incorporating rice, chickens, sheep, and cattle as domesticates), arose social stratification with specialists in pottery, artifacts, and ritual (ibid.:172), including the very widespread Lungshanoid practice of scapulimancy, the characters impressed on which (as the later 'oracle bones') are the foundations of Chinese literacy, whose roots reach back to Yang-shao pottery marks (ibid.:114). It is worth contrasting this 'ritual' basis of Chinese literacy with that of Mesopotamia, which, as has been shown, was organically evolved in connection with the material production process itself. Differential burial practices in the Lungshanoid culture also point to social stratification. But, though Lungshanoid villages are larger, contain pit granaries, and are often surrounded by stamped-earth ramparts, the architectural features of semi-subterranean dwellings and communal longhouses are still found, the former continuing into the succeeding urban phase. Although villages were still self-contained units, Wheatley concludes that

> By the Lung-shan stage, both occupational and sacral distinctions had become more clearly defined, but social relationships were still essentially familial, with kinship as the basis of all groupings and the whole of society permeated by common understandings as to the nature and purpose of life, the latter reflected in an institutionalized ancestor cult.
>
> (Wheatley 1971:30)

When the ancient city of Ao (Ngog) arose out of the Lungshanoid substrata in the vicinity of Cheng-Chou, straddling the rivers Chin-shui and Hsiung-erh, its formation was particularly distinctive, but of a distinctiveness shared with the later Shang cities, such as An-yang (the Great City of Shang) and Lo-yang (in the strategic centre of the 'central plain'). Their distinctiveness lay in areal dimension (approximately 3.2 km^2 for Ao (Wheatley 1971:32)), in the scale of ceremonial buildings and walls associated with elite residential precincts, and in their being non-nucleated cities, clustered around which were dependent settlements containing craftsmen and other servitors of the elite. Indeed Chang (1980:73) having mentioned that 'archaeological sites in the An-yang core are distributed along the River Huan, on both banks, in an area approximately 6 km along the river and 4 km deep' goes on to demonstrate that this is only a kernel. For the greater capital area of which An-yang was, despite its dimensions, only the core,

> at a higher level of organisation had other nodules constituting a larger network. If we take Hsin-hsiang (in the south) to Hsing-t'ai (in the north) as the area of the larger capital, it was then an area about 200 km long from north to south, in the plains east of T'ai-hang Mountains. . . . An-yang was at the spatial centre of this area, about 100 kilometres from each end of it, and archaeologically it was the command nucleus of the vast capital.
>
> (Chang 1980:129)

It will be recognized that such a 'vast capital', encompassing an area at least equivalent to the whole of Sumer and Akkad, has the most profound implications for social structure, which just cannot be 'fundamentally' similar in the village-state to that of the city-state.

In his indispensable study of the Shang, Chang points out that

> walled towns were the principal ruling instruments in Shang China, and they were the residential locales of unilateral kin groups with *tsu* as basic units. The Shang state can be characterised, simply, as the

network of such towns that was under the Shang king's direct control. By 'direct control' we mean that the Shang king was responsible for granting the title to the township and the land that supported the township to the lord who ruled it, and that for this act the king was entitled in return to the lord's services and grains. Such a network was vast – Tung Tso-pin says that he counted close to a thousand town names – and its rule was hierarchical and its perimeters flexible.

(Chang 1980:210)

Tsu refer to the military aspect of the unilineal kin-group's organization, with *shih* its totemic symbol. And

It was the members of *tsu* groups who inhabited the towns; *tsu* were grouped into *tsung* in ritual contexts and into *shih* in terms of political status and political symbols. A male individual was known by the name of his town or his *shih*, but a female individual was usually known by the name of her clan.

(Chang 1980:163)

The Western Chou (i.e. later) poem *Pei shan* stated: 'Everywhere under Heaven/Is no land that is not the king's/To the borders of all those lands/None but is the king's slave' (trans. Arthur Waley, cited Chang 1980:158). And Chang, in common with ancient writers, remarks that what obtained for the Chou was true of the Shang. The fundamental political unit of the Shang state was the *yi*, or town, and in this form, as an administrative centre surrounded by stamped-earth (*hang t'u*) ramparts, was not an organic growth, like the farming villages, but a political creation with features of military colonization. 'The king would send a party out to physically build a town and fill it with people' (Chang 1980:159). Such people would be court officials, relatives, princes, and royal consorts, who in Shang times were politically and even militarily active, and accordingly of high status. This because the kings' recognised spouses came from within the *wang tsu* or the royal lineage, but they came from a tablet unit outside the kings' own' (ibid.:177).

Chang has identified ten 'tablet units' (*kan*), between which kingship shifted intergenerationally in a system of circulating succession between the ten lineages of the ruling *Tzu* clan, grouped into moieties.

Succession did not follow automatic rules except for two: it could not stay within the same *kan* unit, and second, when the kingship stayed within division A or B, it had to be assumed by an heir from another *kan* unit from within the same generation as the former king, but if it went over to the other division it had to go to an heir of the next generation. To phrase this differently: when the kingship passed over to the next generation, it had to move to the opposite division.

(Chang 1980:180–1)

Chang stresses the social and economic stratification obtaining between and within clans, for 'the basic Shang social unit was the *tsu*, and the *tsu*, by virtue of the incessant ramification of its member units, was the seed of social stratification within itself and among one another' (ibid.:227). This resulted in the creation of a lowly 'multitude' (*chung-jen*) who were both the productive, labouring class and the military levies. Further, lineages formed specialized occupational groups[15] of craftsmen and service personnel (ibid.:230) in which case their standing would have been higher.[16]

> . . . 'but agricultural implements of bronze are rare – this is an undeniable fact' (Ch'en Wen-hua). While agricultural implements continued to be made of stone, wood, antler, and bone during the Bronze Age, bronze was used conspicuously for the manufacturing of weapons, ritual paraphernalia (food vessels, wine vessels, and musical instruments), some ornaments, and such carpenter's tools as the axe, adze and chisel. The carpenter's tools were presumably necessary for the construction of wooden chariots, which were the most formidable weapon of the Bronze Age. This pattern of use is highly distinctive of the Chinese Bronze Age, in which bronze was associated primarily with ritual and with war, 'the two principal affairs of the state' (Tso Chuan, entry for 579 B.C.). In other words, if bronze epitomised the way in which scarce resources were used in ancient China, then political culture played a central role in Chinese civilisation at its very inception.
>
> (Chang 1983c:108)

With *tsu* rules as the fundamental law of society and the king, *wang*, the supreme head of all lineages (Chang 1983c:35), Shang, Western Chou (and most probably Hsia) society formed a pyramid, vast in numbers and extent, sketched by Chang as shown in Figure 8.12.

Chang concludes:

> In social organisation and level of societal development, the Hsia, Shang, and Chou shared a very important feature, namely lineages in walled towns serving as the ruling instrument. The Hsia was a dynasty of the Ssu clan, the Shang, the Tzu clan, and the Chou, the Chi clan. All were similarly ruled by dynastic groups within clans, although the rulers of the three dynasties (*san tai*) came from different clans. There were also fundamental similarities in the royal succession rules.
>
> (Chang 1980:353)

Chang then proceeds to correlate the Chinese archaeological sequence with Service's evolutionary scheme, and compares it to the Marxist stages. In Figure 8.13 I have employed, with modification, Chang's (1980:363) sequence for the Sinitic region, and contrasted it with the Near Eastern sequence discussed previously, dropping the Marxist categories for lack of discrimination.

Figure 8.12 Shang economic classes in agricultural production

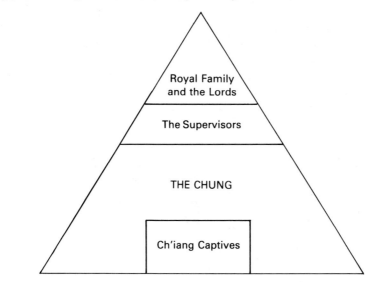

Royal Family
and the Lords

The Supervisors

THE CHUNG

Ch'iang Captives

Source: Chang 1980:231

Figure 8.13 Archaeological cultures and evolutionary stages in China and Mesopotamia

CHINA	level	level	MESOPOTAMIA
Palaeolithic	BAND	BAND	Palaeolithic
Mesolithic			Epipalaeolithic
Yang-shao	TRIBE	egalitarian farming villages	Hassuna, Samarra, Halaf
Lung-shan	CHIEFDOM	emergent stratific- ation	Ubaid
Hsia, Shang, Chou (to 770 BC)	STATE (central- ized bureau- cratic)	STATE many independent city-states	present by Uruk Period (< 4000 BC)
Late Chou, Ch'in, Han			consolidated in the Early Dynastic period

Chapter nine

Modelling societies: modes of production

So far we have been using the concept 'mode of production' to speak not only of the organization of production of disparate societies, but also of the social relations thereby engendered. The usual expression for this latter meaning is 'relations of production'; however, rarely is the specific relationship made explicit, and worse, the *exact* specification of mode and relations (and indeed 'means') of production has never to my knowledge been given a formal model.[1] Instead we all think we know what the concepts mean 'near enough', with the consequence that everyone uses the terms rather differently, and therefore intends something quite different. 'I know what I mean' is not an argument.

> A mode of subsistence *per se* is not a 'mode of production'. The latter includes not only the means for making a living but also the relationships involved: who owns these means, how is production organised, who controls the product and how is it distributed, and who consumes what part of it?
>
> (Leacock and Lee 1982b:7)

The reference of the concept 'mode of production' thus ranges from the specifics of the tools and processes employed in production, to the area of final consumption, posing the questions about what is produced, how is it produced, by and for whom?

If we take as our point of departure the actual labour process of how work is done, then we are dealing with instruments of production – tools, facilities, apparatus – acting upon an 'object of labour' – either previously produced raw materials or land and water directly – instruments and objects interacting only when set in motion by labour power. We thus commence with a 'core block' (Figure 9.1) which together constitute the *forces of production*:

In the societies we have considered above, we observe that the instruments of production, hoes, bows, etc., were usually individual possessions, while the land, and its plants and animals, etc., were common property of the lineage, clan, or village, often 'represented' by

Figure 9.1 Forces of production

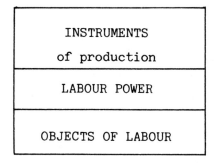

```
┌─────────────────────────────────┐
│         INSTRUMENTS             │
│        of production            │
├─────────────────────────────────┤
│        LABOUR POWER             │
├─────────────────────────────────┤
│      OBJECTS OF LABOUR          │
└─────────────────────────────────┘
```

ancestors, territorial spirits, or indeed gods, as was the communal temple land in Mesopotamia.

So we observe a disjunction, on the one hand between the forms of ownership and control of the instruments and objects of production; and on the other hand, we observe the discrete forms of productive collaboration, such as is necessitated in fishing with nets, which Terray confused with the (overall) mode of production itself. To our 'central core' we consequently must add two other categories as indicated in Figure 9.2, forming the *relations of production*.

Figure 9.2 Relations of production

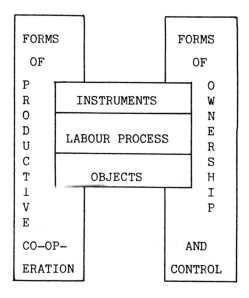

Figure 9.3 Model of mode of production for foraging societies

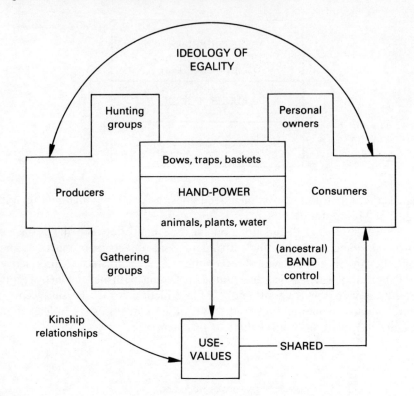

We now have in fact *technical* relations *in* production (left side of Figure 9.2) and social relations of the ownership *of* production (right side).

Finally, we need to specify the social categories that engage in the forms of productive association (and are thereby producers) at the 'input side' as it were.

Output of the means of production is of use-value, centrally means of subsistence, which accrues in the first instance to those who own the means of production or who control them.

Rather than extend our model abstractly we will here (Figure 9.3) show how it applies to the foraging mode of production. For such purposes I am, of course, assuming that there is a foraging mode of production, something upon which there is not necessarily general agreement.

Here, as in acephalous segmentary ('tribal') societies like the Nuer or Dinka, producers and consumers are one and the same, since the conditions of production are vested in them severally and jointly by virtue of their association in a network of (discrete) descent relations, defining

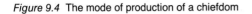

Figure 9.4 The mode of production of a chiefdom

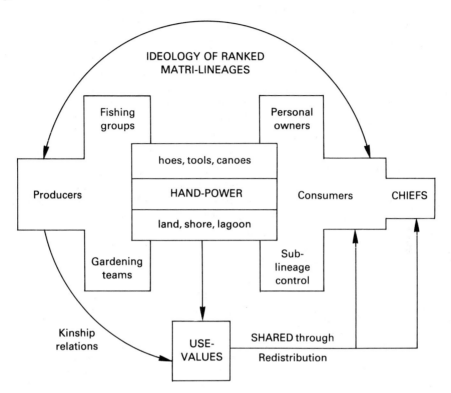

what Fortes (1969:123) calls the 'domain of politico-jural relations' that provide rights to the exploitation of territory.

Since the social categories are related to their conditions of production by the same normative-jural relations as orders persons with regard to one another, we can say with Godelier (1978b:764) that 'relations of kinship function as relations of production' in this mode, 'and that they do so internally', that is, as constitutive of their very *raisons d'être*. Those turn upon 'filiation as the nodal mechanism and crucial relationship of intergenerational continuity and social reproduction', for 'filiation is the mechanism that insures the replacement – physically, socially and psycho-logically – of each generation by the next' (Fortes 1969:256, 264).

Familial production and socio-familial reproduction are thus inextricably linked and so being, engender an ideology of equality reflecting common interests and participation (ibid.:219–49; Bloch 1973:75–87).

If we consider the position of the Trobriand chief I outlined previously, we see him located at the centre of the kinship relations of production as the collective 'brother-in-law' (Figure 9.4).

Since the relations of kinship no longer serve simply to identify producers and consumers, but serve to redistribute between domestic units through matrilateral connection, we call those kinship relations 'redistributional'. Now too, while the ideology of equality continues to unite, to it is superadded the operation of rank, being the relative elevation of the head of the structural unit, the sub-clan, and/or the sub-clan is itself elevated: 'Chieftainship is a combination of two institutions: rank and headmanship of a village community. Each village has its headman' (Malinowski, ed. Young 1979:45). And while the sub-clan is the unit to which rank attaches (ibid.:43), 'at the head of each village community stands the oldest male of the oldest lineage in the sub-clan of the highest rank' (ibid.).

This gives chiefs, even down at the level of headmen, certain prerogatives, certain 'important economic monopolies' as Malinowski calls them (ibid.:51), which ensure that at least important headmen (minor chiefs) get a pre-eminent share of pigmeat, coconut, and betelnut, quite apart from their location in the redistribution network of matrikin. Much of the chiefly revenues are however redistributed again (ibid.:38, 52), and while some of the income will certainly be consumed in and for the chief's establishment, his prerogatives are simply those of rank not class, and so the chiefly household is simply a privileged category of consumer.

Chiefs are entitled to extra revenues; they do not control (i.e. own) the means of production of the population at large. Those remain vested in the institutions of kinship. Chiefs are those enjoying prestige and influence but they have only limited and conditional control. Kings are those with centralized and pre-eminent control over territory and its population.

The Asiatic mode

Under the 'Asiatic mode', as illustrated in Figure 9.5:

a transition to a state society and to an embryonic form of class exploitation has taken place without the development of private ownership of land.

Within this framework the surplus, formerly appropriated by the local communities, now goes in part to the representatives of the higher community.

(Godelier 1978a:224)

Those supreme representatives are embodied in divine Monarchy. Out of the court and courtiers, as is well known, develops a state bureaucracy to monitor and control the state's revenues received either in kind or in labour (corvée) concentrated upon the political infrastructure, such as

Figure 9.5 The Asiatic mode of production

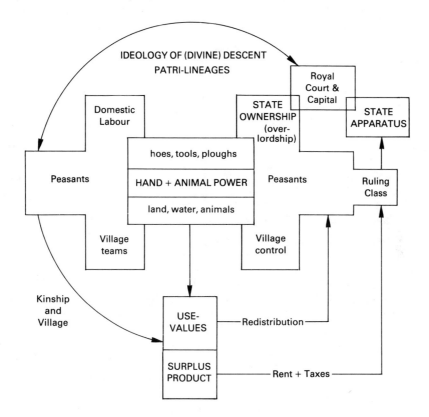

royal roads, ramparts, and garrisons. While Godelier (1978b:767) quite rightly points to the 'relations of domination and exploitation' in origin having presented themselves '*as an exchange* and (in particular) as an exchange of *services*', he necessarily qualifies this to be an exchange of the real means of life from the producers, against the perceived 'invisible realities and forces controlling (in the thought of these societies) the reproduction of the universe and life' (ibid.).

In other words the role of ideology is quite indispensable to this as to the modes of production illustrated previously.

The *real appropriation* (of nature) through the labour process happens under these *presuppositions*, which are not themselves the product of labour, but appear as its natural or divine presuppositions. This form, with the same land-relation as its foundation, can realise itself in very different ways. For example, it is not in the least a contradiction to it that, as in most Asiatic landforms, the *comprehensive unity* standing above all these little communities appears as the higher *proprietor* or as

267

Figure 9.6 Relations of ownership in the pyramidal state

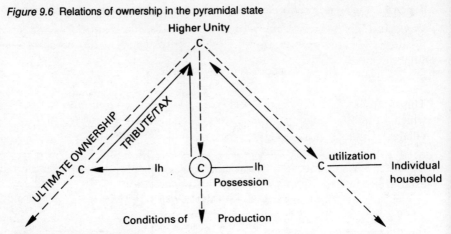

Adapted from Godelier 1978a:223

the sole *proprietor*; the real communities hence only as *hereditary* possessors,

not outright owners, and so they must render tribute to the 'real' or 'true' proprietors (Marx 1973:472–3; original emphasis).

This is the realm of the conical clan become the conical, or rather pyramidal, state illustrated in Figure 9.6 in regard to its juridico-economic aspects.

Here the individual household operates through the communal landholding village C (in Figure 9.6) in exploitation ('appropriation') of the conditions of production. However, at the apex of the system is a supreme community representing all the distinct village communities and which appears to be the ultimate title-holder above all communities, 'owning' them, its 'share' due to its role of guaranteeing all the individual communities their conditions of existence.

The Asiatic mode of production growing directly from clanship is neither logically nor historically bound to Asia. Godelier, for instance, applied the concept most fruitfully to the Inca (1977:63–9, 186–95), and calls for a more suitable appellation than that of 'Asiatic' (1978a:241).

The term proposed here in the light of the foregoing is *village-state mode of production*.

The fundamental reason for this term replacing 'Asiatic' is that it represents a concept and not merely a geographical location or association. The concept which replaces the term 'Asiatic' is that of a society where villages contain the bulk of the population and in which villages form the overwhelming number of units of productive association. In this mode cities are both exceptional and the locus of the ruling authorities of state, centring of course upon the royal capital, 'Pivot of the Four Quarters', and quite unproductive:

Cities proper here form alongside these villages only at exceptionally good points for external trade; or where the head of state and his satraps exchange their revenue (surplus product) for labour, spend it as labour-fund.

(Marx 1973:474)

This contrasts markedly with the city-state of Mesopotamia, for instance, which generally consisted of at least one city with associated towns and villages. Cities here were not islands in a sea of peasant villages.

And this is another point in favour of the term 'village-state' replacing 'Asiatic'; it is commensurable and therefore contrastative with the long-established and conceptually explicit term 'city-state'.

The seminal form in Sumer was, of course, the temple organization which, uniting in itself cosmological and productive functions, facilitated the adaption of post-Neolithic settlers to the demanding ecology of the alluvium and its contiguous semi-arid extensions.

Represented by the temple, then, was the original community organized in what Diakonoff called the 'communal sector' structured through the 'extended patriarchal families or family communes' (1969c:179), which I have identified (above) with the *oikiai* (**é**, *bîtum*).

Associated with this is the long-retained tendency to prevent irrevocable alienation of private [= communal, non-institutional] land and the periodic return of 'sold' land to the seller's clan. It is for precisely this reason that the first acquirers of *irrevocably* alienable land could in practice only be rulers and persons close to them.

(Diakonoff 1976–7:86)

Thus under political and economic pressure a third sector emerged alongside the institutional (palace and temple) and communal sectors. This was the private sector which we will glimpse in the next chapter in its land-dealing and merchandise-trading relationships. Clearly it was formed by the alienation of land from the non-institutional sector, while those without land to work by 'participating in the common property' (ibid.:55) became either clients of the public organizations or the private estates. They were, of course, supplemented over time by 'displaced persons' from elsewhere, quite outside their 'own nome'. And on the lines of the contemporary impact of stratified society upon the less stratified (e.g. Coombs, Dexter, and Hiatt 1982:427–38), we can be sure that if incorporated into the more advanced society, those from the lesser will be absorbed at the lowest levels, which mostly means dependent levels, even if they remain technically free.

'Full chattel slavery was derived from alien elements' (Gelb 1982:90), that is, from those with no kinship nexus that would confer upon them even residual civil or 'social status' in the sense defined above, and which is the sense also applied to true slavery by Finley (1983a:75) in stressing the kinlessness of slaves even at an elementary level; '*quem patrem, qui servos est?*' ('What father [is there], for a slave?')

Merely dependent labour, by contrast, best known from the Helotes of Sparta, retained their own community structure and as such never needed to be replenished from without (ibid.).

'Slavery and serfdom are thus only further developments of the form of property resting on the clan system. They necessarily modify all of the latter's forms. They can do this least of all in the Asiatic form', where, Marx (1973:493) explains, all are subject to, or at the disposition of, a transcendent state. Elsewhere more economic and less political means of subjection prevailed, and there, as in late imperial Italy, a debt-racked peasantry coexisted with true chattel slaves manning imperial factories and mines (Finley, op. cit.:77–9). Thus, with Bloch (1980:129) I do not think that there is any such thing as a 'slave mode of production'. Rather, several modes of production incorporate slavery as a mode of exploitation.

As topographical localization and geographical nucleation in Mesopotamia caused the early crystallization of the city from towns and villages, cities there had necessarily to remain productive. Further, the communal sector was not divorced from the *urbs* and in turn, due in part to that very contiguity, a private sector arose from alienation. The divine status of kings, embodying in their persons what, using White's (1959:310) term, we might call 'the State-Church', arrived only late in Mesopotamia (notably with Šulgi) and in a very attenuated form. This despite the central cultic roles of **ensís** and **lugals**; and there was, as we have seen, a separate corps of priests serving the communal temple(s).

The factors responsible for this city-state type of evolution in Mesopotamia seem to be three:

1 The advent of settlement on the alluvium was by farmers used to the environment and already organized into *oikiai*.
2 There is no real hinterland to the alluvium. Instead there is, as it were, an open frontier (actually an open steppe) in which peoples and influence can run fully the length of the Zagrosian Arc, across and beyond it.
3 Manifestly this was a 'competitive situation', which rising population levels could only accentuate. In conditions of at least latent conflict, settlements tended to nucleate and urbanize behind defensive walls. In so doing the cities would themselves have to remain productive, for although they continued to be at the centre of territory worked by lesser towns and villages, this was none the less insufficiently extensive for a situation to develop in which the 'capital' was simply a centre of unproductive consumption of revenues extracted from the countryside. While 'life was centred on large cities . . . the

cultivation of the fields in the region of a city was conducted from the city' (Leemans 1982:246), just like in the towns and villages of the hinterland (ibid.:248).

There is nothing like 'choice' involved. The city-state was the outcome of a configuration – cultural, social, and techno-environmental – determined by the trajectory from the Neolithic in the Near East.

The final diagram illustrates two sets of relations of production articulated through the control of the ruling class (Figure 9.7). The left-hand set shows the state sector, that of ensial estates (temple and palace); while the right-hand set shows that pertaining to the communal/private sector (cf. Ellis 1976:79–85).

But who were this ruling class? Our specification of a *class* at the outset as those with a shared *position* in the relations of production facilitates their identification. The Mesopotamian city-state was run by, and for the benefit of, its citizens, its free members, those in control of their own lands whether in communal or private ownership. The heads of such 'free' or citizen households, whom we may for convenience call patriarchs, constituted the 'ruling class' whether they did the executive ruling or not, for it is they who were the major beneficiaries of the distribution of property and thus wealth secured by the state. They were quintessentially the 'Assembly Men'.

That the state had its own subservient labour providing its own revenues simply lightened the burden on the communal/private land-holders, analogous to the Athenian state ownership of the silver mines of Laureion (Finley 1973:133–4). But the nature of the dependent labour employed in the two sectors varied, according to Diakonoff (1976–7:71), with ' "genuine" (patriarchal) slaves chiefly in the communal sector and helots exclusively in the state sector'. While the latter seem to have been bound primarily by economic means rather than by means of force as the Spartan helots were – if only for reasons of the difficulty of supervision recognized by Diakonoff (ibid.:78) in Mesopotamia, and which demanded constant military readiness on the part of the Spartans – 'the patriarchal slave', Diakonoff says, 'was a member, albeit without rights, of the family commune as a production group and was an organic component of it. It is precisely in this, above all, that he differs from the classical slave' (ibid.:80). But he also differs too, in that he worked the land with, rather than instead of, his owners, albeit he worked harder and longer (Diakonoff, op. cit.:77 and 79).

'Membership in the *polis* (which we may call citizenship) was inextricably bound up with possession of the land, the obligation of military service, and religion.' Finley here (1983a:89) writes of the fundamental characteristic of membership of the Greek or Roman city (*polis, urbs*); however the description applies equally well to the

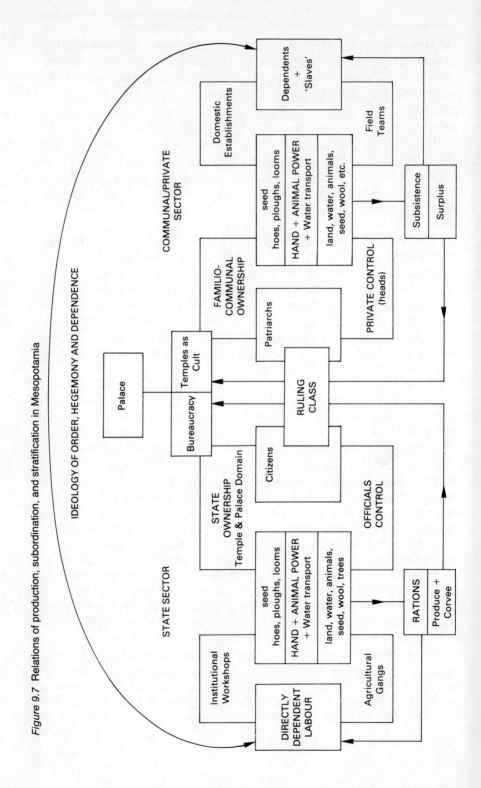

Figure 9.7 Relations of production, subordination, and stratification in Mesopotamia

Mesopotamian. In particular citizenship thus defined was a prerequisite to administrative, official, or scribal office and 'many of them could attain very high social status and in essence had a share in the income from the exploitation of the helots (and later also in the income from taxation of the entire population)' (Diakonoff 1976–7:71). The king could also of course confer office on dependants from his own 'household'.

The military was organized on a bureaucratic and also a militia basis (the *rēdû*) yet the benefits from office and war accrued to officers (Oppenheim 1964:117). Complementary to the palace, with which it overlapped, was the temple as a cult institution and thus focus of ideology. That ideology was one of Order, Hegemony, and Dependence, that in brief can be called 'patriarchal'. Jacobsen summed it up in the words of the Babylonian creation myth *Enuma Elish* as 'benefits and obedience':

When they gave Marduk the kingship
they pronounced to him the formula
of 'Benefits and Obedience':
'From this day forward you shall be
the provider for our sanctuaries,
and whatever you order let us carry out'.

(Jacobsen 1976:180)

'In a similar sense, all kings' dependents, from slaves to the highest officials, are called slaves, just as the ruler himself is said to be a slave of his god or goddess' (Gelb 1982:88). For what is thereby generally denoted is 'a socio-economic dependence of a lower-ranking individual and his household on a higher-ranking individual or his household' (ibid.).

Diakonoff has posited a revealing symmetry between terms whose comprehension has given Assyriology considerable trouble. In so doing, he has thrown much light on the modalities of stratification in Mesopotamia:

In regard to the opposition between 'person in possession of patriarchal authority' vs. 'person under the patriarchal authority of another' we have a neat terminological correspondence in the opposition *bēlum* vs. *wardum* (resp. *amtum*). This is why *wardum* does not necessarily mean 'slave' or even 'servant'; it may just mean 'person under the patriarchal authority of the *bēlum*', or 'person placing himself in such relation to another person as a matter of courtesy';

both of which would be accommodated by the term 'master'.

More important is the opposition between 'person partaking in communal property (= citizen in possession of all civil rights)' vs. 'person under perpetual patriarchal authority and thus not having

273

property of his own, except conditional holdings, etc. (= royal servants or labourers)'. The corresponding terminological opposition is *awīlum* or *mār ālim* (lú, dumu-uru) vs. *muškēnum* (= *arad šarri*, *bunuš malki* in Ugarit, etc.). This is corroborated, among other things, by the fact that the elders of a community as well as the members of a Popular Assembly are always *awīlū* or *mārū ālim*, never *muškēnū(tum)*; note also that there is no mention either of elders or of members of the Popular Assembly among the habitual recipients of rations or land allotments from the state sector at any period later than the archives of Šuruppak,

that is, later than the Early Dynastic period. But most tellingly of all,

Among the royal (and temple) personnel, the sources distinguish the producers of material wealth, *nāši biltim*, from warriors and 'other persons liable to the royal service' (*ilkum aḫûm*).

(Diakonoff 1972:46)

Social strata are thus those with a shared position in the relations of production. Relations of production are structured around ownership or control of, and taxes upon, the means of production, which includes control of labour power directly, as in state corvée.

In Mesopotamia, ownership mostly concerned **oikos** holdings and private estates, while control of temple lands was vested in functionaries on behalf of themselves and the state.

Accordingly we can conclude with Bloch (1980:129), that

The value of the concept mode of production does not lie in the fact that it offers yet another list of types of systems but rather that it focuses on a set of *systematic and analytically revealing interconnections*. These are, as we have seen, the interrelations between the means and techniques of production and relations of production. But it also includes the relation of these to the ideology which is understood as one of the mechanisms of reproduction.

(Bloch 1980:129; my emphasis)

Chapter ten

Ideology and political economy of the Mesopotamian state

> Unfortunately, archaeological data, and even to a considerable extent philological data of the type available to us in Mesopotamia, can nowhere detect the implicit and often unexpressed ideas that regulate the way in which a society behaves and which must be of more relevance to social patterning than either environment or technology.
>
> (Joan Oates 1977:481–2)

Difficult as it is to grapple with something as impalpable as ideology or cosmology, the attempt must be made, given its importance to social structure and individual action.

Cosmology is two things simultaneously: a personal *belief system* and a social *construct system*; but the two are not synonymous. Cosmologies consist of ideologies, which are themselves structured around myths, incorporating empirical facts of some description, such as that baking packed and tempered mud produces bricks; or, in the Mesopotamian case, human beings from fourteen pieces of clay, seven male and seven female (Bottero 1982:24–32).

With the personal belief system the individual situates himself in life as he experiences it: by the social construct system society locates itself in Nature (the 'cosmos') and situates its members in relation to one another. Cosmology is thus a world-view shared to the extent that its holders feel a joint commitment to it because they have come (usually by socialization and not by choice) to interpret their existence through its categories. It is precisely because this is so that cosmological engagement is intrinsic to any stable functioning of society and the state.

From the ideational material supplied by society ready-made (such as its foundation and charter myths)[1] and from the very appearances of how things manifest themselves in social processes (as self-evident events, 'causes', etc.) the individual's own biographical exposure selectively constructs a personal version of the prevailing cosmology.

While, therefore, it is quite possible for individuals to develop a new world-view (e.g. Jesus, Buddha, Marx), for those to become a (social) cosmology they must engage with, and supply more satisfactory answers to, the existential concerns of members of that society (Frend (1959) 1978:282–6; Greeley 1982:97–102).

The existential problem is that of being situated in an environment, social and natural, over whose functioning one has little effective control and of whose logic one will have little comprehension. Thus the environment is encountered as external forces that, in confronting the actor, have somehow to be propitiated (for example by making sacrifices or paying taxes). Collective representations are thus the socially (historically) derived means whereby members of a society cognitively situate themselves in and explain to themselves their common connection with their natural environment as the basis from which all derive subsistence. The totality and shape of social and natural connections perceived form that society's cosmology.

Existential concerns are then those inhering in 'life as lived' by the mortal individual confronting his everyday conditions of existence. Some concerns are kernel in that no member of society can escape his own biological existence and its end, mortality. Other concerns are contingent upon the actual organization of society, with differential benefit to its populace from social institutions. The actual 'crossover linkage' between the kernel and contingent is of course the somatic condition of the individual, his personal state of health, the prerequisite to any possible well-being.

The existential concerns tend to form two clusters, some being intrinsic, that is fundamental, to the life of the individual and others extrinsic or more palpably social. Those concerns are the central issues to which any cosmology must provide satisfying answers. However, the emphases will shift according to historical context – from the millenarian, whereby individual salvation is thought to be produced by total social transformation; to, on the other hand, quietistic beliefs wherein social solutions are the consequence of personal transformations. These are of course polar types and most cosmologies, most of the time, are structured between the two. The existential concerns can be listed as follows:

Fundamental	*Contingent*
mortality =	happiness =
birth	health (the condition of)
death	social vigour and success
health	(by ascriptive or reproductive means)
reproduction	of prestige/wealth/security

We observe, too, that the 'stages', or better, 'conditions' listed in the Fundamental (or kernel) column are what is socially marked by life-crisis ritual ('rites of passage') in which an individual's status is set or recast.

As for the Contingent factors, those are matters of personal prayer, enterprise, and haggling with the gods; especially in Mesopotamia through one's personal god, without whom 'man cannot make his living, the young man cannot move his arm heroically in battle' (Frankfort, Frankfort, Wilson and Jacobsen (1946) 1949:219). A letter to one such personal god asking for his intervention with the high god, Marduk, is revealing in its combination of haggling and pleading:

> To the god my father speak: thus says Apiladad, thy servant:
> 'Why have you neglected me (so)?
> Who is going to give you one (other worshipper) who can take my
>   place?
> Write to the god Marduk, who is fond of you,
> that he may break my bondage;
> then I shall see your face and kiss your feet!
> Consider also my family, grown ups and little ones;
> have mercy on me for their sake, and let your help reach me!'
>
> (Frankfort *et al.* 1949:221)

The benefits, then, to be derived from proper subordination are well summed by Frankfort *et al.* (ibid.:220) as that of the 'dutiful servant' for whom 'service and worship is the way to achieve protection [from the gods]; and it is also the way to earthly success, to the highest values in Mesopotamian life: health and long life, honoured standing in the community, many sons, wealth'.

At the origins of the Chinese writing system (of 'characters') in Shang times, we find the 'oracle-bone script' inscribed on pieces of flat bone or shell and framing a question of immediate concern, the answer to which was found by diviners from the cracks formed when the bone was heated. An example is illustrated in Figure 10.1. Indeed, 'we can see how significant an activity divination was from the fact that the chief ministers of the Shang rulers all seem to have been diviners' (Fairbank, Reischauer, and Craig 1973:28).

While, then, it is perfectly true to say that ideologies are social facts independent of any particular individual, it is certainly not sufficient to their efficacy that ideologies be encountered as external pressure. On the contrary, to work they must be internalized personally to the extent that they become the individual's own way of construing the world and his place in it. So much so that in the process of personalization/socialization the cosmology comes to form the structure of conscience, norms, values, and, to a large extent, actual behaviour. And if we recognize in culture the intergenerational transmission of beliefs, behaviours, and techniques, we may see how cosmology determines the first, shapes the second, and influences the third.

Figure 10.1 Typical inscription from an oracle bone

ORACLE BONE TEXT MODERN CHINESE LITERAL TRANSLATION

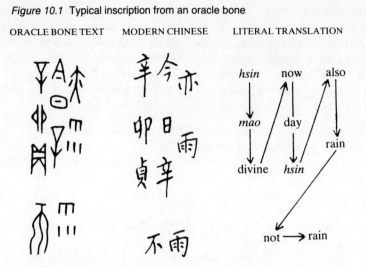

Shang Inscription on Bone The characters are to be read from top to bottom, but the lines in this particular case read from left to right. The meaning of the text is: '[On the day] *hsin-mao*, it is divined whether on this *hsin* day it will rain – or not rain.' Most of the characters in this text are clearly identifiable from their modern forms. The second character in the second column is a picture of the sun with a spot in it, while the second character in the third column as well as the lower right-hand character show rain falling from a cloud. The upper right-hand character, showing a man's armpits (the two spots under the arms), was at this time a homophone for the undepictable word 'also'.

Source: Fairbank, Reischauer, and Craig 1973:25

1 Order and law

Probably the most active thing that cosmology affects is law. Enacted law is generally recognized to depend ultimately on norms intrinsic to society at large, but how it differs is rarely specified, except to say that some sovereign authority is involved in 'making law'. But law is a considerable factor in Mesopotamia, which has the first written law codes and, indeed, the first civil contracts for the transfer of property, in addition to the earliest records of criminal proceedings. As we have seen, above all Mesopotamian kings claimed to be upholders of justice in their proclamations, either those celebrating victory or some pious deed like restoring a temple and, perhaps most pious of all, when proclaiming the *mīšarum* restitution usual on accession and every seven years thereafter. Thus Ur-Nammu (2,112–2,095 BC), the founder of the Third Dynasty of Ur, having declared that 'After An and Enlil had turned over the

Kingship of Ur to Nanna, at that time did Ur-Nammu, son born of (the goddess) Ninsun, for his beloved mother who bore him, in accordance with his [i.e. the god Nanna's] principles of equity and truth . . . ', goes on to show the physical rightness of his course in battle with the ensí of Lagash, whom Ur-Nammu defeated.

> Then did Ur-Nammu, the mighty warrior, king of Ur, king of Sumer and Akkad, by the might of Nanna, lord of the city [of Ur], and in accordance with the true word of Utu, establish equity in the land [and] he banished malediction, violence and strife.
>
> (Finkelstein 1975a:31)

Ur-Nammu then goes on (a) to enunciate measures taken for the general welfare, and (b) to adumbrate many sections of particular redress. Thus he proceeds directly to say that 'By granting immunity in Akkad to the maritime trade from the seafarer's overseer, to the herdsmen from the "oxen-taker", the "sheep-taker" and the "donkey-taker" he set Sumer and Akkad free' – free, it seems, from grasping officials. Ur-Nammu further promoted the general welfare in that 'He fashioned the bronze **silà** measure, he standardised the one **mina** weight (and) standardised the stone weight of a **shekel** of silver in relation to one **mina**' (lines 162–8).

More specifically social measures are found in the claim that 'The orphan was not delivered up to the mighty man: the man of one **shekel** was not delivered up to the man of one **mina**' (ibid.). We do not know just how this was achieved, as some parts of the proclamation, known only from scribal copies, are missing. It may however lie in the specific provisions for restitution that take up the rest of the 'code' which is extant. Thus, following a great deal on adultery and sundry fornication, we read that

> If a man proceeded by force, and plowed the arable field of a(nother) man, and he (i.e. the latter) brought a lawsuit (against him), but he (i.e. the squatter) reacts in contempt, that man will forfeit his expenses.
>
> If a man flooded a field of a(nother) man with water, he shall measure out (for him) three **kur** of barley per **iku** of field.
>
> If a man had leased an arable field to a(nother) man for cultivation, but he (the lessee) did not plough it, so that it turned into wasteland, he shall measure out (to the lessor) three **kur** of barley per **iku** of field.
>
> (Finkelstein 1975a:34)

The king was truly *fons justiciae* (Driver and Miles 1952–5:I.490). He did not merely issue proclamations amending or, more centrally, reaffirming the laws, but he was directly involved in implementation, often acting himself as the court of highest appeal. The preamble to Hammurabi's famous 'code', which is largely taken up with recounting his religious acts in the restoration of temples and so forth, as vindication of the divine favour he has been shown, concludes the introduction to what he calls his *dīnāt mīšarum*, 'verdicts of the just order':

> When Marduk commanded me to give justice to the people of the land and to let (them) have (good) governance, I set forth truth and justice throughout the land (and) prospered the people.
>
> (Driver and Miles 1952–5:II.13)

However, two things should be noted also: the law did *not* apply equally between citizens of substance and lesser men (and even more so, women); and many trials involved ordeal, that is, a physical test, like burning or drowning. One of Ur-Nammu's provisions illustrates both principles:

> If a man accused the wife of a man of fornication and the river (-ordeal) proved her innocent, then the man who had accused her must pay one third of a **mina** of silver.
>
> (Finkelstein 1975a:33)

Mesopotamia was full of law-cases civil and criminal, even marriages necessitating a binding written deed. None the less, there was no police force, no public prosecutor, and no public executioner (Driver and Miles, op. cit.:I.494), those functions falling to the community organs as indicated above. Thus we can see how the political and the legal came together (in 'Justice') to reinforce the legitimacy of rule, even where that bore down unevenly. There was an established social order in which places were ascribed, and its lineaments had to be kept clear, its functioning coherent. If this is done continuity itself assumes value – *nomos* or *mos maiorum* ('the ways of the forefathers') – if only because it is that particular culture into which members are socialized and they know of no other.[2] Those norms (of ideal and expected behaviour) derive from cosmological principles that appeal to continuity itself and the rightness of the present, its 'naturalness', under which the existing order can be postulated as ultimately sanctioned by the gods and nature. The very 'facticity' of prevailing conditions, its palpable actuality, means that it is itself the criterion of 'normality' from which other possibilities are deviations. Legitimate force is then that ostensibly employed in the enforcement of the norms of normalcy.

In Chapter 8 we saw how 'back in time' (for instance genealogically) becomes assimilated to 'upwards' in power and authority, producing super- and sub-ordination. Both the temporal and spatial are 'beyond', and having fused, descend from 'on high'. Thus Anu is the Sumerian god of the sky but he is also simultaneously the father of the gods and the font of authority. Anu is both overarching sky and overarching authority, hence he and Utu, the sun god, are the ultimate arbiters. Authority thus seems to 'descend' to earth as kingship was said to have done, and also as the **me**'s – roles, skills, and offices of civilization – were said to have done.

> Going to law also underlies the great *bît rimki* ritual of purifying the king when he is threatened by the evils involved in an eclipse of the moon. The sunrise ritual takes the form of a full-dress lawsuit before Utu and the assembly of the gods. Utu acts as judge and hears the complaint. Enki guarantees that the verdict will be enforced, a function known as 'overshadowing' the case.
>
> (Jacobsen 1976:86)

This was a necessary recourse, for 'execution was left to the winning party; and for that reason a court would not touch a case unless it was certain that the plaintiff had power behind him, a powerful protector who would guarantee that the judgement would be executed' (Frankfort *et al.*, op. cit.:221).

In the myth *Enki and the World Order*, it was Utu who was put in charge of *all* boundaries, both in heaven and on earth, a particularly important point 'implying that all of the universe was under the same law and the same judge' (Jacobsen 1976:85).[3] And Enki, 'the overshadower' 'decrees the fate':

> Sumer, 'great mountain', 'country of the universe',
> Filled with enduring light, dispensing from
>   sunrise to sunset the **me**'s to (?) the people,
> Your **me**'s are lofty **me**'s, unreachable.
>
> (Kramer 1963:177)

Me's are the norms and techniques of civilization instituted by Enki 'the wise, the knowing', to produce world order at Enlil's behest. Of the hundred or so listed (four times over) in the myth *Inanna and Enki: The Transfer of the Arts of Civilization from Eridu to Uruk*, the first dozen are given in their original order (from Kramer, op. cit.:116):

1 **en**-ship
2 godship
3 the exalted and enduring crown
4 the throne of kingship
5 the exalted sceptre
6 the royal insignia
7 the exalted shrine
8 shepherdship
9 kingship
10 lasting ladyship
11 (the priestly office) 'divine lady'
12 (the priestly office) **ishib**.

Figure 10.2 Cosmic order

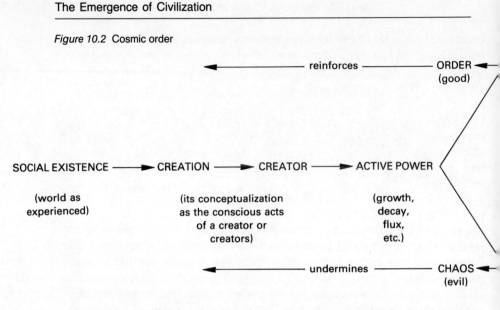

Etymologically [**me**] may be considered as the noun ('being' = manner of being) which corresponds to the verb **me** 'to be'. It is used characteristically of the totality of the functions pertaining to an office or a profession . . . of rites, and of mores. . . . Instructive also is **me-te** 'approaching the norm' = 'proper', 'fitting' (Akkadian *(w)asmu*).

(Jacobsen 1970a:359–60, n.20)

We can thus represent the Mesopotamian view of the fusion of cosmic and social orders, manifested in orderly social relations, as in Figure 10.2.

Order, regularity, and hence stable boundaries in and between natural and social forces as the prerequisite of social life and its reproduction, are by definition 'good', the very archetype of 'goodness'. In Mesopotamian society the king was co-ordinator of cultic and legal structures, the latter, it should be noted, a purely secular system (Speiser 1954:14). None the less,

the cosmos was founded on certain eternal truths which the laws strove to safeguard. These truths applied to the ruler no less than to his subjects. The king, more than anyone else, must be ever watchful to maintain them. The sum of such cosmic and immutable truths was called *kittum*. A king might seek to 'establish' (*šakānum*) the *kittum* just as he was bound to institute *mīšarum* [i.e. restitution, see above].

(Speiser 1954:12)

Those things that conduce to orderly reproduction are virtuous, those tending to undermine it are accordingly evil. As Finley wrote of the unequal but stable incorporation of the lower orders into a (Graeco-Roman) social hierarchy in which they were permanently and institutionally disadvantaged: 'The vast body of religious practices was of course an integral part of the traditional *nomos* or *mos maiorium* that upheld the whole structure, including the right of the elite to dominate' (Finley 1983c:95). Habit, norms, and religion, all of which can be subsumed under the head of 'customary behaviour', thus possess what Bloch (1974:66) has analysed as 'illocutionary force', the power to shape expectations and behaviour by circumventing logic and employing affective devices, formal and positional, so interpellating the individual and inducing him to accept the existing order as both 'natural' and thus inevitable if not necessarily desirable.

But it is not only this 'habitual' or customary dimension which is in play, though it is the most fundamental and omnipresent (Bloch 1975b:3). There is also the reverence that derives from awe of religion or state power, both embodiments of supreme power. Both religion and the state conjoin in a public rhetoric of cult, ceremonial, monument, display, and dispensation, to reinforce the intrinsic aspect of deference and to mobilize that of induced awe. Whereas socialization would tend to elicit assent, public rhetoric of the rulers directed toward the ruled could at the least evoke, and at the most command it. Rhetoric, says Oliver (1971:8) in a phrase that he emphasizes, 'seeks to make motive appeals compulsive'.

We can now envisage how the state appears to hover above society while engaged in a political dialectic with it (Figure 10.3, p. 284).

Here the state manifests its sovereignty, parametrically, by raising military forces for defence (or in the Roman case usually attack) and in conducting inter-state relations generally. For its support the state levies some sort of taxes in labour, kind, or specie. This latter is usually confined to the citizenry properly so-called; those with full political and economic rights, beneath whom there are invariably strata who lack either full political or economic rights. When both are absent the condition is that of slavery, but intermediate we have serfs and clients. The citizenry are represented as undertaking 'horizontal' economic and political transactions, in groups, corporations, or whatever. It is the citizens alone or even just a sub-grouping of those (such as the Roman *nobiles*) who form 'public opinion' amongst themselves, in support of which they then may seek to involve other strata. This is the dialectical counterpart of public rhetoric, and both are focused upon, and contested within, public forums such as councils and law-courts; often one and the same in both Athens and Mesopotamia. Rhetoric proceeds in opposite fashion to religion. Whereas religion seeks ratiocinative justifications for its affective constructs, rhetoric employs ideological elements to obscure the evaluation of evidence.

The political economy of stratified society turns upon the cleavage between the direct producers, i.e. those engaged in the labour process,

Figure 10.3 The political dialectic of the state

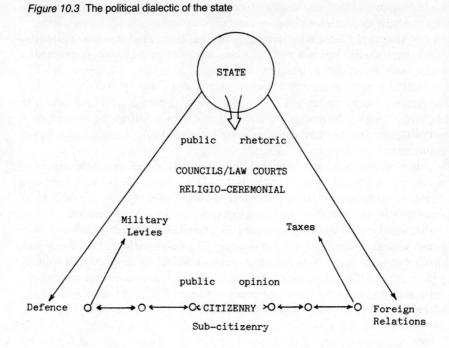

and those who control the conditions of production by regulating access through:

1 *ideological process*: that is, their imputed ability to confer fecundity by ritual means;
2 *by juridical means*: that is, by *rules* deriving from customary possession plus economic acquisition, through purchase or foreclosure;
3 *by physical force*: direct force is of course one possible mode of acquisition. For security, however, it will have to be justified sooner or later by association with modes 1 or 2. Conversely, modes 1 and 2 will at some time have recourse to, or at least will need the background presence of, mode 3.

In practice, for most of the time, in most societies, the mere presence of each will serve to reinforce the others. However, it should be noted that the primary method of surplus extraction varies in each case. In

1 by leaving possession of the means of production and the operation of the labour process in the hands of the direct producers, with surplus extracted *ex post facto*;
2 by the owners operating the labour process themselves, or under their direct supervision. Owners must live on or near the job in this

regime. They are also in a position to, and have an interest in, improving productivity.

3 This is the antithesis of production and engages in none. Revenues are acquired by seizure, threats, or military budgets, and there is a vested interest in warfare.

2 The political terrain

Politics is the contest for public endorsement of private or sectional interests.

It resides not in any one practice or single locus, but is an arena of contest and exchange permeating social life, since what constitutes 'public' varies according to what is sought. Where, however, society is state-ordered, some contests will be directed toward government, since that is then the ultimate locus of authority. But state-directedness must not distract us from the ubiquity of contest-exchange. The major resources for contest-exchange are grouped under the heads of Ideology, Economy, and Physical Force. In the longer term Ideology is paramount because it defines the rules of the game. Rules are however only relatively fixed, since, like all resources, those too are contested.

The political terrain as an arena can be illustrated as in Figure 10.4. It can, and is intended to stand for, contest-exchanges proceeding at all levels of society, and in all its constitutive elements (such as clans and villages), as well as the more usually treated aggregative contest/exchanges in society as a whole. Thus it encompasses ritual promotion by a caste of increased wealth, or the reworking of genealogies in segmentary societies to find a place for cadet lineages, or what a Melanesian 'big-man' has to do to build and retain a following, just as much as contests for government office or over the prerogatives of rulers.

Figure 10.4 The arena of contest-exchanges

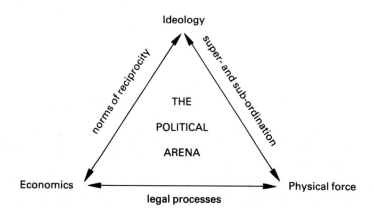

Such a view of the constitution of a political field is extended and reinforced by Barth's (1981) seminal work on ethnic groups and boundaries, developed, amongst others, by Hodder's (1982b) archaeological ethnography.

Implicit in much sociological writing is the assumption that somehow, somewhere, a society developed its own culture in effective isolation, then, due to population growth or migration, came into contact with another society similarly formed, with the two experiencing the mutual differences as a cultural or ethnic boundary between them. Barth has shown this not to be the case, indeed to be the opposite of the case, since

> boundaries persist despite a flow of personnel across them. In other words, categorical ethnic distinctions do not depend on an absence of mobility, contact and information, but do entail social processes of exclusion and incorporation whereby discrete categories are maintained *despite* changing participation and membership in the course of individual life histories.
>
> (Barth 1981:188–9; original emphasis)

Indeed Hodder (op. cit.:56–7) shows that people following the same mode of life and even speaking the same language erect and maintain symbolic lines of demarcation 'especially in the border areas where there is greatest tension and competition, material culture of many forms [being used in those related Kenyan societies] to justify between-group negative-reciprocity and to support the social and economic dependencies within groups'. This last observation is particularly important for the constitution of a political field by marking its boundaries culturally.

Barth (1961:31–3), in his ethnology of pastoral nomads in south Persia, points out how tribes are political, not cultural entities, maintained (and changed) because they assure certain economic-political rights to their members, essentially that enough grazing land will be made available for the flocks of each of the households. The 'ethnicity' of tribes and confederations as manifested culturally by language and origins can thus be very diverse, while the very ethnic designations used are both contingent and plastic. Hence 'aggregational groups are classified ethnically with the political unit with which they are identified', such as 'Arab' tribes of diverse origin that are purely Persian-speaking, or with the 'ethnic group of origin of their original core. The language spoken by the group may well be different from this' (Barth 1961:133).

Boundaries are, then, not historically fixed, objective criteria of origin, for 'ethnic groups are categories of ascription and identification by the actors themselves', selectively maintained (Barth 1981:199). Indeed, of the Bedouin tribes of pre-Islamic Arabia, Lewis remarks that 'God and cult were the badge of tribal identity and the sole ideological expression of the sense of unity and cohesion of the tribe. Conformity to the tribal cult expressed political loyalty. Apostasy was the equivalent of treason' (Lewis 1966:30).

None of this should be a surprise to anthropology. No anthropologist regards moieties, lineages, clans, or any such fundamental structural unit of society as being the result of the meeting or collision of separate entities which then united to form a common system. Correctly they are regarded as the 'organizing principle' of the societies characterized by them; that is, as those elements of the system that assign to each component of the system their respective places. Cognitively for its members such structures form a framework by which the world is ordered. E. Marx writes of the Bedouin that 'while he is capable of interpreting various aspects of his society in an entirely objective fashion, he possesses only one model, or conception, of his total society, namely that of a segmentary political organisation' (E. Marx 1978:61–2).

Consequently it is 'the ethnic *boundary* that defines the group, not the cultural stuff that it encloses' (Barth 1981:204; his emphasis). Ethnicity then can be seen to be the ascription of ascriptions, or the status overranking all other statuses in the precise sense in which both terms are used in Chapter 8.

> In other words, regarded as a status, ethnic identity is superordinate to most other statuses, and defines the permissible constellation of statuses, or social personalities which an individual with that identity may assume. In this respect ethnic identity is similar to sex and rank, in that it constrains the incumbent in all his activities, not only in some defined social situation.
>
> (Barth 1981:206)

Effected by this meta-classification is then the closure of the social field to all but either the existing participants or those who can join only on terms that do not disrupt the game being played.

This enables us to see ethnic identity for what it really is, a set of essentially arbitrary differentia marking out a social boundary that serves as a container for the 'rules of the game'; that is, for the whole mode of life involving the competition for and exchange of economic, ideological, and coercive resources, crystallizing, if stable, a set of cultural values or value orientations (Horowitz 1972:105). Ethnic boundaries thus set the frontiers of what has been termed the political field.

Viewing such boundaries as essentially notional markers also explains the oft-remarked phenomenon of the ethnic plurality possible where established states exist.[4] Since state boundaries are specifically territorial and military, cultural and symbolic modes of interaction are not the definitive ones. Instead different ideological modes obtain (especially as public rhetoric) and stratification mechanisms described in earlier chapters apply. Those beneath the elite would be citizens or subjects, whatever their origins, and only relative utility would be a consideration.

From this we have a possible explanation for the absence of any ethnic conflict to be observed between Sumerians and Akkadians (Jacobsen 1970:187–92; Cooper 1973:245–6). Where the state was in the process of formation or had already arisen on the alluvium prior to the influx of Akkadians, then only considerations of stratification based on relative wealth and power would apply, as was the case late in the third and early in the second millennium BC with the integration of Amorite nomads originally speaking a foreign language (Buccellati 1966:315, 356–7).

Thus Caplice in review of Kraus (1970) writes of

> the recently discovered term by which the Sumerians designated themselves (**dumu.gi$_7$**) mean[s] in practice 'free citizen' and is opposed to 'slave' rather than to a non-Sumerian speaking population group or groups, nor (presuming that such groups were indeed felt as distinct) do we know the Sumerian term by which they may have been designated before Ur III.
>
> (Caplice 1973:526–7)

Indeed of the Ur III period Buccellati notes that

> we seem to lack the very word for 'foreigner'. At least the word which can be used to refer to foreigners, namely **lú kúr** (Akkadian *aḫûm ubāru* and *nakrum*) does not seem to be used anywhere to qualify specific persons in contrast to others who are considered natives. It is interesting to note that this is also true of later periods in Mesopotamian history: the clearest passage where *aḫiūtum* means 'foreigners', as opposed to *aliūtum*, 'citizens (of Aššur)', is in a text coming not from Mesopotamia but Anatolia.
>
> (Buccellati 1966:324)

All of this is further evidence that stratification in Mesopotamia was in no wise 'racial' or 'ethnic', nor an outcome of conquest, but rather an outcome of processes obtaining within and between households. Thus Oates can justly remark that:

> in Mesopotamia both kings and gods were seen simply as heads of rather special households and at least from ED III onwards society was divided basically into two classes, persons under the authority of a household and persons exercising such authority. Labourers in the state sector, whether secular or religious were conceived as under the patriarchal authority of the king or gods.
>
> (Oates 1977:476)

Initially, then, those '**abba**', holding *patria potestas*, held council and power (Frankfort *et al.* 1949:148–9). They were the Assemblymen. The first stage in the loss of their political sovereignty was in treating the

lugal, originally appointed on a temporary or at least reversionary (**bala**) basis by the assembly, as both permanent and equal, thus conceding the sharing of power. This can be called the 'Gilgamesh context' (cf. Jacobsen 1976:184); and indeed according to the account in *Gilgamesh and Agga*, he achieves this by promoting military adventures against the wishes of the 'senate' (cf. Kramer 1963:187–90).

The next stage was that of the assembly functioning as the 'king's parliament', discussing his initiatives, with his the final decision. Such is the 'Sargonic context'. And the third stage of demotion from full sovereignty is the relegation of the assembly to a subsidiary and specialized body of state restricted to resolving breaches of law and custom. This can be termed the 'Hammurabic context', and after the Hammurabic (Old Babylonian) is the era of the territorial state.

The territorial state is the uniquely privileged player in the game of contest-exchanges. Operating on a territory-wide basis within which it claims a monopoly of (at least new) rule-making and enforcement, it can call on social resources unrivalled in breadth and depth. Thus in the economic field it can vary the level of taxes, impose new ones, or even mobilize labour directly. In ideological matters it can build new churches, establish new traditions, and support Vergils, while in military matters it can use the above to conscript, pay mercenaries, and engage in foreign campaigns that may not only be self-financing but internally soothing.

It is the diversity and interplay of resources as much as the scale of any individual one that gives the state its room for manoeuvre *vis-à-vis* all of society's strata and interest groups, thus enabling it to retain the initiative in most circumstances. Indeed its very scale, multi-facetedness, and initiative can make the state appear more a part of natural forces than human powers.

Chapter eleven

Summary and overview

This work has posed the question of why and how permanent settlement, husbandry, and cities developed where and when they did. Answer was given in terms of necessary and sufficient conditions, beginning with the environmental shifts consequent upon the ending of the last Ice Age. In those increasingly permissive conditions of the Holocene Near East, it was indicated that for the very first time *Homo sapiens sapiens* was present to take advantage of an interglacial. But the ending of glacial conditions was itself destabilizing. New adaptations had to be made in an environment that continued to flux differentially for millenniums after the nominal onset of the Holocene neothermal, reaching a temperature 2–3° higher than today's between 5,000 and 3,000 BC, while tree pollen climaxed at 3,500 BC in the Zagros (Bottema 1978:25). It is only about this time that near-modern sea-levels were being attained in the Gulf (Larsen and Evans 1978:236). Some idea of the scale and suddenness of the adaptations that had to be made at the Epipalaeolithic can be gained from the fact that the maximum of the last, Würm, Ice Age was reached only around 21,000 years BP, with sea-level declining about 100 metres (Nützel 1975:104). Regional conditions over this transition are conveniently summarized in Map 11.1.

A rising density of subsistence resources, particularly the grains, led to a downward spiral of mobility until full sedentarization was possible at particularly favoured sites and still employing only wild plants and animals. However, while only a few grass species were intensely exploited, it should be noted that in each area from Anatolia to Khuzistan a different animal species was the main object of the hunt.

In southern Turkey the majority of animal remains from Cayönü and Çatal Hüyük came from cattle (in the earliest levels *Bos primigenius* and in the later, domesticated ox), red deer, sheep and goats. In the Levant the greatest number of animal remains came from gazelle with fox also an important source of meat. At Jarmo and the Deh Luran sites the people hunted mainly wild sheep and goat, but also gazelle,

Map 11.1 Regional conditions during the Late Pleistocene/Early Holocene

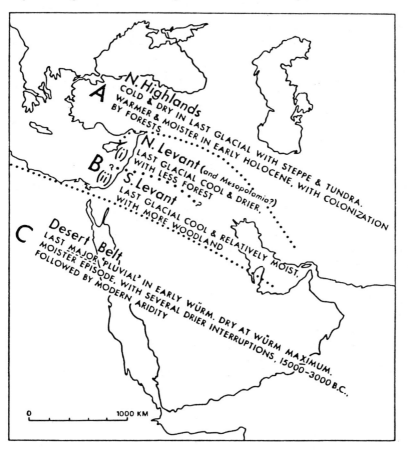

Source: Butzer 1978:7

fox, aurochs, and pig. Beidha is the only site from which the Nubian ibex (*Capra ibex nubiana*) has been identified.

(Clutton-Brock 1978:35)

The same holds of the loci of animal domestication in this most diverse region I have termed the Zagrosian Arc. Here, it was maintained, there was no single 'hearth' for the origins of husbandry from which such techniques diffused. Rather the complementarity of diversity was stressed in the concept of *lateral step-wise progression* whereby innovations made in separate zones connected at different times in different places, forming new syntheses that themselves served as the cores of new departures. Processes of this kind can be seen in the domestication of animals. The earliest domestic goats so far known were found at Asiab, Iran, and date from about 8,000 BC (Bökönyi 1976:21). Domestic sheep with goats have already been noted at Ali Kosh in Deh Luran after about 7,500 BC, while the earliest domestic cattle presently known in the Near East are from Çatal Hüyük in Anatolia, around 6,400 BC (ibid.). Pig is also domesticated in the seventh millennium, with horse and ass significantly later. Domestication of the horse seems to have occurred outside the Near East, in the middle Dnieper area of south Russia during the late fifth or fourth millennium BC (Sherratt 1981:273). Between fourth and third millennia, the ass was domesticated (Bökönyi 1976:21), while the camel may have been domesticated in Arabia at this time (Ripinsky 1975:297).

Most significantly, however, of the five species characteristic of Neolithic animal husbandry in the Near East: sheep and goat, cattle and pig (plus dog, which is Epipalaeolithic), Bökönyi himself observes it to be curious 'that the five species did not appear together at any site in the area before the end of the 7th millennium BC, although many different species combinations occur on many sites' (1976:22). Such a phenomenon is however readily explicable on the basis of 'crossover development' described earlier. Bökönyi (ibid.:21) graphically illustrates the unevenness of domestication and environmental suitability (Map 11.2).

Discussing the secondary exploitation of animals and their products in Eurasia, that is, their later use not for meat but for milk, wool, riding, traction, and pack transport, Sherratt has observed that:

> The development of the economies based on secondary animal exploitation thus began as a mosaic of individual innovations, mostly in the semi-arid areas of the Near East. It was a response to the problem of adapting early forms of farming to new environments, especially open landscapes where it was possible to maintain larger quantities of livestock. These innovations came together during the period of rapid economic change leading to the rise of urban communities, and were disseminated by the expansion of trade routes linking the early states with their resource rich hinterlands.
>
> (Sherratt 1983:100)

In the process of elucidating the origins of farming, two conventional postulates were overturned, one belonging to the nineteenth century and the other current. The nineteenth-century premiss dismissed is that pastoralism precedes and lays the basis for cultivation. In the scheme of Savagery–Barbarism–Civilization then obtaining, the domestication and herding of animals is situated in the 'middle period' of Barbarism by Morgan (1877:26), to whom 'it seems extremely probable . . . that the cultivation of cereals originated in the necessities of feeding the domestic animals'. We have, however, seen that animal and plant domestication went hand-in-hand, and indeed to the extent that nomadic pastoralism

Map 11.2 Sites of the earliest finds of domesticated animals

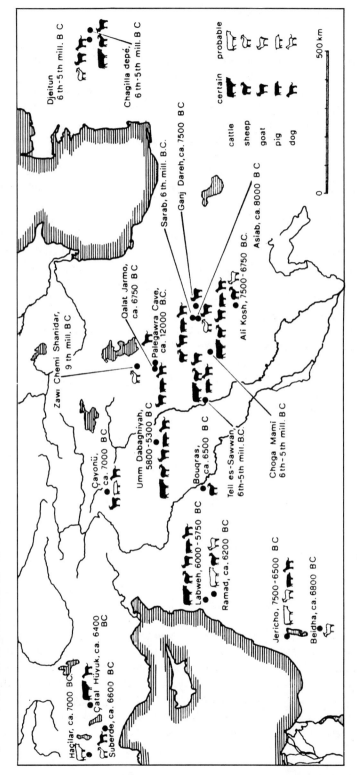

Source: Bökönyi 1976:21

developed it did so in response to an extension of farming beyond the limited amount of hydromorphic terrain available. But further, 'any land that can be found is potential pasture, and extensive farms thus remove extensive areas of pasture from pastoralist use' (Hole 1978:157).

This brings us directly to the current view of the onset of farming, here challenged. This orthodox view basically is that farming originated and flourished in areas of abundant rainfall spreading to cover all the areas capable of supporting 'dry', that is, rainfed, farming. In this view, only when those areas were filled to overflowing would irrigation be attempted, for it would indicate that no areas of rainfed farming, deemed to be preferable, were by that time left, with the 'extra labour' of irrigation merely an unpleasant necessity on otherwise uncultivable lands. This view, it is here maintained, misconstrues the background to the origins of farming outlined in early chapters along with the sequences involved in its emergence (sketched in the flow chart, Figure 3.5, p. 70).

At the outset it was indicated that the Boserup scheme of (extensive) swidden horticulture being intensified into open-field agriculture through decreasing regenerative forest fallow had no relevance to Near Eastern conditions[1] where cereal farming actually originates. Indeed shortly it will be indicated that slash and burn cultivation in forested areas, whether tropical or temperate, was of late advent, and most unlikely to be a seminal point of departure. That distinction belongs to something I have called 'groundwater planting' in Figure 11.2. This in sharp contrast to Childe's view, expressed when discussing the basis of the Urban Revolution:

> At the same time as a population density not exceeding two per square mile [due to 'technical limitations', such as the absence of roads or wheeled vehicles] the normal rural economy of the Neolithic Age was what is now termed slash-and-burn or jhumming, that condemns much more than half the arable land to lie fallow so that large areas were required. As soon as the population of a settlement rose above the numbers that could be supported from the accessible land, the excess had to hive off and found a new settlement.
>
> (Childe (1950) 1974:8)

Sherratt (1980:317), following Flannery (1969:81), considering the sorts of environment encountered, for instance, at Jericho (permanent springs) and Deh Luran (permanent and seasonal marsh) suggests 'that the critical innovation in the cultivation of cereals was their transfer from environments with a winter growth pattern to alluvial, lake edge, riverine or springside locations in which an accelerated (Spring) growth cycle was possible'. In other words, when cereals were first being planted, in contrast to the preceding stage of harvesting naturally occurring wild grains, those still morphologically wild cereals were of necessity transplanted to locations where human groups wanted to be for other reasons. Those included the presence of drinking water, fish, fowl, molluscs, and bodies of standing water to which game animals were also likely to come to drink. Here the significance of the 'broad-spectrum' economy will again be recognized. Soil conditions at desirable sites on small alluvial fans, alongside streams and rivers, and by the margins of lakes and marshes, are naturally hydromorphic;[2] that is, they are very moist throughout most if not all of the year, due either to intrinsically high groundwater or, as in wadis, to seasonal flooding. Such soils, being naturally soft and of fine structure, require little in the way of soil preparation (Sherratt 1980:318), in addition to being in many cases self-fertilizing through seasonal oscillations (which if it included desiccation would also include soil aeration) and local decomposition. Only by transplantation from the grains' natural upland habitats, it has previously been stressed, would the brittle, instantly shattering rachis be replaced by a tough non-shattering rachis.

Hydromorphic soils were optimal for early agriculturalists who were thereby living at a site able to provide all their other requirements in a single location. Year-round sedentarism makes perfect sense in such a context. However, such locations are relatively few and far between in the Near East and hence attempts to recreate hydromorphic conditions would lead to what would otherwise seem to be precocious experiments in irrigation (as at Choga Mami) before enormous tracts of vacant 'dry' arable land had been taken into cultivation. Further, such early irrigation might look like a response to the necessity of agricultural intensification, so lending comfort to population pressure theorists. On the contrary, however, what is known of the size and number of village sites during the early Neolithic leads to the opposite conclusion, namely that 'this pattern would make sense with low population levels and a simple technology' for the hydromorphic locations are the very optimum habitats, 'a narrow zone of maximum productivity' (Sherratt 1980:318). Dry farming, normally taken to be original, would thus be a later development of essentially lower productivity, adoptable only where rainfall was both high and, just as important, dependable. Of the 'wet' Luristan mountains flanking Mesopotamia, Frank Hole, in his ethnoarchaeological investigation there, reports that

> overly wet or overly dry years occur with ominous regularity. A 'normal' year is hard to describe and still harder to find.
> . . . People who live in the area assume that two or three out of five crops will either fail outright or be so poor as to make the work and cost of planting hardly worthwhile.
> . . . In general conditions are better in the mountains than on the Kurdistan Plain. That means that one or two crops out of five may fail.
> (Hole 1978:141)

Figure 11.1 Variations in the discharge of the Tigris and Euphrates, 1925–47

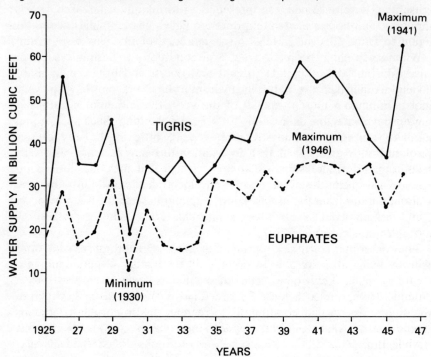

Source: Grigg 1970:180, after Al-Khashab 1958: fig. 11

Kirkbride (1972:4; 1982:14) noted similarly unpredictable conditions when excavating at Umm Dabaghiyah in the Jezirah. Nor are the rivers Tigris and Euphrates predictable in their flow, as seen in the graph in Figure 11.1, albeit based on modern data. 'Over the period 1925–47, deviation from the mean annual supply averaged 24% on the Euphrates and 21% on the Tigris. In a number of years the water supply was inadequate for the crop acreage planted' (Grigg 1970:181). Naturally, the first literate society recorded this as a proverb:

> The sun darkened (but) there rained no rain;
> the rain rained (but) the girdle is not loosened;
> the Tigris is deprived (?) of flood-water (?), it fills not the farmland.
> (Gurney and Kramer, trans. 1976:36; their question marks)

The spread and regionalization of agriculture is seen in Figure 11.2. It will be observed that from the eighth to fourth millenniums agriculture was predominantly on hydromorphic soils, with the notable exception of the Near Eastern steppe. The restricted extent of hydromorphic soils is the most simple and the most general explanation for the advent of specialized nomadic pastoralism. Further, Levy (1983), working in Sinai, has demonstrated that Late Neolithic agriculture there was restricted to water-retentive soils in bottomlands around springs, 'with locally high population levels but with intervening uncultivated areas' (op. cit.:23). When expanding population forced extension away from the springs during the Chalcolithic, settlement was 'situated in the trough-shaped valleys usually along the valley margins in close proximity to the flood plain deposits found in the valley bottoms' (ibid.:25) which constituted a wadi environment.

The very desirability of such hydromorphic locations explains the early colonization and rapid expansion, amounting almost to an explosion, upon the alluvium of Mesopotamia. There river channels flowed between levees which had only to be locally breached to extend the productivity of already moist backslope and swamp areas (see Figure 3.1, p. 50). High and sustained levels of output could thus be attained given the right organizational conditions. For even with high intrinsic productivity and abundance, inter- and intra-annual variability had to be met and buffered in a society for which the grains were the staff of life. Not only were carry-over stocks needed until the next harvest but seed supplies were demanded to produce one, with surpluses on top of those seed supplies required to guard against losses. Over this period too, surpluses were required for exchange against pastoral and other subsistence products while further stores had to be held against years of drought, pests, or growing-season damage, for instance by storms. It might not be fortuitous that the chief executive in the Sumerian pantheon is Enlil, Lord Storm.[3] Such reserves when pooled and organizationally allocated amount to 'social storage', something that does not necessarily mean enormous silo-like storage, but permanent means of organizing production and consumption so that there is always a sure safety margin. The supra-household basis of social storage crystallized into the temples at the nodes of agricultural and social reproduction. In turn the temples, like the precincts of Kulab and Eanna at Uruk, served as the cores of the synoecism that crystallized into cities.

Jacobsen (1980a:74) has hypothesized from the etymologies of Lagash and Ur (the full form of which is Urim) meaning a treasury and its door-post (symbol) respectively, that those cities of the southern alluvium might have their origins in the 'treasuries' at fixed points where tribal valuables were kept during the annual cycle of nomads. 'Such a storehouse, because of its sacred objects, becomes a religious centre at which people gather from afar for religious festivals and – as usual on such occasions – for barter and exchange of goods' (Jacobsen, op. cit.:74). However, the priority of pastoral nomadism has been rejected and further, no 'tribal valuables' theory can explain the location, early date, or deity celebrated in the most venerable site of the area, Eridu, where

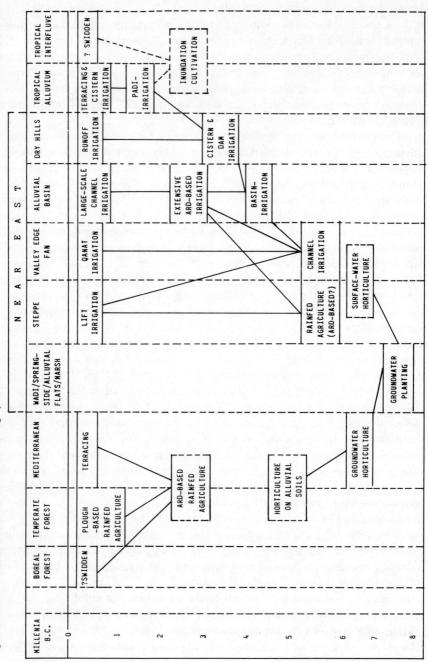

Figure 11.2 The differentiation of old world farming systems

Source: After Sherratt 1980:323

offerings were of fish to its 'owner' Enki, god of the Sweet Waters (Van Buren 1948; 1952). But Jacobsen's etymologies are never to be disregarded, and what it seems they most appropriately designate is the temple's social storage function outlined above.

That this trajectory does indeed follow from the causes stated may be seen by contrast with Australia, and indeed in the contrast of Australia with Tasmania. Having entered the continent at a time whereafter no environmental shocks occurred, *Homo sapiens* received no impulse tending toward qualitative adaptation but instead was able to maintain or even improve upon the prevailing conditions with merely quantitative advances. And if the element of environmental shock was absent, so too was resource diversity through which great changes could be wrought, seen for instance in the absence of any large or medium-sized mammals in Australia, though these were the essential complement of the grain economy in the Near East.[4]

Environmental manipulation undertaken in Australia, such as water-control, 'are not seen as attempts to increase environmental productivity, but to regularise (stabilise) the availability of resources' (Lourandos 1980:246), a stability hard to achieve in the Near East due to ever-shifting parameters, natural and human.[5] In Tasmania, where there was much less topological, faunal, and human diversity and greater environmental stability than obtained in Australia, 'the mainland's vast array of specialised hunting, gathering, food processing and storage methods is not known' (ibid.:256). Indeed recent Tasmanians may even have dropped fishing from their subsistence repertoire (ibid.). It is not irrelevant that no contact between Tasmania and the outside world is thought to have occurred for at least 10,000 years, ironically that span at the beginning of which the Neolithic was forming in the Near East.

Another central proposition advanced was that social organization, technics, and demography were so systematically interrelated that all three moved together in qualitative 'pulses' of change. It was argued that in pre-state societies, where the direct producers are simultaneously the consumers without any mediation by other social strata, decisions on technics by the producers and on demography by the reproducers were taken directly by those immediately involved and were such as to keep those factors in balance, even were that balance to shift over time. Why and how this could occur was demonstrated in the models of Modes of Production developed for pre-state societies.

In post-state societies, however, the case inverts. Now the social configuration is such that the ruling classes have a vested interest in certain techniques of production because they have a guarantee therefrom of certain levels of revenue and bases of power. This disjunction between consumers and producers, between production and the disposition of surplus extracted by and dispensed through political power, is indicated in Figure 11.3.

299

Figure 11.3 Disposition of production by ruling class and the state

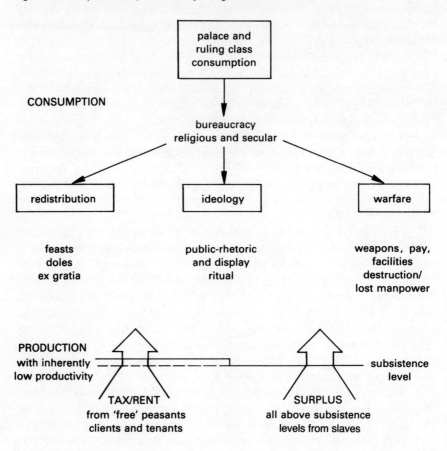

Accordingly, while technics might advance somewhat, nothing can be done that qualitatively transforms the relations of production, for it is they that determine what is produced, by what means, by and for whom, and those decisions determine the level of social productivity. Relations of production are in turn secured by overarching political relations of which the state is the keystone. The state is then 'capping' as it were any fundamental alteration in its structural basis. And as essentially closed systems state-ordered societies remain stable until either internal contradictions accumulate to bursting point or some external shock is received to which the social order is not resilient, or most likely, some external shock opens up fissures along the intrinsic lines of social contradiction which undermine the whole structure.

We can envisage social system collapse by taking the concept literally and not metaphorically. All dynamic systems require energy to create, maintain, and drive them.[6] This is the more so when the system is as complex and hierarchical as human society. For human societies are not just systems formed from relationships to durable hardware, though such are included of course. Societies are essentially systems of human relationships, and those need tending and reiteration at every level, even the simplest (cf. *hxaro* exchanges amongst the !Kung San; Weissner 1982). Inputs are needed of pure energy (food, fuel, etc.) for sheer subsistence, but simultaneously at the level of organization the demand for energy is also heavy, whether this be for keeping stocks, supporting scribes and administrators, priests and the court, or in the human labour required for public monuments, rhetoric, or dynastic wars (*supra*). If we regard culture as information (as in information theory), we can say that information needs organization to trap energy and thus locally to lower entropy (random disorder). In fact stored information *is* organization, whether it be self-replicating like DNA or simply text on a page. 'Since stored information varies inversely with entropy, lowered entropy means a higher capacity to store information' (Gatlin 1972:49). No matter what the form, no organization, no stored information, and without energy no organization can be sustained. Energy, of course, is an input needing constant renewal, and it can only be fixed (and that partially) by organization.[7] Organization, when a certain complexity of information has been reached, is, of course, self-sustaining by being self-replicating and thus energy-seeking.

Should the energy available to the society fall through declining agricultural yields (or greater diversions of resources or incompetence in their handling, competence and confidence being indices of cognitive energy), caused by the likes of diminished rainfall, raised salinity, or sheer overpopulation producing a per capita fall, then problems will be caused for the system of social relations as a whole, and focused upon that set concerned with administration and co-ordination. The characteristic of administration, to which Weber long ago drew our attention, and as we are daily reminded, resides in its hierarchical structure, routinization plus lack of flexibility and imagination. 'Most significantly for the living system, stored information is also the *capacity to combat error*' (Gatlin 1972:51; original emphasis).

In the circumstances of declining yields and perhaps (in this phase) population, the central authority is likely to intensify what it normally does, seeking a 'fix', and so making matters worse. The 'automatic' response is to call for more of the same, redoubled efforts, taxes, sacrifices, wars, etc. Or, especially if headed by an autocrat, to be paralysed by indecision, hoping things will take a turn for the better. Since the underlying causes of the problem(s) may not be known (but will certainly be ramified), policy could just as well lurch from one line to another, and perhaps back again, thus sowing confusion and so confounding resolution. Or the society as a whole may be so constrained by ecology, technology, ideology, and demography, as Harappan civilization seems to have been, that no significant policy alternatives are available to keep existing forms of social complexity in being. In all such cases, that society goes into a spiral of decline, halted by a sudden rupture of the established social fabric. In all those circumstances we are liable to see only the dramatic rupture as if it were itself (or as if its immediate circumstances were) the cause of the ensuing 'dark age' or period of devolution from higher to lower complexity (again clearly seen in the post- or 'sub-Harappan'), forgetting that social equilibrium, where present, can only be *steady state* equilibrium, 'stable in the presence of certain constantly maintained variables, attribute states or values' (Clarke 1978:49).

Causes of the advent of the state are various and highly contingent. They all presuppose, however, as a necessary but not yet sufficient condition, a certain threshold population density produced by settled agriculture (cf. Goody 1977:535–45). While agriculture may produce a population density much less than some particularly well-favoured but highly localized hunter-gatherers (such as those of the northwest coast of North America), only agriculture can sustain a relatively high population density over a wide area and thus, at a regional level, produce high population numbers.[8] Under those circumstances it does not take much to crystallize population around a central place, administrative, cultic, military, or commercial in the first instance, and tending over time to incorporate all those functions in a new synthesis, so developing a further dynamic. A city presupposes, then, both a durable nucleation and a fairly stable relationship to a hinterland, which, depending on circumstances, need not be very large. The previously offered definition of urbanism as a synoecism (*synoikismos*) secreting relations of production appropriate to a dense interdependent population, seems to incorporate Trigger's (1972:582, 578) observations that 'cities occur in complex, socially stratified societies', with 'specialised non-agricultural functions among the generally accepted attributes of urbanism'.

While there can well be chiefdoms without towns and cities (for a large village will do), there cannot be a state in their absence, since the state depends upon the concentration and specialization of power which means the disconnection of ultimate control from the populace as a whole. In short the formation of the state depends upon the replacement of horizontal political relations by vertical ones of super- and subordination. In particular the state's emergence depends upon the severing of kinship bonds (other than the most tenuous rhetorical ones) between ruler and ruled, because the implicit logic of kinship is kinship reciprocity, which will not allow prerogatives, and still less power, without commensurate obligation and reciprocation. But the whole tendency of the state is to develop its own initiative and autonomy. Once arisen the state is concerned to:

(a) ensure and develop the prerogatives of the members that constitute the state;
(b) attend to the reproduction of the society upon which its prerogatives depend (other classes).

The state's responsibilities to reciprocate tend to become intangible, general, and self-defined, turning on its ability to secure external peace (or defence), internal order, and social reproduction, at least notionally. State action thus tends to:

1 allow population to increase further;
2 intensify the division of labour;
3 intensify social stratification; which, either indirectly through the market or directly through exactions,
4 intensifies production still further, encouraging the sequence to recycle from (1).

All of this can be seen in the continual warfare of the city-states of Mesopotamia from the Uruk period forward, and even more drastically in the constant warfare and expansion of the late Roman Republic (Brunt 1971; Hopkins 1978:62).

The city as a *sui-generis* focus and transformational engine should also be remarked. Of the explosive growth of the giant Meso-American city of Teotihuacan, a primate city comparable to ancient Rome in its scale, population, and regional importance, Millon, who mapped it, wrote that: 'The urban revolution culminating in the great metropolis that transformed and soon came to dominate central Mexico is the product of a complex network of intertwined circumstances' (Millon 1974:358–9). Having mentioned its favourable location for food production alongside Lake Texcoco, and its advantageous situation on the best transport route from the Valley of Mexico to the Valley of Puebla, thence to the lowlands along the Gulf of Mexico, Millon none the less maintains that

without a social order responsive to change and a favoured ecological setting, Teotihuacan might have become an important pilgrimage centre. But there would be no reason to expect it to grow into an important economic and political centre or to develop the cultural magnetism of the metropolis. Similarly, Teotihuacan's strategic location, its access to resources of strategic potential, and an expanding market for its exports might provide the basis for an important market centre and a small city-state, but not necessarily for a sacred metropolis with an unparalleled attraction for other Middle American peoples.

(Millon 1974:358–9)

In sum, 'The major sources of the transformation of Teotihuacan seem to have lain in the city itself' (ibid.:356), in the interaction of diverse roles and aspects, developing thereby an internally generated momentum that brought the city to pre-eminence.

It is the failure to form the true, organic, city integrating diversity, to which Coe (1961) attributes the brittleness and precipitate collapse of both Mayan and Cambodian (Khmer) civilizations.

Formed on what Coe terms a 'unilateral' basis in similar tropical (monsoon) forest environments, both were essentially 'one crop, one culture' societies based on single high-yielding staples (maize and rice) with royal, cultic, and sub-centres extracting tithes in kind, plus corvée labour, by ideological-political means. This 'verticality' of relations under conditions of merely mechanical solidarity gives rise to 'a truly pyramidal society' (Coe 1961:73). What marks a truly organic city is not just its internal diversity and complexity, but that its hinterland depends upon it as much as the city is dependent upon its hinterland. An organic city is not a mere consumption centre whose justification is only ideological-political, but one which forms an intrinsic part of the economic life of the region. The archetypal organic city is thus the city-state and the heartland of the true, organic city is Mesopotamia.

In Mesopotamia a continuity was observed from the late sixth millennium (Ubaid) through the Uruk and Early Dynastic periods of the city-states to Sargonic overextension and disarray in the latter part of the third millennium. Resilience prevailed even under the Gutian incursions at the millennium's end. Continuity at Lagash and Uruk meant that reorganization under the Neo-Sumerian hegemony of Ur III resulted in a Sumerian renaissance. Again overextension obtains and confusion follows; yet continuity again prevails through the city-states of Isin and Larsa until the Amorite dynasty of Hammurabi extends hegemony over Sumer and Akkad. In its turn the Amorite dynasty and the High Civilization centred on its capital Babylon gave way to Kassite domination. By then, however (mid 2nd millennium), high civilization had long been widespread in the Eastern Mediterranean.

The immediate beneficiaries of Minoan collapse in the fifteenth century BC were the Mycenaean states of the mainland. But their ascendancy was short-lived in the Eastern Mediterranean, the Trojan War their own epitaph to the Bronze Age, celebrated by Homer early in the Iron Age in the new alphabetic writing derived from the Levant. Temporary records of clay preserved by the fire which destroyed the palace at Pylos in the Peloponnese show that state to be preparing for a sea-borne invasion (at the Gulf of Navarino) which duly came. As Chadwick (1972:233) relates, 'every major Mycenaean site so far excavated shows traces of fire and destruction', and the destructions cluster around a date at the end of the thirteenth century BC. At this time and the beginning of the twelfth

Map 11.3 The centres and routes of transmission of early scripts

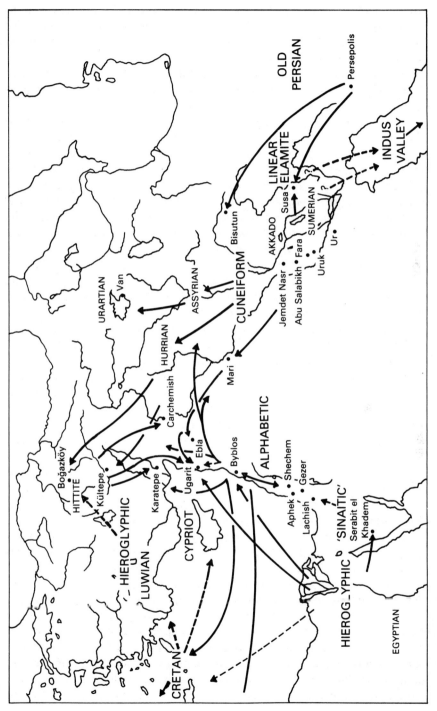

Source: Hawkins 1979:165

century BC the East Mediterranean and Levant were in turmoil. The Hittite empire in Anatolia collapsed about 1,190 BC and what Hutchinson (1962:314) calls 'a motley horde of northerners' overran Syria and Palestine and attacked Egypt. Only by Egypt, the most durable and self-contained of Mediterranean states, were those Aegeo-Anatolians, known to Egyptians as 'Sea Peoples', repulsed. But in thus remaining closed off, Aldred (1961:139) observes of Egypt that 'thereafter she lived on, a Bronze Age anachronism in a world that steadily moved away from her'.

Those are the great upheavals that usher in the Iron Age, whose heroes are the protagonists of Homer. The Homeric epics, products of the immediate post-Bronze Dark Age, were committed to writing in the newly Graecified 'Phoenician' script during the eighth century BC. Emergence of the alphabet is itself a prime example of the mode of contrasting but contiguous development, something well illustrated by Map 11.3 and which is discussed at length in Appendix E.

Although Greek literature first appears in the eighth century BC, it would nevertheless be surprising if the Greek alphabet emerged only at that time. Naveh (1980:22–5) makes a powerful argument for the Greek adoption not of the Phoenician script of the eighth century, but, on the basis of archaisms in, for instance *omicron* (= ayin) with a central dot, and *mu* (= mem) with five strokes of equal length, for the script being adopted in its Proto-Canaanite form, around 1,100 BC. This makes a lot of sense in terms of East Mediterranean historical dynamics.

Prominent among the turbulent 'Sea Peoples' resulting from the collapse of Hittite and Mycenaean states[9] under conditions of drought (Stiebing 1980:16–17) were the Peleset (Philistines) who came to occupy five major cities in Canaan (Ashdod, Ashkalon, Ekron, Gath, Gaza) and indeed gave their name to the territory (Palestine). It is likely that the Peleset came from Caphtor (Amos 9, 7), i.e. Keftiu or Crete, the largest and historically by far the most important island in the Greek culture area. An ostracon (i.e. an inscribed pottery sherd) found at Izbet Sarta, near Tel-Aviv, and dating between 1,200 and 1,000 BC, is inscribed at the top with an abecedary and underneath with four lines of script making no sense in Semitic languages, but which may be Philistine (Naveh 1980:25). Some letters are very similar to the archaic Greek alphabet (ibid.) and it is known that some kind of reoccupation of the drought-stricken, depopulated parts of Greece occurred when the normal weather pattern resumed (Stiebing, op.cit.:19).

But this still leaves several centuries before the emergence of the known Greek script and literature. Recalling the discussion in Chapter 2 and the distinction between invention and innovation, this is not hard to account for. The period from around 1,100 until about 750 BC represents a Dark Age in the Greek world, one of depressed levels of population and economic activity, prior to the advent of the *polis*. The Greek alphabet could then have been 'invented' either in Greece or in 'Palestine' during the Dark Ages, but been confined to relatively few merchant venturers and/or returnees. With the expansion of population, economic activity, and overseas trade accompanying the rise of *poleis*, the alphabet as a demotic medium would have entered into general use.

'The earliest Greek inscriptions come from the city-states which edged both sides of the Aegean, and from their respective colonies; thus the alphabet seems to have spread primarily along the sea trade-routes' (Jeffery 1982:823). By far the largest, most important, and powerful Greek city-state was Athens at 2,500 km^2 (Finley 1983c:16). It was exceptional in mainland Greece because of the country's small size overall, many mountains, and restricted arable land. There were however no such restrictions upon the Roman city-state which, having first subordinated Etruscan central Italy in the fourth century BC, was able thereafter to proceed down the peninsula absorbing the Greek-founded cities during the third century BC (by 272 BC);[10] proceeding to bitter wars with Carthage for control of the West Mediterranean, till by 146 BC Rome was the only 'world power', having destroyed both Carthage and Corinth.

Greece was swallowed during the second century BC, by which time Rome itself had lost the internal constitution of a city-state. Devastating civil wars lasted until the Republican political forms were transformed into the Principate under Augustus in the first century AD. He, concentrating in one person *auctoritas* and *mos maiorum*, supposedly on the basis of a *consensus universorum* delegated to the Princeps by the Senate and populace, alone wielded *imperium*, supreme power.

The expansion of the Empire under such forms of government at the centre are too well known to need recounting, suffice it to say that by the time of Augustus the whole Mediterranean seaboard had been conquered by Rome, including the Levant.

> In the final three hundred years of the Republic there were probably not a dozen when a Roman army was not engaged abroad. For the last two centuries, it has been estimated that the median of adult male citizens involved in any year was 13%, rising as high as 35% in some years.
>
> (Finley 1983c:17)

This then is the apotheosis of the citizen-militia of the city-state, its phalanxes become Roman legions and its hinterland world empire. None the less 'One of the most enduring legacies of Rome's rule were her towns' (Frederiksen 1969:151), for 'the provincial municipalities were the basic units of the Roman Empire, which was a vast experiment in local self-government' (Sherwin-White 1969:83). Yet despite advances in military technique gleaned, often at great cost, from action all over the known world, it has been indicated how little productive technique, technics, advanced other than at the beginning of this period.

Reece (1969) has cogently argued that the Graeco-Roman world lacked many of the physical requisites for sustained technical development such as characterized Europe of the Industrial Revolution. Those are:

1   cultural attitudes conducive to technological progress;

2(a) sufficient existing productive resources, particularly agricultural, to permit a significant fraction (say 10 per cent) of total 'national' income to be put regularly into productive investment; which must be coupled with, as *sine qua non* –

2(b) the disposition to engage in productive investment instead of idle consumption (for example military or luxury expenditure);

3   a sufficient density of population over a large enough area;

4   a sufficient supply of raw materials (such as iron ore) with energy resources for their working;

5   a sufficient transport potential to move raw materials and to network markets.

Though the cultural factors were somewhat less debilitating in Greece than Rome (with, for instance, the Greek penchant for original enquiry), Greek populations were generally too small and scattered and, with a few notable exceptions such as Athens and Corinth, their wealth too little. And as the Mediterranean littoral is notably deficient in accessible minerals and has few navigable or all-year reliable rivers, this inhibits both the supply of raw materials, their working into finished products using water-power, and the linking of populations into market networks beyond the coastal strips.

Both Greece and Rome shared those problems common to the Mediterranean, though the disposable wealth of Rome, Republican or Imperial, was much greater than even an aggregated Greece. Later Rome had access to the mineral and other resources, not least hydraulic, of transalpine Europe and the Balkans. However, despite an agricultural productivity high both by the standards of medieval Europe and even some countries of the modern Mediterranean (Reece 1969:38–9), the cultural inhibitions referred to earlier, coupled with high levels of political, military, and luxury consumption, meant that such access bolstered the existing system rather than inducing techno-economic transformations. Environmental limitations were indeed inherent structural problems, but the system of social relations that early formed on that basis meant that they could not subsequently be overcome.

Coal was used both in Roman Britain and northern Gaul, but 'there is only one certain reference to coal in the whole of Latin literature, and that comes in the "Collectanea Rerum Memorabilium" of Iulius Solinus, an obscure writer probably of the third century A.D.' (Reece 1969:44–5). Coal was thus ignored at the centre and overexploitation of a single resource, wood, continued unabated. It could be argued that given distances and terrain it was impossible to bring significant supplies of coal into the Mediterranean; yet tin was brought from Cornwall and other minerals were exported from Britain to the Continent. For his military campaigns in the Channel, Caesar had fleets of ships specially built to local designs when those brought from the Mediterranean proved totally unsuitable. Had there been a perceived economic necessity, ships could likewise have been specially built to move coal.

But coal is not the only example of local technics being ignored and allowed to lapse. At the other end of the Empire in Mesopotamia, the millenniums-old use of naturally occurring bitumen (petroleum) products was supplanted under Rome by the use of tar and pitch, again tree products (Leemans 1960b:217). After all, when Roman society was in process of formation, Italy was well clad in trees. Thereafter the pattern was set, and as Rome could expand continually, it did not have to effect techno-economic changes to survive.

For a qualitative breakthrough, a 'first', such as the Industrial Revolution of mid-eighteenth to nineteenth centuries AD, all those factors mentioned, social and physical, must be present and also cohere, as they did in Britain upon the basis of centuries of mercantile and agrarian transformations, themselves part of the cultural and political revolutions which the civil and religious wars represented. In their turn those techno-economic and politico-cultural factors were the outcomes of the long, slow, but organic development of medieval Europe from the Dark Age following the collapse of Rome, through a unique 'feudal' synthesis of elements cultural (literacy, religion, learning) and techno-logical, drawn originally from the Graeco-Roman Iron Age and the Near Eastern Bronze Age.

From Dark Age interludes the old civilizations are never reborn, for from such periods new syntheses emerge subsuming (and losing) pre-existing elements, social and technical, in a qualitatively new configuration with its own dynamics, contradictions, and growth potential. In Mesopotamia we were able to examine the first such decisive crystallization.

The pantheon of the Sumerian city-state

The following is a simplified outline which minimizes the true complexity. Most major deities were worshipped in some or in most, if not all, the cities of Sumer and Akkad. Lesser gods and manifestations, plus much merging and elaboration, are here overlooked to highlight the principal actors.

God/Goddess	Role	City (& named shrine)	Other names or roles
Nammu	Ocean, chaos, primeval fluid	Ur	'The mother who gave birth to heaven and earth' (and Enki)
An(u)	Sky, the heavens an.gal 'the great above'	Uruk (É-anna – the House of Heaven – temple of An and Inanna)	Authority, Father of the gods; begetter of Enki
Inanna	Fecundity, plenty, 'numen of the store-house', 'queen of heaven'	Uruk, Lagash, Zabalam, Ur (É-anna 'the house of heaven'), Agade Shuruppak	Ishtar, Baba, 'Venus/ Aphrodite', peace and war, Morning and Evening Star
Enki	Sweet (fertilizing) waters (nagbu) 'wisdom', 'knowing' i.e. god of craftsmen	Eridu (É-apsu) (É-engura) Assur, Isin Larsa, Mari, Nippur, Ur, Uruk	Ea (antagonist of Ninhursaga), helper of humans

God/Goddess	Role	City (& named shrine)	Other names or roles
Enlil	Storm, power, enforcement, ·the lower air 'King of the Lands'	Nippur (É-kur)	Akk: Ellil Brother of Ninhursaga 'Prime Minister' to his father An's 'Presidential' role
Geshtinanna	'Lady of wine'	Lagash	Sister of Dumuzi, alternates with him in the underworld
Marduk	Gods' warrior with many of Enlil's characteristics	Babylon (É-sagila) É-temenanki his ziggurat	Of merely local significance until hegemony of Babylon
Utu	Sun, justice, judgeship 'shown with a sword'	Larsa (É-babbar 'the shining house') Sippar and Eridu	Shamash, Babbar. Utu is the brother of Inanna, son of Nanna and Ningal
Nanna	Moon, Father of Inanna	Ur, Urum (É-kišnugal)	Sin, Suen (the result of the rape of Ninlil by Enlil)
Ningal	Goddess of reeds (lit. 'The Great Lady')	Ur (É-karzida)	Also called Zirru. Wife of Nanna and mother of Inanna
Ningirsu	Rainstorms, rainclouds	Lagash (É-Ninnu)	God of hoe
Ninurta	Mountain rains, floods	Girsu, Nippur (É-šumeša)	God of plough 'farmer of Enlil'
Ninhursaga	'Numen of the stony ground', 'lady of the rocks', 'mother of all children'	Kesh and Adab (É-mah) Lagash Tell Ubaid	Called 'Mama' Nintur or Ninmah; originally called 'Ki' = Earth (i.e. mother

God/Goddess	Role	City (& named shrine)	Other names or roles
			earth) or Urash
Ninsuna	Lady of the wild cattle	Uruk (Kullab)	Mother of Dumuzi (and Gilgamesh). Also called Sirtur
Ninlil	Grain goddess	Nippur (Tummal) Shuruppak	Wife of Enlil called Sud originally
Nisaba	Goddess of scribes (and grain)	Uruk and Eresh	Mother of Ninlil Wife of Ningirsu
Ninisina	Goddess of medicine and healing	'Lady of Isin' (É-galmah)	Bau at Lagash (spouse of Ningirsu)
Dumuzi	'The divine shepherd', god of flocks, the steppe (edin) and as Amaushumgalanna of the date-clusters. Also called Ululu	Badtibira, Umma, Zabalam, Uruk	*Hieros gamos* with Inanna. They are the archetypal couple of procreation Geštinanna is his sister.
Ereshkigal	Queen of the underworld (but note etymology)		Elder sister of Inanna. Nergal her reluctant consort

Nin = Lady (cf. 'Our Lady' in Catholic tradition). En = Master or Lord

Myths/gods are, of course, plastic over time and changed circumstances, not least political. Thus Marduk and Ashur were the city gods of Babylon and Ashur respectively, which when risen to overall hegemony with their cities were likewise promoted into a place similar to Enlil's.

For a full account, with excellent bibliography, see Gwendolyn Leick (1991): *A Dictionary of Ancient Near Eastern Mythology* (Routledge).

Appendix B

Inanna and Dumuzi of the dates

Reviewing the baked clay figurines from Tell es-Sawwan, Joan Oates (1966:150) observes, in regard to a male terracotta, that 'the inlaid shell eyes found on this and on many of the stone statues are astonishingly reminiscent of the much later Sumerian technique'. Best-known perhaps are the figurines from Tell Asmar (ancient Eshnunna) where the largest of a very striking group of varying dimensions is the god Ninurta, 'Lord of the Thunderstorm' (cf. Frankfort 1970:46–9).

However, the eyes of early female figurines are quite different, indeed one can say diametrically opposed, for whereas the males manifest a wide-eyed stare, with the iris pronounced, female figurines are shown without any modelling to eyeball or socket, the eyes rendered merely as a slit in an appliqué blob, and are therefore referred to as 'coffee-bean eyes'. Thus speaking still of the female figurines from the Samarran site of Tell es-Sawwan, Oates remarks that although

> the 'coffee-bean' eyes are equally without contemporary parallel in Mesopotamia . . . they too resemble a later Mesopotamian type, in this instance the late Ubaid 'lizard-headed' figurines, although the appliqué eyes of the latter are more oblong in shape. Moreover, many of the latter display pointed bitumen headdresses comparable with those on some of the Sawwan stone figurines.
>
> (Oates 1966:150)

Oates (1966:n.19) cites J. G. D. Clark as suggesting that the 'coffee-bean' eye moulded in clay is a poor-man's substitute for the cowrie shells used at Jericho to model eyes in skulls, in which teeth are also present. But the Mesopotamian examples are highly stylized clay and stone figurines, not human skulls. However, if the 'coffee-bean' eyes are taken as 'date-stone' eyes, another possibility presents itself, namely that what is represented at Tell es-Sawwan is a forerunner of Inanna, goddess of fecundity and the storehouse, specifically the date storehouse. The crucial Sumerian fertility cult was that involving sexual intercourse between Inanna and Dumuzi Amaushumgalanna ' "the one great source of the date clusters" (**ama-ušum.gal-ana(.ak)**) and refers to the so-called heart of palm, the enormous bud which the palm tree sets each year' (Jacobsen 1976:26). The Ubaidian figurines referred to above as 'lizard-headed' include a male (from Eridu; cf. Seton Lloyd 1978:47) bearing a 'mace' which could well be an implement for pollinating date-palm (which is best done artificially), while he has appliquéd blobs on his shoulders that may represent ripe dates (cf. 'Inanna and Šulgi: a Sumerian fertility song', S. N. Kramer (1969), which has many references to dates. The tree itself is, of course, of particular importance as a constructional material, and, indeed, in iconography).

The spread of farming from the Near East

Zvelebil has criticized Ammerman and Cavalli-Sforza's 'wave of advance' model (1984), despite its admitted simplicity and elegance, because it 'provides no real explanation for the adoption of farming in Europe' and, he claims, it makes some

> untenable assumptions which include the minimal view of hunter-gatherers (1984:9), the assumption that the discontinuity in settlement pattern and lithic assemblages between the Mesolithic and the Neolithic are the norm, rather than the exception (ibid.:46–7, 55), the assumption that pottery and food production were introduced simultaneously (ibid.:46) and the assumption of little or no overlap between the Mesolithic occupation and the onset of early farming (ibid.:60).
>
> (Zvelebil 1986b:9)

Other criticisms include the indicators chosen to type sites as belonging to the Neolithic, and these points are well taken. However, as to the first criticism, that the model provides no real explanation for the adoption of farming in Europe, this is indeed the case, but it is not an objection, since such an explanation is not the aim of the model, *which is rather to measure the rate of spread of farming from the Near East nuclear area.* This is modelled 'as if' the Neolithic was spread demically (and genetic mapping tends to support this empirically); yet the 'wave of advance' model does not depend on the diffusion of farming by waves of Near Eastern farmers, but on the transmission of farming intergenerationally by localized 'random-walk' movements.

There is no doubt that Zvelebil's own models (1986b:11–12) are superior to anything thus far in conceptualizing the social mechanisms of the spread of agriculture in Europe (or anywhere for that matter). However the Ammerman and Cavalli-Sforza model did not set out to tackle this but to measure rate of spread from a putative centre. The absence of a uniform radial wave front is not fatal to this, its use is a simplifying assumption. What would be fatal would be evidence of independent domestication in Europe and the adoption of village farming on that basis. But Zvelebil (1986c:181), in my view rightly, denies the reality of this, so I would conclude with him (1986b:9) that the demic wave of advance model, which despite its shortcomings, 'amounts to a quantified and well argued, if somewhat biased, case for the introduction of farming to Europe by farmer colonization', none the less 'gives us a conditional standard of the rate of farming colonization against which the actual spread of farming can be compared' (1986c:175). And, since it deals with the social geography of 'the actual spread of farming', Zvelebil's model does not contradict, but rather complements, that of Ammerman and Cavalli-Sforza.

Support of and from the early temple

Nicholas Postgate reminds us that temples formed 'a sort of "joint company" from whose capital the community which supports it is able to profit' (1972:814). With their reserves of food, grain, and equipment, temples would have been able to replace sudden losses or to bridge lean seasons and could themselves undertake long-distance exchange. 'In this way they functioned as "emergency granaries" for the community, and if justly run, prevented profiteering at the expense of the peasant' (ibid.). As a co-operative society the temple could thus assist the peasants in retaining their independence, as well as acting corporately in its own interest as an organization administered by cultic and secular officials. Too often in the past the temple has been regarded as incorporating virtually all community life within its domain, something recently manifest in the question of 'bevelled-rim' ration bowls, so called.

In a deft statistical re-examination of the evidence on those 'bevelled-rim' bowls in the Uruk period, Beale (1978:289–313) has neatly reversed the assumption that they were ration bowls in which temple dependants received their subsistence. Those poorly made friable bowls, chaff or grit tempered, acquired their bevelled rims through being formed in moulds dug into the ground, knife-trimmed, and fired at low temperature. G. A. Johnson (1973), following suggestions by Nissen (1970), supported the ration-bowl view with the postulate that bowls from his survey of Susa and Khuzistan clustered around three modal volumes: 0.9, 0.65, and 0.45 litres. Those, Johnson argued, allocated standard rations to men, women, and children for corvée labour, institutionally administered, on the lines of the ration system known from historic times (cf. Gelb 1965). Beale measured separately mould volumes, (levelled) inside volumes, and heaped volumes and could find no significant distribution, with *every* bowl size between 0.4 and 0.95 litres being common (Beale, op. cit.:290). As there were no generally accepted size standards for bevelled-rim bowls, despite geographical and stratigraphic tests, he concluded that 'the variability is simply too great for one to accept a theory of standardised bowl capacities' (ibid.:293). Also the bowls were generally too small to serve as ration containers when 75 per cent of those from Khuzistan would have been too small to hold even a woman's daily ration, and 23 per cent would have been large enough to hold only an infant's ration. 'These statistics imply that men would not have been involved at all in the centrally organised labour system, which seems very unlikely' (ibid.:296).

Given the bowls' small but variable size, poor and *ad hoc* construction, and the fact that they are found *unbroken* and in great numbers at temples, shrines, and administrative buildings, it seems much the most likely that they were in fact *offering bowls* by which food was donated by the community to the temple and counter-prestated (see below). Given the vast numbers unearthed from Yahya in the east to the Amuq plain in the west which agree only in being crudely mould-made, we seem to have domestically made vessels fired in a household oven and offered to the temple with domestically produced contents. On other occasions the bowls were buried (also intact) domestically as votive offerings.

Beale (ibid.:307) reminds us that as soon as we have textual evidence, we find the temples receiving almost every available type of food, grain, beer, bread, sheep, dates, fruit, vegetables, fish, and so forth, offered frequently and in considerable quantities. Such offering ceremonies were often represented in Sumerian art, such as covers the famous metre-high alabaster vase from proto-literate Uruk, illustrated by Frankfort (1956:26) and Seton Lloyd (1961:39). There too we find Inanna seated before the double reed bundles that always identify her and which served as the pictographic prototype of her cuneiform character in the historic period (Frankfort, op. cit.:27). Indeed as the acme of the ceremony, she is there presented with a large basket of fruit by someone Seton Lloyd (op. cit.) calls 'the leader of the procession, probably a king', but who is probably the **En** at this date (*c.* 3,500–3,250 BC). Further, the very sign for the **En**, Beale (1978:307,n.64) suggests, might have originated as the pictographic representation of a stack of presentation bowls.

However, the Sumerian sign for bread (**NINDA**) has the conical shape of the bevelled-rim bowl, plus the appearance (a parallel line) of something having risen above the rim. In association with a schematic human head, the sign **GU₇**, 'to eat', is formed.

Therefore bevelled-rim bowls are likely in origin to be bread-baking containers, perhaps for highly prized wheaten white bread, using **eša**, a special flour made from emmer. Either such loaves or ones made from ordinary flour could have been counter-prestated to the community on special days, and regularly supplied (presumably using ordinary flour), to its dependants. The Temple Hymns indicate that making good bread was cultically important. Thus in the story of Adapa,

The blameless, the clean of hands, the ointment priest, the observer of rites.
With the bakers he does the baking

With the bakers of Eridu he does the baking;
Bread and water for Eridu daily he provides . . .

(Pritchard 1958:76)

Independently, both Schmidt (1982) and Millard (1987) have suggested that bevelled-rim bowls were indeed bread-making containers, Millard associating this with the availability of yeast by Uruk (Level XII) times, the bowls continuing in this form until Uruk IV. He remarks:

> With yeast, the dough can be mixed in various ways to produce loaves of differing consistencies, all more tasty and satisfying than the unleavened flat loaves or 'quick' bread of the *tannur*. If the dough was prepared in a semi-liquid form, containers would be essential. Put into the moulds to prove, the dough could be most easily baked in the same containers. If the bread mould theory is correct, the advent of the bevelled-rim bowls may be seen to mark the introduction of leavened loaves on a large scale. Whether some improved process in working with yeast or control over the function of the oven led to this new fashion cannot be told.

(Millard 1988:55)

Support for the baking-container view comes both from archaeology and ethnology. In his discussion of Uruk pottery from Eridu, Ur, and Al-Ubaid, Al-Soof (1973:21) notes that Uruk-period graves, in addition to handled cups and shallow saucer-like bowls, also contained wheel-made 'flower pot'-like bowls, all three types indicating provisions for the journey to the afterlife. Today bread can be found, even commercially, baked in flower pots. This makes all the more suggestive Al Soof's statement that 'Both early and late Uruk types were present almost equally at Eridu. Unlike Warka, and in fact unlike the majority of other Mesopotamian sites, the crude bevelled-rim votive [*sic*] bowls occurred rather late, while "flower pots" were found in an earlier context' (1973:21).

Here then we have an archaeologically defined sequence, where one bowl type is directly succeeded by another, the potential uses of both coinciding with bread-baking activities ethnologically known in urban Europe and in contemporary Near Eastern villages. For in regard to her 'Observations gathered in Syrian villages from 1980–1985', Seeden states that 'stone bread moulds for special festive breads were cut in Busra until just a generation ago, *while clay moulds are still being made by the local potter women [sic!] . . . and indeed are found in every household in the village*' (1986:296; my emphasis). Further, Millard's (1988:51–2) artefactual and lexical comparisons with late fourth and third millennium Egypt strongly support the bread-mould hypothesis, reinforced by the association with beer-making in both Egypt and Mesopotamia.[1]

The interactive evolution of alphabetic script

During the third and second millenniums, the Near East was dominated by two writing systems: Egyptian, usually called hieroglyphic, which, when not used monumentally was written on papyrus; and Sumero-Akkadian cuneiform, written with a stylus on clay.

Both began pictographically, representing the object they wished to designate visually, and by the early third millennium they had already moved on to the ideographic principle whereby ideas associated with a term (say, foot) are also designated by the sign in addition to and by extension of its basic referent (thus 'foot' of a mountain; but also stand, walk, go, etc.). Both pictograms and ideograms are called logograms, i.e. (whole) word-signs, distinguishing them from the later syllabaries[1] whereby only single syllables are represented whether or not these are whole words, which in both Sumerian and Chinese they very often are. As a script evolves, however, usually it comes to incorporate both logograms and syllabograms and, in the case of Sumerian, 'class determinatives' showing how a sign should be read, by indicating to what class of referents it belonged, such as MAN (for professions or nationalities), WOMAN (for female names), FLESH (for parts of the body), WOOD (trees, woods, and wooden artefacts), and so forth (Hawkins 1979:138). The mis-called 'radicals' perform analogous classificatory functions in Chinese as semantic or phonetic determinatives; the latter specifying which pronunciation (and thus meaning) of a graph is intended, the former an element indicating which homophonic alternative.

Egyptian and Mesopotamian scripts are, then,

both mixed logographic scripts, both using class determinatives formed from common logograms as aids to reading. The essential internal difference of the two lay in their syllabaries; for while both formed these in the same way (namely by the rebus-principle of stripping a logogram of its semantic content and using it to write the syllable which its syllabary suggests), the cuneiform syllabary was based on the monosyllabic structure of Sumerian, supplemented by similar Akkadian roots, but the hieroglyphic syllabary reflected the Egyptian word structure,

the consonantal skeleton of the syllable without reference to the vowels, a feature shared by Semitic orthographies (Hawkins, op. cit.:146). They differ too in their social applications. While Egyptian seems to have its origins in ritual and ceremonial contexts (like the Chinese) Sumero-Akkadian is, as we have seen, rooted in practical accounting needs.[2] Cuneiform also, despite the cursive versions of hieroglyphic later developed, was applied much more widely than hieroglyphic, rapidly forming a corpus of literature, mathematics, and so forth. By as early as c. 2,500 BC Mesopotamian cuneiform had already been borrowed to write the copious 'proto-Canaanite' documents of Ebla (Tell Mardikh, in Syria) and a few centuries later was again borrowed at the other end of the Mesopotamian province to write Elamite (the Susa area of southwest Iran).[3] In contrast Egyptian hieroglyphic was never borrowed to write another language.

Generally speaking, when, over the next thousand or more years, societies became literate in the Near East, they did so by employing a version of Mesopotamian cuneiform for writing their own languages. And while Egyptian papyruses circulated in its areas of influence, the international language of diplomacy from the Sargonic period onward was cuneiform Akkadian. But the area where Akkadian and Egyptian influences overlapped most continuously was the Levantine seaboard. Its ports were the major direct points of contact between Mesopotamia and Egypt, and not by sailing right around the Arabian Peninsula as During-Caspers imagines (1971–2:43). Between Egypt and Syria there was early and continual overland contact through Sinai (M. Wright 1985:240).

Ugarit (Ras Shamra) and the signally titled Byblos (which means 'papyrus' in Greek) are the cities on the Syrian seaboard where the contrast between the mutations of hieroglyphic and cuneiform secreted alphabetic script in the later part of the second millennium. In Ugarit are found no less than five separate scripts: Egyptian, Akkadian, Hittite hieroglyphs, Cypro-Minoan, and a fifth script

the remarkable Ugaritic 'Cuneiform Alphabet', written also on clay tablets found in large numbers and dating to the period c. 1,400–1,200 BC. The language written is mostly Ugaritic, a West Semitic language, though it is important to note that the script was also used to write Hurrian. Ugaritic was used, in contrast to the international and diplomatic Akkadian, for local documentation (letters, legal and administrative texts), but above all for literacy, mythological, and ritual texts. Scattered examples of the Ugaritic script found on various sites in Syria and Palestine attest to its wide dissemination.

(Hawkins 1979:159)

The Ugaritic was a thirty-letter, essentially vowelless alphabet, though Ugaritic scribes did introduce three vowel sounds: *a*, *i*, *u*, used for initial sounds (ibid.:161). From the fourteenth to the eleventh centuries BC different alphabets were employed for a variety of purposes, including graffiti, throughout Canaan (Millard 1976:135). The number of letters needed to fit local dialects varied, with Phoenician needing only twenty-two. None the less, 'it is beyond doubt that the Byblian, Palestinian, Phoenician, and Aramaic scripts are all related, the Byblian being the most archaic' (ibid.:133). It was, however, the twenty-two-character consonantal alphabet that the Greeks subsequently borrowed and to which they added letters for distinct vowels, to function solely as vowels, entirely supplanting the previous mode of a character standing for 'consonant + vowel'.

The Ahiram coffin text and tomb inscription from Byblos is the oldest text in the linear alphabet to yield continuous sense (ibid.:135), and does so in a script developed for writing ink on papyrus in an area long within the Egyptian cultural sphere. The Ahiram text date is around 1,000 BC, and the inscription on the wall of his tomb shaft reads: 'Beware! Behold (there is) disaster for you down there' (Hawkins 1979:164).

Although disseminated only during the Iron Age, notably via Greece, the alphabet has its origins in the Bronze Age Levant around the middle of the second millennium. Millard suggests the sort of process involved:

> Picture a Canaanite scribe in a mercantile centre, trained to write Egyptian with pen and ink on papyrus, aware of cuneiform, and, maybe, other scripts. None of them really suit his native language; all are quite complicated to write. All have signs for syllables, some having many more than a single range for consonant + vowel. An adequate simple syllabary of consonant + vowel sounds for a semitic language would need towards one hundred signs. Now the Egyptian signs used phonetically as syllables leave the vowels unspecified. Other devices in the script guide the reader, and, although they are essential, the vowel signs serve normally to modify the basic sense of the consonantal roots. The scribe, having observed how series of syllables are expressed in Egyptian, and perhaps in some other scripts, too, decides to create a set of syllabic signs for his own tongue. Some of the Egyptian signs owe their syllabic value to the initial phoneme of the name of the object they depict, some to the strongest phoneme in the name. The scribe does not adopt the Egyptian signs, but instead creates his own, drawing on names of objects for their initial phonemes only. Thus a simple picture of water, *mayim* or a very similar form, represents m + any vowel, a head, *resh*, r + any vowel, and so forth. Eventually he has one sign for each consonantal sound in his language.
>
> (Millard 1986:394)

This directly linguistic system was produced exactly where the interactionist postulate would predict: in an area where major writing systems overlapped, namely the Levant. By contrast, although Chinese characters evolved and were both rationalized and simplified, the monopoly of the Chinese system in East Asia meant that a parallel process could not take place there.

The Greeks called their script *phoinikeia*: 'Phoenician letters', and with the Greeks it was truly revolutionary. Early in the Iron Age, namely by the end of the eighth century BC, both Homer and Hesiod had happened. For this was a new demotic literacy, addressing not other scribes but a general public. Accordingly, 'the earliest existing Greek inscriptions are public statements: they explain some object, or intention, to a reading public' (Jeffery 1982:831).

The Ages System

Though the modern stone–bronze–iron succession, with its ethnographic parallels, derives ultimately from Mercati (1541–93) whose *Metallotheca* was suppressed until 1717, the first recorded 'Ages System' is, of course, that contained in Hesiod's *Works and Days*. It is, as is only to be expected of the eighth century BC, a mytho-moral system describing successive 'races (*genos*) of men'. Degeneration results in mankind now inhabiting a cold black Age of Iron, whereas originally there had been a Golden Age at the beginning of time, for 'both gods and men began the same' (Hesiod 1973:62). This was followed by a 'race' or Age of Silver, whose childish irresponsibility caused them to be 'hidden away' by Zeus and replaced by a 'race of bronze' who 'loved the groans and violence of war' and by whom 'black iron was not known' (ibid.:63).

Great soldiers, they were captured by black Death,

to be replaced by a fourth race of men,

> more just and good,
> A godlike race of heroes, who are called
> The demi-gods – the race before our own.
> Foul wars and dreadful battles ruined some;
> Some sought the flocks of Oedipus, and died
> In Cadmus' land, at seven-gated Thebes;
> And some, who crossed the open sea in ships,
> For fair-haired Helen's sake, were killed at Troy.
>
> (Hesiod 1973:63–4)

All of which is a fair description of the late Bronze Age Aegean in its period of collapse, engendering the displaced 'Sea Peoples', as against Hesiod's own 'Race of Bronze' who ate no bread. The impression that Hesiod's 'race before our own', who are 'more just and good' (as were the times and land they inhabited) is a dim recollection of Minoan and Mycenaean relative peace and plenty, is strengthened by Hesiod's association of some of them

at the earth's edge.
And there they live a carefree life, beside
The whirling Ocean, on the Blessed Isles.

(ibid.)

Both (impressionistic) location and conditions sound very much like those of the Atlantis legends familiar to us from Plato (*Timaeus* and *Critias*), while J. V. Luce (1969) has convincingly argued for conditions in, and the sudden collapse of, Minoan Crete as the basis for the Atlantis legends.

Notes

Preliminary

1 Later Sumer with Akkad adjoining to the north = Babylonia.
2 In my usage the Near East as a whole (i.e. the land bounded by the Red, Mediterranean, Black, and Caspian Seas, and the Persian Gulf) constitutes a *region*, composed of *areas*, such as Mesopotamia, which consists of *zones*, such as the marsh 'sealand'.
3 By ethnology is meant a monographic report on a particular society; while by ethnography is meant theoretical discussion based upon such reports.
4 They may also wish to see my (1987) article in *Man*, 22(2):331–59, entitled 'Models of social evolution: trajectories from the Neolithic to the state'.
5 An anachronistic term for Mesopotamian textual scholarship deriving from the nineteenth-century origins of the subject.

Chapter 1: Introduction

1 In areas such as Western Europe where a distinct stage between Palaeolithic and Neolithic is discerned, this is called the Mesolithic (cf. Clark 1980).
2 Archaeology has its own procedures and problems which are irreducible because it is working to recover as complete a material record as possible, while ethnology deals with people in living societies. There the potential 'record' is so great as to demand selection by the ethnologist in the first instance, and too often he/she pays scant attention to the physical aspects of society, as though 'social' was a synonym for 'immaterial'.
3 Like Binford (1968b:269), '*Process*, as I understand it, refers to the dynamic relationships (causes and effects) operative among components of a system or between systematic components and the environment.'
4 By *evolution* I understand the increasing complexity of entities seen as systems; that is, increases in the number of sub-systems. Carneiro (1973:90) deploys a modified Spencerian definition of evolution, where: 'Evolution is a change from a relatively indefinite, incoherent homogeneity to relatively definite, coherent heterogeneity, through successive differentiations and integrations.' Both definitions see the evolutionary process as the cumulative emergence of heightened states of organization (information structure) over time.
5 Lesser's 'Evolution in social anthropology' was read before the annual meeting of the American Anthropological Association in 1939, and published only in 1952. Carneiro (1973:94) cites Steward's article 'Cultural causality and law: a

trial formulation of the development of early civilisations' (1949) as the decisive post-war contribution to restoring interest in evolution in anthropology. He calls Steward's article 'a landmark in the history of evolutionism', though he 'dates the resurgence in cultural evolutionism from 1943, the year in which Leslie A. White's *Energy and the Evolution of Culture* appeared' (in *American Anthropologist*). However, in their *History of American Archaeology*, Willey and Sabloff observe that 'the theory of cultural evolutionism was generally anathema as late as the 1950's' (1974:182) and until it had been accepted the New Archaeology, combining as it did 'cultural evolutionary theory, systems theory and logico-deductive reasoning' (ibid.:189), could not have emerged. That it did so when it did, they attribute to parallel advances in ecology, geography, and sociology, tending 'toward scientific thinking and away from humanism in the social sciences' (ibid.:187), as much as to internal technical developments that took place in what they call the Classificatory-Historical Period (1940–60), which preceded the Explanatory Period (1960 to date) of American archaeology.

6 Signally, one of the longest-running and most copied scribal exercises in Sumer was precisely a list of occupations categorized by their ranking in the socio-economic hierarchy. Here emic and etic meet in the world's first complex society.

7 Descent traced through only one parent; i.e. either the male or the female line; i.e. unilineal.

8 But see Thucydides (II:15). Before the formation of the Attic city-state, he writes, the city of Athens 'consisted of the present citadel [the acropolis] and the district beneath it to the south. This is shown by the fact that the temples of the other deities, as well as Athene, are in the citadel and even those that are outside it are mostly situated in this quarter of the city, as that of the Olympian Zeus, of the Pythian Apollo, of Earth and of Dionysus in the marshes. There were also ancient temples in this quarter.'

Chapter 2: The premisses of social succession

1 cf. Barth (1956:1079–89) for the classic statement: 'Ecological relationships of ethnic groups in Swat, North Pakistan'.

2 Which, if it does not derive from, certainly has its most sustained exposition in W. H. Oswalt's *Habitat and Technology: The Evolution of Hunting* (1973:168–72).

3 cf. Van Arsdale (1978) for a review of infanticide in the New Guinea context.

4 *c.* 200 square metres.

5 *c.* 10,000 BC.

6 i.e. *c.* 16,000–10,000 BC.

7 This is equivalent to the maintenance of a young bovine as against sheep or goat on the same area.

8 There the Bronze Age extends from around 3,000 BC to about 1,000 BC.

9 This is all the more remarkable because 'inventing' the windmill only involved bringing together two well-established technologies, namely the application of ships' sails to the mill. K. D. White's indispensable *Roman Farming* (1970:453) refers to 'lack of incentives to change, especially methods of cultivation. In the basic techniques, innovation was rare, and technical improvements, such as the wheeled plough and the Gallic harvesting machine, which originated outside the Mediterranean region, remained isolated and did not "catch on". There is also some evidence, which is both sporadic in its incidence, and

difficult to interpret, of lack of concern for increasing productivity' (1970:453). Chapter 9 of the present volume takes those points further.

10 Perhaps 'mutation', to contrast with 'succession'.

11 Though he has elsewhere (e.g. 'Origins and ecological effects of early domestication in Iran and the Near East', 1969) provided excellent ones.

12 See Rindos (1985) for a powerful account of the evolution of the capacity for culture.

Chapter 3: The ecology of the Zagrosian Arc

1 Now the rivers Dijlah and Furat.

2 Ranging from 1,200 to 1,800 cc, with a mean around 1,350 cc (Holloway (1974) 1975:73).

3 Indeed, Russell (1988:48–50) has collected evidence from Roman to modern times in both the Mediterranean and northern Europe, showing the figure for typical wheat yields stubbornly, and with amazing uniformity, stuck around 50–54 kg per dunam. He contends (1988:109) 'that there would appear to be no variations in wheat yields prior to the late eighteenth and early nineteenth centuries AD, which could not be attributed to regional differences in soil fertility, the use of fertiliser, climate, and [the incidence of] rainfall or irrigation'. Russell (1988:111) takes prehistoric mean yields on average quality land to be 50 kg/du for wheat and 60 kg/du for barley, because of good agreement in wide-ranging data. *Inter alia* 'the mean wheat yield of 52.8 kg/du derived from Titow's Medieval British Data closely approximates the 53.5 kg/du mean wheat yield derived from Columella's first century AD data on land of average quality in Roman Italy (II.9.1, III.3.4). These figures also fall close to the 50 kg/du average wheat yield calculated by Meyerson (1955:55, 1960:18) from seventh century AD papyri recovered from the Byzantine town of Nessana in the Negev desert of southern Israel. The possibility that a wheat yield of around 50–54 kg/du may reflect a realistic productivity division between the yields expected on "marginal" and "optimal" lands for wheat cultivation would again gain support from Meyerson's informant data on the yields expected by Bedouin cultivators in the central Negev in the late 1950's.'

4 At least this is the orthodox view. However, the early occurrence of bread wheat at widely separated sites like Tell es-Sawwan, Tepe Sabz, and Hacilar, taken with the fact that no less than sixteen varieties of goatface grass are known in contemporary Iraq (Al-Rawi 1964), casts strong doubt on the 'northern connection' in the formation of bread wheat.

5 Using Harlan's data Russell (1988:127–8) has calculated the post-encounter caloric return-rates to be 2,378 kcal/hr for 1.1 hours hand-stripping wild einkorn, even adding 0.4 hr for threshing, winnowing, and milling, those last based on ethnographic examples. Using a flint sickle for the 0.9 hr now needed to collect 1 kg of wild einkorn and adding the same 0.4 hr processing time, results in 2,744 kcal/hr. In either case an hour's work produces sufficient calories (plus some of the protein) for one adult for 24 hrs; obviously a very high rate of productivity and very attractive to foraging populations.

6 At least seasonally. For the pattern of mobility/settlement this involves, see Figure 4.2 and discussion.

7 This is quite unusual, since tell mounds in the Near East are normally formed by the decay of mud-brick structures, with rebuilding on top of the old debris forming successive levels.

8 Indeed, the occurrence of emmer in Phase IA, dating from 7,800 to 7,600 BC (Van Zeist and Bakker-Heeres 1979:163), would make this the earliest find of cultivated wheat so far. Aswad Phase IA is contemporary in its lithic industry with Mureybet III (de Contenson 1979:155), while Phase IB, 7,600–7,300 BC, corresponds to the industry of Mureybet IVA.

9 Russell (1988:33) argues that, using trap corrals, 'prehistoric hunters could have captured and initially controlled wild herds in such a fashion as to be able to isolate the phenotypically most desirable individuals for use as the founding members in subsistence herds'. This is indeed 'counter-intuitive' as it presupposes that the prehistoric hunters had a model of the domestication process in mind. On the other hand, an early milk production strategy, as Russell (1988:35) postulates on energetic grounds, would serve as a basis of, and rationale for, keeping herds.

Chapter 4: The origin and growth of villages

1 There is, however, an underlying Natufian settlement on the site (Kirkbride 1967:10).

2 Quaternary = Pleistocene + Holocene; i.e. *c.* 2 million years so far.

3 Poplar poles, covered by reeds and mud, are the traditional roofing for pre-cement-block village houses in the area (Copeland 1979:253).

4 If this date is sustained, then not only are the Zawi Chemi sheep the earliest manifesting domestication, but indeed represent the earliest domesticated animals, other than dog, anywhere.

5 'Black Mountain': a local name for this part of the Zagros.

6 Dates were revised by Hole (1977:27) on the basis of the newly known half-life of C^{14}. These are the ones given here, and not those originally published in Hole, Flannery, and Neely (1969). Correspondences are listed in Table 4.1.

7 J. Oates (1983:262–3) expresses doubts about the correspondence of Surkh with Samarra, but such correlations, even more than radio-carbon datings, are always provisional (cf. Hole 1987; Voigt 1987). Merpert and Munchaev (1987:19), having observed correspondences between Hassuna features and the Sefid and Surkh phases on the Deh Luran plain, remark that 'The lower levels of Yarim Tepe I (i.e. in Northern Mesopotamia) appear to be contemporary with the Sefid phase in Deh Luran and the two lower levels of Tell es-Sawwan (which precede the appearance of Samarran painted ceramics).'

8 Which is no longer merely an extended kinship unit.

9 Whose origins almost certainly lie in the Khabur Plains area, north of Jebels Sinjar and Abd Al-Azziz, but south of the mountain front. This area, known to third-millennium Sumer as **Subir** (later **subartu**), and which then contained important cities like Tell Leilan, receives from 300 mm to over 450 mm rainfall (to the north), and so is well suited to early rainfed farming. The plain contains many Halaf sites, notably the type site of Ras el ʿAin.

10 See the comments of Nissen (1987) on the construction of chronology from textual sources.

11 This settling-down sequence is the explanation given by Merpert and Munchaev (1973:100–1) for the characteristic Halaf tholoi, and for the presence of round-houses alongside rectilinear ones in Hassuna settlements, with rectangular houseforms later dominant there.

12 Originating with Mortensen (1972:294) and developed by Henry (1975:382) for the Levant.
13 Oates (1980:308) suggests a population of 50–100 persons as an average for fully agricultural villages of 1 hectare in the most fertile parts of northern Iraq, from the early sixth to the late fifth millennium.
14 Or, ignoring synchronicity, 2.5 per generation; say one new domestic unit beginning its reproductive cycle. If population was thereby cumulatively allowed to rise to 0.4 persons/km^2 and beyond (Ammerman and Cavalli-Sforza 1984:121), then this new family, assuming neolocal residence on average only 1 km distant, would be a component of a demic front with others behaving similarly. This is discussed immediately below.
15 Note absolute decline in both area and population of the Northern Enclave over this half millennium, while in the same period the population of the Southern Enclave more than quadrupled while the area went up by around 50 per cent.
16 cf. the systematic neglect of children leading to their deaths among the New York Iroquois, discussed above.

Chapter 5: The heartland of cities

1 Probably a reference to the freshwater springs which bubble up in the sea around Bahrain, i.e. Dilmun (Heidel 1951:62 n.7).
2 Below it is argued to take the form of *oikiai*, internally and inter-stratified households.
3 The Assyriological convention is to use Roman lower-case letters for Sumerian words, italic lower case for Akkadian (often in brackets after the Sumerian), while upper-case Roman letters (CAPITALS) are employed where the precise or agreed reading of an element has not been established, for this is how the ideogram or cuneiform sign is represented.
4 Gelb (1973:84) describes their ambiguous status as that of 'soldiers/workers' thus 'indicating the double nature of their employment, as soldiers in time of war and as workers, mainly in agriculture, in time of peace. This dual usage of the term **erín** is reflected in the use of the terms for their officers, as in the following sources: **sagana erín-na** "general", **nu-banda** "captain", and **ugula** "sergeant" applied to the army . . . ; **sagana**, **nu-banda**, and **ugula** for either soldiers or workers . . . ; and **nu-banda** "overseer" and **ugula** "foreman" for workers.' **Nu-banda**, 'captain' or 'overseer' was in charge of a 'century' of **erín**, each **i-dab$_5$** (of ten members) led by a **ses-gal**, or foreman (Maekawa 1976:16–17). **Erín** obviously functioned as the most mobile form of labour and army reserve.
5 This is the long-established reading for his name which still appears in histories. However it is now usually rendered 'Uruinimgina', although some prefer to reproduce the uncertain element thus: UruKAgina.

Chapter 6: The institutions of urbanism

1 'The Arua Institution'; Gelb (1972) is discussed in detail below.
2 See ch. 5, n. 5.
3 Probably the circuit wall of the temple precinct.
4 This is Kramer's own estimate and is certainly too small; 57,600 gallons is scarcely worth having for irrigation and barely enough as a reserve of drinking water in the Near East.

5 Neck-stocks were one of the usual means of dealing with prisoners of war before deciding their fate (Gelb 1973:72).

6 That is, from the Mediterranean to the Gulf.

7 Literally, 'sons of Akkad'.

8 Meluhha = the Indus (Basham 1971:19).

9 Magan = Baluchistan or Oman, probably the latter; but either or both might be so designated in different periods.

10 Dilmun = Bahrain (Bibby 1970:220–1).

11 Dagan = West Semitic weather god; head of the pantheon at Ebla.

12 Although such a despotic monarchy could not be long sustained (Hallo and Simpson 1971:102).

13 This is the precise sense in which the term 'status' is used in other chapters of the present volume.

14 R. B. Rowton (1980:298n.) suggests the Old Babylonian period was one of 'incipient capitalism' which 'took the form of loans on excessively high interest'. However, usury and the resulting debt-bondage were far from new and it is hard to see why 'Babylonian society was entirely unprepared to deal with [it]'. Rowton (op. cit.:298) also reckons that Hammurabi had succeeded in doing away with the city-state system 'once and for all', but couldn't make empire stick. 'Instead, Babylonia once again lapsed into a long process of trivial obscurity, although in this case the decline was a gradual process.' It had also much to do with Kassite irruptions, and not to mention this is like overlooking similar events in the collapse of Rome; though many factors, of which usury was no doubt one, tore Old Babylonian society apart.

15 However, see Powell 1985 for more recent computations that show rather higher sustained averages.

16 1 sìla = 1 litre is a usual working equivalence. 1 sìla = 620g dry.

17 Indeed the 'Mari' nomads often had villages of their own, occupied at least seasonally (Matthews 1978:110–12) and/or as a retreat from government control. Agriculture could also be undertaken, as when the Mari government supplied ploughs and other agricultural equipment in exchange for a share in the harvest, seemingly a quite common practice (ibid.:86). With what he calls a 'symbiosis hypothesis', Fritz (1987:98–9) sees such a process as best accounting for the range of evidence for Israelite settlement of Palestine, dismissing both 'conquest' and 'revolution' hypotheses.

18 The goddess of grain.

19 About 20 lbs of locally processed wool is required for a rug (gilim) c. 2.25 × 1.50 m made by traditional weaving methods in a contemporary Zagros village (Watson 1979:174).

20 A similar set of dispositions obtained during the Sargonic period, and probably earlier than that also (Foster 1982c).

Chapter 7: Theories of the state

1 A full treatment of the statuses/offices distinction is given early in Chapter 8.

2 Despite Steward's pioneering work in this field; cf. his *Theory of Culture Change*, 1955.

3 Which Flannery subsumes under the head: 'cultural ecology' (1972a:400) but differentiates from the traditional or 'pre-information' ecologists like Steward, while he identifies with Rappaport's approach.

4 None of which is intended to be dismissive of the systems approach as such, rather to indicate what its limits and uses are, stated by Johnson (1978:91) to

be 'attempts to describe various organisational approaches to system growth, not explain that growth'.

5 And conversely through their warfare, for which they also mobilize a lot of resources, they can also destroy them. The Roman destruction of, for instance, Carthage, is deservedly as famous as Roman aqueducts.

6 cf. Halstead (1981a:334) for Greece: 'The observed spacing between Neolithic settlements may rather reflect the need for access to wild foods in years of bad harvests, while the broadening of the subsistence base to include, in particular, olive cultivation may have taken place for a similar reason.' Indeed Meillassoux ((1972) 1978b:161) regards this as axiomatic.

7 For whom 'production for exchange seems to be a constant factor in evolution' (1977b:204), and by whom 'It can easily [sic] be argued that since the rise of the great commercial civilisations of the Middle East, the collapse of individual states and empires and even the general crises of the entire area including the Mediterranean have been economic in nature and much like the one we are experiencing today (ecce!) not simply a question of running out of energy sources' (Eckholm and Friedman 1981:617).

8 Such an approach Brumfiel (1983:263) calls 'structural', since 'certain socio-cultural systems, because of their inherent structural properties, are dynamic' and 'structurally induced social conflict has both a political and an economic basis in political systems where leadership is instituted in weak, but permanent offices' that is, in chiefdoms. While responding to certain ecological possibilities and constraints, it is the social structure as an emergent complex that develops according to strains and opportunities set up in its own continuing operation.

9 Accordingly, 'there is good evidence for agricultural festivals during which the king performed activities related to the plough, its oxen, and the first opening of the furrows' (M. Civil 1976:84).

Chapter 8: From status to state

1 So much so, indeed, that Begler (1978:595) divides nominally egalitarian (hunter-gatherer) societies into two types according to how egalitarian they really are. Truly egalitarian societies are those (few) like the Pygmy or, less likely, Bushman, where 'there are no socio-centric statuses, other than those based on the transient characteristic of age, which are vested with authority', and where something like symmetrical rights for each sex obtains. By contrast, 'at the other end of the egalitarian spectrum of egalitarian societies, we find what we might call "semi-egalitarian societies". In these societies, exemplified by the Eskimo and the Aborigines, the egalitarian mode of interaction obtains only within the boundaries of each sex. The relations between the sexes are characterised by differential ranking of males and females whereby males are vested with definite, albeit limited, authority over females.'

2 In terms of 'achieved' status, one could speak of the status of a doctor being not his prestige (although that obtains), but his/her assumed technical capacity to cure, formally specified. Thus he/she is 'licensed for' medicine and the practitioner's status turns upon this sense of 'capacity'.

3 The *Domestic Unit* is the locus of procreation and basic socialization of the individual. It is procreation licensed as a component of social reproduction, and is thus the fundamental cultural institution.

The *Household* is the means by which the domestic unit engages in physical exchanges with the natural and human environment.

4 See discussion in Legros (1988:16), for whom 'A stratified structure is a possibility that some people may succeed in instituting in any economic context. Its form will simply vary according to the sort of production techniques which are in place.'

5 *Filiation* is the public recognition of children as proper members of the domestic unit. It involves a 'package of jurally, ritually and morally validated credentials' (Fortes 1969:262) through which parents transmit status to their children. *Marriage* marks the formation of an enterprise (household/domestic unit) conferring upon the partners rights in each other's productive and reproductive capacities.

6 This use of the term 'tribe' to characterize the 'kinship idiom' as the basic means of social structuration should not be confused with (left-over) nineteenth-century notions of the tribe as a political unit with leaders, etc. When this is intended, I use the term 'chiefdom'. The kinship order is not, however, a seamless web, but a composition of relatively discrete units (such as clans, lineages, or households), produced by some principles of filiation.

7 This is the condition of equal weight being given to descent from either male or female parent. This produces not lineages but 'stocks', whereby each pair of parents gives their children access to four stocks. Accordingly every ego (and his/her siblings) has a unique set of relations called 'kindred', which cannot normally be a corporate group.

8 'Prestige is first acquired by an individual by lavishness in fulfilling ritual obligations. This prestige is then converted into recognised status by validating retrospectively the rank of the individual's lineage. This last is largely a matter of manipulating the genealogical tradition' (Leach 1970:164).

9 Though the term 'brideprice' has for some decades been replaced by 'bridewealth' it is the term applied by Friedman; and Leach insists that it is strictly accurate in the case of 'Ordinary Jinghpaw' marriage: 'In this case the bridewealth transactions can correctly be described as a "brideprice"; ownership of the physical person of the bride and all rights that adhere to her are transferred in exchange for the goods of the marriage payment. In this situation, as Professor Gluckman has predicted, divorce is impossible' (Leach 1961b:119).

10 cf. Kirsch (1973:11–13) for whom the pursuit of such blessings are the mainsprings of action not only amongst the Kachin but throughout 'upland S.E. Asia' in which the various peoples 'can be viewed as sharing a single generalised culture' (ibid.:36) despite a certain structural variability, which latter will be taken up shortly.

11 Kirsch suggests that 'We might characterise "autocratic" [i.e. gumsa-type] societies as those in which ritual advantages have "piled-up" or been "captured" by individuals (or by lineage segments)' (1973:26).

12 Hence the importance in North China of the tree food crops: jujube (*Zizyphus jujuba*), persimmon (*Diaspyros kaki*), chestnut (*Castanea mollisima*), and hazelnut (*Corylus heterphylla*); plus the succulents, peach (*Prunus persica*) and apricot (*Prunus armeniaca*) (Li 1983:34–5). And while the brassicas were always important, mallow (*Malva verticillata*) seems to have been an especially important northern vegetable, as 'in ancient times vegetable oils were not available, so mulcilaginous vegetables like mallow were a required part of the diet' (ibid.:36).

13 A contemporary rice-growing pottery Neolithic culture exists called Ch'ing-lien-kang. To it belong over 500 sites extending over 100,000 km^2 in the coastal provinces of Shantung, Kiansu, Anwei, Chekiang, and the lower Yangtze Valley (Pearson 1983:125–6). This culture is preceded by horizons of

an earlier culture at Ho-mu-tu, a large site some 50 km from the sea south of Hangchow bay in Chekiang province. There in a rice-growing and pottery-making context, possibly domestic oxen, pigs, dogs, and water buffalo occur, around 5,000 BC (Meacham 1983:158–9).

Concentrating upon the hegemony of Central Plains civilization is in no way intended to suggest that Neolithic and post-Neolithic cultures only developed in that area, when in fact independent and parallel developments were taking place in several parts of East Asia. Accordingly, with Meacham, I would stress that 'the elements probably unique to Early Shang – kingship, priesthood, an organised military, urban settlement, writing – mark the radically new epoch entered by the progenitors of Shang civilisation' (Meacham 1983:169).

What I have sought to outline is the cultural and ecological basis for this 'radical departure'.

14 Unless otherwise differentiated, the author thus referred to is Chang Kwang-chih, i.e. K. C. Chang.
15 Something I have hypothesized for Harappan social organization (Maisels 1984c).
16 Literally, too, as some artisanal groups, such as of craftsmen in bronze, jade, or some types of pottery, would be entitled to high-status *hang-t'u* platforms for their houses. Aristocratic dwellings and ritual structures were erected on such platforms, often of great dimensions.

Chapter 9: Modelling societies: modes of production

1 Godelier (1977:168, 174), Friedman and Rowlands (1977b:203), and Friedman (1974:445) provide diagrammatic outlines of relations of production or 'social formations' (Friedman, loc. cit.). However the latter states that 'there is nothing implied in [his] hierarchy other than a set of functional distinctions' (ibid.) and I take this to be the general usage, not being aware of other attempts to apply diagrammatic methods to develop an operational model.

Chapter 10: Ideology and political economy of the Mesopotamian state

1 Foundation myths are those about how the particular society came into existence (which may or may not be distinct from human origin myths); while charter myths are those explaining what makes the particular society what it is, i.e. special. Thus Magna Carta and English democracy.
2 Conversely, Finley (1983c:123–6) cogently argues that it was the constitutional contrast between the Greek city-states, between the Greek-speaking world and barbarians, and indeed the condition of rapid political flux of state constitutions within city-states like Athens, which provoked and sustained the classic tradition of enquiry in politics and social philosophy.
3 Even Enlil was bound by the **me**'s he had caused to be uttered.
4 For plurality in a native African state, see Gluckman (1959) and Hodder (1981) on Barotseland; for the Roman Republic and Empire, see Sherwin-White (1967).

Chapter 11: Summary and overview

1 This is not to suggest that destruction of forest for fuel, timber, etc. did not occur, still less that it was not locally devastating, as it currently is in parts of Iran (Hole 1978:148; Watson 1979:240). In Jordan it is gallery forest and ravine woodland that seems to have suffered most (Harlan 1982:71–7). Rowton's review (1967b) is indispensable on Near Eastern woodlands.

2 And indeed seem to be those, with alluvial soils on valley bottoms, exploited by the LBK cultures in the early Neolithic of Europe also (Howell 1987:98–105).

3 Jacobsen (1980a:74) states that it is 'significant that in Nippur (the only pre-Uruk settlement in the region) Enlil, god of the older, sacred parts of the site was god of the hoe; while his son Ninurta, god of the city area itself, was god of the plough'. While Ninurta in fact means 'Lord Plough' he is also god of the floodstorm.

4 Of Meso-America, Bray suggests that 'what may have delayed the advent of settled life is simply the lack of a staple crop. Archaeological specimens of maize from dry caves (from 5,000 BC to the Spanish conquest) show that more than three thousand years of genetic selection were needed to develop races capable of sustaining full-time agriculture' (Bray 1979:79).

5 This is not to suggest that there were *no* secular changes in Australia; secular changes are always under way. Lourandos (1985:403) argues for 'a general amplification of socioeconomic behaviour' in the last four or five thousand years, viewing this 'as fuelled by the demands of social relations and merely stimulated by environmental factors' (ibid.:408).

6 Technically energy is the capacity to do work, and work is the capacity to produce changes of condition, that is, of state or position, where state = form.

7 Thus stored information, I_s, or information density may be defined as $D_1 + D_2$, where D_1 is divergence from equiprobability and D_2 divergence from independence, their sum providing a measure of how much entropy has been lowered from the maximum entropy condition (Gatlin 1972:49). When the sum is divided by log a, we have a measure of the 'redundancy'. Simply, information is any signal to which an entity can respond. Raw energy, such as sunlight, is also information, but the structure of a cell capable of photosynthesis depends on a prior (evolutionary) organization of information.

8 The ceiling for hunter-gatherers over large territories is usually taken to be 1 per square mile (Lee and Devore 1968:11). Agriculture, as Lee and Devore observe (ibid.), is easily able to exceed this figure by factors of ten to 1,000. There is an intermediate level, however, which is worth noticing, for I believe this might be a threshold at or beneath which neither urbanism nor the state is possible. It is the single-figure population densities of pastoral populations, of which the following is a sample (from Allan 1965:309; the Nuer figure from Evans-Pritchard 1940:110): Tanganika Masai: 2.0/square mile; Fulani 2.4/square mile; Turkana 3.3/square mile; Kenya Masai 4.3/square mile; Nuer 5.5/square mile; Somali 5.8/square mile; Mukogodo 6.0/square mile.

Of course the pastoralist way of life militates against urbanism at least as much as their overall population densities, unless of course they are involved in the conquest of agricultural populations. With hunter-gatherers' density at less than unity, 'pure' pastoralists at less than 10 per square mile, and agriculturalists easily ten-times that figure, we seem to have *quantum levels* for qualitatively distinct modes of production, something to be expected from their typical trophic levels, since each type specializes in a different level of the food chain (cf. Odum 1975:64–8).

9 Intriguingly, it may be that Phoenician long-distance sailing was a product of Syrian coastal cities, hitherto restricted in sailing technique and routes, having learned Mycenaean techniques and routes (Liverani 1987:73 n.11). The merchant ship which went down off Ulu Burun in Turkey early in the fourteenth century already hints at the 'internationalization' of crews (Bass 1987). And the technology manifested at the Sea Peoples' (Sikuli) port of Dor in Palestine from the thirteenth century forward, supports the idea of 'transferred technics' (Raban 1987:126).

10 The Battle of Beneventum was the defeat of Pyrrhus and the Greek cities of southern Italy.

Appendix D

1 Indeed Millard (1988:57) suggests that those related yeast-using techniques were diffused from Mesopotamia, as also the idea of writing and sealing employing cylinder seals; the last two often suggested, but now appearing increasingly likely, to derive from Mesopotamian originals.

Appendix E

1 Cretan Linear A and B scripts are also syllabaries. Gelb (1963:252), who denies the validity of the term 'ideogram', defines the *Rebus Principle* as that process 'by which word signs which are difficult to draw are written by signs expressing words which are similar in sound and are easy to draw. Thus, in Sumerian, the word *ti*, 'life', is expressed by the picture of an arrow which also is *ti* in Sumerian.'

2 Egyptian hieratic and demotic scripts on papyrus were, however, later applied to purposes of administration; hieroglyphs used monumentally were called 'god's words' (Baines 1983:581).

3 Finkelstein calls the 'cuneiform world' that 'broad territorial span encompassing Asia Minor and the Syrian coastal region in the West to the western portion of Iran in the East which, for extended periods of time, utilised the Babylonian cuneiform writing system and were in this respect influenced by the cultural traditions of the cuneiform homeland in Babylonia and Sumer in the lower half of the Tigris and Euphrates valley' (Finkelstein 1974:606 n.8).

Bibliography

Abrams, P. and Wrigley, E.A. (eds) (1978) *Towns in Societies: Essays in Economic History and Historical Sociology*, Cambridge: Cambridge University Press.

Acsadi, G.Y. and Nemeskeri, J. (1970) *History of Human Life Span and Mortality*, Budapest: Akademiai Kiado.

—— (1974) '*History of Human Life Span and Mortality*: Authors' precis and reviews', *Current Anthropology* 15(4):495–507.

Adams, Richard N. (1981) 'Natural selection, energetics and "cultural materialism" ', *Current Anthropology* 22(6):603–24.

Adams, Robert McC. (1962) 'Agriculture and urban life in early southwestern Iran', *Science* 136:109–22.

—— (1965) *Land Behind Baghdad: A History of Settlement on the Diyala Plains*, Chicago: University of Chicago Press.

—— (1966) *The Evolution of Urban Society: Early Mesopotamia and Prehispanic Mexico*, Chicago: Aldine.

—— (1974) 'Anthropological perspectives on ancient trade', *Current Anthropology* 15(3):239–58.

—— (1975) 'The Mesopotamian social landscape: a view from the frontier', in Charlotte B. Moore (ed.), *Reconstructing Complex Societies*, Bulletin of the American Schools of Oriental Research, Supplement 20, 1–20.

—— (1978) 'Strategies of maximisation, stability and resilience in Mesopotamian society, settlement and agriculture', *Proceedings of the American Philosophical Society* 122:329–35.

—— (1981) *Heartland of Cities: Surveys of Ancient Settlement and Land Use on the Central Floodplain of the Euphrates*, Chicago: University of Chicago Press.

—— (1982) 'Property rights and functional tenure in Mesopotamian communities', in Dandamayev *et al.* (eds), 1–14.

—— (1983a) 'Natural and social science paradigms in Near Eastern prehistory', in T. C. Young *et al.* (eds) (1983), 369ff.

—— (1983b) 'The Jarmo stone and pottery vessel industries', in Braidwood *et al.* (eds) (1983), 209–32.

Adams, Robert McC. and Nissen, H.J. (1972) *The Uruk Countryside: The Natural Setting of Urban Society*, Chicago: University of Chicago Press.

Air Ministry Meteorological Office (1958) *Tables of Temperature, Relative Humidity and Precipitation for the World. Part V: Asia*. London: HMSO.

Akkermans, P.M.M.G. (1987) 'A late neolithic and early Halaf village at Sabi Abyad, Northern Syria', *Paléorient* 13(1):23–40.

Akkermans, P.A., Van Loon, M.N., Roodenberg, J.J., and Waterbolk, H.T.

(1982) 'The 1976–7 excavations at Tell Bouqras', *Les Annales archéologiques arabes syriennes*, 45–57.

Alden, John R. (1982) 'Trade and politics in proto-Elamite Iran', *Current Anthropology* 23(6):613–40.

Aldred, Cyril (1961) *The Egyptians*, London: Thames & Hudson.

Alexander, Richard D. (1975) 'The search for a general theory of behavior', *Behavioral Science* 20:77–100.

Algaze, G. (1986) 'Habuba on the Tigris: archaic Nineveh reconsidered', *Journal of Near Eastern Studies* 45(2):125–37.

Al-Khalesi, Y.M. (1977) 'Tell al-Fakhar (Khurruhanni), a *Dimtu*-settlement (excavation report)', *Assur* 1(6):81–122.

—— (1978) *The Court of Palms: A Functional Interpretation of the Mari Palace*, Bibliotheca Mesopotamica, vol. 8, Malibu, Calif.: Undena.

Al-Khashab, W.H. (1958) *The Water Budget of the Tigris and Euphrates Basin*, Chicago: Department of Geography Research Paper no.54, University of Chicago.

Allan, J. (1974) 'The Bagundji of the Darling basin: cereal gatherers in an uncertain environment', *World Archaeology* 5(3):309–22.

Allan, William (1965) *The African Husbandman*, Edinburgh: Oliver & Boyd.

Allchin, B. (1972) 'Hunters or pastoral nomads? Late stone age settlement in western and central India', in P.J. Ucko *et al.* (eds), 115–19.

Allchin, B. and Allchin R. (1982) *The Rise of Civilisation in India and Pakistan*, Cambridge: Cambridge University Press.

Allen W.L. and Richardson, J.B. (1971) 'The reconstruction of kinship from archaeological data: the concepts, the methods and the feasibility', *American Antiquity* 36(1):41–53.

Almagor, Uri (1978) 'Gerontocracy, polygyny and scarce resources', in J.S. La Fontaine (ed.) (1978a), 139–59.

Al-Rawi, Ali (1964) *Wild Plants of Iraq*, Baghdad: Government Press.

Al-Soof, B.A. (1973) 'Uruk pottery from Eridu, Ur and Al-Ubaid', *Sumer* 29:17–22.

Alster, B. (1972) *Dumuzi's Dream: Aspects of Oral Poetry in a Sumerian Myth*, Mesopotamia 1, Copenhagen Studies in Assyriology, Copenhagen: Akademisk Forlag.

—— (1975) *Studies in Sumerian Proverbs, Mesopotamia 3*, Copenhagen Studies in Assyriology, Copenhagen: Akademisk Forlag.

Amiet, P. (1979) 'Archaeological discontinuity and ethnic duality in Elam', *Antiquity* 53:195–204.

Ammerman, A.J. and Cavalli-Sforza, L.L. (1973) 'A population model for the diffusion of early farming in Europe', in Colin Renfrew (ed.) (1973b), 343–57.

—— (1984) *The Neolithic Transition and the Genetics of Populations in Europe*, Princeton, N.J.: Princeton University Press.

Andrewes, A. (1965) 'The growth of the city-state', in H. Lloyd-Jones (ed.), *The Greek World*, Harmondsworth: Penguin, 26–65.

Angel, J.L. (1972) 'Ecology and population in the eastern Mediterranean', *World Archaeology* 4:88–105.

Asch, M.I. (1979) 'The ecological-evolutionary model and the concept of Mode of Production', in D.H. Turner and G.A. Smith (eds) (1979), 81–99.

Auge, M. (1978) 'Status, power and wealth: relations of lineage dependence and production in Alladian society', in D. Seddon (ed.), 389–412.

Aurenche, O., Evin, J., and Hours, F. (eds) (1987) *Chronologies in the Near East: Relative Chronologies and Absolute Chronology 16,000–4,000 B.P.*, 2 vols

(CNRS International Symposium, Lyon, November 1986), BAR International Series 379.

Austin, M.M. and Vidal-Naquet, P. (1977) *Economic and Social History of Ancient Greece: An Introduction*, London: Batsford.

Bader, N.O., Merpert, N. Ya., and Munchaev, R.M. (1981) 'Soviet expedition's surveys in the Sinjar Valley', *Sumer* 37(1–2):55–110.

Bailey, A. and Llobera, J.R. (eds) (1981) *The Asiatic Mode of Production*, London: Routledge & Kegan Paul.

Bailey, F.G. (1961) ' "Tribe" and "caste" in India', *Contributions to Indian Sociology* 5:7–19.

—— (1963) 'Closed social stratification in India', *Archives of European Sociology* 4:107–24.

Bailey, G. (ed.) (1983) *Hunter-Gatherer Economy in Prehistory: A European Perspective*, Cambridge: Cambridge University Press.

Bailkey, N. (1967) 'Early Mesopotamian constitutional development', *American Historical Review* 72(4):1211–36.

Baines, J. (1983) 'Literacy and ancient Egyptian society', *Man* 18:572–99.

Baker, H.G. (1970) *Plants and Civilisation*, London: Macmillan.

Balsdon, J.P.V.D. (ed.) (1969) *Roman Civilisation*, Harmondsworth: Penguin.

Banton, M. (ed.) (1965) *Political Systems and the Distribution of Power*, ASA Monograph no.2, London: Tavistock.

Barnard, A. (1979) 'Kalahari Bushmen settlement patterns', in P.C. Burnham and R.F. Ellen (eds), 131–44.

—— (1980a) 'Basarwa settlement patterns in the Ghanzi ranching area', *Botswana Notes and Records* 12:137–49.

—— (1980b) 'Sex roles among the Nharo Bushmen of Botswana', *Africa* 50(2):115–24.

—— (1983) 'Contemporary hunter-gatherers: current theoretical issues in ecology and social organisation', *Annual Review of Anthropology* 12:193–214.

Barrau, J. (1958) *Subsistence Agriculture in Melanesia*, Honolulu: Bernice P. Bishop Museum Bulletin no.219.

Barth, F. (1953) *Principles of Social Organisation in Southern Kurdistan*, Oslo: Universitets Ethnografiske Museum Bulletin no.7.

—— (1956) 'Ecologic relationships of ethnic groups in Swat, North Pakistan', *American Anthropologist* 58(6):1079–89.

—— (1961) *Nomads of South Persia: The Basseri Tribe of the Khamseh Confederacy*, London: Allen & Unwin.

—— (1964) 'Herdsmen of S.W. Asia', in P.B. Hammond (ed.), 63–84.

—— (1981) 'Ethnic groups and boundaries', in *Process and Form in Social Life: Selected Essays of Frederik Barth*, London: Routledge & Kegan Paul, I, 198–227.

Barton, G.A. (1929) *Royal Inscriptions of Sumer and Akkad*, New Haven, Conn.: Yale University Press.

Bar-Yosef, O. (1980) 'Prehistory of the Levant', *Annual Review of Anthropology* 9:101–33.

—— (1983) 'The Natufian of the southern Levant', in T.C. Young *et al.* (eds), 11–42.

—— (1986) 'The walls of Jericho: an alternative interpretation', *Current Anthropology* 27(2):157–62.

Bar-Yosef, O. and Goren, N. (1973) 'Natufian remains in Hayonim Cave', *Paléorient* 1:49–68.

Bar-Yosef, O. and Vogel, J.C. (1987) 'Relative and absolute chronology of the epi-palaeolithic in the south of the Levant', in O. Aurenche *et al.* (eds), part i, 219–45.

Basham, A.L. (1971) *The Wonder that was India: A Survey of the History and Culture of the Indian Subcontinent before the Coming of the Muslims*, Glasgow: Fontana.

Bashilov, V.A., Bolshakov, O.G., and Kouza, A.V. (1980) 'The earliest strata of Yarim Tepe I', *Sumer* 26(1,2):43–64.

Bass, G.F. (1987) 'Oldest known shipwreck (Ulu Burun)', *National Geographic* 172(6):693–732.

Bates, D.G. and Lees, S.H. (1977) 'The role of exchange in productive specialisation', *American Anthropologist* 79:824–41.

Batto, B.F. (1980) 'Land tenure and women at Mari', *Journal of the Economic and Social History of the Orient* 23(3):207–39.

Bayliss, Miranda (1973) 'The cult of the dead in Assyria and Babylonia', *Iraq* 35:115–27.

Beale, T.W. (1978) 'Bevelled-rim bowls and their implications for change and economic organisation in the later 4th millennium B.C.', *Journal of Near Eastern Studies* 37(4):289–313.

Begler, E.B. (1978) 'Status and authority in egalitarian society', *American Anthropologist* 80:860–72.

Beidelman, T.O. (ed.) (1971) *The Translation of Culture: Essays to E.E. Evans-Pritchard*, London: Tavistock.

Bender, Barbara (1975) *Farming in Prehistory: From Hunter Gatherer to Food-producer*, London: John Baker.

—— (1978) 'Gatherer-hunter to farmer: a social perspective', *World Archaeology* 10:204–22.

—— (1981) 'Gatherer-hunter intensification', in A. Sheridan and G. Bailey (eds), 149–57.

Berndt, R.R. (1951) 'Ceremonial exchange in West Arnhem Land', *Southwestern Journal of Anthropology* 7:156–76.

Berry, B.J.L. (1961) 'City size distributions and economic development', *Economic Development and Cultural Change* 9:573–87.

Betts, A. (1987) 'Djebel es Shubi: a Natufian site in eastern Jordan', *Paléorient* 13(1):101–5.

Bibby, G. (1970) *Looking for Dilmun*, London: Collins.

Bicchieri, M.G. (ed.) (1972) *Hunters and Gatherers Today*, New York: Holt, Rinehart & Winston.

Biggs, R.D. (1973) 'Pre-Sargonic riddles from Lagash', *Journal of Near Eastern Studies* 32:26–33.

—— (1974) *Inscriptions from Tell Abu Salabikh*, Chicago: Oriental Institute of the University of Chicago.

Binford, L.R. (1968a) 'Post-Pleistocene adaptations', in L.R. Binford and S.R. Binford (eds) (1968), 313–41.

—— (1968b) 'Some comments on historical versus processual archaeology', *Southwestern Journal of Anthropology* 24:267–75.

—— (ed.) (1977) *For Theory Building in Archaeology*, New York: Thomas Crowell.

—— (1980) 'Willow smoke and dogs' tails: hunter-gatherer settlement systems and archaeological site formation', *American Antiquity* 45(1):4–20.

—— (1983) *In Pursuit of the Past: Decoding the Archaeological Record*, London: Thames & Hudson.

Binford, L.R. and Binford, Sally R. (eds) (1968) *New Perspectives in*

Archaeology, Chicago: Aldine.

Binford, L.R. and Chasko, J. (1976) 'Nunamiut demographic history: a provocative case', in E.B.W. Zubrow (ed.), 63–143.

Bintliff, J. (1982) 'Settlement patterns, land tenure and social structure: a diachronic model', in Colin Renfrew and A. Shennan (eds), 106–11.

Birdsell, J.B. (1957) 'Some population problems involving Pleistocene man', *Population Studies: Animal Ecology and Demography*, Cold Spring Harbor Symposia on Quantitative Biology 22:47–69.

—— (1973) 'A basic demographic unit', *Current Anthropology* 14:337–56.

Bloch, M. (1971) 'Decision-making in councils among the Merina of Madagascar', in A. Richards and A. Kuper (eds), 29–63.

—— (1973) 'The long term and the short term: the economic and political significance of the morality of kinship', in J. Goody (ed.), 75–87.

—— (1974) 'Symbols, song, dance and features of articulation: Is religion an extreme form of traditional authority?', *European Journal of Sociology* 15:55–81.

—— (ed.) (1975a) *Marxist Analyses and Social Anthropology*, ASA Studies 2, London: Malaby Press.

—— (ed.) (1975b) *Political Language and Oratory in Traditional Society*, London: Academic Press.

—— (1975c) 'Introduction', in M. Bloch (ed.) (1975b), 1–28.

—— (1975d) 'Property and the end of affinity', in M. Bloch (ed.) (1975a), 203–28.

—— (1976) 'The past and present in the present', *Man* (n.s.) 12:278–92.

—— (1977) 'The disconnection between power and rank', in J. Friedman and M.J. Rowlands (eds) (1977a), 303–40.

—— (1980) 'Modes of production and slavery in Madagascar: two case studies', in James L. Watson (ed.), *Asian and African Systems of Slavery*, Oxford: Basil Blackwell, 100–34.

Boardman, J. (1976) 'The olive in the Mediterranean: its culture and use', *Philosophical Transactions of the Royal Society of London* B275:187–96.

Boardman, J., Brown, M.A., and Powell, T.G.E. (eds) (1971) *The European Community in Later Prehistory – Studies in Honour of C.F.C. Hawkes*. Totowa, N.J.: Rowman & Littlefield.

Bohannan, P. and Bohannan, Laura (1968) *Tiv Economy*, London: Longman.

Bohannan, P. and Middleton, J. (eds) (1968) *Kinship and Social Organisation*, American Museum Sourcebooks in Anthropology Q10, New York: Natural History Press.

Bohrer, V.L. (1972) 'On the relation of harvest methods to early agriculture in the Near East', *Economic Botany* 24:145–55.

Bokonyi, S. (1976) 'Development of early stock rearing in the Near East', *Nature* 264:19–23.

—— (1977) *The Animal Remains from Four Sites in the Kermanshah Valley, Iran: Asiab, Sarab, Dehsavar and Siahbid*, Oxford: BAR Supplementary Series No.34.

Bongaarts, J. (1980a) 'The fertility inhibiting effects of intermediate fertility variables', Paper prepared for the Seminar on the Analysis of Birth Histories, London: IUSSP.

—— (1980b) 'Does malnutrition affect fecundity: a summary of the evidence', *Science* 208:564–9.

Bonte, P. (1977) 'Non-stratified social formations among pastoral nomads', in J. Friedman and M.J. Rowlands (eds) (1977a), 173–200.

Bordes, F. (1968) *The Old Stone Age*, trans. J.E. Anderson, London: Weidenfeld & Nicolson.

Boserup, Ester (1965) *The Conditions of Agricultural Growth: The Economics of Agrarian Change under Population Pressure*, Chicago: Aldine.

Bottema, S. (1978) 'The Late Glacial in the eastern Mediterranean and the Near East', in W.C. Brice (ed.), 15–28.

Bottero, J. (1982) 'La Création de l'homme et sa nature dans la poème d'Atrahasis', in M.A. Dandamayev *et al.* (eds), 24–32.

Bottero, J., Cassin, E., and Vercoutter, J. (eds) (1967) *The Near East: The Early Civilisations*, London: Weidenfeld & Nicolson.

Boyce, A.J. (ed.) (1972) *The Structure of Human Populations*, Oxford: Oxford University Press.

Braidwood, L.S. (1983) 'Appendix. Additional remarks on the Jarmo obsidian', in L.S. Braidwood *et al.* (eds), 285–8.

Braidwood, L.S., Braidwood, R.J., Howe, B., Reed, C.A., and Watson, P.J. (eds) (1983) *Prehistoric Archaeology along the Zagros Flanks*. Oriental Institute Publications no.105, Chicago: Oriental Institute of the University of Chicago.

Braidwood, R.J. (1972a) 'The agricultural revolution', in C.C. Lamberg-Karlovsky (ed.) (1972), 71–9.

—— (1972b) 'Prehistoric investigations in southwestern Asia', *American Philosophical Society Proceedings* 116(4):310–20.

—— (1975) *Prehistoric Men*, 8th edn, Glenview, Ill.: Scott, Foresman.

—— (1983a) 'The site of Jarmo and its archaeological remains', in L.S. Braidwood *et al.* (eds) (1983), 155–208.

—— (1983b) 'Jarmo chronology', in L.S. Braidwood *et al.* (eds) (1983), 537–40.

—— (1983c) 'Miscellaneous analyses of materials from Jarmo', in L.S. Braidwood *et al.* (eds) (1983), 541–4.

Braidwood, R.J. and Braidwood, L.S. (1960) *Excavations in the Plain of Antioch. I: The Earlier Assemblages*, Oriental Institute Publications no.61, Chicago: Oriental Institute of the University of Chicago.

Braidwood, R.J. and Çambel, H. (1976) 'An early farming village in Turkey (Çayönü Tepesi)', in B.M. Fagan (ed.), 125–31.

Braidwood, R.J. and Howe, B. (1960) *Prehistoric Investigations in Iraqi Kurdistan*, Oriental Institute Studies in Ancient Oriental Civilisation no.31, Chicago: Oriental Institute of the University of Chicago.

—— (1962) 'Southwestern Asia beyond the lands of the Mediterranean littoral', in R.J. Braidwood and G.R. Willey (eds) (1962a), 132–46.

Braidwood, R.J. and Reed, C.A. (1957) 'The achievement and early consequences of food production: a consideration of the archaeological and natural-historical evidence', in *Population Studies: Animal Ecology and Demography*, Cold Spring Harbor Symposia on Quantitative Biology 22:19–31.

Braidwood, R.J. and Willey, G.R. (eds) (1962a) *Courses Toward Urban Life: Archaeological Considerations of Some Cultural Alternatives*, Edinburgh: Edinburgh University Press.

—— (1962b) 'Conclusions and afterthoughts', in R.J. Braidwood and G.R. Willey (1962a), 330–59.

Brannigan, K. (1970) *The Foundations of Palatial Crete: A Survey of Crete in the Early Bronze Age*, London: Routledge & Kegan Paul.

Bray, W. (1977) 'From foraging to farming in early Mexico', in J.V.S. Megaw (ed.), 225–50.

—— (1979) 'From village to city in Mesoamerica', in P.R.S. Moorey (ed.), 78–102.

Bray, W. and Trump, D. (1972) *The Penguin Dictionary of Archaeology*, Harmondsworth: Penguin.

Breasted, J.H. (1916) *Ancient Times*, Boston: Ginn and Co.

Brew, J.O. (ed.) (1968) *One Hundred Years of Anthropology*, Cambridge, Mass.: Harvard University Press.

Brice, W.C. (ed.) (1978) *The Environmental History of the Near East and Middle East since the last Ice Age*, London: Academic Press.

Brinkman, J.A. (1977) 'Chronological appendix', in A.L. Oppenheim, 335–48.

—— (1984) 'Settlement surveys and documentary evidence: regional variation and secular trend in Mesopotamian demography', *Journal of Near Eastern Studies* 43(3):169–80.

Bronson, B. (1977) 'The earliest farming: demography as cause and consequence', in C.A. Reed (ed.), 23–48.

Browman, D.L. (ed.) (1980) *Early Native Americans: Prehistoric Demography, Economy and Technology*, The Hague: Mouton.

Brumfiel, Elizabeth M. (1983) 'Aztec state making: ecology, structure and the origin of the state', *American Anthropologist* 85:261–84.

Brunt, P.A. (1971) *Italian Manpower 225 BC – AD 14*, Oxford: Oxford University Press.

Brush, S.B. (1975) 'The concept of carrying capacity for systems of shifting cultivation', *American Anthropologist* 77:799–811.

Buccellati, G. (1966) *The Amorites of the Ur III Period*, Naples: Instituto Orientale di Napoli.

—— (ed.) (1978–82) *Bibliotheca Mesopotamica: Primary Sources and Interpretative Analyses for the Study of Mesopotamian Civilisation and its Infleunce from Late Prehistory to the End of the Cuneiform Tradition*, vols 8 (1978), 13 (1981), and 14 (1982). Published under the auspices of the International Institute for Mesopotamian Area Studies, Malibu, Calif.: Undena.

Buccellati, G., Kelly-Buccellati, M., and Michalowski, P. (eds) (1979) *Monographs of the Ancient Near East I*. Published under the auspices of the International Institute for Mesopotamian Area Studies, Malibu, Calif.: Undena.

Buringh, P. (1957) 'Living conditions in the lower Mesopotamian plain in ancient times', *Sumer* 13(1–2):30–46.

Burney, C. and Long, D.M. (1971) *The Peoples of the Hills. Ancient Ararat and the Caucasus*, London: Weidenfeld & Nicolson.

Burnham, P.C. (1979) 'Permissive ecology and structural conservatism in Gbaya society', in P.C. Burnham and R.F. Ellen (eds), 185–202.

Burnham, P.C. and Ellen, R.F. (eds) (1979) *Social and Ecological Systems*, ASA Monograph no.18. London: Academic Press.

Butzer, K. (1978) 'The late prehistoric environmental history of the Near East', in W.C. Brice (ed.), 5–12.

Cadogan, G. (1980) *Palaces of Minoan Crete*, London: Methuen.

Calvet, Y. (1987) 'L'apport de Tell el 'Oeilli à la chronologie d'Obeid', in O. Aurenche *et al.* (eds), part ii, 465–72.

Calvot, D. (1969) 'Deux documents inédits de Selluš Dagan', *Revue d'Assyriologie* 63:101–14.

Çambel, H. and Braidwood, R. J. (eds) (1980) *Prehistoric Research in South East Anatolia*, Istanbul: Joint Istanbul/Chicago Universities Publication.

Campbell, A.H. (1965) 'Elementary food production by the Australian aborigines', *Mankind* 6:206–11.

Caplice, R. (1973) Review of Kraus, F.R., *Sumerer und Akkader: Ein Problem der altemesopotamischen Geschichte, Orientalia* 42:526–7.

Carneiro, R.L. (1967) 'On the relationship between size of population and complexity of social organisation', *Southwestern Journal of Anthropology* 23:234–43.

—— (1970) 'A theory of the origin of the state', *Science* 169:733–8.

—— (1973) 'The four faces of evolution', in J.J. Honigmann (ed.), 89–110.

—— (1978) 'Political expansion as an expression of the principle of competitive exclusion', in R. Cohen and E.R. Service (eds), 205–23.

Carneiro, R.L. and Hilse, D.F. (1966) 'On determining the probable rate of population growth during the Neolithic', *American Anthropologist* 68:177–81.

Cashdan, Elizabeth (1983) 'Territoriality among human foragers: ecological models and an application to four Bushmen groups', plus 'Comments', *Current Anthropology* 24(1):47–66.

Caspers, E.C.L. During (1971–2) 'New archaeological evidence for maritime trade in the Persian Gulf during the Late Protoliterate Period', *East and West* 21:21–44.

Casteel, R.W. (1972–3) 'Two static maximum population-density models for hunter-gatherers: a first approximation', *World Archaeology* 4:19–39.

Castellino, G.R. (1972) *Two Sulgi Hymns (B.C.)*, Rome: Instituto di Studi del Vinco Oriente, Universita di Roma.

Cauvin, J.C. (1972) 'Nouvelle fouilles à Tell Mureybet (Syrie) 1971–72 Rapport Preliminaire', *Les Annales archéologiques arabes syriennes* 22:105–15.

—— (1973) 'Découverte sur l'Euphrate d'un village natoufien du IXe millénaire av. J.-C. à Mureybet (Syrie)', Note de M. Jacques Cauvin, presentée par M. Jean Piveteau, *C.R. Acad. Sc. Paris* t.276:1985–7.

—— (1977) 'Les fouilles de Mureybet (1971–74) et leur signification pour les origines de la sedentarisation au Proche-Orient', *Annual of the American Schools of Oriental Research* 44:19–48.

Cauvin, J.C. and Cauvin, M.C. (1983) 'Origines de l'agriculture au Levant: facteurs biologiques et socio-culturels', in T.C. Young *et al.* (eds), 43–56.

Centre National de la Recherche Scientifique (1980) *L'Archéologie de l'Iraq du début de l'Epoque Néolithique à 333 avant notre ère*, Colloques Internationaux du CNRS no.580, Paris: Editions du CNRS.

—— (1981) *Préhistoire du Levant: Chronologie et organisation de l'espace depuis les origines jusqu'au VIe millénaire*, Colloques Internationaux du CNRS, no.598, Paris: Editions du CNRS.

Chadwick, J. (1972) 'Life in Mycenaean Greece', in C.C. Lamberg-Karlovsky (ed.), 225–33.

—— (1976) *The Mycenaean World*, Cambridge: Cambridge University Press.

Chang, K.C. (1974) 'Urbanism and the king in ancient China', *World Archaeology* 6(1):1–14.

—— (1976) *Early Chinese Civilisation: Anthropological Perspectives*, Cambridge, Mass.: Harvard University Press.

—— (1977) *The Archaeology of Ancient China*, 3rd edn, New Haven and London: Yale University Press.

—— (1980) *Shang Civilisation*, New Haven and London: Yale University Press.

—— (1983a) 'Sandai archaeology and the formation of states in Ancient China: processual aspects of the origins of Chinese civilisation', in D.N. Keightley (ed.) (1983a), 495–521.

—— (1983b) 'Concluding remarks', in D.N. Keightley (ed.) (1983a), 565–81.

—— (1983c) *Art, Myth and Ritual. The Path to Political Authority in Ancient China*, Cambridge, Mass. and London: Harvard University Press.

—— (1983d) 'Settlement patterns in Chinese archaeology: a case study from the Bronze Age', in E.Z. Vogt and R.M. Leventhal (eds) (1983), 361–74.

Chang, Te-Tzu (1983) 'The origins and early cultures of the cereal grains and food legumes', in D.N. Keightley (ed.) (1983a), 65–94.

Charvat, P. (1974) 'Pre-Sargonic Adab', *Archivi Orientalni* 43:161–6.

Childe, V.G. (1944) 'Archaeological ages as technological stages', Huxley Memorial Lecture, *Journal of the Royal Archaeological Institute* 74:7–24.

—— (1950) 'The urban revolution', *Town Planning Review* 21(1):3–17.

—— (1958) *The Prehistory of European Society*, London: Cassell.

—— (1965) *Man Makes Himself*, 4th edn, Glasgow: Collins.

—— (1974) 'The urban revolution', in J.A. Sabloff and C.C. Lamberg-Karlovsky (eds), *The Rise and Fall of Civilisations*, Menlo Park, Calif.: Cummings.

Chisholm, M. (1968) *Rural Settlement and Land Use: An Essay in Location*, London: Hutchinson.

Christenson, A.L. (1980a) 'Change in the human niche in response to population growth', in T.K. Earle and A.L. Christenson (eds) (1980), 31–72.

—— (1980b) 'Subsistence change: bibliographic overview', in T.K. Earle and A.L. Christenson (eds) (1980), 243–55.

Civil, M. (1976) 'The song of the ploughing oxen', in B.L. Eichler (ed.), 83–95.

Claesson, H.J.M. and Skalnik, P. (eds) (1978) *The Early State*, The Hague: Mouton.

Clark, G. (1952) *Prehistoric Europe: The Economic Basis*, London: Methuen.

—— (1960) *Archaeology and Society*, London: Methuen.

—— (1973) *Stone Age Hunters*, London: Book Club Associates.

—— (1976) 'Prehistory since Childe', The First Childe Memorial Lecture, *Bulletin of the Institute of Archaeology* 13:1–21.

—— (1980) *Mesolithic Prelude: The Palaeolithic-Neolithic Transition in Old World Prehistory*, Edinburgh: Edinburgh University Press.

Clark, W.E. Le Gros (1971) *The Antecedents of Man: An Introduction to the Evolution of the Primates*, 3rd edn, Edinburgh: Edinburgh University Press.

Clarke, D.L. (1976) 'Mesolithic Europe: the economic basis', in Sieveking *et al.* (eds), 449–81.

—— (1978) *Analytical Archaeology*, 2nd edn, London: Methuen (1st edn 1968).

Clarke, W.C. (1966) 'From extensive to shifting cultivation: a succession from New Guinea', *Ethnology* 5(4):347–59.

Clutton-Brock, J. (1978) 'Early domestication and the ungulate fauna of the Levant during the Prepottery Neolithic Period', in W.C. Brice (ed.), 29–40.

—— (1981) *Domesticated Animals from Early Times*, London: British Museum Natural History/Heinemann.

Clutton-Brock, J. and Grigson, C. (eds) (1984) *Animals and Archaeology. Vol. 3: Early Herders and their Flocks*, BAR International Series 202, Oxford.

Clutton-Brock, J. and Uerpmann, H.-P. (1974) 'The sheep of early Jericho', *Journal of Archaeological Science* 1(3):261–74.

Coale, A.J. (1975) 'The history of human population', in S.H. Katz (ed.), 459–69.

Cockburn, T.A. (1971) 'Infectious diseases in ancient populations', *Current Anthropology* 12:45–62.

Coe, M.D. (1961) 'Social typology and tropical forest civilisations', *Comparative Studies in Society and History* 4:65–85.

Cohen, M.N. (1975) 'Population pressure and the origins of agriculture. An archaeological example from the coast of Peru', in S. Polgar (ed.), 79–121.

—— (1977) *The Food Crisis in Prehistory: Overpopulation and the Origins of Agriculture*, New Haven: Yale University Press.

Cohen, M.N., Malpass, R.S., and Klein, H.G. (eds) (1980) *Biosocial Mechanisms of Population Regulation*, New Haven, Conn.: Yale University Press.

Cohen, R. and Middleton, J. (eds) (1967) *Comparative Political Systems: Studies in the Politics of Pre-Industrial Societies*, American Museum Sourcebooks in Anthropology Q4, New York: Natural History Press.

Cohen, R. and Service, E.R. (eds) (1978) *Origins of the State: The Anthropology of Political Evolution*, Philadelphia: Institute for the Study of Human Issues.

Colson, E. (1979) 'In good years and bad: food strategies of self-reliant societies', *Journal of Anthropological Research* 35:18–29.

Colson, E. and Gluckman, M. (eds) (1959) *Seven Tribes of British Central Africa*, corrected edn, Manchester: Manchester University Press.

Contenson, de H. (1971) 'Tell Ramad, a village of Syria of the 7th and 6th millennia B.C.', *Archaeology* 24(3):278–85.

—— (1979) 'Tell Aswad (Damascene)', *Paléorient* 5:153–6.

—— (1983) 'Early agriculture in western Asia', in T.C. Young *et al.* (eds), 57–74.

Coombs, H.C., Dexter, B.G., and Hiatt, L.R. (1982) 'The outstation movement in aboriginal Australia', in E. Leacock and R.B. Lee (eds) (1982a), 427–39.

Cooper, J.S. (1973) 'Sumerian and Akkadian in Sumer and Akkad', *Orientalia* 42:239–46.

—— (1983) *The Curse of Agade*, Baltimore: Johns Hopkins University Press.

Cooper, J.S. and Heimpel, W. (1983) 'The Sumerian Sargon legend', *Journal of the American Oriental Society* 103:67–82.

Copeland, L. (1979) 'Observations on the prehistory of the Balikh Valley, Syria, during the 7th to 4th millennia B.C.', *Paléorient* 5:251–75.

Copeland, L. and Hours, F. (1983) 'Les rapports entre l'Anatolie et la Syrie du nord à l'époque des premières communautés villageoises de bergers et de paysans (7,600–5,000 B.C.)', in T.C. Young *et al.* (eds), 75–90.

—— (1987) 'The Halafian, their predecessors and their contemporaries in northern Syria and the Levant: relative and absolute chronologies', in O. Aurenche *et al.* (eds), part ii, 401–25.

Cordell, L.S. and Beckerman, S.J. (eds) (1980) *The Versatility of Kinship*, New York: Academic Press.

Cotterell, A. (ed.) (1980) *The Encyclopedia of Ancient Civilisations*, New York: Mayflower Books.

Cowgill, G.L. (1975a) 'On causes and consequences of ancient and modern population changes', *American Anthropologist* 77:505–25.

—— (1975b) 'Population pressure as a non-explanation', *American Antiquity* 40(2):127–31.

Crawford, H.E.W. (1977) *The Architecture of Iraq in the Third Millennium B.C.*, *Mesopotamia* 5, Copenhagen Studies in Assyriology, Copenhagen: Akademisk Forlag.

—— (1978) 'The mechanics of the obsidian trade', *Antiquity* 205:129–32.

Crawford, V.E. (1954) *Sumerian Economic Texts from the First Dynasty of Isin*, New Haven, Conn.: Yale University Press.

Crumley, C.L. (1976) 'Toward a locational definition of state systems of settlement', *American Anthropologist* 78:59–73.

Curtis, J. (ed.) (1982) *Fifty Years of Mesopotamian Discovery: The Work of the British School of Archaeology in Iraq*, London: British School of Archaeology in Iraq.

Dahlberg, F. (1976) 'More on mechanisms of population growth', *Current Anthropology* 17:164–6.

Dalton, G. (ed.) (1967) *Tribal and Peasant Economies: Readings in Economic*

Anthropology, American Museum Sourcebook in Anthropology Q2, New York: Natural History Press.

—— (ed.) (1971) *Studies in Economic Anthropology*, Washington: American Anthropological Association.

—— (1977) 'Aboriginal economies in stateless societies', in T.K. Earle and J.E. Ericson (eds), 191–212.

—— (1981) 'Anthropological models in archaeological perspective', in I.R. Hodder *et al.* (eds), 17–48.

Dandamayev, M.A. (1979) 'State and temple in Babylonia in the first millennium B.C., in *State and Temple in the Ancient Near East II*, (ed.) E. Lipinski, 589–96.

—— (1982) 'The Neo-Babylonian elders', in M.A. Dandamayev *et al.* (eds), 38–41.

Dandamayev, M.A., Gershevitch, I., Klengel, H., Komoroczy, G., Larsen, M.T., and Postgate, J.N. (eds) (1982) *Societies and Languages of the Ancient, Near East. Studies in Honor of I.M. Diakonoff*, Warminster: Aris & Phillips.

Daniel, G. (1964) *The Idea of Prehistory*, Harmondsworth: Penguin.

—— (1968) 'One hundred years of old world prehistory', in J.O. Brew (ed.), 57–93.

Davidson, T.E. (1977) 'Regional variation within the Halaf ceramic tradition', unpublished PhD thesis, University of Edinburgh.

Davidson, T.E. and McKerrell, H. (1976) 'Pottery analysis and Halaf period trade in the Khabur headwaters region', *Iraq* 38:45–56.

Davis, P.H., Harper, P.C., and Hedge, I.C. (eds) (1971) *Plant Life of South West Asia*, Edinburgh: Botanical Society of Edinburgh.

Delougaz, P. (1938) 'A short investigation of the temple at Tell al-Ubaid', *Iraq* 5:1–11.

—— (1940) *The Temple Oval at Khafajah*, Chicago: University of Chicago Press.

Denham, W.D. (1974) 'Population structure, infant transport, and infanticide among Pleistocene and modern hunter-gatherers', *Journal of Anthropological Research* 30:191–8.

Diakonoff, I.M. (1954) 'Sale of land in Pre-Sargonic Sumer', Moscow: Papers presented by the Soviet Delegation to the 23rd International Congress of Orientalists.

—— (1969a) (ed.) *Ancient Mesopotamia: A Socio-Economic History. A Collection of Studies by Soviet Scholars*, Moscow: Nauka Publishing House.

—— (1969b) 'Editor's Preface', in I.M. Diakonoff (1969a), 8–16.

—— (1969c) 'The rise of the despotic state in ancient Mesopotamia', in I.M. Diakonoff (ed.) (1969a), 173–203.

—— (1971) 'On the structure of Old Babylonian society', in H. Klengel (ed.), 15–31.

—— (1972) 'Socio-economic classes in Babylonia and the Babylonian concept of social stratification', in D.O. Edzard (ed.), 41–52.

—— (1974) *Structure of Society and State in Early Dynastic Sumer*, summary and translation of selected passages by the author, Monographs on the Ancient Near East I, fascicle 3, Malibu, Calif.: Undena.

—— (1975) 'The rural community in the ancient Near East', IVth International Congress on Economic History, Copenhagen 1974, *Journal of Economic and Social History of the Orient* 18:121–33.

—— (1976–7) 'Slaves, helots and serfs in early antiquity', *Soviet Anthropology and Archaeology* 15:50–102.

—— (1982) 'The structure of Near Eastern society before the middle of the 2nd millennium B.C.', *Oikumene* 3:1–100. Budapest: Akademiai Kiado.

—— (1985) 'Extended families in Old Babylonian Ur', *Zeitschrift für Assyriologie und verwandte Gebiete* 75(1):47–65.

Diamond, S. (ed.) (1979) *Toward a Marxist Anthropology: Problems and Perspectives*, The Hague: Mouton.

Dickeman, M. (1975) 'Demographic consequences of infanticide in man', *Annual Review of Ecology and Systematics* 6:107–37.

Divale, W.T. (1972–3) 'Systematic population control in the Middle and Upper Palaeolithic: inferences based on contemporary hunter-gatherers', *World Archaeology* 4:222–37.

Dixon, J.E., Cann, J.R., and Renfrew, A.C. (1979) 'Obsidian and the origins of trade', in C.C. Lamberg-Karlovsky (ed.), 108–16.

Dollfus, G. (1983) 'Rémarques sur l'organisation de l'espace dans quelques agglomérations de la Susiane du Ve millénaire', in T.C. Young *et al.* (eds), 283–314.

Douglas, Mary (ed.) (1973) *Rules and Meanings*, Harmondsworth: Penguin.

Drekmeier, C. (1962) *Kingship and Community in Early India*, Stanford, Calif.: Stanford University Press.

Driver, G.R. and Miles, J.C. (1952–5) *The Babylonian Laws, I: Commentary, II: Text*, Oxford: Clarendon Press.

Ducos, P. (1969) 'Methodology and results of the study of the earliest domesticated animals in the Near East (Palestine)', in P.J. Ucko *et al.* (eds), 265–75.

—— (1970) 'The Oriental Institute Excavations at Mureybit, Syria: preliminary report on the 1965 campaign. Part IV: Les Restes d'Equidés', *Journal of Near Eastern Studies* 29(4):273–89.

Dumond, D.E. (1961) 'Swidden agriculture and the rise of Maya civilisation', *Southwestern Journal of Anthropology* 17(4):301–16.

—— (1965) 'Population growth and cultural change', *Southwestern Journal of Anthropology* 21(4):302–24.

—— (1970) 'Competition, cooperation, and the folk society', *Southwestern Journal of Anthropology* 26:261–86.

—— (1975) 'The limitation of human population: a natural history', *Science* 187:713–21.

—— (1976a) 'Response to Zubrow', *American Anthropologist* 78:896.

—— (1976b) 'Review of Zubrow', *American Anthropologist* 78:710–11.

Dunnell, R.C. and Wenke, R.J. (1980) 'Cultural and scientific evolution: some comments on "The Decline and Rise of Mesopotamian Civilisation" ', *American Antiquity* 45(3):605–9.

Durkheim, E. (1964) *The Division of Labour in Society*, New York: Free Press.

Earle, T.K. (1977a) *Economic and Social Organisation of a Complex Chiefdom*, Ann Arbor: University of Michigan.

—— (1977b) 'A reappraisal of redistribution: complex Hawaiian chiefdoms', in T.K. Earle and J.E. Ericson (eds), 213–29.

—— (1980) 'A model of subsistence change', in T.K. Earle and A.L. Christenson (eds), 1–29.

Earle, T.K, and Christenson, A.L. (eds) (1980) *Modelling Change in Pre-Historic Subsistence Economies*, New York: Academic Press.

Earle, T.K. and Ericson, J.E. (eds) (1977) *Exchange Systems in Prehistory*. London: Academic Press.

Eckholm, K. and Friedman, J. (1981) 'Comment on R.N. Adams, "Natural selection, energetics and 'cultural materialism' " ', *Current Anthropology* 22(6):616–17.

Edelberg, L. (1966–7) 'Seasonal dwellings of farmers in north-western Luristan', *Folk* 8–9:373–401.

Edmondson, M.S. (1961) 'Neolithic diffusion rates', *Current Anthropology* 2:21–102.

Edzard, D.O. (1957) *Die 'Zweite Zwischenzeit' Babyloniens*, Wiesbaden: Harrossowitz.

—— (1959–60) 'Enmebaragesi von Kiš', *Zeitschrift für Assyriologie N.F.* 19:9–26.

—— (ed.) (1972) *Gesellschaftsklassen im Alten Zweistromland und in dem angrenzenden Gebieten*, Munich: *XVIII Rencontre Assyriologique Internationale*.

—— (1974a) 'Problèmes de la royauté dans la Période Présargonique', *Rencontre Assyriologique Internationale* 29:143–9.

—— (1974b) 'History of Mesopotamia and Iraq', *Encyclopaedia Britannica* 11:1963–79.

Eichler, B.L. (1973) *Indenture at Nuzi: The Personal Tidennutu Contract and its Mesopotamian Analogues*, Yale Near East Researches no.5, New Haven, Conn.: Yale University Press.

—— (ed.) (1976) *Cuneiform Studies in Honour of S.N. Kramer*, Neukirchen-Vluyn: Verlag Butzon & Becker, Neukirchener Verlag.

Eisenstadt, S.N. (1965) *Essays on Comparative Institutions*, New York: John Wiley & Sons.

Ellis, Maria de J. (1976) *Agriculture and the State in Ancient Mesopotamia: An Introduction to the Problems of Land Tenure*, Philadelphia: Occasional Publications of the Babylonian Fund no.1.

Ellison, Rosemary (1978) 'A study of diet in Mesopotamia (*c.* 3000–600 B.C.) and associated techniques and methods of food production', unpublished thesis, University of London.

—— (1981) 'Diet in Mesopotamia: the evidence of the Ration Texts (*c.* 3000 B.C.–1400 B.C.)', *Iraq* 43:35–43.

—— (1983) 'Some thoughts on the diet of Mesopotamia from *c.* 3000–600 B.C.', *Iraq* 45(1):146–50.

Ellison, R., Renfrew, J., Brothwell, D., and Seeley, N. (1978) 'Some food offerings from Ur, excavated by Sir Leonard Woolley, and previously unpublished', *Journal of Archaeological Science* 5(2):167–77.

El-Waïlly, F. and Abu es-Soof, B. (1965) 'The excavations at Tell es-Sawwan. First preliminary report', *Sumer* 21:17–32.

Ember, C.R., Ember, M., and Pasternak, B. (1974) 'On the development of unilineal descent', *Journal of Anthropological Research* 30(2):69–94.

Engelbrecht, W. (1987) 'Low population density among prehistoric Iroquois', *American Antiquity* 52(1):13–27.

Engels, F. (1884) *Origin of the Family, Private Property and the State*, 1940 edn, London: Lawrence & Wishart.

Erasmus, C.J. (1955) 'Changing folk beliefs and the relativity of empirical knowledge', *Southwestern Journal of Anthropology* 8:411–28.

Erinç, S. (1980) 'Human ecology in south east Anatolia', in H. Çambel and R T Braidwood (eds), 73 80.

Evans, G. (1958) 'Ancient Mesopotamian assemblies', *Journal of the American Oriental Society* 78:1–11 and 114–15.

Evans, J.D. (1971) 'Neolithic Knossos: the growth of a settlement', *Proceedings of the Prehistoric Society* 37(2):95–117.

Evans-Pritchard, E.E. (1940) *The Nuer*, Oxford: Clarendon Press.

—— (1951) *Social Anthropology*, London: Cohen & West.

—— (1981) *A History of Anthropological Thought*, ed. A. Singer, London and Boston: Faber & Faber.

Fagan, B.M. (ed.) (1976) *Avenues to Antiquity. Readings from 'Scientific American'*, San Francisco: W.H. Freeman.

Fairbank, J.K., Reischauer, E.O., and Craig, A.M. (1973) *East Asia: Tradition and Transformation*, London: Allen & Unwin.

Falkenstein, A. (1979) *The Sumerian Temple City. Monographs of the Ancient Near East I*, fascicle I, Malibu, Calif.: Undena.

Faris, J.C. (1979) 'Social evolution, population, and production', in S. Diamond (ed.), 421–55.

Fernea, R.A. (1970) *Shaykh and Effendi: Changing Patterns of Authority Among the Shabara of Southern Iraq*, Cambridge, Mass.: Harvard University Press.

Ferrara, A.J. (1973) *Nanna-Suen's Journey to Nippur*, Rome: Biblical Institute Press.

Finegan, J. (1979) *Archaeological History of the Ancient Middle East*. Boulder, Col.: Westview Press.

Finkelstein, J.J. (1963) 'The antedeluvian kings: a University of California tablet', *Journal of Cuneiform Studies* 17:39–51.

—— (1970) 'On some recent studies in cuneiform law', Review article, *Journal of the American Oriental Society* 90(2):243–56.

—— (1974) 'The West, the Bible and the ancient east: apperceptions and categorisations', *Man* 9(4):591–608.

—— (1975a) 'Laws of Mesopotamia', in J.B. Pritchard (ed.) (1975), 31–41.

—— (1975b) 'Mesopotamian legal documents', in J.B. Pritchard (ed.) (1975), 70–82.

Finkelstein, J.J. and Greenberg, M. (eds) (1967) *Oriental and Biblical Studies. Collected Writings of E.A. Speiser*, Philadelphia: University of Pennsylvania Press.

Finley, M.I. (1962) *The World of Odysseus*, Harmondsworth: Penguin.

—— (1973) *The Ancient Economy*, London: Chatto & Windus.

—— (1977) *Aspects of Antiquity: Discoveries and Controversies*, 2nd edn, Harmondsworth: Penguin.

—— (ed.) (1978) *Studies in Ancient Society*, Past and Present Series, London: Routledge & Kegan Paul.

—— (1981) *Early Greece: The Bronze and Archaic Ages*, 2nd edn, London: Chatto & Windus.

—— (1983a) *Ancient Slavery and Modern Ideology*, Harmondsworth: Penguin.

—— (1983b) *Economy and Society in Ancient Greece*, ed. R.P. Saller and B.D. Shaw, London: Chatto & Windus.

—— (1983c) *Politics in the Ancient World*, Cambridge: Cambridge University Press.

Flannery, K.V. (1965) 'The ecology of early food production in Mesopotamia', *Science* 147:1247–56.

—— (1969) 'Origins and ecological effects of early domestication in Iran and the Near East', in P.J. Ucko and G.W. Dimbleby (eds), 72–100.

—— (1971) 'Archaeological systems theory and early Mesopotamia', in S. Streuver (ed.), 80–100.

—— (1972a) 'The cultural evolution of civilisations', *Annual Review of Ecology and Systematics* 3:399–426.

—— (1972b) 'The origins of the village as a settlement type in Mesoamerica and the Near East: a comparative study', in P.J. Ucko *et al.* (eds), 23–53.

—— (1973) 'The origins of agriculture', *Annual Review of Anthropology* 2:271–310.

—— (1983) 'Early pig domestication in the Fertile Crescent: A retrospective look', in T.C. Young et al. (eds), 163–88.

Flannery, K.V. and Wheeler, J.C. (1967) 'Animal bones from Tell es-Sawwan, Level III (Samarra Period)', *Sumer* 23:179–82.

Flannery, K.V. and Wright, H.T. (1966) 'Faunal remains from the "hut sounding" at Eridu, Iraq', *Sumer* 22:61–3.

Flew, A. (ed.) (1970) Thomas Robert Malthus, *An Essay on the Principle of Population*, Harmondsworth: Penguin.

Fogg, W.H. (1983) 'Swidden cultivation of foxtail millet by Taiwanese Aborigines: a cultural analogue of the domestication of *Setaria italica* in China', in D.N. Keightley (ed.), 95–115.

Foley, R. (1981) 'Off-site archaeology: an alternative approach for the short-sited', in I.R. Hodder et al. (eds), 157–83.

Forde, C.D. (1934) *Habitat, Economy and Society: A Geographical Introduction to Ethnology*, London: Methuen.

Forest, C. (1980) 'Rapport sur les fouilles de Kheit Qasim III – Hamrin', *Paléorient* 6:221–4.

—— (1984) 'Kheit Qasim III: The Obeid settlement', *Sumer* 40:(1–2):119–21.

Forest, J.D. (1983) 'The Obeid 4 architecture', *Sumer* 39:20–3.

—— (1984) 'Kheit Qasim III – an Obeid settlement', *Sumer* 40:85.

Forge, A. (1972) 'Normative factors in the settlement size of Neolithic cultivators (New Guinea)', in P.J. Ucko et al. (eds), 363–76.

Forrest, W.G. (1966) *The Emergence of Greek Democracy: The Character of Greek Politics, 800–400 B.C.*, London: Weidenfeld & Nicolson.

Fortes, M. (1959) 'Descent, filiation and affinity: a rejoinder to Dr. Leach', *Man* 59:193–7 and 206–12.

—— (1962) 'Ritual and office in tribal society', in M. Gluckman (ed.), 53–88.

—— (1965) 'Some reflections on ancestor worship in Africa', in M. Fortes and G. Dieterlen (eds), 122–44.

—— (1966) *Totem and Taboo*, Presidential Address 1966, Faculty of Archaeology and Anthropology, Cambridge.

—— (1969) *Kinship and Social Order: The Legacy of Lewis Henry Morgan*, London: Routledge & Kegan Paul.

—— (1970) *Time and Social Structure and Other Essays*, LSE Monographs on Social Anthropology no.40, London: Athlone Press.

—— (1972) 'Kinship and the social order: the legacy of L.H. Morgan', Book Review, *Current Anthropology* 13(2):285–7 and 293–6.

—— (1983) *Rules and the Emergence of Society*, RAI Occasional Paper no. 39.

Fortes, M. and Dieterlen, G. (eds) (1965) *African Systems of Thought*, Oxford: Oxford University Press.

Fortes, M. and Evans-Pritchard, E.E. (1940) *African Political Systems*, Oxford: Oxford University Press.

Foster, B.R. (1977) 'Commercial activity in Sargonic Mesopotamia', *Iraq* 13:31–43.

—— (1982a) 'Archives and record-keeping in Sargonic Mesopotamia', *Zeitschrift für Assyriologie* 72(1):1–27.

—— (1982b) *Umma in the Sargonic Period*, Memoirs of the Connecticut Academy of Arts and Sciences no.20.

—— (1982c) *Administration and Use of Institutional Land in Sargonic Sumer, Mesopotamia* 9, Copenhagen Studies in Assyriology, Copenhagen: Akademisk Forlag.

Frankfort, H. (1956) *The Birth of Civilisation in the Near East*, New York: Doubleday.

—— (1970) *The Art and Architecture of the Ancient Orient*, Pelican History of Art Series, Harmondsworth: Penguin.

—— (1978) *Kingship and the Gods: A Study of Ancient Near Eastern Religion as the Integration of Society and Nature*, Chicago: University of Chicago Press.

Frankfort, H., Frankfort, H.A., Wilson, J., and Jacobsen, T. (1949) *Before Philosophy: The Intellectual Adventure of Ancient Man*, Harmondsworth: Penguin.

Frankfort, H., Jacobsen, T., and Lloyd, S. (1940) *The Gimilsin Temple and the Palace of the Rulers at Tell Asmar*, Oriental Institute Publications no.43, Chicago: Oriental Institute of the University of Chicago.

Frayne, D. (1983) 'Šulgi, the runner', *Journal of the American Oriental Society* 103(4):739–48.

Frederiksen, M.W. (1969) 'Towns and houses', in J.P.V.D. Balsdon (ed.), 151–68.

Freeman, J.D. (1968) 'On the concept of kindred', in P. Bohannan and J. Middleton (eds), 255–72.

Freeman, L.C. and Winch, R.F. (1957) 'Societal complexity: an empirical test of a typology of societies', *American Journal of Sociology* 62:461–6.

Freeman, M. (1971) 'A social and economic analysis of systematic female infanticide', *American Anthropologist* 73:1011–18.

Frend, W.H.C. (1978) 'The failure of the persecutions in the Roman Empire', in M.I. Finley (ed.), 263–87.

Fried, M.H. (ed.) (1959) *Readings in Anthropology*, 2 vols, New York: Thomas Crowell.

—— (1967) *The Evolution of Political Society: an Essay in Political Anthropology*, New York: Random House.

—— (1978) 'The state, the chicken and the egg: or what came first', in R. Cohen and E.R. Service (eds), 35–48.

—— (1983) 'Tribe to state or state to tribe in Ancient China?', in D.N. Keightley (ed.) (1983a), 467–93.

Friedman, J. (1974) 'Marxism, structuralism and vulgar materialism', *Man* (n.s.) 9(4):444–69.

—— (1975) 'Tribes, states and transformations', in M. Bloch (1975a), 161–202.

—— (1979) *System, Structure and Contradiction in the Evolution of 'Asiatic' Social Formations*, Social Studies in Oceania and S.E. Asia no.2, Copenhagen: National Museum of Denmark.

Friedman, J. and Rowlands, M.J. (eds) (1977a) *The Evolution of Social Systems*, London: Duckworth.

—— (1977b) 'Notes towards an epigenetic model of the evolution of "civilisation" ', in J. Friedman and M.J. Rowlands (1977a), 201–6.

Frisch, R. and McArthur, J. (1974) 'Menstrual cycles: fatness as a determinant of minimum weight for height etc.', *Science* 185:949–51.

Fritz, Volkmar (1987) 'Conquest or settlement: the Early Iron Age in Palestine', *Biblical Archaeologist* 50(2):84–100.

Gamble, C. (1982) 'Leadership and "surplus" production', in Colin Renfrew and S. Shennan (eds), 100–5.

Gandara, M. (1987) 'Observations about the theoretical term "Archaic State" ', in L. Manzanilla (ed.), 209–16.

Garfinkel, Y. (1987) 'Burnt lime products and social implications in the Pre-Pottery B Neolithic villages of the Near East', *Paléorient* 13(1):69–76.

Garlan, Y. (1969) *War in the Ancient World: A Social History*, London: Chatto & Windus.

Garrod, Dorothy A.E. (1957) 'The Natufian culture: the life and economy of a Mesolithic people in the Near East', *Proceedings of the British Academy* 43:211–27.

Garrod, D.A.E. and Bate, D. (1937) *The Stone Age of Mt Carmel: Excavations at the Wadi Mughara*, vol.1, Oxford: Clarendon Press.

Gatlin, L.L. (1972) *Information Theory and the Living System*, New York and London: Columbia University Press.

Geertz, C. (1963) *Agricultural Involution: The Process of Ecological Change in Indonesia*, Berkeley, Calif.: University of California Press.

Gelb, I.J. (1961) *Old Akkadian Writing and Grammar*, 2nd edn, revised and enlarged, Chicago: University of Chicago Press.

—— (1963) *A Study of Writing*, Berkeley: University of California Press.

—— (1965) 'The ancient Mesopotamian ration system', *Journal of Near Eastern Studies* 24:230–43.

—— (1967a) 'Approaches to the study of ancient society', *Journal of the American Oriental Society* 87:1–8.

—— (1967b) 'Growth of a herd of cattle in ten years', *Journal of Cuneiform Studies* 21:64–9.

—— (1969) 'On the alleged temple and state economies in ancient Mesopotamia', in *Studi in Onore di Eduardo Volterra 6*, Rome: Guiffre Editore, 137–54.

—— (1972) 'The Arua institution', *Revue d'assyriologie et d'archéologie orientale* 66:1–38.

—— (1973) 'Prisoners of war in early Mesopotamia', *Journal of Near Eastern Studies* 32:70–98.

—— (1976) 'Quantitative evaluation of slavery and serfdom', in B.L. Eichler (ed.), 195–207.

—— (1979) 'Household and family in ancient Mesopotamia', in E Lipinski (ed.), *State and Temple Economy in the Ancient Near East I*, 1–98.

—— (1982) 'Terms for slaves in ancient Mesopotamia', in M.A. Dandamayev *et al.* (eds), 81–95.

Geller, M.J. (1985) *Forerunners to Udug-Hul: Sumerian Exorcistic Incantations*, Stuttgart: Franz Steiner Verlag Wiesbaden.

Gellner, E. (ed.) (1980) *Soviet and Western Anthropology*, London: Duckworth.

Gibson, McG. (1982) 'A re-evaluation of the Akkad Period in the Diyala region on the basis of recent excavations at Nippur and in the Hamrin', *American Journal of Archaeology* 86(4):531–8.

Gibson, McG. and Biggs, R.D. (eds) (1977) *Seals and Sealing in the Ancient Near East*, Bibliotheca Mesopotamia, vol.6, Malibu, Calif.: Undena.

Gibson, McG. and Downing, T. (1974) *Irrigation's Impact on Society*, Tucson, Arizona: University of Arizona Press.

Gilbert, A.S. (1983) 'On the origins of specialised nomadic pastoralism in Western Iran', *World Archaeology* 15(1):105–19.

Glass, D.V. 'Introduction' to 1953 edn of Thomas Robert Malthus, *An Essay on the Principle of Population*, London: Watts.

Glotz, G. (1929) *The Greek City and Its Institutions*, London: Kegan Paul, Trench, Trubner & Co.

Gluckman, M. (1959) 'The Lozi of Barotseland in north-western Rhodesia', in E. Colson and M. Gluckman (eds), 1–93.

—— (ed.) (1962) *Essays on the Ritual of Social Relations*, Manchester: Manchester University Press.

Godelier, M. (1977) *Perspectives in Marxist Anthropology*, trans. Robert Brain, Cambridge: Cambridge University Press.

—— (1978a) 'The concept of the "Asiatic Mode of Production" and Marxist models of social evolution', in D. Seddon (ed.), 207–57.

—— (1978b) 'Infrastructures, societies, and history', *Current Anthropology* 19(4):763–71.

—— (1979a) 'Epistemological comments on the problems of comparing modes of production and societies', in S. Diamond (ed.), 71–92.

—— (1979b) 'On infrastructures, societies and history: reply', *Current Anthropology* 20(1):108–11.

—— (1980) 'The emergence and development of Marxism in anthropology in France', in E. Gellner (ed.), 3–17.

Goetze, A. (1962) 'Two Ur-Dynasty tablets dealing with labor', *Journal of Cuneiform Studies* 16:13–16.

—— (1963) 'Sakkanakkus of the Ur III empire', *Journal of Cuneiform Studies* 17:1–31.

Gonen, R. (1975) *Weapons of the Ancient World*, London: Cassell.

Goodenough, W.H. (1956) 'Residence rules', *Southwestern Journal of Anthropology* 12:22–37.

—— (1968) 'A problem in Malayo-Polynesian social organisation', in A.P. Vayda (ed.), 133–49.

—— (1970) *Description and Comparison in Cultural Anthropology*, The Lewis Henry Morgan Lectures for 1968, Cambridge: Cambridge University Press.

Goody, J. (ed.) (1958) *The Developmental Cycle in Domestic Groups*, Cambridge Papers in Social Anthropology no.1, Cambridge: Cambridge University Press.

—— (ed.) (1973) *The Character of Kinship*, Cambridge: Cambridge University Press.

—— (1976) *Production and Reproduction: A Comparative Study of the Domestic Domain*, Cambridge Studies in Social Anthropology no.17, Cambridge: Cambridge University Press.

—— (1977) 'Population and polity in the Voltaic Region', in J. Friedman and M.J. Rowlands (eds) (1977a), 535–45.

—— (1980) *Technology, Tradition and the State in Africa*, London: Hutchinson.

Goring-Morris, A.N. and Bar-Yosef, O. (1987) 'A late Natufian campsite from the western Negev, Israel', *Paléorient* 13(1):107–13.

Gough, K. (1971) 'Nuer kinship: a re-examination', in Beidelman (ed.), 79–121.

Gould, P.R. (1963) 'Man against his environment: a game theoretic framework', *Annals of the Association of American Geographers* 53:290–7.

Gould, R.A. (ed.) (1978a) *Explorations in Ethnoarchaeology*, School of American Research Advanced Seminar Series, Albuquerque: University of New Mexico Press.

—— (1978b) 'From Tasmania to Tucson: new directions in ethnoarchaeology', in R.A. Gould (1978a), 1–10.

—— (1980) *Living Archaeology*, New Studies in Archaeology, Cambridge: Cambridge University Press.

Gouldner, A.W. and Peterson, R.A. (1962) *Notes on Technology and the Moral Order*, Indianapolis: Bobbs-Merrill.

Gourou, P. (1971) *The Tropical World*, London: Longman.

Graham, J.W. (1979) *The Palaces of Crete*, Princeton, N.J.: Princeton University Press.

Gray, J. (1964) *The Canaanites*, London: Thames & Hudson.

Grayson, A.K. (1970) 'Chronicles and the Akitu festival', *Rencontre Assyriologique Internationale* 17:160–70.

Greeley, A.M. (1982) *Religion: A Secular Theory*, New York: Free Press.

Green, M.W. (1980) 'Animal husbandry at Uruk in the Archaic Period', *Journal of Near Eastern Studies* 39(1):1–19.

Greengus, S. (1969) 'The Old Babylonian marriage contract', *Journal of the American Oriental Society* 89:505–32.

Grigg, D. (1970) *The Harsh Lands: A Study in Agricultural Development*, London: Macmillan.

Gurney, O.R. and Kramer, S.N. (1976) *Oxford Editions of Cuneiform Texts*, vol.V, Oxford: Oxford University Press.

Guterbock, H.G. and Jacobsen, T. (1965) *Studies in Honour of Berno Landsberger on his Seventy-fifth Birthday*, Assyriological Studies no.16, Chicago: University of Chicago Press.

Haas, J. (1982) *The Evolution of the Prehistoric State*, New York: Columbia University Press.

Haggett, Peter (1972) *Geography: A Modern Synthesis*, New York: Harper & Row.

Hallo, W.W. (1963a) 'Critical review of W.F. Leemans: "Foreign trade in the Old Babylonian Period as revealed by texts from Southern Mesopotamia" ', *Journal of Cuneiform Studies* 17:59–60.

—— (1963b) *Early Mesopotamian Royal Titles: A Philologic and Historical Analysis*, American Oriental Series, vol.43, New Haven, Conn.: Yale University Press.

—— (1963c) 'Royal hymns and Mesopotamian unity', *Journal of Cuneiform Studies* 17:112–18.

—— (1963d) 'On the antiquity of Sumerian literature', *Journal of the American Oriental Society* 83(2):167–76.

—— (ed.) (1968) *Essays in Memory of E.A. Speiser*, New Haven: American Oriental Society.

—— (1970) 'Antedeluvian cities', *Journal of Cuneiform Studies* 23:57–67.

—— (1973) 'The date of the Fara Period: a case study in the historiography of early Mesopotamia', *Orientalia* 42:228–38.

—— (1976) 'Toward a history of Sumerian literature', in S.J. Lieberman (ed.), 181–203.

—— (1977) 'Seals lost and found', in McG. Gibson and R.D. Biggs (eds), 55–60.

—— (1979) 'God, king and man at Yale', in E. Lipinsky (ed.), I, 99–111.

Hallo, W.W. and Simpson, W.K. (1971) *The Ancient Near East: A History*, New York: Harcourt-Brace.

Halstead, Paul (1981a) 'Counting sheep in Neolithic and Bronze Age Greece', in I.R. Hodder *et al.* (eds) (1981), 307–39.

—— (1981b) 'From determinism to uncertainty: social storage and the rise of the Minoan Palace', in A. Sheridan and G. Bailey (eds), 187–213.

Halstead, P. and O'Shea, J. (1982) 'A friend in need is a friend indeed: social storage and the origins of social ranking', in Colin Renfrew and S.J. Shennan (eds), 92–9.

Hammond, Norman (ed.) (1974) *Mesoamerican Archaeology: New Approaches*, London: Duckworth.

—— (1986) 'The emergence of Maya civilisation', *Scientific American* 255: 98–107.

Hammond, P.B. (ed.) (1964) *Cultural and Social Anthropology: Selected Readings*, New York: Macmillan.

Handwerker, W. Penn (1983) 'The first demographic transition: an analysis of subsistence choices and reproductive consequences', *American Anthropologist* 85:5–27.

Hansman, J. (1973) 'A periplus of Magan and Meluhha', *Bulletin of the School of Oriental and African Studies* 36:554–87.

Hardin, G. (1960) 'The comparative exclusion principle', *Science* 131:1292–7.

Harding, Thomas G. (1967) *Voyagers of the Vitiaz Strait: A Study of a New Guinea Trade System*, Seattle: University of Washington Press.

Harlan, J.R. (1967) 'A wild wheat harvest in Turkey', *Archaeology* 20:197–201.

—— (1975) *Crops and Man*, Madison, Wisc.: American School of Agronomy/Crop Science Society of America.

—— (1977) 'The origins of cereal agriculture in the Old World', in C.A. Reed (ed.), 357–83.

—— (1982) 'The Garden of the Lord: a plausible reconstruction of natural resources of southern Jordan in the Early Bronze Age', *Paléorient* 8(1):71–7.

Harlan, J.R. and Zohary, D. (1966) 'Distribution of wild wheats and barley', *Science* 153:1074–80.

Harner, M.J. (1970) 'Population pressure and the social evolution of agriculturalists', *Southwestern Journal of Anthropology* 27:67–86.

—— (1975) 'Scarcity, the factors of production and social evolution', in S. Polgar (ed.), 123–38.

Harris, D.R. (1969) 'Agricultural systems, ecosystems and the origins of agriculture', in P.J. Ucko and G.W. Dimbleby (eds), 3–15.

—— (1977) 'Settling down: an evolutionary model for the transformation of mobile bands into sedentary communities', in J. Friedman and M.J. Rowlands (eds) (1977a), 401–17.

Harris, M. (1959) 'The economy has no surplus?', *American Anthropologist* 61:185–99.

—— (1971) *Culture, Man and Nature*, New York: Thomas Y. Crowell.

—— (1975) *Cows, Pigs, Wars and Witches*, London: Fontana.

—— (1978) *Cannibals and Kings: The Origins of Cultures*, London: Fontana.

Harris, R. (1975) *Ancient Sippar: A Demographic Study of an Old Babylonian City, 1894–1595 B.C.*, Istanbul: Uitgaven van het Nederlands Historisch Archeol. Instituut.

—— (1976) 'On kinship and inheritance in Old Babylonian Sippar', *Iraq* 38:129–32.

Hassan, F.A. (1973) 'On mechanisms of population growth during the Neolithic', *Current Anthropology* 14(5):535–42.

—— (1975) 'Determination of size, density and growth rate of hunting-gathering populations', in S. Polgar (ed.), 27–52.

—— (1979) 'Demography and archaeology', *Annual Review of Anthropology* 8:137–60.

—— (1981) *Demographic Archaeology*, New York: Academic Press.

Hassan, F.A. and Robinson, S.W. (1987) 'High precision radiocarbon chronometry of Ancient Egypt, and comparisons with Nubia, Palestine and Mesopotamia', *Antiquity* 61:119–35.

Haviland, W.A. (1970) 'Tikal, Guatemala and Mesoamerican urbanism', *World Archaeology* 2:186–98.

Hawkes, C. (1954) 'Archaeological theory and method: some suggestions from the Old World', *American Anthropologist* 56:155–68.

Hawkes, J. (1974) *Atlas of Ancient Archaeology*, London: Heinemann.

Hawkes, J.G. (1969) 'The ecological background of plant domestication', in P.J. Ucko and G.W. Dimbleby (eds), 17–29.

Hawkins, D. (1979) 'The origin and dissemination of writing in western Asia', in P.R.S. Moorey (ed.), 128–65.

Hayden, B. (1981) 'Research and development in the Stone Age: technological transitions among hunter-gatherers', *Current Anthropology* 22(5):519–48.

Hecker, H.M. (1975) 'The faunal analysis of the primary food animals from Pre-Pottery Neolithic Beidha', PhD thesis, Faculty of Political Science, Columbia University, New York.

Heidel, A. (1963) *The Babylonian Genesis: The Story of Creation*, 2nd edn, Chicago: University of Chicago Press.

Heizer, R.F. (1960) 'Agriculture and the theocratic state in lowland southeastern Mexico', *American Antiquity* 26(2):215–22.

Helbaek, H. (1965) 'Early Hassunan vegetable food at Tell es-Sawwan near Samarra', *Sumer* 20:45–8.

—— (1966) 'Pre-Pottery Neolithic farming at Beidha', *Palestine Exploration Quarterly* 98:61–6.

—— (1969) 'Plant collecting, dry-farming and irrigation agriculture in prehistoric Deh Luran', in F. Hole *et al.* (eds), 383–426.

—— (1971) 'The origin and migration of rye, *Secale cereale L.*: a Palaeo-ethnobotanical study', in P.H. Davis *et al.* (eds), 265–80.

Henry, D.O. (1973) 'The Natufian of Palestine: its culture and ecology', unpublished PhD thesis, Southern Methodist University, Dallas.

—— (1975) 'The fauna in Near Eastern archaeological deposits', in F. Wendorf and A.E. Marks (eds), 379–85.

Henry, D.O., Leroi-Gourhan, A., and Davis, S. (1981) 'The excavation of Hayonim Terrace: an examination of terminal Pleistocene climatic and adaptive changes', *Journal of Archaeological Science* 8(1):33–58.

Herre, W. and Rohrs, M. (1977) 'Zoological considerations on the origins of farming and domestication', in C.A. Reed (ed.), 245–79.

Herrmann, G. (1968) 'Lapis Lazuli: the early phases of its trade', *Iraq* 30:21–57.

Hesiod (1973), *Hesiod and Theognis*, trans. D. Wender, Harmondsworth: Penguin.

Hesse, B. (1982) 'Slaughter patterns and domestication: the beginnings of pastoralism in western Iran', *Man* 17:403–17.

—— (1984) 'These are our goats: the origins of herding in west central Iran', in Clutton-Brock and Grigson (eds), 243–64.

Hiatt, B. (1967–8) 'The food quest and the economy of the Tasmanian aborigines', *Oceania* 38:99–133 and 190–219.

Higgs, E.S. (ed.) (1972) *Papers in Economic Prehistory: Studies by Members and Associates of the British Academy Major Research Project in the Early History of Agriculture*, Cambridge: Cambridge University Press.

Higgs, E.S. and Jarman, M.R. (1972) 'The origins of animal and plant husbandry', in E.S. Higgs (ed.), 3–13.

Higgs, E.S. and Vita-Finzi, C. (1972) 'Prehistoric economies: a territorial approach', in E.S. Higgs (ed.), 27–36.

Hijara, I.H. (1973) 'Fouilles de Tell Qalinj Agha', *Sumer* 29:13–34.

—— (1980) 'The Halaf Period in Northern Mesopotamia', PhD thesis, Institute of Archaeology, University of London.

Hill, J.N. (ed.) (1977) *The Explanation of Prehistoric Culture Change*, Albuquerque: University of New Mexico Press.

Hinz, W. (1972) *The Lost World of Elam*, London: Sidgwick & Jackson.

Hirth, K.G. (1978) 'Interregional trade and the formation of prehistoric gateway communities', *American Antiquity* 43:35–45.

Hitchcock, R.K. (1982) 'Patterns of sedentism among the Basarwa of eastern Botswana', in E. Leacock and R.B. Lee (eds) (1982a), 233–67.

Ho, Ping-Ti (1975) *The Cradle of the East: An Inquiry into the Indigenous Origins of Techniques and Ideas of Neolithic and Early Historic China, 5000–1000 B.C.*, Hong Kong: Chinese University of Hong Kong/Chicago: University of Chicago Press.

—— (1977) 'The indigenous origins of Chinese agriculture', in C.A. Reed (ed.), 413–84.

Hocart, A.M. (1954) *Social Origins*, London: Watts & Co.

Hockett, C.F. and Ascher, R. (1964) 'The human revolution', *Current Anthropology* 5:135–67.

Hodder, I.R. (1981) 'Society, economy and culture: an ethnographic case', in I.R. Hodder *et al.* (eds), 67–96.

—— (ed.) (1982a) *Cambridge Seminar on Symbolic and Structural Anthropology*, Cambridge: Cambridge University Press.

—— (1982b) *Symbols in Action: Ethnoarchaeological Studies of Material Culture*, Cambridge: Cambridge University Press.

Hodder, I.R., Isaac, G., and Hammond, N. (eds) (1981) *Patterns of the Past. Studies in Honour of D.L. Clarke*, Cambridge, Cambridge University Press.

Hodges, H. (1970) *Technology in the Ancient World*, Harmondsworth: Penguin.

Hole, F. (1966) 'Investigating the origins of Mesopotamian civilisation', *Science* 153(3736):605–11.

—— (1977) *Studies in the Archaeological History of the Deh Luran Plain: The Excavation of Chagha Sefid*, University of Michigan Memoirs of the Museum of Anthropology no.9, Ann Arbor: University of Michigan Press.

—— (1978) 'Pastoral nomadism in western Iran', in R.A. Gould (ed.) (1978a), 127–67.

—— (ed.) (1980a) *Archaeological Perspectives on Iran: From Prehistory to the Islamic Conquest*, Albuquerque: University of New Mexico Press.

—— (1980b) 'The prehistory of herding: some suggestions from ethnography', in *L'Archéologie de l'Iraq du début de l'époque néolithique à 333 avant notre ère*, Paris: Editions du CNRS, 119–27.

—— (1983) 'Symbols of religion and social organisation at Susa', in T.C. Young *et al.* (eds), 315–34.

—— (1987a) 'Chronologies in the Iranian Neolithic', in O. Aurenche *et al.* (eds), part i, 353–67.

—— (1987b) 'Issues in Near Eastern chronology', in O. Aurenche *et al.* (eds) part ii, 559–63.

Hole, F., Flannery, K.V., and Neely, J.A. (1969) *Prehistory and Human Ecology of the Deh Luran Plain: An Early Village Sequence from Khuzistan, Iran*, University of Michigan Memoirs of the Museum of Anthropology no.1, Ann Arbor: University of Michigan Press.

—— (1971) 'Prehistory and human ecology of the Deh Luran plain (excerpts)', in S. Streuver (ed.), 252–311.

Holling, C.S. (1973) 'Resilience and stability of ecological systems', *Annual Review of Ecology and Systematics* 4:1–23.

Holloway, R.L. (1975) 'The casts of fossil hominid brains', in S.H. Katz (ed.), 69–78.

Homans, G.C. (1958) 'Social behavior as exchange', *American Journal of Sociology* 58:597–606.

Honigmann, J.J. (ed.) (1973) *Handbook of Social and Cultural Anthropology*, Chicago: Rand McNally.

Hood, S. (1971) *The Minoans: Crete in the Bronze Age*, London: Thames & Hudson.

Hopf, M. and Bar-Yosef, O. (1987) 'Plant remains from Hayonim Cave, Western Galilee', *Paléorient* 13(1):117–20.

Hopkins, K. (1978) 'Economic growth and towns in Classical antiquity', in P. Abrams and E.A. Wrigley (eds), 35–77.

Horowitz, M.M. (1972) 'Ethnic boundary maintenance among pastoralists and farmers in the western Sudan (Niger)', in W. Irons and N. Dyson-Hudson (eds), 105–14.

Hours, F. and Copeland, L. (1983) 'Les rapports entre l'Anatolie et la Syrie du Nord à l'époque des premières communautés villageoises de bergers et de paysans, 7600–5000 B.C.', in T.C. Young *et al.* (eds), 75–87.

Howe, B. (1983) 'Karim Shahir', in L.S. Braidwood *et al.* (eds), 23–154.

Howell, J.M. (1987) 'Early farming in northwestern Europe', *Scientific American* 257(5):98–105.

Huber, L.G.F. (1983) 'The relationship of the painted pottery and Lungshan cultures', in D.N. Keightley (ed.) (1983a), 177–216.

Humphreys, S.C. (1972) 'Town and country in ancient Greece', in P.J. Ucko *et al.* (eds), 763–8.

Huot, J.-L., Bachelot, L., Braun, J.P., Calvet, Y., Cleuziou, Y., Forest, J.D., and Seigne, J. (1978) 'Larsa – Rapport préliminaire sur la septième campagne à Larsa et la première campagne à Tell el'Oeili (en 1976)', *Syria* 55:183–223.

Hutchinson, Sir J. (ed.) (1974) *Evolutionary Studies in World Crops*, Cambridge: Cambridge University Press.

Hutchinson, R.W. (1962) *Prehistoric Crete*, Harmondsworth: Penguin.

Ingold, T. (1983) 'The significance of storage in hunting societies', *Man* (n.s.) 18(3):553–71.

Iraqi Principal Bureau of Statistics (1954) *Report on the Agriculture and Livestock Census of Iraq, 1952–53*, vol.I, Baghdad: Al-Akhbar House.

Irons, W. and Dyson-Hudson, N. (eds) (1972) *Perspectives on Nomadism*, Leiden: E.J. Brill.

Isserlin, B.S.J. (1982) 'The earliest alphabetic writing', *Cambridge Ancient History*, III(1):794–818.

Jacobsen, T. (1943) 'Primitive democracy in ancient Mesopotamia', *Journal of Near Eastern Studies* 2:159–72.

—— (1949) 'Mesopotamia', in H. Frankfort *et al.* (eds), 137–234.

—— (1953) 'The myth of Inanna and Bilulu', *Journal of Near Eastern Studies* 12:160–87.

—— (1957) 'Early political development in Mesopotamia', *Zeitschrift für Assyriologie, Neue Folge* 18(52):91–140.

—— (1970a) *Toward the Image of Tammuz (and Other Essays)*, ed. W.L. Moran, Cambridge, Mass.: Harvard University Press.

—— (1970b) 'On the textile industry at Ur under Ibbi-Sin' in T. Jacobsen (1970a), 216–29 (first published 1953).

—— (1970c) 'Early political development in Mesopotamia', in T. Jacobsen (1970a), 132–56.

—— (1970d) 'Notes', in T. Jacobsen (1970a), 319–470.

—— (1976) *The Treasures of Darkness: A History of Mesopotamian Religion*. New Haven, Conn.: Yale University Press.

—— (1980a) 'Akkad', in A. Cotterell (ed.), 84–9.

—— (1980b) 'Sumer', in A. Cotterell (ed.), 72–3.

—— (1982) *Salinity and Irrigation Agriculture in Antiquity. Diyala Basin Archaeological Projects: Report on Essential Results 1957–58*, Bibliotheca Mesopotamica, vol.14, Malibu, Calif.: Undena.

Jacobsen, T. and Adams, R. McC. (1958) 'Salt and silt in ancient Mesopotamian agriculture', *Science* 128:1251–8.

Jankowska, N.B. (1969a) 'Extended family commune and civil self-government in Arrapha in the 15th and 14th century B.C.', in I.M. Diakonoff (ed.), 253–76.

—— (1969b) 'Communal self-government and the king of the state of Arrapha', *Journal of the Economic and Social History of the Orient* 12:233–82.

Jarman, M.R. (1976) 'Early animal husbandry', *Philosophical Transactions of the Royal Society of London*, B275:85–97.

Jasim, S.A. (1985) *The Ubaid Period in Iraq: Recent Excavations in the Hamrin Region*, BAR International Series no.267, 2 vols, Oxford.

Jasim, S.A. and Oates, J. (1986) 'Early tokens and tablets in Mesopotamia: new information from Tell Abada and Tell Brak', *World Archaeology* 17(3):348–61.

Jeffery L.H. (1976) *Archaic Greece: The City-States c.700–500 B.C.*, London: Methuen.

—— (1982) 'Greek alphabetic writing', *Cambridge Ancient History* III(1), 819–33.

Jochim, M.A. (1983) 'Palaeolithic cave art in ecological perspective', in G. Bailey (ed.), 212–19.

John, A.M. (1985) 'Comment' on Scott and Johnston, *Current Anthropology* 26(4):469.

Johnson, D. (1969) *The Nature of Nomadism: A Comparative Study of Pastoral Migrations in S.W. Asia and Northern Africa*, Department of Geography Research Paper no.118, Chicago: University of Chicago Press.

Johnson, G.A. (1973) *Local Exchange and Early State Development in S.W. Iran*, Ann Arbor Anthropology Papers 51, Ann Arbor: University of Michigan Press.

—— (1975) 'Locational analysis and the investigation of Uruk local exchange systems', in J.A. Sabloff and C.C. Lamberg-Karlovsky (eds), 285–339.

Jones, A.H.M. (1972) *Constantine and the Conversion of the Empire*, Harmondsworth: Penguin.

Jones, R. (1978) 'Why did Tasmanians stop eating fish?', in R.A. Gould (ed.) (1978a), 11–47.

Jones, T.B. (ed.) (1969) *The Sumerian Problem*, New York: Wiley.

—— (1976) 'Sumerian administrative documents: an essay', in S.J. Lieberman (ed.), 41–61.

Jones, T.B. and Snyder, J.W. (1961) *Sumerian Economic Texts from the Third Ur Dynasty*, Minneapolis: University of Minnesota Press.

Kang, S.T. (1972) *Sumerian Economic Texts from the Drehem Archive*, Urbana: University of Illinois Press.

Kantor, H.J. (1984) 'The ancestry of the divine boat (Sirsir?) of Early Dynastic and Akkadian glyptic', *Journal of Near Eastern Studies* 43(4):227–80.

Katz, S.H. (ed.) (1975) *Biological Anthropology*, Readings from *Scientific American*, San Francisco: W.H. Freeman.

Kees, H. (1961) *Ancient Egypt: A Cultural Topography*, London: Faber & Faber.

Keightley, D.N. (1977) 'Ping Ti Ho and the origins of Chinese civilisation', Review article, *Harvard Journal of Asiatic Studies* 37:381–411.

—— (1978) 'The religious commitment: Shang theology and the genesis of Chinese political culture', *History of Religions* 17:211–25.

—— (ed.) (1983a) *The Origins of Chinese Civilisation*, Berkeley, Calif.: University of California Press.

—— (1983b) 'The Late Shang state: when, where and what', in D.N. Keightley (ed.) (1983a), 532–64.

Kenyon, K.M. (1959) 'Some observations on the beginnings of settlement in the

Near East', *Journal of the Royal Anthropological Institute* 89(1):35–43.

—— (1969) 'The origins of the Neolithic', *The Advancement of Science* 26: 144–60.

—— (1980) *Archaeology of the Holy Land*, 4th edn, London: Benn.

Keppie, L. (1984) *The Making of the Roman Army*, London: Batsford.

Killick, R.G. and Roaf, M.D. (1979) 'Excavations at Tell Madhur', *Sumer* 25:534–42.

Kilmer, A.D. (1972) 'The Mesopotamian concept of overpopulation', *Orientalia* (n.s.) 41:160–77.

—— (1976) 'Speculations of Umul, the first baby', in B.L. Eichler (ed.), 265–70.

King, V.T. (1981) 'Marxist analysis and Highland Burma: a critical commentary', *Cultures et développement* 13:675–88.

—— (1983) 'Imaginary Kachins', *Man* (n.s.) 18(2):405–6.

Kirchhoff, P. (1968) 'The principles of clanship in human society', in M. Fried (ed.), *Readings in Anthropology*, vol.II, New York: Thomas Y. Crowell, 260–70.

Kirkbride, D. (1966) 'Five seasons at the Pre-Pottery Neolithic site of Beidha in Jordan: a summary', *Palestine Exploration Quarterly*, 98th year, 8–61.

—— (1967) 'Beidha 1965: an interim report', *Palestine Exploration Quarterly*, 99th year, 5–13.

—— (1968) 'Beidha: early Neolithic village life south of the Dead Sea', *Antiquity* 42:263–74.

—— (1972) 'Umm Dabaghiyah', *Iraq* 24:3–15.

—— (1973) 'Umm Dabaghiyah', *Iraq* 25:1–7 and 205–9.

—— (1974) 'Umm Dabaghiyah', *Iraq* 26:85–92.

—— (1975) 'Umm Dabaghiyah', *Iraq* 27:3–10.

—— (1982) 'Umm Dabaghiyah', in J. Curtis (ed.), 11–21.

Kirkby, M.J. (1977) 'Land and water resources of the Deh Luran and Khuzistan plains', Appendix I in F. Hole (1977), 251–88.

Kirsch, T.A. (1973) *Feasting and Social Oscillation: Religion and Society in Upland S.E. Asia*, Ithaca, N.Y.: Cornell University S.E. Asia Program.

Kislev, M.E. (1984) 'Emergence of wheat agriculture', *Paléorient* 10(2):61–70.

Klaits, J. and Klaits, B. (eds) (1974) *Animals and Man in Historical Perspective*, New York: Harper.

Klein, J. (1981) *The Royal Hymns of Shulgi King of Ur*, Philadelphia: American Philosophical Society.

Klengel, H. (ed.) (1971) *Beitrage zur sozialen Struktur des alten Vorderasien*, Berlin: Akademie-Verlag.

Kohl, P. (1987) 'The ancient economy, transferable technologies and the Bronze Age world system: a view from the northeastern frontier of the Ancient Near East', in M. Rowlands *et al.* (eds), 13–24.

Kohl, P.L. (1978) 'The balance of trade in southwestern Asia in the mid-third millennium B.C.', *Current Anthropology* 19(3):463–92.

Kolata, G. (1974) '!Kung hunter gatherers: feminism, diet and birth control', *Science* 185:932–4.

Komoroczy, G. (1976) 'Work and strike of the gods', *Oikumene* 1, Berlin: Akademiai Kiado.

Kottak, C.P. (1972) 'Ecological variables in the origin and evolution of African states: the Buganda example', *Comparative Studies in Society and History* 14:351–80.

Kramer, C. (1979) 'An archaeological view of a contemporary Kurdish village: domestic architecture, household size and wealth', in C. Kramer (ed.),

Ethnoarchaeology: Implications of Ethnography for Archaeology, New York: Columbia University Press. 139–63.

—— (1980) 'Estimating prehistoric populations: an ethno-archaeological approach', in *L'Archéologie de l'Iraq du début de l'Époque Néolithique à 333 avant notre ère*, Paris: Editions du CNRS, 315–34.

—— (1983) 'Spatial organization in contemporary southwest Asian villages and archaeological sampling', in T.C. Young *et al.* (eds), 347–68.

Kramer, S.N. (1961a) *History Begins at Sumer*, London: Thames & Hudson.

—— (1961b) *Sumerian Mythology*, New York: Harper & Row.

—— (1963) *The Sumerians*, Chicago: University of Chicago Press.

—— (1968) 'Review of Adams: *Evolution of Urban Society*', *Journal of Near Eastern Studies* 27:326–30.

—— (1969) 'Innana and Šulgi: a Sumerian fertility song', *Iraq* 31:18–23.

—— (1974) 'Kingship in Sumer and Akkad: the ideal king', in P. Garelli (ed.), *Le Palais et la royauté (XIXe Rencontre Assyriologique Internationale)*, Paris: Librairie Orientaliste Paul Geuthner, 163–76.

—— (1977) 'Commerce and trade: gleanings from Sumerian literature', *Iraq* 39:59–66.

—— (1979) *From the Poetry of Sumer*, Berkeley: University of California Press.

Kraus, F.R. (1954) 'Le rôle des temples depuis la Troisième Dynastie d'Ur jusqu'à la Première Dynastie de Babylone', *Journal of World History* 1:518–45.

—— (1970) *Sumerer und Akkader: Ein Problem der altmesopotamischen Geschichte*, Amsterdam: North-Holland.

Kraybill, N. (1977) 'Pre-agricultural tools for the preparation of foods in the Old World', in C.A. Reed (ed.), 485–521.

Kroeber, A.L. (1940) 'Stimulus diffusion', *American Anthropologist* 42(1):1–20.

Kuper, A. (1973) *Anthropologists and Anthropology: The British School 1922–1972*, Harmondsworth: Penguin.

Lafargue, P. (1891) *The Evolution of Property: From Savagery to Civilisation*, Glasgow: Socialist Labour Press.

La Fontaine, J.S. (ed.) (1978a) *Sex and Age as Principles of Social Differentiation*, ASA Monograph no.17, London: Academic Press.

—— (1978b) Editor's 'Introduction', in J.S. La Fontaine (1978a), 1–20.

Lamberg-Karlovsky, C.C. (ed.) (1972) *Old World Archaeology: Foundations of Civilisation*, Readings from *Scientific American*, San Francisco: W.H. Freeman.

—— (1975) 'Third millennium modes of exchange and modes of production', in J.A. Sabloff and C.C. Lamberg-Karlovsky (eds), 341–68.

—— (1978) 'The Proto-Elamites on the Iranian plateau', *Antiquity* 52:114–20.

—— (ed.) (1979) *Hunters, Farmers and Civilisation: Old World Archaeology*, Readings from *Scientific American*, San Francisco: W.H. Freeman.

Lambert, W.G. (1974) 'The seed of kingship', in P. Garelli (ed.), *Le Palais et la royauté (XIXe Rencontre Assyriologique Internationale)*, Paris: Librairie Orientaliste Paul Geuthner, 427–40.

Lambert, W.G. and Millard, A.R. (1969) *Atra-hasis: The Babylonian Story of the Flood*, Oxford: Oxford University Press.

Landsberger, B. (1979a) 'Three essays on the Sumerians', trans. and intro. M. de J. Ellis, in G. Buccellati *et al.* (eds) (1979), 23–40.

—— (1979b) 'The conceptual autonomy of the Babylonian world', trans. T. Jacobsen, B. Foster, and H. von Siebenthal, intro. T. Jacobsen, in G. Buccellati *et al.* (eds) (1979), 57–72.

Larsen, C.E. (1975) 'The Mesopotamian delta region: a reconsideration of Lees and Falcon', *Journal of the American Oriental Society* 95(1):43–57.

—— (1987) 'Commercial networks in the Ancient Near East', in M. Rowlands *et al.* (eds), 47–56.

Larsen, C.E. and Evans, G. (1978) 'The Holocene geological history of the Tigris-Euphrates-Karun delta', in W.C. Brice (ed.), 227–44.

Larsen, M.T. (1967) *Old Assyrian Caravan Procedures*, Istanbul: Nederlands Historisch-archaeologisch Instituut in het Nabiye Oesten.

—— (1976) *The Old Assyrian City State and its Colonies, Mesopotamia* 4, Copenhagen Studies in Assyriology, Copenhagen: Akademisk Forlag.

—— (ed.) (1979) *Power and Propaganda: A Symposium on Ancient Empires, Mesopotamia* 7, Copenhagen Studies in Assyriology, Copenhagen: Akademisk Forlag.

Laslett, P. (1956) 'The face to face society', in P. Laslett (ed.), *Philosophy, Politics and Society*, Oxford: Basil Blackwell, 157–84.

—— (1971) *The World We Have Lost*, Cambridge: Cambridge University Press.

Leach, E.R. (1961a) *Rethinking Anthropology*, LSE Monograph on Social Anthropology no.22, London: Athlone Press.

—— (1961b) 'Aspects of bridewealth and marriage stability among the Kachin and Lakher', in E.R. Leach (1961a), 114–23.

—— (1961c) *Pul Eliyah, A Village in Ceylon: A Study in Land Tenure and Kinship*, Cambridge: Cambridge University Press.

—— (1970) *Political Systems of Highland Burma: A Study in Kachin Social Structure*, LSE Monograph on Social Anthropology no.44, London: Athlone Press.

—— (1973a) 'Complementary filiation and bilateral kinship', in J. Goody (ed.), (1973), 53–8.

—— (1973b) 'Concluding address', in Colin Renfrew (ed.), 761–71.

—— (1983) 'Imaginary Kachins (Correspondence)', *Man* (n.s.) 18(1):191–7.

Leacock, E. (1979) 'Class, commodity and the status of women', in S. Diamond (ed.), 185–99.

—— (1982) 'Relations of production in band society', in E. Leacock and R.B. Lee (eds) (1982a), 158–70.

Leacock, E. and Lee, R.B. (eds) (1982a) *Politics and History in Band Societies*, Cambridge: Cambridge University Press.

—— (1982b) 'Introduction', in E. Leacock and R.B. Lee (eds) (1982a), 1–20.

Le Blanc, S.A. and Watson, P.J. (1973) 'A comparative statistical analysis of painted pottery from seven Halafian sites', *Paléorient* 1:117–33.

Le Breton, L. (1957) 'The early periods at Susa, Mesopotamian relations', *Iraq* 19:79–124.

Lee, R.B. (1968) 'What hunters do for a living, or, how to make out on scarce resources', in R.B. Lee and I. DeVore (eds) (1968a), 30–48.

—— (1972a) 'Population growth and the beginnings of sedentary life among !Kung Bushmen', in B. Spooner (ed.), 329–42.

—— (1972b) 'Work effort, group structure and land-use in contemporary hunter-gatherers', in P.J. Ucko *et al.* (eds), 177–85.

—— (1980) 'Lactation, ovulation, infanticide and women's work: a study of hunter-gatherer population regulation', in M.N. Cohen *et al.* (eds), 321–48.

—— (1981) 'Is there a foraging mode of production?', *Canadian Journal of Anthropology* 2(1):13–19.

—— (1982) 'Politics, sexual and non-sexual in an egalitarian society', in E. Leacock and R.B. Lee (eds) (1982a), 37–59.

Lee, R.B. and DeVore, I. (eds) (1968a) *Man the Hunter*, Chicago: Aldine.

—— (1968b) 'Problems in the study of hunter-gatherers', in R.B. Lee and

I. DeVore (1968a), 3–12.

—— (eds) (1976) *Kalahari Hunter-Gatherers: Studies in the !Kung San and their Neighbours*, Cambridge, Mass.: Harvard University Press.

Leeds, A. (1969) 'Ecological determinants of chieftainship among the Yaruro Indians of Venezuela', in A.P. Vayda (ed.) (1969a), 377–94.

Leeds, A. and Vayda, A.P. (eds) (1965) *Man, Culture and Animals: The Role of Animals in Human Ecological Adjustments*, Washington, D.C.: American Association for the Advancement of Science, Publication no.78.

Leemans, W.F. (1954) *Legal and Economic Records from the Kingdom of Larsa*, Leiden: E.J. Brill.

—— (1960a) *Foreign Trade in the Old Babylonian Period: As Revealed by Texts from Southern Mesopotamia. Studia et Documenta ad Jura Orientis Antiqui Pertinentia VI*, Leiden: E.J. Brill.

—— (1960b) 'The trade relations of Babylonia and the question of relations with Egypt in the Old Babylonian Period', *Journal of the Economic and Social History of the Orient* 3:21–37.

—— (1960c) 'Miscellanea: some marginal remarks on ancient technology', *Journal of the Economic and Social History of the Orient* 3:217–37.

—— (1968) 'Old Babylonian letters and economic history: a review article with a digression on foreign trade', *Journal of the Economic and Social History of the Orient* 11:171–226.

—— (1982) 'The pattern of settlement in the Babylonian countryside', in M.A. Dandamayev *et al.* (eds), 246–9.

Lees, G.M. and Falcon, N.L. (1952) 'The geographical history of the Mesopotamian plain', *Geographical Journal* 118:24–39.

Lees, S.H. and Bates, D.G. (1974) 'The origins of specialised nomadic pastoralism: a systematic model', *American Antiquity* 39:187–93.

Legge, A.J. (1977) 'The origins of agriculture in the Near East', in J.V.S. Megaw (ed.), 51–67.

Legros, D. (1977) 'Chance, necessity and mode of production: a Marxist critique of cultural evolutionism', *American Anthropologist* 79:26–41.

—— (1988) 'Comment' on Testart, *Current Anthropology* 29(1):15–17.

Lemche, N.P. (1979) '*Andurārum* and *Mišarum*: comments on the problem of social edicts and their application in the ancient Near East', *Journal of Near Eastern Studies* 38(1):11–22.

Leroi-Gourhan, A. (1979) 'Analyse pollinique à Tell Aswad', *Paléorient* 5:170–4.

—— (1981) 'Analyse pollinique de Zawi Chemi', Appendix III in R.L. Solecki, 77–80.

Lesser, A. (1952) 'Evolution in social anthropology', *Southwestern Journal of Anthropology* 8:134–46.

—— (1961) 'Social fields and the evolution of society', *Southwestern Journal of Anthropology* 17:40–8.

Levine, L.D. and McDonald, M.M.A. (1982) 'The Neolithic and Chalcolithic periods in the Mahidasht', *Iran* 15:39–50.

Levy, T.E. (1983) 'The emergence of specialised pastoralism in the southern Levant', *World Archaeology* 15(1):15–36.

Levy, T.E. and Alon, D. (1983) 'Chalcolithic settlement patterns in the northern Negev desert', *Current Anthropology* 24(1):105–7.

Lewis, B. (1966) *The Arabs in History*, 4th edn, London: Hutchinson.

Li, Hui-Lin (1983) 'The domestication of plants in China: ecogeographical considerations', in D.N. Keightley (ed.) (1983a), 21–65.

Lieberman, S.J. (ed.) (1976) *Sumerological Studies in Honor of Thorkild*

Jacobsen on his 70th Birthday, June 7, 1974, Assyriological Studies no.20, Chicago: Oriental Institute of the University of Chicago.

—— (1980) 'Of clay pebbles, hollow balls, and writing: a Sumerian view', *American Journal of Archaeology* 84:339–58.

Linton, R. (1936) *The Study of Man*, New York: Appleton-Century.

Lipinski, E. (ed.) (1979) *State and Temple Economy in the Ancient Near East*, 2 vols, Proceedings of the International Conference Organized by the Katholieke Universiteit Leuven, 10–14 April 1978, published as *Orientalia Lovaniensa Analecta*, 6, Leuven: Departement Orientalistiek Leuven.

Liverani, M. (1979) 'Three Amarna essays', intro. and trans. M.L. Jaffe, in G. Buccellati *et al.* (eds), 73–106.

—— (1982) 'Ville et campagne dans le royaume d'Ugarit. Essai d'analyse économique', in M.A. Dandamayev *et al.* (eds), 250–8.

—— (1987) 'The collapse of the Near Eastern regional system at the end of the Bronze Age: the case of Syria', in M. Rowlands *et al.* (eds), 66–73.

Lloyd, S. (1960) 'Ur, Al-ʿUbaid, ʿUqair and Eridu: an interpretation of evidence from the flood-pit', *Iraq* 22(1):23–31.

—— (1961) *The Art of the Ancient Near East*, London: Thames & Hudson.

—— (1978) *The Archaeology of Mesopotamia: From the Old Stone Age to the Persian Conquest*, London: Thames & Hudson.

Lloyd, S. and Safir, F. (1943) 'Tell Uqair: excavations by the Iraqi Government Directorate of Antiquities in 1940 and 1941', *Journal of Near Eastern Studies* 2:131–58.

—— (1945) 'Tell Hassuna', *Journal of Near Eastern Studies* 4:255–89.

—— (1947) 'Eridu: preliminary report on the first season's excavations', *Sumer* 3:84–111.

—— (1948) 'Eridu: a preliminary report on the second season's excavations', *Sumer* 4:115–27.

Lloyd, S., Safir, F., and Mustafa, M.A. (1981) *Eridu*, Baghdad: State Organisation of Antiquities and Heritage.

Lourandos, H. (1980) 'Change and stability? Hydraulics, hunter-gatherers and population in temperate Australia', *World Archaeology* 11(3):245–64.

—— (1985) 'Intensification and Australian prehistory', in T.D. Price and J.A. Brown (eds), 385–423.

Lowrie, R.H. (1946) 'Evolution in cultural anthropology: a reply to Leslie White', *American Anthropologist* (n.s.) 48:223–33.

Lubbock, J. (Lord Avebury) (1865) *Prehistoric Times as Illustrated by Ancient Remains and Customs of Modern Savages*, London: Williams & Norgate.

Luce, J.V. (1969) *The End of Atlantis: New Light on an Old Legend*, London: Thames & Hudson.

—— (1975) *Homer and the Heroic Age*, London: Futura.

McArthur, N. (1970) 'The demography of primitive populations', *Science* 167:1097–101.

McNairn, B. (1980) *The Method and Theory of V. Gordon Childe*, Edinburgh: Edinburgh University Press.

MacNeish, R.S. (1972) 'The evolution of community patterns in the Tehuacán valley of Mexico and speculations about the cultural processes', in P.J. Ucko *et al.* (eds), 67–93.

—— (1977) 'The beginning of agriculture in Central Peru', in C.A. Reed (ed.), 753–801.

Maddin, R., Muhly, J.D., and Wheeler, T.S. (1979) 'How the Iron Age began', in C.C. Lamberg-Karlovsky (ed.), 293–300.

Maddock, K. (1973) *The Australian Aborigines: A Portrait of their Society*, London: Allen Lane.

Maekawa, K. (1973–4) 'The development of the **é-mí** in Lagash during the Early Dynastic III', *Mesopotamia* 8–9:77–144.

—— (1974) 'Agricultural production in ancient Sumer: chiefly from Lagash materials', *Zinbun* 13:1–60.

—— (1976) 'The Erín-people in Lagash of Ur III times', *Revue assyriologique* 70:9–44.

Maine, H.S. (1883) *Dissertations on Early Law and Custom*, London: John Murray.

Maisels, C.K. (1984a) 'The origins of settlement, agriculture and the city-state in Mesopotamia', PhD thesis, Department of Social Anthropology, University of Edinburgh.

—— (1984b) 'Dualism between the desert and the sown: aspects of pastoral/ agrarian relations in the ancient Near East', paper given to the Conference on Duality, Traditional Cosmology Society, University of Stirling, September 1984.

—— (1984c) 'Indus civilization in comparative perspective with the Near East', unpublished MS.

—— (1985) 'Ensi and Lugal: the institution of kingship in Sumer and Akkad', paper given to the Conference on Kingship, Traditional Cosmology Society, University of Edinburgh, August 1985.

—— (1986) 'Ideology and cosmology: existential conditions and social order', unpublished MS.

—— (1987) 'Models of social evolution: trajectories from the Neolithic to the state', *Man* 22(2):331–59.

Malinowski, B. (1922) *Argonauts of the Western Pacific*, London: Routledge & Kegan Paul.

—— (1929) *The Sexual Life of Savages in North-Western Melanesia*, London: Routledge & Kegan Paul.

—— (1968) 'Kula: the circulating exchange of valuables in the archipelagoes of eastern New Guinea', in A.P. Vayda (ed.), 407–20.

—— (1979) *The Ethnology of Malinowski: The Trobriand Islands 1915–1918*, ed. M.W. Young, London: Routledge & Kegan Paul.

Mallowan, M.E.L. (1965a) *Early Mesopotamia and Iran*, London: Thames & Hudson.

—— (1965b) 'The mechanics of ancient trade in Western Asia', *Iran* 3:1–17.

Malthus, T.R. (1970) *An Essay on the Principle of Population*, ed. A. Flew, Harmondsworth: Penguin.

Manzanilla, L. (ed.) (1987) *Studies in the Neolithic and Urban Revolutions*, The V. Gordon Childe Colloquium, Mexico 1986, BAR S349, Oxford.

Marfoe, L. (1987) 'Cedar forest to silver mountain: social change and the development of long-distance trade in early Near Eastern societies', in M. Rowlands *et al.* (eds), 25–35.

Margueron, J.-C. (1967) *Mesopotamia*, Archaeologia Mundi, Geneva: Nagel.

—— (1984) 'Le célèbre palais de Zimri-lim', *Les Dossiers de l'histoire et l'archeologie* 80:38–45.

Marshall, L. (1967) '!Kung Bushman bands', in R. Cohen and J. Middleton (eds), 15–43.

Martin, H.P. (1972) 'The tablets of Shuruppak', *Compte rendu de la rencontre assyriologique* 20(181):173–7.

Marx, E. (1978) 'The ecology and politics of nomadic pastoralists in the Middle

East', in W. Weissleder (ed.) (1978b), 41–74.

Marx, K.H. (1918) *Capital*, Chicago: Charles Kerr.

—— (1973) *Grundrisse: Foundations of the Critique of Political Economy*, Harmondsworth: Penguin.

Marx, K.H. and Engels, F. (1976) *The German Ideology*, London: Lawrence & Wishart.

Mason, L. (1968) 'Suprafamilial authority and economic process in Micronesia', in A.P. Vayda (ed.) (1968), 299–329.

Matthews, R.J. and Postgate, J.N. (with a contribution by E.J. Luby) (1987) 'Excavations at Abu Salabikh, 1985–86', *Iraq* 49:91–119.

Matthews, V.H. (1978) *Pastoral Nomadism in the Mari Kingdom (ca. 1830–1760 B.C.)*, American Schools of Oriental Research Series no.3, Cambridge, Mass.: Harvard University Press.

Mattiae, P. (1979) 'Ebla in the period of the Amorite Dynasties and the Dynasty of Akkad: recent archaeological discoveries at Tell Mardikh', in G. Buccellati *et al.* (eds), 104–7.

—— (1980) *Ebla: An Empire Rediscovered*, London: Hodder & Stoughton.

Meacham, W. (1983) 'Origins and development of the Yüeh Coastal Neolithic: a microcosm of culture change on the mainland of East Asia', in D.N. Keightley (ed.) (1983a), 147–75.

Meeker, B.F. (1971) 'Decisions and exchange', *American Sociological Review* 36:485–95.

Megaw, J.V.S. (ed.) (1977) *Hunters, Gatherers and First Farmers Beyond Europe: An Archaeological Survey*, Leicester: Leicester University Press.

Meillassoux, C. (1972) 'From reproduction to production: a Marxist approach to economic anthropology', *Economy and Society* 1:93–105.

—— (1978a) ' "The economy" in agricultural self-sustaining societies: a preliminary analysis', in D. Seddon (ed.), 127–57.

—— (1978b) 'The social organisation of the peasantry: the economic basis of kinship', in D. Seddon (ed.), 159–69.

Meldgaard, J., Mortensen, P., and Thrane, H. (1964) 'Excavations at Tepe Guran, Luristan', *Acta Archaeologia* 34:97–133.

Mellaart, J. (1972) 'Anatolian settlement patterns', in P.J. Ucko *et al.* (eds), 279–92.

—— (1975) *The Neolithic of the Near East*, London: Thames & Hudson.

Merpert, N.Y. and Munchaev, R.M. (1972) 'Early agricultural settlements in northern Mesopotamia', *Soviet Archaeology* 3:141–69.

—— (1973) 'Early agricultural settlements in the Sinjar plain, N. Iraq', *Iraq* 35:93–119.

—— (1987) 'The earliest levels at Yarim Tepe I and Yarim Tepe II in Northern Iraq', *Iraq* 49:1–36.

Merpert, N.Y., Munchaev, R.M., and Bader, N.O. (1981) 'Investigations of the Soviet expedition in northern Iraq, 1976', *Sumer* 37:22–54.

Meyers, J.T. (1971) 'The origins of agriculture: an analysis of three hypotheses', in S. Struever (ed.), 101–21.

Millar, J.A. (1771) *The Origin of the Distinction of Ranks or an Inquiry into the Circumstances which give rise to Influence and Authority in the different Members of Society*, Edinburgh: W. Blackwood.

Millard, A.R. (1976) 'The Canaanite linear alphabet and its passage to the Greeks', *Kadmos* 15:130–44.

—— (1986) 'The infancy of the alphabet', *World Archaeology* 17:390–8.

—— (1988) 'The bevelled-rim bowls: their purpose and significance', paper given at the Inaugural Conference of the British Association for Near Eastern Archaeology, University of Manchester, December 1987, *Iraq* 50:49–57.

Millon, R. (1974) 'The study of urbanism at Teotihuacan, Mexico', in N. Hammond (ed.), 335–62.

Mitchell, J.C. (1956) *The Yao Village: A Study in the Social Structure of a Nyasaland Tribe*, Manchester: Manchester University Press for the Rhodes-Livingstone Institute.

Moholy-Nagy, H. (1983) 'Jarmo artifacts of pecked and ground stone and of shell', in L.S. Braidwood *et al.* (eds) (1983), 289–346.

Moore, A.M.T. (1979) 'A pre-Neolithic farmers' village on the Euphrates', *Scientific American* 241(2):62–70.

—— (1982) 'Agricultural origins in the Near East: a model for the 1980s', *World Archaeology* 14(2):224–36.

—— (1983) 'The first farmers in the Levant', in T.C. Young *et al.* (eds), 91–112.

Moore, H.C. (1954) 'Cumulation and cultural processes', *American Anthropologist* 56:347–57.

Moorey, P.R.S. (1964) 'The plano-convex building at Kish and early Mesopotamian palaces', *Iraq* 26:83–98.

—— (1976) 'The late prehistoric administrative building at Jemdet Nasr', *Iraq* 38:95–106.

—— (ed.) (1979) *The Origins of Civilisation*, Wolfson College Lectures 1978, Oxford: Clarendon Press.

—— (1982) 'The archaeological evidence for metallurgy and related technologies in Mesopotamia, c.5,500–2,100 B.C.', *Iraq* 44:13–38.

—— (1985) *Materials and Manufacture in Ancient Mesopotamia: The Evidence of Archaeology and Art*, BAR S237, Oxford.

—— (1986) 'The emergence of the light, horse-drawn chariot in the Near East c.2000–1500 B.C.', *World Archaeology* 18(2):196–215.

—— (1987) 'On tracking cultural transfers in prehistory: the case of Egypt and lower Mesopotamia in the fourth millennium BC', in Rowlands *et al.* (eds), 36–46.

Morales, V.B. (1983) 'Jarmo figurines and other clay objects', in L.S. Braidwood *et al.* (eds), 369–424.

Moran, W.L. (ed.) (1970) *Toward the Image of Tammuz (and Other Essays)*, Collected essays of Thorkild Jacobsen, Cambridge, Mass.: Harvard University Press.

—— (1971) 'Atrahasis: the Babylonian story of the flood', *Biblica* 52:51–61.

Morgan, L.H. (1877) *Ancient Society*, Chicago: Charles H. Kerr.

Mortensen, P. (1964) 'Additional remarks on the chronology of early village-farming communities', *Sumer* 20:28–36.

—— (1970) 'Tell Shimshara. The Hassuna Period', *Hist. Filos. Skr. Dan. Yid. Selsk.* 5:1–148.

—— (1972) 'Seasonal camps and early villages in the Zagros', in P.J. Ucko *et al.* (eds), 293–7.

—— (1983) 'Patterns of interaction between seasonal settlements and early villages in Mesopotamia', in T.C. Young *et al.* (eds), 207–30.

Moseley, M.E. (1975a) 'Chan Chan: Andean alternative of the preindustrial city', *Science* 187(4173):219–25.

—— (1975b) 'Prehistoric principles of labor organization in the Moche valley, Peru', *American Antiquity* 40:191–6.

Mosse, C. (1969) *The Ancient World at Work*, Ancient Culture and Society Series, London: Chatto & Windus.

Muhly, J.D. (1973) *Copper and Tin: The Distribution of Mineral Resources and the Nature of the Metals Trade in the Bronze Age*, Hamden, Conn.: Archon Books.

—— (1976) 'Supplement to "Copper and Tin" ', *Transactions of the Connecticut Academy of Arts and Sciences* 46:77–136.

Mulvaney, D.J. (1976) 'The prehistory of the Australian aborigine', in B.M. Fagan (ed.), 76–84.

Mulvaney, D.J. and Golson, J. (eds) (1971) *Aboriginal Man and Environment in Australia*, Canberra: Australian National University Press.

Murdock, G.P. (1949) *Social Structure*, New York: Free Press.

—— (1968) 'Cognatic forms of social organisation', in P. Bohannan and J. Middleton (eds), 235–53.

Mylonas, G.E. (1977) *Mycenae: A Guide to its Ruins and its History*, Athens: n.p.

Naroll, R. (1956) 'A preliminary index of social development', *American Anthropologist* 58:687–715.

Naroll, R. and Divale, W.T. (1976) 'Natural selection in cultural evolution: warfare vs. peaceful diffusion', *American Ethnologist* 3(1):97–129.

Naveh, J. (1980) 'The Greek alphabet: new evidence', *Biblical Archaeologist* 43(1):22–5.

Nettleship, M., Givens, R., and Nettleship, A. (eds) (1975) *War, Its Causes and Correlates*, The Hague: Mouton.

Nicholas, I.M. (1987) 'The function of bevelled-rim bowls: a case study at the TUV Mound, Tal-e Malyan, Iran', *Paléorient* XIII/2:61–72.

Nissen, H.J. (1970) 'Grabung in den Quadraten K/LXII in Uruk Warka', *Baghdader Mitteilungen* 5:101–91.

—— (1972) 'The city wall of Uruk', in P.J. Ucko *et al.* (eds), 793–8.

—— (1979) 'Short remarks on early state formation in Babylonia: an answer to Steiner and Westenholz', in M.T. Larsen (ed.), 145–50.

—— (1980) 'The mobility between settled and non-settled in early Babylonia: theory and evidence', in *L'Archéologie de l'Iraq du début de l'Époque Néolithique à 333 avant notre ère*, Paris: Editions du CNRS, 285–90.

—— (1983) 'Political organization and settled zone: a case study from the ancient Near East', in T.C. Young *et al.* (eds), 335–46.

—— (1987) 'The chronology of the proto and early historic periods in Mesopotamia and Susiana', in O. Aurenche *et al.* (eds), part ii, 607–14.

Nugent, D. (1982a) 'Closed system and contradiction: the Kachin in and out of history', *Man* (n.s.) 17:508–27.

—— (1982b) 'Correspondence', *Man* (n.s.) 18(1):200–6.

Nutzel, W. (1975) 'The formation of the Arabian Gulf from 14,000 B.C.', *Sumer* 31:101–10.

Oates, D. (1968) *Studies in the Ancient History of Northern Iraq*, Oxford: Oxford University Press.

—— (1987) 'Excavations at Tell Brak 1985–86', *Iraq* 49:175–91.

Oates, D. and Oates, J. (1976a) 'Early irrigation agriculture in Mesopotamia', in G. de G. Sieveking *et al.* (eds) (1976), 109–35.

—— (1976b) *The Rise of Civilisation*, Making of the Past Series, Oxford: Phaidon.

Oates, J. (1960) 'Ur and Eridu: the prehistory', *Iraq* 20:32–50.

—— (1966) 'The baked clay figurines from Tell es-Sawwan', *Iraq* 28:146–53.

—— (1968) 'Prehistoric investigations near Mandali, Iraq', *Iraq* 30:1–20.

—— (1969) 'Choga Mami 1967–68: a preliminary report', *Iraq* 31:115–52.

—— (1973) 'The background and development of early farming communities in Mesopotamia and the Zagros', *Proceedings of the Prehistoric Society (London)* 39:147–81.

—— (1977) 'Mesopotamian social organisation: archaeological and philological evidence', in J. Friedman and M.J. Rowlands (eds) (1977a), 457–85.

—— (1978–9) 'Religion and ritual in sixth-millennium B.C. Mesopotamia', *World Archaeology* 10(2):117–24.

—— (1979) *Babylon*, London: Thames & Hudson.

—— (1980) 'Land use and population in prehistoric Mesopotamia', in *L'Archéologie de l'Iraq du début de l'Époque Néolithique à 333 avant notre ère*, Paris: Editions du CNRS, 303–14.

—— (1982) 'Choga Mami', in J. Curtis (ed.), 22–9.

—— (1983) 'Ubaid Mesopotamia reconsidered', in T.C. Young *et al.* (eds), 251–82.

—— (1987a) 'Ubaid chronology', in O. Aurenche *et al.* (eds), part ii, 473–82.

—— (1987b) 'A note on Ubaid and Mittani pottery from Tell Brak', *Iraq* 49:193–8.

Oates, J., Davidson, T.E., Kamilli, D., and McKerrell, H. (1977) 'Seafaring merchants of Ur?', *Antiquity* 51:221–34.

Odum, E.P. (1975) *Ecology*, 2nd edn, New York: Holt, Rinehart & Winston.

Oliver, D.L. (1967) *A Solomon Island Society: Kinship and Leadership among the Siuai of Bougainville*, Boston: Beacon Press.

Oliver, R.T. (1971) *Communication and Culture in Ancient India and China*, Syracuse, N.Y.: Syracuse University Press.

Olszewski, D. (1986) *The North Syrian Late Epipalaeolithic*, BAR S309, Oxford.

Oppenheim, A.L. (1954) 'The seafaring merchants of Ur', *Journal of the American Oriental Society* 74:6–17.

—— (1964) *Ancient Mesopotamia: Portrait of a Dead Civilisation*, Chicago and London: University of Chicago Press.

—— (1966) 'Mesopotamia in the early history of alchemy', *Revue d'assyriologie* 60:29–45.

—— (1967) 'A new look at the structure of Mesopotamian society', *Journal of the Economic and Social History of the Orient* 10:1–16.

—— (1969) 'Mesopotamia – land of many cities', in M. Lapidus (ed.), *Middle Eastern Cities*, Berkeley and Los Angeles: University of California Press.

—— (1970) *Glass and Glassmaking in Ancient Mesopotamia*, New York: Corning.

Orans, M. (1966) 'Surplus', *Human Organisation* 25:24–32.

Orme, B. (1981) *Anthropology for Archaeologists*, London: Duckworth.

O'Shea, J.M. (1981) 'Coping with scarcity: exchange and social storage', in A. Sheridan and G. Bailey (eds), 167–83.

Oswalt, W.H. (1973) *Habitat and Technology: The Evolution of Hunting*, New York and London: Holt, Rinehart & Winston.

Palmer, L.R. (1961) *Mycenaeans and Minoans*, London: Faber & Faber.

Pearson, R. (with Shyh Charng Lo) (1983) 'The Ch'ing-lien-kang culture and the Chinese Neolithic', in D.N. Keightley (ed.) (1983a), 119–45.

Peebles, C.S. and Kus, S.M. (1977) 'Some archaeological correlates of ranked societies', *American Antiquity* 42:421–48.

Peoples, J.G. (1982) 'Individual or group advantage? A reinterpretation of the Maring ritual cycle', *Current Anthropology* 23(3):291–310.

Perkins, A.L. (1949) *The Comparative Archaeology of Early Mesopotamia*, Chicago: University of Chicago Press.

Perkins, D. (1964) 'The prehistoric fauna from Shanidar, Iraq', *Science* 144:1565–6.

—— (1966) 'The fauna from Madamagh and Beidha', *Palestine Exploration*

Quarterly 98:68–72.

Perkins, D. and Daly, P. (1968) 'A hunters' village in Neolithic Turkey', *Scientific American* 219:97–106.

Perrot, J. (1983) 'Terminologie et cadre de la préhistoire récente de Palestine', in T.C. Young *et al.* (eds), 113–22.

Petersen, W. (1975) 'A demographer's view of prehistoric demography', *Current Anthropology* 16(2):227–46.

Peterson, N. (1976) 'Ethnoarchaeology in the Australian Iron Age', in G. de G. Sieveking *et al.* (eds), 265–75.

—— (1979) 'Territorial adaptations among desert hunter-gatherers: !Kung and Australians compared', in P.C. Burnham and R.F. Ellen (eds), 111–29.

Pettinato, G. (1979) 'Old Canaanite cuneiform texts of the third millennium recovered during the 1974 season at Tell Mardikh = Ebla (1975)', in G. Buccellati *et al.* (eds), 141–58.

Phillipson, D.W. (1985) *African Archaeology*, Cambridge: Cambridge University Press.

Philsooph, H. (1971) 'Primitive magic and mana', *Man* (n.s.) 6(2):182–203.

Piggott, S. (1965) *Ancient Europe: From the Beginnings of Agriculture to Classical Antiquity*, Edinburgh: Edinburgh University Press.

Pleket, H.W. (1967) 'Technology and society in the Graeco-Roman world', *Acta Historiae Neerlandica* 2:1–25.

Polanyi, K. (1957) *The Great Transformation*, 11th edn, Boston: Beacon Press.

Polanyi, K., Arensberg, C.M., and Pearson, H.W. (eds) (1957) *Trade and Markets in the Early Empires*, Glencoe, Ill.: Free Press.

Polgar, S. (1972) 'Population history and population policies from an anthropological perspective', *Current Anthropology* 13:203–11 and 260–2.

—— (ed.) (1975) *Population, Ecology and Social Evolution*, The Hague: Mouton.

Pollock, S. (1987) 'Abu Salabikh, the Uruk mound', *Iraq* 49:121–41.

Possehl, G.L. (ed.) (1982) *Harrapan Civilisation – A Contemporary Perspective*, Warminster: Aris & Phillips.

Postan, M.M. (1972) *The Medieval Economy and Society*, Harmondsworth: Penguin.

Postgate, J.N. (1972) 'The role of the temple in the Mesopotamian secular community', in P.J. Ucko *et al.* (eds), 811–25.

—— (1980a) 'Excavations at Abu Salabikh, 1978–9', *Iraq* 42:87–113.

—— (1980b) 'Palm trees, reeds and rushes in Iraq ancient and modern', in *L'Archéologie de l'Iraq du début de l'époque néolithique à 333 avant notre ère*, Paris: Editions du CNRS, 99–109.

—— (1982) 'Abu Salabikh', in J. Curtis (ed.), 48–61.

—— (1983) 'Excavations at Abu Salabikh, 1983', *Iraq* 46:95–113.

Postgate, J.N. and Moon, J.A. (1982) 'Excavations at Abu Salabikh, 1981', *Iraq* 44:103–36.

—— (1984) 'Excavations at Abu Salabikh, a Sumerian city', *National Geographic Reports* 17(Year 1976):721–43.

Pounds, N.J.G. (1971) 'The urbanisation of the Classical world', *Ekistics* 182 (Jan.):22–35.

Powell, M.A. (1977) 'Sumerian merchants and the problem of profit', *Iraq* 39:23–9.

—— (1978a) 'A contribution to the history of money in Mesopotamia prior to the invention of coinage', in B. Hruska and G. Komoroczy (eds), *Festschrift Lubor Matous* II, Budapest, 211–43.

—— (1978b) 'Non-slave labour in Sumer', in M. Flinn (ed.), *Proceedings of the Seventh International Economic History Congress*, Edinburgh: Edinburgh University Press, 169–77.

—— (1979) 'Ancient Mesopotamian weight metrology: methods, problems and perspectives', in M.A. Powell and R.H. Sack (eds), 71–109.

—— (1985) 'Salt, seed and yields in Sumerian agriculture. A critique of the theory of progressive salinisation', *Zeitschrift für Assyriologie* 75(1):7–38.

Powell, M.A. and Sack, R.H. (eds) (1979) *Studies in Honor of Tom B. Jones*. Neukirchen-Vluyn: Verlag Butzon & Becker Kevelaer, Neukirchener Verlag.

Price, B.J. (1977) 'Shifts of production and organisation: a cluster-interaction model', *Current Anthropology* 18:209–33.

—— (1978) 'Secondary state formation: an explanatory model', in R. Cohen and E.R. Service (eds), 161–86.

Price, T.D. and Brown, J.A. (eds) (1985) *Prehistoric Hunter-Gatherers: The Emergence of Cultural Complexity*, London: Academic Press.

Pritchard, J.B. (ed.) (1969) *Ancient Near East Texts Relating to the Old Testament*, 3rd edn, Princeton, N.J.: Princeton University Press.

—— (1975) *The Ancient Near East*, vol. II, Princeton, N.J.: Princeton University Press.

Raban, A. (1987) 'The harbor of the Sea Peoples at Dor', *Biblical Archaeologist* 50(2):118–26.

Radcliffe-Brown, A.R. (1952) *Structure and Function in Primitive Society*, London: Cohen & West.

Raikes, R.L. (1966) 'Beidha: prehistoric climate and water supply', *Palestine Exploration Quarterly* 98:68–72.

Rappaport, R. (1969) 'Ritual regulation of environmental relations among a New Guinea people', in A.P. Vayda (ed.) (1969a), 181–201.

Ratnagar, S. (1981) *Encounters: The Westerly Trade of the Harappa Civilisation*, Delhi: Oxford University Press.

Raven, P. (1971) 'The relationships between "Mediterranean" floras', in P.H. Davis *et al.* (eds), 120–34.

Redfield, R. and Singer, M.B. (1954) 'The cultural role of cities', *Economic Development and Cultural Change* 13:53–73.

Redman, C.L. (1978) *The Rise of Civilisation: From Early Farmers to Urban Society in the Ancient Near East*, San Francisco: W.H. Freeman.

——(1983) 'Regularity and change in the architecture of an early village', in T.C. Young *et al.* (eds), 189–206.

Redman, C.L., Berman, M., Curtin, F., Langhorne, W., Versaggi, N., and Wanser, J. (1978) *Social Archaeology: Beyond Subsistence and Dating*, London and New York: Academic Press.

Reece, D.W. (1969) 'The technological limits of the ancient world', *Greece and Rome* 16:32–47.

Reed, C.A. (ed.) (1977) *The Origins of Agriculture*, The Hague: Mouton.

Renfrew, Colin (1972) *The Emergence of Civilisation: The Cyclades and the Aegean in the Third Millennium BC*, London: Methuen.

—— (1973a) *Before Civilisation*, Harmondsworth: Penguin.

—— (ed.) (1973b) *The Explanation of Culture Change: Models in Prehistory*, London: Duckworth.

—— (1975) 'Trade as action at a distance: questions of interaction and communication', in J.A. Sabloff and C.C. Lamberg-Karlovsky (eds), 3–59.

—— (1977a) 'The later obsidian of Deh Luran: the evidence of Chagha Sefid', Appendix II in F. Hole (1977), 289–311.

—— (1977b) 'Space, time and polity', in J. Friedman and M.J. Rowlands (eds) (1977a), 89–112.

—— (1982) *Problems in European Prehistory*, Edinburgh: Edinburgh University Press.

—— (1984) *Approaches to Social Archaeology*, Edinburgh: Edinburgh University Press.

Renfrew, Colin and Cherry, J.F. (eds) (1986) *Peer Polity Interaction and Socio-Cultural Change*, New Directions in Archaeology Series, Cambridge: Cambridge University Press.

Renfrew, Colin, Dixon, J.E., and Cann, J.R. (1966) 'Obsidian and early cultural contact in the Near East', *Proceedings of the Prehistoric Society* 32:30–72.

Renfrew, Colin and Shennan, S. (eds) (1982) *Ranking, Resource and Exchange: Aspects of the Archaeology of Early European Society*, Cambridge: Cambridge University Press.

Renger, J. (1973) 'Who are all those people?' *Orientalia* 42:259–73.

—— (1976) 'The daughters of Urbaba: some thoughts on the succession to the throne during the 2nd dynasty of Lagash', in B.L. Eichler (ed.), 367–9.

Reviv, H. (1969) 'On urban representative institutions and self-government in Syria-Palestine in the 2nd half of the second millennium B.C.', *Journal of the Economic and Social History of the Orient* 12:281–97.

Richards, A. and Kuper, A. (eds) (1971) *Councils in Action*, Cambridge Papers in Social Anthropology no.6, Cambridge: Cambridge University Press.

Rindos, D. (1980) 'Symbiosis, stability and the origins of agriculture: a new model', *Current Anthropology* 21:751–72.

—— (1984) *The Origins of Agriculture: An Evolutionary Perspective*, New York: Academic Press.

—— (1985) 'Darwinian selection, symbolic variation and the evolution of culture', *Current Anthropology* 26:65–88.

—— (1987) 'Darwinian evolution and cultural change: the case of agriculture', in L. Manzanilla (ed.), 69–79.

Ripinsky, M.M. (1975) 'The camel in ancient Arabia', *Antiquity* 49:295–8.

Ripley, S. (1980) 'Infanticide in Langurs and man: adaptive advantage or social pathology?', in M.N. Cohen *et al.* (eds), 349–90.

Roaf, M.D. (1982) 'The Hamrin sites', in J. Curtis (ed.), 40–7.

—— (1984a) 'Ubaid houses and temples', *Sumer* 43(1–2):80–90.

—— (ed.) (1984b) 'Tell Madhhur – a summary report on the excavations', *Sumer* 43:110–26.

Roth, E.A. (1981) 'Sedentarism and changing fertility patterns in a North Athapascan Isolate', *Journal of Human Evolution* 10:413–25.

Roux, G. (1964) *Ancient Iraq*, Harmondsworth: Penguin.

Rowlands, M., Larsen, M.T., and Kristiansen, K. (eds) (1987) *Centre and Periphery in the Ancient World*, New Directions in Archaeology Series, Cambridge: Cambridge University Press.

Rowton, M.B. (1967a) 'Watercourses and water rights in the official correspondence from Larsa and Isin', *Journal of Cuneiform Studies* 21:267–74.

—— (1967b) 'The woodlands of ancient western Asia', *Journal of Near Eastern Studies* 26:261–77.

—— (1969) 'The Abu Amurrim', *Iraq* 31:68–73.

—— (1973a) 'Autonomy and nomadism in Western Asia', *Orientalia* 42:247–58.

—— (1973b) 'Urban autonomy in a nomadic environment', *Journal of Near Eastern Studies* 32:201–15.

—— (1974) 'Enclosed nomadism', *Journal of the Economic and Social History of the Orient* 17(1):1–30.

—— (1976) 'Dimorphic structure and topology', *Oriens Antiquus* 15:17–31.

—— (1977) 'Dimorphic structure and the parasocial element', *Journal of Near Eastern Studies* 36(3):181–98.

—— (1980) 'Pastoralism and the periphery in evolutionary perspective', in *L'Archéologie de l'Iraq du début de l'Époque Néolithique à 333 avant notre ère*, Paris: Editions du CNRS, 291–301.

Runciman, W.G. (1982) 'Origins of states: the case of Archaic Greece', *Comparative Studies in Society and History* 24:351–77.

Russell, K.W. (1988) *After Eden: The Behavioural Ecology of Early Food Production in the Near East and North Africa*, BAR S391, Oxford.

Ruyle, E.E. (1973) 'Slavery, surplus and stratification on the northwest coast: the ethnoenergetics of an incipient stratification system', *Current Anthropology* 14(5):603–17.

Ryder, M.L. (1969) 'Changes in the fleece of sheep following domestication (with a note on the coat of cattle)', in P.J. Ucko and G.W. Dimbleby (eds), 495–521.

Sabloff, J.A. and Lamberg-Karlovsky, C.C. (eds) (1975) *Ancient Civilization and Trade*, School of American Research Advanced Seminar Series, Albuquerque: University of New Mexico Press.

Safir, F. (1950) 'Eridu: a preliminary report on the third season's excavations', *Sumer* 6:27–38.

Sahlins, M. (1968) 'Poor man, rich man, big man, chief: political types in Melanesia and Polynesia', in A.P. Vayda (ed.) (1968), 157–76.

—— (1974) *Stone Age Economics*, London: Tavistock.

—— (1976) *Culture and Practical Reason*, Chicago: University of Chicago Press.

Sahlins, M. and Service, E.R. (eds) (1960) *Evolution and Culture*, Ann Arbor: University of Michigan Press.

Salim, S.M. (1962) *Marsh Dwellers of the Euphrates Delta*, London: Athlone Press.

Salisbury, R. (1966) 'Politics and shell-money finance in New Britain', in M.J. Swatz *et al.* (eds), 113–28.

—— (1968) 'Early stages of economic development in New Guinea', in A.P. Vayda (ed.) (1968), 486–500.

Saller, R.P. and Shaw, B.D. (eds) (1981) *Economy and Society in Ancient Greece*, Harmondsworth: Penguin.

Salzman, P.C. (1967) 'Political organization among nomadic peoples', *Proceedings of the American Philosophical Society* 3(2):115–31.

Sandars, N.K. (1985) *The Sea Peoples: Warriors of the Ancient Mediterranean*, London: Thames & Hudson.

Sanders, W. and Webster, D. (1978) 'Unilinealism, multilinealism, and the evolution of complex societies', in C.L. Redman *et al.* (eds), 249–302.

Sanlaville, P. (ed.) (1985) *Holocene Settlement in North Syria*, Maison de l'Orient Méditerranéen, Lyon, France: CNRS – Université de Lyon 2, BAR S238.

Sasson, J.M. (1976) 'The **ENGAR/ikkarum** at Mari', in B.L. Eichler (ed.), 401–10.

Saxon, E.C. (1974) 'The mobile herding economy of Kebarah Cave, Mt. Carmel: an economic analysis of the faunal remains', *Journal of Archaeological Science* 1(1):27–45.

Scheffler, H.W. (1966) 'Ancestor worship in anthropology; or, observations on descent and descent groups', *Current Anthropology* 7(5):541–51.

Schmandt-Besserat, D. (1979) 'The earliest precursor of writing', in C.C. Lamberg-Karlovsky (ed.), 152–61.

Schmidt, K. (1982) 'Zur Verwendung der Mesopotamischen "Glockentöpfe" ', *Archäologisches Korrespondenzblatt* 12:317–19.

Schoeninger, M.J. (1981) 'The agricultural "revolution": its effects on human diet in prehistoric Iran and Israel', *Paléorient* 7(1):73–91.

Scott, E.C. and Johnston, F.E. (1985) 'Science, nutrition, fat, and policy: tests of the critical fat hypothesis', *Current Anthropology* 26(4):463–73.

Seddon, D. (ed.) (1978) *Relations of Production: Marxist Approaches to Economic Anthropology*, London: Frank Cass.

Seedon, H. (1986) 'Aspects of prehistory in the present world: observations gathered in Syrian villages from 1980–1985', *World Archaeology* 17(2):289–303.

Service, E.R. (1968) 'The prime mover of cultural evolution', *Southwestern Journal of Anthropology* 24:396–409.

—— (1971a) *Cultural Evolutionism: Theory in Practice*, New York: Holt, Rinehart & Winston.

—— (1971b) *Primitive Social Organization*, New York: Random House (first published 1962).

—— (1975) *Origins of the State and Civilization: The Process of Cultural Evolution*, New York: Norton.

—— (1978) 'Classical and modern theories of the origins of government', in R. Cohen and E.R. Service (eds), 21–34.

Shack, W.A. and Cohen, P.S. (eds) (1979) *Politics in Leadership: A Comparative Perspective*, Oxford: Clarendon Press.

Shanin, T. (ed.) (1971) *Peasants and Peasant Society*, Harmondsworth: Penguin.

Sharp, L. (1964) 'Technological innovation and culture change: an Australian case', in P.B. Hammond (ed.), 84–94.

Shaw, W.H. (1978) *Marx's Theory of History*, London: Hutchinson.

Sheridan, A. and Bailey, G. (eds) (1981) *Economic Archaeology: Towards an Integrated Approach*, BAR International Series 96, Oxford.

Sherratt, A. (1980) 'Water, soil and seasonality in early cereal cultivation', *World Archaeology* 2(3):313–29.

—— (1981) 'Plough and pastoralism: aspects of the secondary products revolution', in I.R. Hodder *et al.* (eds), 261–305.

—— (1983) 'The secondary exploitation of animals in the Old World', *World Archaeology* 15(1):90–104.

Sherwin-White, A.N. (1967) *Racial Prejudice in Imperial Rome*, Cambridge: Cambridge University Press.

Sieveking, G. de G., Longworth, I.H., and Wilson, K.E. (eds) (1976) *Problems in Economic and Social Archaeology*, London: Duckworth.

Silverbauer, G. (1981) *Hunter and Habitat in the Central Kalahari Desert*, Cambridge: Cambridge University Press.

—— (1982) 'Political process in G/wi bands', in E. Leacock and R.B. Lee (eds) (1982a), 23–35.

Simmons, I.G. (1974) *The Ecology of Natural Resources*, London: Edward Arnold.

Singh, P. (1974) *Neolithic Cultures of Western Asia*, London: Seminar Press.

Skinner, J.H. (1968) 'Chipped stone finds: the Oriental Institute excavations at Mureybit, Syria, Part II', *Journal of Near Eastern Studies* 27(4):282–90.

Smelser, N.J. (1959) 'A comparative view of exchange systems', *Economic Development and Cultural Change* 4:173–82.

Smith, C.A. (1976) 'Exchange systems and the spatial distribution of elites', in *Regional Analysis. Vol. II: Social Systems*, New York: Academic Press, 309–74.

Smith, M.G. (1977) 'Conditions of change in social stratification', in J. Friedman and M.J. Rowlands (eds) (1977a), 29–47.

Smith, P.E.L. (1971) 'Iran 9000–4000 B.C.: the Neolithic', *Expedition* 13:6–13.

—— (1972) 'Land use, settlement patterns and subsistence agriculture: a demographic perspective', in P.J. Ucko *et al.* (eds), 409–25.

—— (1972–3) 'Changes in population pressure in archaeological explanation', *World Archaeology* 4:5–17.

Smith, P.E.L. and Young, T.C. (1983) 'The force of numbers', in T.C. Young *et al.* (eds), 141–62.

Smith, R.T. (1956) *The Negro Family of British Guiana: Family Structure and Social Status in the Villages*, London: Routledge & Kegan Paul.

Smith, S. (1969) 'Babylonian time reckoning', *Iraq* 31:74–81.

Smith, W.R. (1907) *The Religion of the Semites*, rev. edn, London: A. & C. Black.

Snodgrass, A. (1986) 'Interaction by design: the Greek city-state', in Colin Renfrew and J.F. Cherry (eds), 47–58.

Solecki, R.L. (1979) 'Contemporary Kurdish winter-time inhabitants of Shanidar Cave, Iraq', *World Archaeology* 10(3):318–30.

—— (1981) *An Early Village Site at Zawi Chemi-Shanidar*, Bibliotheca Mesopotamica, vol. 13, Malibu, Calif.: Undena.

Solecki, R.L. and Solecki, R.S. (1983) 'Late Pleistocene – early Holocene', in T.C. Young *et al.* (eds), 123–40.

Solecki, R.S. (1963) 'Prehistory in Shanidar valley, N. Iraq', *Science* 139:179–93.

Southall, A. (1965) 'A critique of the typology of states and political systems', in M. Banton (ed.), 113–40.

—— (ed.) (1973) *Urban Anthropology*, New York: Oxford University Press.

Speiser, E.A. (1954) 'Authority and law in Mesopotamia', *Journal of the American Oriental Society*, Supplement 17: *Authority and Law in the Ancient Orient*, 8–15.

Spooner, B. (1963) 'The function of religion in Persian society', *Iran* 1:83–96.

—— (1969) 'Politics, kinship and ecology in S.E. Persia', *Ethnology* 8(2):139–52.

—— (ed.) (1972) *Population Growth: Anthropological Implications*, Cambridge, Mass.: MIT Press.

Sproat, G.M. (1868) *Scenes and Studies of Savage Life*, London: Smith Elder.

Stampfli, H.R. (1983) 'The fauna of Jarmo, with notes on animal bones from Matarrah, the Amuq and Karim Shahir', in L.S. Braidwood *et al.* (eds), 431–4.

Stanner, W.E.H. (1959) 'On Aboriginal religion. I: The lineaments of sacrifice', *Oceania* 30(2):108–27.

Stauder, J. (1972) 'Anarchy and ecology: political society among the Majangir', *Southwestern Journal of Anthropology* 28:153–68.

Steinkeller, P. (1977) 'Seal practice in the Ur III Period', in McG. Gibson and R.D. Biggs (eds), 41–53.

—— (1981) 'The renting of fields in early Mesopotamia and the development of the concept of "interest" in Sumerian', *Journal of the Economic and Social History of the Orient* 24:113–45.

Stekelis, M. and Yisraeli, T. (1963) 'Excavations at Nahal Oren, preliminary report', *Israel Exploration Journal* 13:1–12.

Stenning, D.J. (1958) 'Household viability among the pastoral Fulani', in J. Goody (ed.), 92–119.

Stevens, J.H. (1978) 'Post-pluvial changes in the soils of the Arabian Peninsula', in W.C. Brice (ed.), 263–74.

Stevenson, H.N.C. (1943) *The Economics of the Central Chin Tribes*, Bombay: Times of India Press.

—— (1954) 'Racial and social problems in Burma', *Proceedings of the Scottish*

Anthropological and Folklore Society 5(1):19–37.

Steward, J.H. (1949) 'Cultural causality and law: a trial formulation of the development of early civilisations', *American Anthropologist* 51:1–27.

—— (1955) *Theory of Culture Change: The Methodology of Multilinear Evolution*, Urbana: University of Illinois Press.

Steward, J.H. and Murphy, R.F. (eds) (1977) *Evolution and Ecology: Essays on Social Transformation*, Urbana: University of Illinois Press.

Stewart, O.C. (1956) 'Fire as the first great force employed by man', in W.L. Thomas, Jr (ed.), 115–33.

Stiebing, W.H. (1980) 'The end of the Mycenaean Age', *Biblical Archaeologist* 43(1):7–21.

Stiles, D. (1977) 'Ethnoarchaeology: a discussion of methods and applications', *Man* (n.s.) 12:87–103.

Stordeur, D. (1974) 'Objets dentés en os de Mureybet (Djezireh, Syrie) des phases IB à III: 8400–7600 B.C.', *Paléorient* 2:437–42.

Stott, D.H. (1969) 'Cultural and natural checks on population growth', in A.P. Vayda (ed.) (1969a), 90–115.

Streuver, S. (ed.) (1971) *Prehistoric Agriculture*, American Museum Sourcebooks in Anthropology Q15, New York: Natural History Press.

Struve, V.V. (1969a) 'The problem of the genesis, development and disintegration of the slave societies in the ancient orient', in I.M. Diakonoff (ed.), 17–69.

—— (1969b) 'Some new data on the organisation of labour and on social structure in Sumer during the reign of the IIIrd Dynasty of Ur', in I.M. Diakonoff (ed.), 127–72.

Stuart, D.E. (1980) 'Kinship and social organization in Tierra del Fuego', in L.S. Cordell and S.J. Beckerman (eds), 269–84.

Sussman, R.W. (1972) 'Child transport, family size and increase in human population during the Neolithic', *Current Anthropology* 13:258–9.

Swartz, M.J., Turner, V.W., and Tuden, A. (eds) (1966) *Political Anthropology*, Chicago: Aldine.

Sweet, L.E. (1960) *Tell Toqaan: A Syrian Village*, Anthropological Papers no.14, Ann Arbor: University of Michigan Museum of Anthropology.

Tait, D. (1956a) 'The family, household, and minor lineage of the Konkomba. Part I: Development and structure', *Africa* 26(3):219–45.

—— (1956b) 'The family, household, and minor lineage of the Konkomba. Part II: The functions of the household', *Africa* 26(4):332–42.

Taylor, W.W. (1948) *A Study of Archaeology*, American Anthropological Association Memoir no.9, Carbondale: University of Minnesota Press.

Taylour, L.W. (1983) *The Mycenaeans*, London: Thames & Hudson.

Testart, A. (1982) 'The significance of food storage among hunter-gatherers: residence patterns, population densities, and social inequalities', *Current Anthropology* 23(5):523–37.

—— (1987) 'Game sharing systems and subsistence systems among hunter-gatherers', *Man* (n.s.) 22(2):287–304.

—— (1988) 'Some major problems in the social anthropology of hunter-gatherers', *Current Anthropology* 29(1):1–32.

Textor, R.B. (1967) *A Cross-Cultural Summary*, New Haven, Conn.: Human Relations Area File Press.

Thomas, W.L., Jr (ed.) (1956) *Man's Role in Changing the Face of the Earth*, 2 vols, Chicago: University of Chicago Press.

Thommeret, J. (1983) 'Carbon 14 dates from Tell El 'Oueili', *Sumer* 39:67.

Thompson, R.C. (1920) 'Abu Shahrain in Mesopotamia in 1918', *Archaeologica*

70(1918–20):101–44.

Thomsen, C.J. (1836) *Ledetraad til Nordisk Oldkyndighed* (English trans. 1848), Copenhagen: National Museum.

Thucydides (1943) *The Peloponesian War*, ed. and trans. R.W. Livingstone, Oxford: Oxford University Press.

Tilley, C. (1981) 'Conceptual frameworks for the explanation of socio-cultural change', in I.R. Hodder *et al.* (eds), 363–86.

Torrence, R. (1983) 'Time budgeting and hunter-gatherer technology', in G. Bailey (ed.), 11–23.

Trigger, B. (1978) *Time and Traditions: Essays in Archaeological Interpretation*, Edinburgh: Edinburgh University Press.

Turner, D.H. (1972) 'Determinants of urban growth in pre-industrial societies', in P.J. Ucko *et al.* (eds), 575–99.

—— (1978) 'Ideology and elementary structures', *Anthropologica* (n.s.) 20(1–2): 223–47.

Turner, D.H. and Smith, G.A. (eds) (1979) *Challenging Anthropology: A Critical Introduction to Social and Cultural Anthropology*, Toronto: McGraw-Hill, Ryerson.

Tyumenev, A.I. (1969a) 'The working personnel on the estate of the temple of ^{d}Ba-U in Lagaš during the period of Lugalbanda and Urukagina (25th–24th century B.C.)', in I.M. Diakonoff (ed.), 88–126.

—— (1969b) 'The state economy of ancient Sumer', in I.M. Diakonoff (ed.), 70–87.

Ucko, P.J. and Dimbleby, G.W. (eds) (1969) *The Domestication and Exploitation of Plants and Animals*, London: Duckworth.

Ucko, P.J., Tringham, R., and Dimbleby, G.W. (eds) (1972) *Man, Settlement and Urbanism*, London: Duckworth.

Uphill, E. (1972) 'The concept of the Egyptian palace as a "ruling machine" ', in P.J. Ucko *et al.* (eds), 721–34.

Van Arsdale, P. (1978) 'Population dynamics among hunter-gatherers of New Guinea: data, methods, comparisons', *Human Ecology* 6(4):435–67.

Van Buren, E.D. (1948) 'Fish-offerings in ancient Iraq', *Iraq* 10:101–21.

—— (1952) 'Places of sacrifice ("Opferstatten")', *Iraq* 14:76–92.

Van Dijk, J. (1965) 'Une insurrection générale au pays de Larsa avant l'avènement de Nuradad', *Journal of Cuneiform Studies* 19:1–25.

—— (1983) *LUGAL UD ME-LÁM-bi NIR-ĞÁL. Le récit épique et didactique des Travaux de Ninurta, du Déluge et de la Nouvelle Création. Tome I: Introduction. Texte Composite. Traduction*, Leiden: E.J. Brill.

Van Driel, G. and Van Driel-Murray, C. (1983) 'Jebel Aruda, the 1982 season of excavation, interim report (1)', *Akkadica* 33:1–26.

Van Loon, M. (1966) 'Mureybit: an early village in inland Syria', *Archaeology* 19:215–16.

—— (1968) 'The Oriental Institute excavations at Mureybit, Syria: preliminary report on the 1965 campaign', *Journal of Near Eastern Studies* 27(4):265–90.

Van Zeist, W. (1969) 'Reflections on prehistoric environments in the Near East', in P.J. Ucko and G.W. Dimbleby (eds), 35–46.

—— (1970) 'The Oriental Institute excavations at Mureybit, Syria: preliminary report on the 1965 campaign: the palaeobotany', *Journal of Near Eastern Studies* 29:167–76.

—— (1976) 'On macroscopic traces of food plants in S.W. Asia (with some reference to pollen data)', *Philosophical Transactions of the Royal Society of London*, B275:27–41.

Van Zeist, W. and Bakker-Heeres, J.A.H. (1975) 'Evidence for linseed cultivation before 6,000 B.C.', *Journal of Archaeological Science* 2(3):215–29.

—— (1979) 'Some economic and ecological aspects of the plant husbandry at Tell Aswad', *Paléorient* 5:161–9.

Van Zeist, W. and Bottema, S. (1977) 'Palynological investigations in Western Iran', *Palaeohistoria* 19:19–85.

Van Zeist, W. and Casparie, W.A. (eds) (1984) *Plants and Ancient Man*, Rotterdam and Boston: A.A. Balkema.

Van Zeist, W., Woldring, H., and Stepert, D. (1975) 'Late Quaternary vegetation and climate of southwestern Turkey', *Palaeohistoria* 17:53–143.

Vayda, A.P. (1967) 'Pomo trade feasts', in Dalton (ed.), 494–500.

—— (ed.) (1968) *Peoples and Cultures of the Pacific: An Anthropological Reader*, New York: Natural History Press.

—— (ed.) (1969a) *Environment and Cultural Behaviour: Ecological Studies in Cultural Anthropology*, Austin: University of Texas Press.

—— (1969b) 'Expansion and warfare among swidden agriculturalists', in A.P. Vayda (ed.) (1969a), 202–20.

Vertesalji, P.P. (1987) 'The chronology of the Chalcolithic in Mesopotamia (6,000–3,000 B.C.)', in O. Aurenche *et al.* (eds), part ii, 483–523.

Vogt, E.Z. and Leventhal, R.M. (1983) *Prehistoric Settlement Patterns: Essays in Honour of H. Gordon Willey*, Albuquerque: University of New Mexico Press and Peabody Museum of Archaeology and Ethnology, Harvard University.

Voigt, M. (1987) 'Relative and absolute chronologies for Iran between 6,500 and 3,500 cal. B.C.', in O. Aurenche *et al.* (eds), part ii, 615–46.

Walters, S.D. (1970) *Water for Larsa: An Old Babylonian Archive Dealing with Irrigation*, New Haven, Conn.: Yale University Press.

Walton, K. (1969) *The Arid Zones*, London: Hutchinson.

Watkins, T. (1978) 'Comment' on Kohl, *Current Anthropology* 19(3):485.

Watkins, T. and Baird, D. (1987) *Qermez Dere: The Excavation of an Aceramic Neolithic Settlement near Tel Afar, N. Iraq*, Edinburgh: University of Edinburgh Department of Archaeology Project Paper no.6.

Watkins, T. and Campbell, S. (1987) 'The chronology of the Halaf culture', in O. Aurenche *et al.* (eds), part ii, 427–64.

Watson, P.J. (1978) 'Architectural differentiation in some Near Eastern communities, prehistoric and contemporary', in C.L. Redman *et al.* (eds), 131–58.

—— (1979) *Archaeological Ethnography in Western Iran*, Viking Fund Publications in Anthropology no.57, Tucson: University of Arizona Press.

—— (1980) 'The theory and practice of ethnoarchaeology with special reference to the Near East', *Paléorient* 6:55–64.

—— (1983a) 'The Halafian culture: a review and synthesis', in T.C. Young *et al.* (eds), 231–50.

—— (1983b) 'A note on the Jarmo plant remains', in L.S. Braidwood *et al.* (eds), 501–4.

Weadock, P.N. (1975) 'The Giparu at Ur', *Iraq* 37:101–28.

Webb, M.C. (1975) 'The flag follows trade: an essay on the necessary interaction of military and commercial factors in state formation', in J.A. Sabloff and C.C. Lamberg-Karlovsky (eds), 155–209.

Webster, D. (1975) 'Warfare and the evolution of the state: a reconsideration', *American Antiquity* 40:464–70.

—— (1976) 'On theocracies', *American Anthropologist* 78:812–28.

Weiss, H. (1975) 'Kish, Akkad and Agade' (review article), *Journal of the*

American Oriental Society 95:434–53.

—— (1985) 'Tell Leilan on the Habur Plains of Syria', *Biblical Archaeologist* 48(1):5–34.

Weiss, H. and Young, T.C. (1975) 'The merchants of Susa: Godin V and plateau–lowland relations in the late fourth millennium B.C.', *Iran* 13:1–17.

Weissleder, W. (1978a) 'Aristotle's concept of political structure and the state', in R. Cohen and E.R. Service (eds), 187–203.

—— (ed.) (1978b) *The Nomadic Alternative: Modes and Models of Interaction in the African-Asian Deserts and Steppes*, The Hague: Mouton.

Weissner, P. (1982) 'Risk, reciprocity and social influences on !Kung San economics', in E. Leacock and R.B. Lee (eds) (1982a), 61–8.

Wendorf, F. and Marks, A.E. (eds) (1975) *Problems in Prehistory: North Africa and the Levant*, Southern Methodist University Contributions in Anthropology no.13, Dallas, Texas: Southern Methodist University Press.

Wenke, R.J. (1981) 'Explaining the evolution of cultural complexity: a review' *Advances in Archaeological Method and Theory* 4:79–127.

Wertime, T.A. and Muhly, J.D. (eds) (1980) *The Coming of the Age of Iron*, New Haven, Conn.: Yale University Press.

Westenholz, A. (1975a) *Early Cuneiform Texts in Jena*, Copenhagen: Munksgaard.

—— (1975b) *Old Sumerian and Old Akkadian Texts in Philadelphia Chiefly from Nippur. Part 1: Literary and Lexical Texts and the Earliest Administrative Documents from Nippur*, Bibliotheca Mesopotamica, vol.1, Malibu, Calif.: Undena.

—— (1979) 'The Old Akkadian Empire in contemporary opinion', in M.T. Larsen (ed.), 107–24.

Wheatley, P. (1971) *The Pivot of the Four Quarters: A Preliminary Enquiry into the Origins and Character of the Ancient Chinese City*, Edinburgh: Edinburgh University Press.

Wheeler, M. (1956) *Archaeology from the Earth*, Harmondsworth: Penguin.

White, J.P. (1971) 'New Guinea and Australian prehistory: the "Neolithic problem" ', in D.J. Mulvaney and J. Golson (eds), 182–95.

White, J.P. and O'Connell, J.F. (1979) 'Australian prehistory: new aspects of antiquity', *Science* 203:21–8.

White, K.D. (1970) *Roman Farming*, London: Thames & Hudson.

White, L.A. (1943) 'Energy and the evolution of culture', *American Anthropologist* 45:335–56.

—— (1949) *The Science of Culture: A Study of Man and Civilization*, New York: Grove Press.

—— (1959) *The Evolution of Culture: The Development of Civilization to the Fall of Rome*, New York: McGraw-Hill.

—— (1960) 'Foreword', in M. Sahlins and E.R. Service (eds), v-viii.

White, Lynn A. (1970) 'Medieval uses of air', *Scientific American* 223(2):92–100.

Whitehouse, R.D. (ed.) (1983) *Macmillan Dictionary of Archaeology*, London: Macmillan.

Whyte, R.O. (1983) 'The evolution of the Chinese environment', in D.N. Keightley (ed.) (1983a), 1–19.

Willey, G.R. and Phillips, P. (1958) *Method and Theory in American Archaeology*, Chicago: University of Chicago Press.

Willey, G.R. and Sabloff, J.A. (1974) *A History of American Archaeology*, London: Thames & Hudson.

Williams, E. (1987) 'Complex hunter-gatherers: a view from Australia', *Antiquity* 61:310–21.

Wilmsen, E.N. (ed.) (1972) *Social Change and Interaction*, Museum of Anthropology Papers no.46, Ann Arbor: University of Michigan Press.

Wilson, J.V.K. (1985) *The Legend of Etana – A New Edition*, Warminster: Aris & Phillips.

Wing, E.S. and Brown, A.B. (1980) *Palaeonutrition: Method and Theory in Prehistoric Foodways*, London: Academic Press.

Wittfogel, K. (1956) 'Hydraulic civilisations', in W.L. Thomas, Jr (ed.), 152–64.

—— (1957) *Oriental Despotism: A Comparative Study of Total Power*, New Haven, Conn.: Yale University Press.

—— (1971) 'Developmental aspects of hydraulic societies', in S. Streuver (ed.), 557–71 (first published 1955).

—— (1981) *Oriental Despotism*, new edition, with new foreword by author, New York: Vintage Books.

Wobst, H.M. (1976) 'Locational relationships in Palaeolithic society', *Journal of Human Evolution* 5:49–58.

Woodburn, J. (1972) 'Ecology, nomadic movement and the composition of the local group among hunters and gatherers: an East African example and its implications', in P.J. Ucko *et al.* (eds), 193–206.

—— (1979) 'Minimal politics: the political organization of the Hadza of North Tanzania', in W.A. Shack and P.S. Cohen (eds), 244–66.

—— (1980) 'Hunters and gatherers today and reconstruction of the past', in E. Gellner (ed.), 95–117.

—— (1982) 'Egalitarian societies', *Man* (n.s.) 17:431–51.

Woosley, A.I. and Hole, F. (1978) 'Pollen evidence of subsistence and environment in ancient Iran', *Paléorient* 4:59–70.

Wright, G.A. (1971) 'Origins of food production in S.W. Asia: a survey of ideas,' *Current Anthropology* 12:447–77.

Wright, H.E. (1968) 'Natural environment of early food production north of Mesopotamia', *Science* 161:334–9.

—— (1977) 'Environmental change and the origin of agriculture in the Old and New Worlds', in C.A. Reed (ed.), 281–318.

—— (1980) 'Problems of absolute chronology in prehistoric Mesopotamia', *Paléorient* 6:93–8.

Wright, H.T. (1969) *The Administration of Rural Production in an Early Mesopotamian Town*, University of Michigan Anthropology Papers no.38, Ann Arbor: University of Michigan Press.

—— (1972) 'A consideration of interregional exchange in Greater Mesopotamia: 4000–3000 B.C.', in E.N. Wilmsen (ed.), 95–105.

—— (1978) 'Toward an explanation of the origin of the state', in R. Cohen and E.R. Service (eds), 49–68.

—— (1981) *An Early Town on the Deh Luran Plain: Excavations at Tepe Farukhabad*, Memoirs of the Museum of Anthropology no.13, Ann Arbor: University of Michigan Press.

Wright, H.T. and Johnson, G.A. (1975) 'Population, exchange, and early state formation in southwestern Iran', *American Anthropologist* 77:267–89.

Wright, H.T., Neely, J.A., Johnson, G.A., and Speth, J. (1975) 'Early 4th millennium developments in S.W. Iran', *Iran* 13:129–41.

Wright, M. (1985) 'Contacts between Egypt and Syro-Palestine during the Protodynastic period', *Biblical Archaeologist* 48(4):240–53.

Wymer, J.J. (1982) *The Palaeolithic Age*, Croom Helm Studies in Archaeology, London: Croom Helm.

Yanagisako, S.J. (1979) 'Family and household: the analysis of domestic groups',

Annual Review of Anthropology 8:161–205.
Yasin, W. (1970) 'Excavations at Tell es-Sawwan, 1969 (6th season)', *Sumer* 24:3–11.
Yellen, J.E. (1977) *Archaeological Approaches to the Present: Models for Reconstructing the Past*, New York: Academic Press.
Yellen, J.E. and Harpending, H. (1972–3) 'Hunter-gatherer populations and archaeological inference', *World Archaeology* 4:244–53.
Yesner, D.R. (1980) 'Maritime hunter gatherers: ecology and prehistory', *Current Anthropology* 21:727–50.
—— (1983) 'On food storage among hunter-gatherers', *Current Anthropology* 24(1):119–20.
Yoffee, N. (1977) *The Economic Role of the Crown in the Old Babylonian Period*, Bibliotheca Mesopotamica, vol.5, Malibu, Calif.: Undena.
—— (1978) 'On studying Old Babylonian history. A review article', *Journal of Cuneiform Studies* 30(1):18–32.
—— (1979) 'The decline and rise of Mesopotamian civilisation: an ethno-archaeological perspective on the evolution of social complexity', *American Antiquity* 44(1):5–35.
—— (1981) *Explaining Trade in Ancient West Asia*, Monographs on the Ancient Near East II, fascicle 2, Malibu, Calif.: Undena.
Yonah, M.A. and Shatzman, I. (1976) *Illustrated Encyclopaedia of the Classical World*, Maidenhead: Sampson Low.
Young, M.W. (ed.) (1979) *The Ethnology of Malinowski: The Trobriand Islands 1915–1918*, London: Routledge & Kegan Paul.
Young, T.C., Smith, P.E.L., and Mortensen, P. (eds) (1983) *The Hilly Flanks and Beyond: Essays on the Prehistory of Southwestern Asia (Presented to Robert J. Braidwood)*, Studies in Ancient Oriental Civilisation no.36, Chicago: Oriental Institute of the University of Chicago.
Zagarell, A. (1986) 'Trade, women, class, and society in ancient Western Asia', *Current Anthropology* 27(5):415–30.
Zarins, J. (1978) 'The domesticated Equidae of third millennium B.C. Mesopotamia', *Journal of Cuneiform Studies* 30:3–17.
Zelinsky, W. (1970) 'Beyond the exponentials: the role of geography in the Great Transition', *Economic Geography* 46:498–535.
Zeuner, F.E. (1974) 'The origins and stages of animal domestication', in J. Klaits and B. Klaits (eds), 117–43.
Zipf, G.K. (1949) *Human Behaviours and the Principle of Least Effort*, Cambridge, Mass.: Addison-Wesley.
Zohary, D. (1969) 'The progenitors of wheat and barley in relation to domestication and agricultural dispersal in the Old World', in P.J. Ucko and G.W. Dimbleby (eds), 47–66.
—— (1971) 'The origin of S.W. Asiatic cereals: wheats, barley, oats, rye', in P.H. Davis *et al.* (eds), 235–60.
Zohary, D., Harlan, J.R., and Vardi, A. (1969) 'The wild diploid progenitors of wheat and their breeding value', *Euphytica* 18:58–65.
Zohary, D. and Spiegel-Roy, P. (1975) 'Beginnings of fruit growing in the Old World', *Science* 187:319–27.
Zubrow, E.B.W. (ed.) (1976) *Demographic Anthropology: Quantitative Approaches*, School of American Research Advanced Seminar Series, Albuquerque: University of New Mexico Press.
Zvelebil, M. (ed.) (1986a) *Hunters in Transition: Mesolithic Societies of Temperate Eurasia and their Transition to Farming*, New Directions in

Archaeology Series, Cambridge: Cambridge University Press.

—— (1986b) 'Mesolithic prelude and Neolithic revolution', in M. Zvelebil (ed.), 5–15.

—— (1986c) 'Mesolithic societies and the transition to farming', in M. Zvelebil (ed.), 167–88.

Index